P9-DDU-896

GARCILASO de la VEGA was born in Peru in 1539, the son of an Inca princess and a Spanish conquistador. He was a convert to Catholicism, leaving his native Peru for good at the age of twenty-one. But before leaving he took copious notes, listening to all the members of his mother's family, visiting the Indian villages, investigating the minutest aspects of the decaying Empire. In Spain he took part in the wars against the Italians and Moors, and late in life he retired to a religious vocation in Cordoba. At the age of 69 he had published the first part of the Royal Commentaries, recalling the land of his birth and the glory of Peru. Once he began to write, he never stopped until his death in 1010. He is today celebrated as one of the greatest of South American writers, certainly the first and most national.

This edition of the Royal Commentaries is edited and introduced by the famous explorer, Alain Gheerbrant, author of *JOURNEY TO THE FAR AMAZON.*

THE INCAS

The Royal Commentaries of the Inca

GARCILASO de la VEGA

Translated by
MARIA JOLAS
from the critical, annotated French edition, edited and introduced by
ALAIN GHEERBRANT

A DISCUS BOOK/PUBLISHED BY AVON BOOKS

AVON BOOKS
A division of
The Hearst Corporation
959 Eighth Avenue
New York, New York 10019

Copyright © 1961 by The Orion Press, Inc.
Published by arrangement with the Orion Press, Inc.
Library of Congress Catalog Card Number: 61-14189.
ISBN: 0-380-45542-0

All rights reserved, which includes the right
to reproduce this book or portions thereof in
any form whatsoever. For information address
The Orion Press, Inc., 125A East 19th Street,
New York, N.Y. 10003.

First Printing (Avon Library Edition), November, 1964
Third Printing (Discus Edition), June, 1971
Fifth Printing

DISCUS TRADEMARK REG. U.S. PAT. OFF. AND IN
OTHER COUNTRIES, MARCA REGISTRADA, HECHO EN
U.S.A.

Printed in the U.S.A.

CONTENTS

ILLUSTRATIONS

The Drawings of Guaman Poma

Map

The designs at the beginnings of Books I, III, V, VIII are drawn after figures taken from the Sun Door at Tiahuanaco. The designs at the beginning of Books VII, IX, X are Trujillo in origin. The one at the beginning of Book IV is Mochica in origin. Those of Books II and VI are Tiahuanaco and Pacasmayu, respectively, in origin.

INTRODUCTION

GARCILASO "EL INCA"

Today, when the annual feast of the Sun is revived in the ancient Inca city, a feast that is a source of joy for tourists and of emotion for the Indians, it is no exaggeration to say that the entire population talks of the Inca Garcilaso, whom they piously and rather naïvely associate with the greatest figures of the past. The Calle Garcilaso is one of the principal avenues of the new city, between the Calle Manco Capac and the Calle Pachacutec. Here, two steps from the hotel where Americans usually stay, is the "old Cuzco Bazaar" which sells postcards of the Sun, and tapestry or terra cotta likenesses of the Incas. The young "Cuzceños" get their sports training at the "Garcilaso Stadium" and, at school, they are taught the story of the Inca Garcilaso, Peru's leading writer. Finally, in the heart of the old town, no visitor should miss the *casa* Garcilaso, where our author himself will act as guide and let us attend the bullfights given four hundred years ago, on the main square of the city.

At that time—that was in 1553, Garcilaso was therefore fourteen years old—the fratricidal struggles of the first conquistadors had ended in bloodshed, like those of Huascar and Atahualpa. Indeed, it looked as though, from the last Incas to the first Spaniards, the same tragic story had repeated itself. The reigns of Pizarro and Almagro had been quite as ephemeral as those of Huaina Capac's sons; hardly had they thought they held the Empire in their hands, when it had eluded them, with their lives. They had been superseded by men of haughty mien, sparing of gesture and word, from a legal rather than a military background. Under their rod of iron, thousands and thousands of Indians were digging in the mountains and scraping the beds of the rivers, in order that thousands and thousands of cargos of gold and silver might keep moving towards the coast, where they were awaited by the potbellied galleons of H.M. Charles V, supreme lord of all Spanish possessions, supreme master of the former kingdoms and provinces of Peru. From Quito to Chile, there was no longer an Empire, but a sort of huge farm, dotted with churches, schools and courthouses: conquest had given way to colonialism.

This had happened little by little with the passing years, while, one after the other, with the regularity of a pendulum, the heads of the last rebels had fallen under the knife of the executioner. To the end of his days the Inca Garcilaso never forgot those years during which Spanish justice had mowed down his childhood dreams, replacing them in his adolescence and maturity with a world without miracles; when it was not a case of the last miracle workers doing away with each other.

In 1541, three years after the elder Almagro was executed, a handful of partisans forced their way into Francisco Pizarro's palace in Lima and assassinated the Peruvian conqueror as well as his half-brother, Martín de Alcantara. The body of the most famous of all the conquistadors was thrown out into the street and buried at night by a Negro slave. . . . The same year Pedro de Alvarado, who had been in Mexico with Cortez before coming to Peru with Captain Garcilaso, father of the poet, ended his astonishing adventures in a stupid accident. Our Inca was two years old at the time.

In 1542, Don Diego de Almagro the younger, for whom Pizarro's head was not enough, aimed as well at the Peruvian crown. He met the royal armies at Chupas, was beaten, then beheaded. Before surrendering, however, with his lance he nailed the first white man to tread upon Peruvian soil to the gun carriage of a cannon. This man was the stupendous, legendary figure Pedro de Candia, whom Garcilaso, in one of his most brilliant passages, shows us walking alone and unarmed through the streets of Tumbez, while the wild beasts that had been unleashed to devour him lay down at his feet when they saw the cross in his hand: rather like in a Byzantine hagiography. By now, Garcilaso was three years old.

Who remained among the conquistadors after the battle of Chupas? Francisco Pizarro, Juan Pizarro, Martín de Alcantara were dead; Ferdinand Pizarro was rotting in a Spanish jail; the two Almagros, father and son, were dead; Alvarado was dead. The only one left, among those who had been the "great of the great," was Gonzalvo Pizarro, a friend of the Garcilaso family. The young Inca knew him well, having gone to school with his son, whose mother was also an Indian princess. And very often, in the evening or on Sundays, the two children would play together or run races under the watchful eye of the old warrior. In these moments, no doubt, Gonzalvo saw the future of the two schoolboys in the light of his own past. For how could he imagine what the real future was to be when, already, he was no longer able to see the real present? Figures, accounts, all the cold reality of this colony, were not the affair of a Pizarro. It was one thing to organize an Empire, but quite another to domesticate the prodigious Peru whose image haunted this old man still. He had shod his horses with silver and gold; he had fought and won, a thousand to one; he had seen with his own eyes and weighed with his own hands the fabulous ransom of Atahualpa, richer than all the treasures of the old world. He knew that masses of white clouds scatter every morning over the crests of the cordillera; but he also knew that they form again every evening. How could he admit that an implacable present had won for all time over his fabulous past? Did he realize even that he himself had been an assassin of grandeur? Even madder than he, although older, his companion in arms, Carvajal, who was a terrible old man, encouraged him to hurl back the newly arrived Spaniards into the sea and to recapture Peru. In 1543, together, they raised a small army and attacked the troops of Viceroy Nunez Vela. Luck was with them and, after a few hours' fighting, the viceroy surrendered his sword to Gonzalvo, who had him properly beheaded.

But time was on the side of the new order, and Madrid, like a giant spider, kept tirelessly mending the immense net which finally began to tighten about Pizarro.

In 1548, a new emissary of Charles V, La Gasca, announced that he was going to "restore order in Peru." Gonzalvo Pizarro and Carvajal were soon in their saddles. They stayed in them until the day of their execution in the middle of the main square of Cuzco. "That day," Garcilaso wrote later, "we left school early to go and watch the execution of those two gentlemen. Gonzalvo's head was carried by messenger to the Lima gallows, nearly a thousand miles from Cuzco, in order that everyone should know about it. As for Carvajal, who had rebelled not only against men but also against God—he had refused confession, he was hanged and quartered, despite the fact that he was eighty-one years old, and his body was strewn, piece by piece, along Cuzco's four streets." La Gasca wanted to finish entirely with the past. But even this penalty seemed insufficient to him. He also ordered all the soldiers who had fought with the last Pizarro to be whipped in public, "which greatly scandalized the Indians." What a spectacle indeed, to see these hardened veterans, naked, submitting publicly to a punishment that was crueler than death! No doubt, the notaries, the scribes, and the inquisitors returned home satisfied and relieved. But the Indian people, taking upon themselves the humiliation inflicted upon those who had succeeded in conquering them—the Indian people felt deep shame. For although the new colonial order had little use for grandeur, considered as just another source of disorder, the Indians could not forget their love for those to whom they had surrendered, and to whom they had delegated their own former grandeur.

"A few days later," Garcilaso wrote, "it being Sunday, we went for a walk in the country, my school friends and I, along the Collasuyu road, which runs south of Cuzco. There were a dozen or so children, all half-breeds, the eldest of whom was not over twelve years old. A piece of Carvajal's body was lying in a field: 'Let's go and look at Carvajal!' we all shouted. And very soon, there we were beside it. It was a piece of thigh from which the fat had dripped onto the ground in a large pool. The flesh itself was green, already putrid.

" 'Shall we touch it?' said one boy. 'No,' said another. 'Let's do,' said a third.

"And so we were divided into two camps. Finally, the most daring among us stepped forward. 'Watch me, I'll do it!' he said. And he laid his hand down so hard on the piece of corpse that his entire thumb sank into it.

" 'Shame on you!' we shouted, drawing back. 'It's disgraceful! Dirty! Disgusting! Carvajal is going to kill you for your audacity!'

"The child ran to a nearby brook and washed his fingers and hand in it as hard as he could. Then we all went home.

"The following day, Monday, when we met at school, his thumb was so swollen and black that it looked as if he were wearing the finger of a glove. That evening the swelling had spread to his entire hand, as far as the wrist. And the next day it had reached his elbow, with the result that he was finally obliged to tell his father the truth. Doctors were called who treated and bandaged it, and gave him all kinds of antidotes. Nevertheless, the child all but died, and for four months he was unable to hold a pen in hand.

"And that," concluded Garcilaso, "is what old Carvajal did after he died. Nor was it very unlike what he had done during his lifetime."

Thus ends the tale of the conquistadors in Peru, and one could add that, with them, there disappeared a late shoot of the Middle Ages which had burgeoned in the soil of the New World as a result of the unusual atmosphere of adventure and isolation in which these conquerors lived. Its blooming lasted nearly twenty years, at a time when the first result of this same conquest had been to bring about a golden age in Renaissance Spain.

For this renaissance to be felt in the former Empire of the Incas, it was essential that the chaos of the early years should subside, and trade with the parent state increase. This had been accomplished in the second half of the sixteenth century, when young Garcilaso, who was a precocious lad, left his childhood behind him to enter into adolescence. On the recommendation of Las Casas, who pleaded the cause of the Indians, Charles V had just promulgated the famous *Leyes Nuevas,* or New Laws, which did away with Indian slavery, and attributed to them the same rights and duties as to all other vassals of His Majesty.

Thanks to the normalizing, innovating current that followed this event, Garcilaso was given the same education in Cuzco that the sons of gentlemen enjoyed in Spain, an institution of learning, especially devoted to instructing young half-breeds of noble descent, having been founded there by priests. Here it was that the future historian of the Andes became familiar with the New Testament, Christian Revelation, Latin, the classical humanities, and all that a wellborn young man of that time was supposed to know. Things went so far, and so fast, in fact, that in 1551, the first university in the New World was founded in Lima, with classes in theology, medicine, jurisprudence, mathematics, Latin, Aristotelian philosophy, and the Quechua language. All of which goes to show the very special interest—today it would be called a development program—that Spain took in Peru. This fortunate state of affairs was to be of great assistance in making our young Inca feel that history had not forgotten him in its forward march.

Meanwhile, Captain Garcilaso, having survived with some difficulty the vicissitudes of the preceding years, was now in favor with the viceroy who, in 1553, named him governor of the city of Cuzco. From then on, he kept open house, and his home became quite naturally the meeting place of all those who arrived from Spain, whether they were men of arms, letters, or law. In this society, the Inca Garcilaso, having discovered that he was the son of a highborn gentleman, also became aware of the refinements of his century, and we can imagine with what rapt attention he listened to the conversation of the gentlemen and ladies of quality who were the guests of the governor, his father. It was through them, in fact, that he first entered into contact with his second country, for he had also begun to read the polite literature of the time, and one guesses that he must have witnessed an astonishing symbiosis within himself, between the imaginary adventures of Amadis, going forth in search of an ideal island, and the very real adventures experienced by his father and his father's companions, when they had encountered the Incas, his other relatives. At the same time, in his mother's home, they too told him stories of their past.

For, alas, those exceptional times having become merely a memory, the inevitable had happened and, once more, the two bloods that had joined together and blended in his veins, were now divided between two houses. As a result of scruples, today we should say, of "complexes," created by the society of these new gentlemen with whom he was in frequent contact, Captain Garcilaso had left ñusta Isabel, and married a real Spanish woman, from Spain. To Garcilaso "El Inca," it must have seemed that the new Peru, which he himself incarnated, was already disintegrating.

But the Inca Garcilaso was equally respectful and proud of both his origins. Quite precociously, he knew what a changing thing is human fortune—he who only yesterday had helped his father flee the justiciaries of the moment. He perhaps understood, too, with that innate patience that is in the blood of every Indian, that all mixtures must be tested and retested before they can constitute, for all time, a new body. Lastly, the Christian God and the Revelation, in addition to his natural tendencies, helped him to reconcile, through religion, the opposing elements which must necessarily have clashed in him at times. And thus it was that Garcilaso "El Inca" became neither a rebel nor a melancholy dreamer, but a man of action, fully aware of things and serious, with a seriousness that is often acquired earlier than we think. For many details of his writings lead us to believe that, already when he was quite young, he had sensed that the unusual circumstances of his birth—even that of being a half-breed, which might, in the eyes of certain less clear-sighted persons, seem nothing but a handicap—would, on the contrary, help him to find a special niche in the historic upheaval that was taking place, and which was justified in his conscience by the teachings of Christ.

Without this conviction, the actual divorce that separated his parents (who, it must be recalled, had never been legally married) would quite naturally have led him to choose between Spain and Peru of the Incas, in other words, to refuse both the present and the future, of which he himself was a forerunner; to destroy the rich alloy taking place within himself; and, finally, to ignore the very thing that was to lend a novelty of tone and a significance to his work that can only increase with the passing centuries.

But on the contrary: already as an adolescent, we see him equally attached to all that both houses, which were equally dear to him, held for him and taught him.

In the very first lines of the *Royal Commentaries* he returns to this period of his life to tell us how, in the home of the princess, his mother, he questioned the older members of the family, the last of the Incas; how he was taught and made his own the word-of-mouth tradition of his ancestors; how, thanks to his knowledge of the Quechua language, he was able to question people in the market places and in the streets, even in the ruins of ancient Cuzco; in other words, how he began to collect the enormous amount of material out of which he was to construct his vast work. He neglected nothing of what he saw; everything Spanish interested him; but everything Inca interested him more, and throughout his investigations, he gave first place to the witnesses of their waning civilization. He tried out the local medicines on himself; had himself taught the use of the quipu; and, despite his fervent Catholic faith, took part in the sacrificial ceremonies that certain former priests of the Sun continued to perform in secret, and noted what he saw with almost scientific care. In Coricancha, in Sacsahuaman, everywhere, in fact, where only yesterday he had played with his little school friends, he returned now, pen in hand, looking for the traces of history.

That he had already begun to take notes at this time, there is no doubt. Otherwise, as C. R. Markham has remarked, how could he have named three hundred and twenty towns of old Peru, fifty years later, without making a single mistake as to their location? And we should be inclined to add, how could he remember, when he came to write it all down, so many details, so many anecdotes which, in his telling, lose nothing of their vividness? The human memory, however vast, would not suffice to make this possible. And the correspondence that, after settling in Europe, he kept up with relatives and friends who had remained in Peru, could not, by itself, have been the only source of the invaluable, living raw material that enters into the *Royal Commentaries*.

The last years that Garcilaso spent in Peru—he left it never to return at the age of twenty-one—were therefore of great importance to his own development, and essential to the work he was to write. Not only did he take notes, but already, he was making his choice of what he wanted to recall. Today he is reproached for his partiality. I agree with Baudin, however, that this is not only comprehensible but enlightening; not merely because, as he says, it reveals "the state of mind of the Indians who lived in a state of perpetual hankering for the past," but because, in addition to a certain melancholy, which has its charm, Garcilaso, in making this choice, sought to give voice to everything which, in the case of the first Spaniards as well as in that of the Incas, might justify both the present and the future of Peru. Garcilaso made his choice, and occasionally even went too far, either in the role of a son determined to defend the memory of his ancestors, or in that of a Christian who is convinced that the downfall of one side and the demands of the other have served humanity by extending belief in Christ's redemption to the Peruvian Indians.

Indeed, there is more in the *Royal Commentaries* than just reflection of the soul of a vanquished people, as the oft-quoted Menendez y Pelayo stated. There is as well something that is more alive, more instructive, more significant for us today than merely that. Garcilaso believed in the future, and his thought was that of a man of the future who refuses to deny, on one side or the other, the things his young country may be proud of; and in this, as a man of the sixteenth century, he was incredibly ahead of his time. For it must be reiterated that Garcilaso did not reject the forward march of history and, although he took his sustenance from the past, he also spoke of the present, and wanted to assist in the realization of the future. He knew that this "vanquished people" would continue to form the great mass of Peruvian humanity, and it was for this reason that he insisted so fervently, at that critical time, upon its past grandeur, and was inclined to forget the elements of this past that had disturbed his conscience. Such was his vocation, and he owed it to the fact that he was a half-breed; nor is there any doubt in the minds of the people of the Andes, for whom the Inca Garcilaso is the "leading Peruvian writer." And despite the separation of four centuries, the astonishing modernity of his subject relates him today to the youngest among Latin American writers.

No one today would say of a writer like Miguel Angel Asturias that his work is nothing but melancholy nostalgia for a distant past. On the contrary, it constitutes a lyrical endeavor, which is so violent that, at times, it appears to be desperate, to recapture the forgotten forces of ancient Guatemala, to breathe their spirit into a modern body that, otherwise, risks desiccation and decay through depersonalization.

In every line of Garcilaso's great work, the "Peruvian personality" is also present, even when the Spaniards occupy the center of the stage. In this connection, the following passage, among a hundred others from the *Royal Commentaries*, is significant. It tells how the first hospital to be opened for the Indians in the New World was founded in Cuzco. This took place, he tells us, in 1555 or 1556, when he himself was therefore sixteen or seventeen years old. The idea of building a hospital with Spanish funds originated with a former Franciscan friar who, one Lenten Sunday, speaking from the pulpit of the Cuzco cathedral, unfolded his plan to his parishioners with these words: "Gentlemen," he said, "today at one o'clock, accompanied by our governor, I plan to take up a house-to-house collection for this purpose. I hope that, on this occasion, you will show yourselves to be as open-handed and generous as you were strong and brave in the conquest of this country . . ." This, added Garcilaso, in order that everyone, conquistadors and others alike, might, in this manner, repay the indefeasible debt they had contracted towards the Peruvian people.

Is it necessary to emphasize that reflections which reply as precisely as this to questions that are being asked with increasing insistence in our twentieth century, are not to be found in the works of all the chroniclers of the Spanish conquest? It is easy to understand therefore, why, after the emancipation of Latin America, the young republics built upon the former Empire of the Incas proclaimed the glory of the Inca Garcilaso with a fervor that has not yet died down; why, too, Madrid thought it best to forbid his work on the new continent at the very beginning of the disturbances that preceded the wars of independence. But to come back to the founding of the Cuzco hospital, it should be added that that evening the younger Garcilaso acted as secretary to his father, the governor, keeping an account of the funds collected. This example of cooperation between civil and religious authorities, for a humanitarian purpose, impressed him so strongly that, fifty years later, he reproduced this account for us, without having forgotten so much as a maravedi!

We have now reached the critical moment when Garcilaso was obliged to leave his first homeland to go to Europe. In 1556, Captain Garcilaso resigned from his post of governor, and in 1559, he died a natural death, which was more or less exceptional for a conquistador. Events followed fast one upon the other. The Inca's mother, Princess Isabel Chimpu Occlo, was the next to die. The father's property went to the children he had had by his Spanish wife, and that of his mother was confiscated, despite the laws and ordinances promulgated by Charles V. Garcilaso was twenty, or perhaps twenty-one, when he decided to appeal to the only higher authority that might hear his claim for what was due him, and that was the Emperor, or rather King Philippe II, since, five years earlier, Charles V had renounced the crown and the vanities of this world to enter holy orders. Did Garcilaso have other motives for leaving? We know of at least one other, which undoubtedly fits in quite well with all we have just told about him, and which we possess in his own words:

". . . After my father's death, I left for Spain, where I tried to obtain a papal bull permitting me to transport his bones from the place where they were and to commit them, as I did, to the Church of San Isidore of Seville, where they were buried to the glory of God, who, I pray, will grant him His mercy."

This Christian God who, for Garcilaso, is also the great Pachacamac, invisible yet present in all the hazards of existence, was to give the young man a great surprise before he left his native city, one that Garcilaso tells with all the grandeur and simplicity required. "Before leaving," he wrote, "I went to take leave of my learned friend, Polo de Ondegardo:

" '. . . Since you are leaving for Spain,' he said, 'come with me into this room; here you will see some of your own people, whom I had dug up, and about whom you might speak once you're there.'

"There were five bodies, three of which were those of kings and two of queens . . . It was thought that one of them was the Inca Viracocha . . . The second was the great Tupac Yupanqui, and the third, Huaina Capac [Tupac Yupanqui and Huaina Capac, it will be recalled, were the grandfather and paternal uncle of Princess Isabel] . . . All of these bodies were so well preserved that not a hair, not an eyebrow, not an eyelash was missing. I remember having touched one finger of Huaina Capac's hand: it was as hard as wood . . . The bodies were so light that the Indians carried them easily in their arms . . . And all the Indians who saw them pass knelt down immediately, sobbing, their faces bathed in tears . . . Many Spaniards, too, took off their hats . . . which touched the Indians so much that they did not know how to express their feeling."

How these faces of a past epoch were to haunt him! This was in 1560. Then, forty-nine years later, in 1609, thanks to Garcilaso who, by that time, was himself an old man, they came to life again and told their story not only to Spain, but to the entire Old World.

Garcilaso left Cuzco for Lima by muleback, traveling along the Chinchasuyu road. Until the very last moment, the sound of his mule's hoofs knocking against the pavings of this fine road, finer than any in ancient Rome, recalled the grandeur of his Emperor ancestors, whose faces he had just seen. And for another fifty-six years, this monotonous sound kept echoing in his memory, until his death, when it too died away . . .

AN IMAGINARY ACCOUNT OF CUZCO, APRIL 12, 1539

To begin with, the fratricidal, criminal struggle between the two Incas, had ended in bloodshed, as had been predicted. Atahualpa had hardly taken possession of Huascar before the emissaries of Viracocha had landed in Tumbez; and the Viracochas had killed Atahualpa.

Like a headless body, the Tahuantinsuyu, the Inca Empire, was without an Emperor; this, too, had been written in the ancient predictions. And now those strange, bearded, ironclad beings, the Viracochas, had entered Cuzco, the capital of the Incas, brandishing thunderbolts. That was hardly more than five years ago: that was as if it were yesterday . . . They had violated the silence of the sacred city; they had pillaged it; they had destroyed its temples, its convents, its palaces. The time of bloodshed had been followed by a time of shame, and nothing had been spared; the great deeds of the sons of the Sun had disappeared in smoke, and the name of the god-star was no longer mentioned. That, too, had been predicted. All the last reigning kings had known it; the *amautas*, philosopher-advisers to the Inca, and the soothsayers had expected it: that was how it had to happen, and a thing was done that could never be undone.

There had been a faint glimmer of hope and brief opposition in the face of fate: that was the day when Pizarro and the Almagro, the leaders of the Viracochas, had promised Manco, Huascar's brother, that he would soon don the scarlet *llautu*, the Inca insignia of supreme power. But a few months later, when he reminded them of their promise, the Viracochas took the prince and threw him, in irons, into a Sacsahuaman dungeon; and that was their only reply.

Then Manco, seeing that they attached so little importance both to his life and to their own word, began to wonder if these Viracochas were not simply men, as certain people had begun to whisper. He therefore decided to answer cunning with cunning, and force with force, in order to test them. With a few soft words, he had himself freed and fled to the mountains. When he came back, stealthily, in the dead of night, he was no longer alone: two hundred thousand warriors, the most formidable army that had ever been raised in the Tahuantinsuyu, accompanied him. As in the heyday of the great Pachacutec, or of the conqueror Tupac Yupanqui, every man had his cotton armor, his shield and his offensive weapons: *macanas* made of hard wood, with a sharp-edged double cord like the cord of the obsidian, bronze and gold bludgeons, lances, javelins, slings, bows and arrows. The entire city was asleep when, after crossing ridge after ridge, they came in view of the valley and surrounded it. The two or three hundred Spanish were sleeping, too. Now it was going to be seen whether they were gods or men. The Inca had resin-dipped arrows lighted and let them fly by the thousand at the straw roofs of the imperial city. The whole place burst into flames, and the battle began. Hours, days, soon months passed. And in the end, it was not the Incas but the Viracochas who had the upper hand. Manco's last general threw himself off the top of the Muyu Marca, the high tower of the Sacsahuaman fortress . . . and Manco himself fled a second time to the mountains, from where he never returned . . .

From then on there was no more hope. The Spaniards were not only the masters of Cuzco, but of all Tahuantinsuyu, from Quito to Atacama. In his secret retreat Manco was perhaps free, but now it was quite certain that the Incas would never recover their Empire. The facts had confirmed all the ancient predictions, and Huaina Capac's pronouncement had proved to be true: the newcomers were stronger than the Incas in everything, and there was therefore nothing to do but to obey them. Only three years earlier Cuzco had been in flames: that was as if it were yesterday . . .

The time of bloodshed had been followed by a time of shame: Cuzco, like its princes, had lost its crown. Don Francisco Pizarro, the leader of the Spaniards, had drawn a new city in the sand, beside the sea, in the Yunca country, near the temple of Rimca, the famous oracle having become silent like all the oracles of the Empire. He had called it the City of Kings [today Lima], and he had decided that, like himself, it would rule over the whole of Peru, replacing Cuzco and the Incas. Proud Cuzco had been reduced to melancholy silence, like the entire *puna* of the Andes. That was the time of shame.

But now the Viracochas themselves—they who fought

like gods—had begun to sin like men. Their priests were everywhere, threatening death to those who still mentioned the names of Pachacamac, the invisible creator of the universe; of Inti, the Sun-god, father of the Inca line; of their mother Mamaquilla, Our Mother, the Moon; of Mamacocha, Mother of the waters; of Mamapacha, the Earth-mother. In their place, they taught the names of God the Father, invisible creator of all things; of His Son Jesus Christ, Savior of the human race; of Mary, Holy Virgin, Our Lady, His Mother . . .

All the Spanish went down on one knee and took off their metal headgear when they heard these sacred names, and yet, just like the last Incas, they had now become divided into two camps and were fighting among themselves. Less than a year before, Francisco Pizarro had seized Almagro and had him publicly executed before the Spanish and the Indians, without fearing the wrath of the Eternal, whether he be called God or Pachacamac. What was going to happen? Were the Viracochas also going to disappear and lose the Empire, as the Incas had done? And who, then, would reign over Peru, that great body twice beheaded? Juan Pizarro was dead, Diego de Almagro was dead. The past was dead, the present was a reign of terror, what did the future hold? The world must be in parturition, it must be about to bring forth an entirely new epoch, else this was the end, for everybody and everything.

Such was the situation, and such were the questions that people must have been asking in Cuzco, on that 12th of April, 1539, when the first bells set up on the ruins of the Temple of the Sun started to ring out in full peal. And a murmur began to go the rounds by word of mouth: the ñusta Chimpu Occlo had given birth to a child: a male child.

The ñusta, or Princess Chimpu Occlo, whose first name, since her conversion to the new gods, was Isabel, was a first cousin of Huascar and of Manco, daughter of Prince Hualpa Tupac Inca Yupanqui, niece of the great King Huaina Capac—the one who had predicted the arrival of the Spaniards—and granddaughter of Tupac Yupanqui, the great conqueror. But the father of the child she had just brought into the world was neither a Capac, nor a Tupac, not even a member of the "long-eared" race;

he was an hidalgo, captain in the army of His Majesty, the Emperor Charles.

An *hidalgo: hijo de algo,* the son of something. There are epochs—like men—whose pride is so great that they are defined by a word that is intentionally unassuming. And the fact is that, with this single word, the conquistador captain, standing beside the ñusta Isabel at his son's baptism, conferred upon him all the grandeur of Spain's greatest century. The blood that flowed in his veins was worthy of that of the Incas. He belonged to the Vargas and the Velas, whose family trees had already borne a number of famous scions, men of letters and men of arms. Offsetting the great Pachacutec, the Tupac Inca Yupanqui, and the twelve Emperors of Tahuantinsuyu, were two great poets, Jorge Manrique and Garcilaso de la Vega, the elected friend of Charles V, and a large number of other noble lords who had fought against the infidel for the glory of greater Spain: the Marquis de Santillone, and García Pérez de Vargas, the liberator of Andalusia, and García Lasso, Commander of Montizon, who was killed by the Moors at Granada in 1458 . . .

The child born of the fusion of two such illustrious bloods received his father's name: Garcilaso de la Vega. He later supplemented it with a single epithet, "El Inca," which should suffice to make it unforgettable.

GARCILASO "EL HIDALGO"

In 1561, young Garcilaso arrived in Madrid where he requested audience at the court of Philippe II and before the Indian Council, in order to present his claims for restitution of his mother's estate. He also sought royal favor, in view of services rendered by his father.

"What!" came the answer. "You dare to claim royal favor, when your father helped Gonzalvo Pizarro to flee the king's justice by lending him his own horse during the battle of Huarina? All historians agree on this point. Do you dare to deny their testimony?"

"To give up one's own horse in favor of a friend," replied Garcilaso, "and in such dangerous circumstances, is certainly not a crime, but rather a noble action, the sign of a great and generous nature. I shall remember it always with pride. And to those who allege that this gesture was accomplished in opposition to the king's service, I shall reply that, in itself, it is sufficiently glorious and honorable to deserve respect rather than to incur opprobrium!"

But the proud arguments of this young man were of no avail against the Spanish administration. The past, which he thought he had left far behind him, and for which, after all, he was in no way responsible, had suddenly reappeared to bar his path. We can imagine his bitterness: "All my life," he complained later, "I have had to suffer the consequences of an error that was never committed." For the moment, the fact of being an Inca was of no more use to him. But he was also an hidalgo. All that remained for him, therefore, was to enter the only career that is always open to men of his station, the army, in which he served with honor.

"I served His Majesty with four captain's commissions . . . two from King Philippe II and two from his brother, H.S.H. Don Juan of Austria. And in spite of this fact, the former periods of disgrace I had been subjected to were such that, never again, did I dare make the slightest claim."

It is not known exactly where his campaigns led this second Captain Garcilaso. Doubtless, he went first to fight in Italy, which would explain the fact that his first literary effort was a translation of the *Dialoghi d'Amore* by Leone il Ebreo. Then, like so many other gentlemen from the same families as himself, he probably fought against the infidel. Since the discovery of America—which had coincided with the capture of Granada—one might have expected that the struggle between the Spanish and the Arabs would have finally come to an end. But it had lasted so long, and the memory of it had remained so vivid, that early historians of the New World, from Mexico to Cuzco, frequently called the Indians "Moors," and their temples "mosques." Now, some seventy years after Christopher Columbus had made his discovery, we see the sons of these pseudo-Moors combating the real ones. How Christianity, like a constantly increasing whirlwind, was little by little successful in drawing all the peoples and all the races on earth into its centrifugal struggles is only too well known. The Inca Garcilaso combating the Barbary peoples, was but one example among many.

THE INCA OF CORDOVA

It seems to have been in 1587, when Don Juan of Austria died, that Garcilaso left the army. He turned up first in Seville, then in Cordova, where he settled definitely in 1589, at the age of fifty. The sound and the fury of the closing years of his great century hardly reached him now:

"I came back from the war with such losses and such debts that it was impossible for me to ask for another audience at court, and I therefore preferred to withdraw into loneliness and poverty, in order to lead the calm and peaceful life of a disillusioned man who has taken leave of this fickle world and expects nothing more from it."

The descendant of the conquistadors and the Incas had been transformed into a hermit. This did not mean, however, that he had given up all ambition. Already, in the introduction to his first original work, *La Florida del Inca,* he reassures us on this point:

"I have no reason to regret that fortune has not always smiled on me, since I am indebted to this fact for the opening up of my literary career which, *I believe* [italics our own] will give me wider and more lasting fame than might be expected from any sort of material success."

This point then is certain: once the Inca had started writing, he never stopped until he died in 1616. By that time, he had attained his goal so completely that people said, and they say still, in all Spanish libraries, "El Inca," when they mean "El Inca Garcilaso de la Vega." To see one's name familiarly shortened by posterity is the unmistakable mark of success.

In 1609, three years after *La Florida,* which recounts the Spanish wars in Florida, the first part of the *Royal Commentaries* appeared in Lisbon, where Garcilaso had first come into contact with the Old World. The second part appeared in Cordova one year after the author's death. In 1600, or thereabouts, the Inca had become a member of the clergy, and his last work was dedicated to "Our Lady, the Very Immaculate Virgin Mary, Mother of God."

Today, in the Cordova Cathedral, visitors may still decipher the following inscription on one of the gravestones:

EL INCA GARCILASO
DISTINGUISHED MAN DESERVING OF
PERPETUAL MEMORY; OF ILLUSTRIOUS
BLOOD; EXPERT WRITER; SON OF GARCILASO
DE LA VEGA, OF THE HOUSES OF THE DUKES
DE FERIA Y INFANTADO; AND OF ELIZABETH
PALLA; FLORIDA COMMENTATOR; TRANSLATOR
OF LEONE IL EBREO; COMPOSER OF THE ROYAL
COMMENTARIES, LIVED IN CORDOVA, WITH DEEP
RELIGIOUS CONVICTION; DIED AN EXEMPLARY
DEATH; CONTRIBUTED TO THIS CHAPEL; WAS
BURIED IN IT; LEFT HIS ESTATE FOR THE
LIBERATION OF SOULS IN PURGATORY; THE LORDS
OF THIS CITY WERE HIS PERMANENT PATRONS
AS ALSO THE HEAD OF THIS HOLY CHURCH.
DIED APRIL 22, 1616
MAY HIS SOUL REST IN GOD

SURVIVAL OF THE INCA GARCILASO

The Inca had not been mistaken. Although his life had been, after all, an obscure one, his works were destined to bring him "wider and more lasting fame than might be expected from any sort of material success," the only fame that had seemed to him to be worthy of himself and of his ancestors.

The *Royal Commentaries* were translated for the first time into French, and were published in Paris, between 1633 and 1658. They soon crossed the Channel and appeared in English in 1688. Indeed, for two centuries, despite its many awkward passages, the French translation was regularly re-edited, both in Paris and, curiously enough, in Amsterdam.

It is well known that the baroque style which, in the eighteenth century, influenced all forms of art and thought, took its principal sustenance from tales of travel and discovery. Distant peoples, those who entered into our history during that serious and at the same time quite frivolous century, were of equal interest to the man in the street, the salons and the philosophers. For the latter, who were soon to lay the foundations of what were later called the "human sciences," the *Royal Commentaries* constituted a unique source of study and information, for neither Zarate nor Las Casas, translated at roughly the same time, had opened up the way, as Garcilaso had done, to a great civilization, the very existence of which was unknown. And in 1778, when Marmontel published his book entitled *Les Incas,* all he did really was to plagiarize Garcilaso, accentuating his melancholy to suit the pre-romantic tastes of the time. For the artists and the salons, the *Commentaries* belonged quite naturally between what were then fashionably referred to as "*turqueries*" and "*chinoiseries.*" And undoubtedly when, in 1735, Rameau composed his famous opera *Les Indes Galantes,* in which the "Inca" may be seen beside the "Grand Turk," he was already acquainted with the works of Garcilaso, either directly or indirectly. Two years later, in 1737, a reprinting of the *Royal Commentaries* was enhanced with engravings, one of which was based on a design by Boucher, representing the heroes of the Tahuantinsuyu as some sort of orientalized Romans, which was how the Parisians of that time imagined them to be. When we recall the quite positive notions concerning the Peruvian past that obtained in Spain at that same epoch, this time-lag between Paris and Madrid may well seem surprising, in view of the fact that, as they said then, "the Pyrenees no longer existed." But it should not be forgotten that, despite this famous dictum, the Spanish kings were far from having opened their frontiers, at least as regarded "their" America, and that neither La Condamine nor Humboldt, the first two important non-Spanish travelers to explore the cordillera of the Andes, had yet set out. The explanation of this was that the suspicious government of Spain still refused visas to foreigners wishing to visit her colonies in the New World.

This, then, explains why the *Royal Commentaries* had such a great success during two centuries, as also why everything Garcilaso had written was taken quite literally, as gospel truth. He could not be attacked for the reason that he could not be contradicted; and he could not be contradicted for the reason that once the Pyrenees had been left behind, Garcilaso was practically the only individual who represented Peru.

Slowly at first, then more rapidly, things began to change with the coming of the nineteenth century. La Condamine, Humboldt, then Darwin, returned from South America with important, entirely new observations. Along with her material power, Spain had not only lost the spiritual monopoly she had assumed over half of the New World, but she had now finally given access to the invaluable stock of manuscripts that had accumulated, since the early days of the conquest, in Seville and in Madrid. In addition to this fact, from Mexico to Cuzco, the mere treasure hunters were beginning to be replaced by archaeologists; Humboldt frequently spoke the language of the ethnologists, and he was followed by Spruce, d'Orbigny, Prescott, and Markham. In other words, the human sciences had emerged from their chrysalis and the new tools afforded by these branches of study now made it possible, thanks to a vast material of cross references, to undertake a critical examination of the *Commentaries*. In Madrid, in London (Hakluyt), and in Paris (Ternaux-Compans), specialized collections rescued a number of vitally important documents from oblivion, and in some cases translated them before they had been published in the original version. The second part of the *Crónica del Perú*, by Cieza de Leon, which is entirely devoted to the history of the Incas, was discovered at this time. Indeed, all this material was so important, and the archives scattered not only throughout Spain, but throughout all Europe, were so rich, that these publications continued to appear until the twentieth century. After the works of Polo de Ondergardo, the two Molinas, and the irreplaceable Cobo, Sarmiento was first brought out in Berlin, in 1906, and Guaman Poma's *Nueva Crónica* which, to everyone's astonishment, was discovered in Copenhagen, was first published in Paris in 1928. The numerous drawings by Guaman Poma that are reproduced in the present volume will permit the reader to understand the unusual importance of this work which, quite deservedly, is considered to be the first and only Peruvian codex.

As a result of all this, not only were the Inca's *Commentaries* no longer taken literally, but criticism of him was all the more severe in view of the fact that, until then, he had been universally adopted. He continued, of course, to be recognized as a classic writer who had been the first to write about Peru. But the burgeoning "science of man" sought to build on solid foundations, and because Garcilaso was an essential writer, it became as pitiless with him as the preceding centuries had been indulgent.

In Spain itself, after having passed through numerous editions that ran through the middle of the eighteenth century, Garcilaso went through a long eclipse, for reasons of a political, rather than of a scientific, nature. The revolts of the Inca, Tupac Amaru, which, after a century and a half of "Pax Hispanica," created disturbances in Peru and Bolivia, led the Spanish government to forbid the *Royal Commentaries* in all the Iberian colonies. The point has already been mentioned, and we shall not insist upon the symbolic value that was attached both to this writer and to his works in Latin America as soon as the former crown colonies threw off Spanish tutelage.

In Paris, Garcilaso was not retranslated, and editions of his works were gradually exhausted during the nineteenth century. However, the *History of Peru*, by the American W. H. Prescott, which was directly inspired by Garcilaso and by Cieza de Leon, was translated into French in 1867, and through it, Garcilaso's work was guaranteed continued existence. Indeed, it met with such success that still today, despite the fact that it has become quite obsolete, certain authors continue to refer to it.

The impetus given by Prescott made itself felt for a long time in Great Britain and we are undoubtedly indebted to him for the only modern translation of the *Commentaries*, which is, however, already nearly a hundred years old since its author, the well-known English authority on the Americas, Sir C. S. Markham, brought it out in London in 1869. We may surmise that it, too, is obsolete, which is one of the facts that prompted the present critical edition. Markham translated the first part of the Inca's work, consisting of nine books. I shall explain later how and why I have added a tenth.

In the notes at the end of this volume, I have attempted to point out and, insofar as this is possible, to correct the principal mistakes and lacunae in the Inca's own text. These observations are based upon the most recent learned publications, and to a lesser extent, on my own personal observations. I shall try now to outline briefly the different sorts of errors encountered, and their causes. I shall then return, in greater detail, to the presentation of this edition.

It should be recalled, first of all, that Garcilaso showed great partiality. An explanation has already been given of how his dual personality of half-breed and convinced

Christian inclined him to minimize and, occasionally even, to neglect mention of everything which, in the government and life of the Inca Emperors, as also of the first Peruvian conquistadors, seemed to him to be morally unjustifiable. We must, however, understand one point, and that is that if Garcilaso made such an attempt to justify the desire for conquest of first one and then the other, it was with no intention of opposing them to each other but, on the contrary, of bringing them together, by considering their accomplishments as two successive stages in the forward march of humanity from the darkness of earliest times till the only total civilization which, for this Christian Inca, must derive from the teachings of Christ. According to him, the people of Tahuantinsuyu lived, before the time of the Incas, "in a state of savagery, without gods or laws, without houses or villages." Despite their own ignorance of the real faith, the Incas raised these peoples from their bestial state and made them into real men, capable at least of receiving the Christian Revelation that was soon to be brought to them by the Spaniards, themselves the legitimate successors, in the eyes of God, to the Incas.

This very personal interpretation of history necessarily impelled Garcilaso to deny the existence in Peru of any pre-Inca civilizations; whereas certain of the most famous among them still flourished on the Pacific coast after the arrival of the Spanish, and were themselves a thousand years old when the Cuzco Empire was scarcely more than two hundred years old. Need we say that this was not merely a matter of prejudice, but also the result of quite justifiable ignorance. It should be recalled as well, to give one example, that the most fantastic suppositions on the subject of the origins of the "mysterious" Tiahuanaco civilization were still current at the beginning of the twentieth century. But Garcilaso's responsibility, although not implicated elsewhere, is very great when he attributes to the Incas the invention of certain techniques which they only took over and developed, however brilliantly. This was particularly true in the case of canals for irrigation purposes, terraced planting (the origins of which are little known), and the famous quipus, concerning the use of which Garcilaso is inclined to embroider somewhat. He likewise alters the figures of the Peruvian hall of fame, occasionally attributing their only paternity to the Incas, and again presenting them as a prefiguration of the Christian God and His heavenly throng. Finally, he mentions human sacrifice only in regions outside Inca jurisdiction, when we know that young people, both boys and girls, were sacrificed—true enough, under exceptional circumstances—to the divinities of the Cuzco temple.

However, the consequences of Garcilaso's prejudices, the omissions, exaggerations, and confusion, did not alter the fact that in his philosophy and in his very conception of history, he remains astonishingly original and ahead of his time. For several centuries were to pass before the idea of helping the human animal to attain to human dignity and, consequently, that of the mission and moral duty of rulers, was revived. The first cause of this unusual viewpoint seems to have been Garcilaso's own social status as a half-breed who, as has already been emphasized, had succeeded in resolving in God (one might say dialectically), the antagonisms that existed between his bloods and his cultures. Nor did his conception of Christianity keep him from being constantly concerned with the future of his country. It might even be said that, as a result of this unusual success, Garcilaso today takes on a third timeliness, following upon those that the eighteenth, the nineteenth, and the early part of the twentieth centuries conferred upon him. He was a fashionable writer, then a learned writer. Today he deserves to become once more in Europe and America what he has never ceased to be in Latin America: that is, a writer who is indispensable to all men of good will. He is not only the "son of a vanquished people." He wants to be, as well, and above all, the leading thinker of a people that has grown rich and taken its place in history, at the cost of a sacrifice that the future must justify.

Garcilaso has also frequently been reproached for the rather fanciful and, at times, confused manner in which he describes the successive Inca conquests. He starts out at the beginning of the work by attributing a number of definite victories to the early Emperors of the dynasty, when it is not even known today whether Manco Capac and Sinchi Roca really existed. Further on, when his account approaches the dawn of actual historic times, he gives credit to the Inca Viracocha for the accomplishments of the Inca Pachacutec, and makes two successive kings of one and the same Inca, son of the latter. In our notes, we have pointed out the mistakes that result from this confusion. It is hard to say what caused it. All we know for certain is that Garcilaso had been living away from Peru for forty years before he started writing his book, and this may well have been the source of a confusion which he shared with many Spanish historians.

Garcilaso's partiality with regard to his paternal ancestors—conquistadors and early colonists—should be considered. For here, too, he reacts historically neither as an Indian, nor as a Spaniard, but as a half-breed. He does not question the right of conquest which the Pope gave to Charles V, and for him the conquistadors, like the Indians, are heroes whose memory he seeks to respect. No doubt his fear of being considered too partial, because of his Indian blood, explains why he is much less severe towards the Spanish conquerors than Las Casas, who had no reason to share his scruples, had allowed himself to be. Garcilaso doesn't mention the extortionate methods of the conquistadors and the colonists. Nor does he mention the enslavement of the Indians, which lasted a long time both in Peru and elsewhere, despite the *Leyes Nuevas*, under the iniquitous *Encomiendas* regime. He doesn't even name the more than famous Potosí silver mines in which countless Indians died in slave labor to satisfy Spanish greed. Indeed, he partially absolves his ancestors of this greed, having seen that most of the early conquerors paid for it with their lives, and that only a few obtained any lasting profit from it. The only mention he makes of it is in connection with the destruction of the monuments of old Peru which, according to him, the Spanish would have done well to keep and maintain, since the very presence of these monuments, in future centuries, would only have enhanced the glory of those who had conquered so great an Empire. But he also stigmatizes this heedless greed, when he tells of the herds of llamas, guanacos, and vicuñas, as well as the other natural wealth of the country, such as the fertilizer known as guano, all of which the Spaniards exhausted entirely in a few decades, whereas a wise and provident Inca policy had husbanded them and made them fructify. Here, as in the case of destruction of the ancient monuments, Garcilaso takes the liberty of judging his ancestors, not too severely, it is true, but without excusing them.

Here then, somewhat cursorily presented, we see what

were the origins as well as the spirit of the mistakes made by Garcilaso, and because of which he has been reproached with not being an "objective" witness of the past. On the scientific plane, however, these mistakes in no way alter the fact that the Inca's work is so filled with information that is either new or not to be found elsewhere, and contains such precision, such wealth of detail, that the *Royal Commentaries* continue to occupy first place on the shelves of any Latin American library.

But, above all, none of these criticisms can change the fact that Garcilaso remains an irreplaceable writer, not only for scientific and literary reasons—his style is on a par with that of the greatest sixteenth century writers—but above all, for reasons that transcend all technical considerations. There are those who consider that, independent of all discussion Garcilaso is one of the great storytellers of his time. Shall we say that he is, above all, a great dramatist who is haunted by the struggle between what is destined to perish and what is eternal. Explanation of the dramatic construction of the *Commentaries* will follow, but it should be recalled that the Inca died in the same year as did Shakespeare and Cervantes. In conclusion, it may be added, too, that in his life as well as in his work, the problems he posed and those he succeeded in solving, while seeking and making ready after his own fashion a future for his country that would leave both Spanish and Indians to the past, lend a timeliness to his personality that, in the middle of the twentieth century, is greater even than the timeliness he enjoyed in the middle of the sixteenth century. For our world of today, which is becoming more and more crossbred and is therefore faced with options that would reject the march of history, needs, and will continue to need as much, if not more, men who, like him, have sought to do better than merely to choose.

Garcilaso was indulgent towards everything he loved and respected; he refused to choose therefore between the two bloods that ran in his veins. Also, although proud of all human accomplishment, as of all spiritual victory, he was in reality one of the most modest writers of his time.

From earliest childhood on, he witnessed events that were amongst the bloodiest in history, and indeed his life itself never ceased to be inwardly dramatic. But he succeeded in overcoming all the obstacles in his path without self-indulgence or bitterness. And the final cry of the *Royal Commentaries*, JESUS, A HUNDRED THOUSAND TIMES JESUS, which he addressed to future generations with such fervor and distress, before laying down his pen forever, is worthy of his most ecstatically devout contemporaries: Santa Teresa de Avila, San Juan de la Cruz, and all those who, from Castile to Aragon, made of the sixteenth century, the Golden Age of Spanish civilization.

THE INCA TRAGEDY

and the presentation of this edition.

As already stated, the only modern translation of the *Comentarios reales,* which is that made into English by Sir C. S. Markham in 1869, includes only the first part of the Inca's work, composed of nine books, to which we have now added a tenth. This tenth book, which ends the present volume, is the complete translation of the first book of the second part of the *Comentarios.*

It should be recalled that the first part of the *Comentarios* is limited to the history of the Incas which, for Garcilaso, ends with the fratricidal struggle between Huaina Capac's two sons, Huascar and Atahualpa, before the arrival of the Spaniards. The second part, entitled *Historia General de Peru,* tells of Spanish Peru as the author knew it, beginning with Pizarro's maiden voyage and ending with the close of the civil wars between the conquistadors and the first administrators sent out from Madrid. The first book of this second part finishes with the deaths of the last independent Inca kings, Huascar and Atahualpa, in 1532-1533, and today this date is generally conceded to mark the end of the Tahuantinsuyu Empire and the beginning of modern times in Peru. This reason alone would have sufficed, therefore, to justify adding this book to the nine preceding ones.

But perhaps by more than anything else our decision was dictated by the dramatic construction of Garcilaso's work, history and tragedy, as we have already pointed out, being indissolubly linked together in his conception of Peru's entry into the modern world, and consequently, in the very structure of the *Commentaries* as well. After a lengthy introduction, which is both legendary and documentary—he wants to make the reader understand what ancient Peru really was—the actual tragedy starts with the reign of the Inca Yahuar Huacac (Weep-blood), his son Viracocha Inca, and the Chanca rebellion. A fissure has become evident in the immutable law according to which Emperors, who are charged with a divine mission, must be perfect in all things. And for the first time, the young Empire is threatened. Thus the first act ends with the victory of the Emperor Viracocha, after which, against a Shakespearian background, we are shown menacing shadows while Heaven predicts both triumphs to come and, rather more vaguely, sin and eventual downfall.

In the second act, the power of the sons of the Sun-god attains to its highest point, with the great Pachacutec and his son, Tupac Inca Yupanqui. The Tahuantinsuyu practically reaches its definitive frontiers, and it looks as though nothing, ever again, will succeed in impeding the course of the pitiless governmental machine that has been set in motion by the Emperors.

Huaina Capac's reign is the subject of the third act. Once again, the peoples who are subject to the crown have become roused to action; once again the "backdrop" of destiny becomes alive with moving shadows, ghosts, and threats. There is a continual crescendo of signs till, as the Inca lies dying, after having divided his Empire between Huascar and Atahualpa, divine law notwithstanding, he himself predicts the arrival of the Spaniards, the "Viracochas," whom the Supreme Being, the great "Pachacamac" (who might have come from the Old Testament), is going to send on earth to punish the guilty Incas.

In the fourth act, the tragedy that had been brewing breaks out. Atahualpa, defying Heaven, attacks his reigning brother, Huascar, overthrows him and dares to take him prisoner. Inca blood has begun to flow throughout the length and breadth of Peru, from Cuzco to the Equator. We are reminded of Thebes. And thus ends the first part of the *Comentarios reales,* or the *History of the Incas.*

But the tragedy is not yet finished. A last act is missing, and we find it in its entirety in the first book of the second part of the *Comentarios.*

When the curtain next rises, the vengeful "Viracochas" enter upon the scene. Just when the powerful Atahualpa thinks he has become the master of his fate, Francisco Pizarro—a sort of *deus ex machina*—comes and sits down at his table like the Commander in *Don Giovanni.* Atahualpa was to maintain his challenge until the end, and having himself fallen into the hands of the newcomers, he sent his secret emissaries to assassinate his brother in his distant prison. It was at this point that the Spaniards, after a rigged trial, executed the last Inca. When the curtain falls, therefore, everything is finished: both Empire and dynasty have definitely disappeared.

During this last act, Garcilaso does not deny that the Spaniards, from a human standpoint, behaved wrongly. He insists upon their arguments, their disagreements, and their hesitations at the time of Atahualpa's "trial." They were not justified, according to his idea, given their role of messengers of God. And if they were to exceed their mandate, the same divine justice that condemned the Incas would turn pitilessly against them. This is the theme of a second tragedy that unfolds in the other books of the second part of the *Royal Commentaries,* a tragedy that simply repeats, in a more secular way, the outline of the first one, based, this time, on the civil wars among the Spaniards and the punishment meted out to the conquistadors who, in their turn, also lose the Empire. The *Commentaries* end, as we said before, with the setting up of a colonial regime in the former Tahuantinsuyu provinces. For this reason, we have stopped there.

In the course of this work, we have taken the liberty of lightening the Inca's text in a few places. The most important of these changes consisted in dropping the first fourteen chapters of Book I of the *History of the Incas* (Pages 11-38, EMECE edition, Buenos Aires). Here Garcilaso, as was customary among the historians of his time, presents the origin of Peru in the light of the Bible, and it is not until Chapter Fourteen, "Origin of the Incas, kings of Peru," that he really approaches his subject. We also cut a few chapters in Books VIII and IX, some of which deal with the flora and fauna native to Peru, while others speak of the first plants and animals brought to Peru by the Spaniards (wheat, grapevines, horses, sheep, and so forth). Lastly, we have here and there dropped or shortened the occasionally tedious intercessions of Jesus Christ our Lord, the Virgin Mary, and the Holy Apostles.

Garcilaso's style is noble and rugged, at the same time that it possesses great elegance. The few flowers of speech he uses are of wrought iron, and one is constantly aware of a Latin construction beneath the form and organization of his sentences. From his vocabulary and from his way of using it, we sense that this man, who wielded both the pen and the sword, had also become a genuine humanist, and we have striven never to forget this point in making this attempt at translation and transposition. Our desire to leave to his words the full, absolute sense that Garcilaso gives them may, at times, have resulted in a certain unavoidable awkwardness, which we ask the reader to excuse.

The aim of our critical and reference notes, as we explained earlier, has been to bring this edition of the *Royal Commentaries* up-to-date, from the documentary standpoint, and in line with the most recent scientific findings. This meant venturing upon treacherous ground, for there are not a few points concerning which far more enlightened persons than ourselves would have hesitated to make definite pronouncements, particularly as regards the chronology of the civilizations of ancient Peru. In all doubtful cases, therefore, we have merely mentioned the hypotheses that are most commonly accepted by specialists in American culture, without risking judgments that are not entirely founded.

The drawings of Guaman Poma de Ayala come from his *Nueva crónica y buen gobierno*, a manuscript chiefly prized for its illustrations. They make it the only Peruvian codex, but the accompanying notes are also of great interest, as they supplement the drawings and explain many of their details. The translation of extracts from the commentaries, appearing in this edition on the back of the illustrations, endeavors to preserve the conversational style of the author whose neologisms and awkward turns of speech give piquancy and character to his comments. Guaman Poma is naïve in expression but far from stupid. It is hoped that the reader will enjoy his spontaneous remarks on the main figures described by Garcilaso. As will be seen, the half-caste Guaman Poma has no scruples; he takes as many liberties with people as with style. He is just as outspoken about the kings, queens, and important personages of the Inca Empire as about the conquistadors, missionaries, and colonists. This must have been somewhat unusual in the days of the Holy Inquisition and the Pax Hispanica.

In conclusion, we should like to take this opportunity to thank all those who kindly helped us with their advice and counsel, especially Mlle Friedberg, ethno-botanist and assistant at the Muséum national d'Histoire naturelle, M. Henri Lehmann, assistant director in charge of the American department of the Musée de l'Homme, and M. Henry Reichlen, attached to the Centre national de la Recherche scientifique.

A. G.

BOOK ONE

Which treats of the origin of the Incas; of the life, works, and conquests of their first king, Manco Capac, and of the founding of the imperial city of Cuzco

After having experimented with several ways of relating from the very beginning the story of the Incas, who were Peru's natural rulers, it has seemed to me that, in reality, nothing could be simpler or surer than to tell what I have many times had the opportunity of hearing as a child, from my mother's lips, or from those of her uncles and others of our closest relatives.

At that time, my mother was living in her native city, Cuzco, and every week, the members of her family who had escaped Atahualpa's cruelty, of which I shall tell in time, came to visit her. On these occasions, the conversation turned almost invariably to the origins of our kings and to their majesty. It also concerned the grandeur of their empire, their conquests and noble deeds, their government in war and peace, and the very wise laws that they had promulgated for the welfare of their subjects and vassals. In short, nothing of what these great lords had done for our country was forgotten.

Then, leaving grandeur behind, my relatives would return to the present, and here they wept over their dead kings and their lost empire. Indeed, I do not believe that there was a single one of these conversations that did not end in tears and wailing, while all those present kept repeating: "Once we were kings, now we are vassals!"

Being but a child, I came and went freely amongst them, and I listened to what they said with the rapt attention with which, at this age, one listens to fairy tales.

And so the months and the years passed, and soon I was sixteen or seventeen years old. Then one day, while they were talking together as was their custom, I went up to the eldest of them and said:

"Inca, my uncle, you have no written records, how then can you remember these things of the past, and what can you know about the origins and beginnings of our kings? The Spanish and the nations that are their neighbors possess books; they know their entire history, and can even say how many thousands of years ago God created heaven and earth. But you who have none, how are you able to tell us of our past? Who was the first Inca? What was his name? From whom was he descended? How did he come to reign? With what men and what arms did he conquer this great empire? In other words, what is the source of our wealth, and of our great feats?"

The Inca, who was delighted with my questions, for he loved to talk about these things, turned towards me. I made ready to listen to him more attentively than ever, and here is what he told me:

"My nephew," said he, "I shall answer you with the greatest pleasure, because it is important for you to have heard these things and you should preserve them in your heart. Know then that, at one time, all the land you see about you was nothing but mountains and desolate cliffs. The people lived like wild beasts, with neither order nor religion, neither villages nor houses, neither fields nor clothing, for they had no knowledge of either wool or cotton. Brought together haphazardly in groups of two and three, they lived in grottoes and caves and, like wild game, fed upon grass and roots, wild fruits, and even human flesh. They covered their nakedness with the bark and leaves of trees, or with the skins of animals. Some even went unclothed. And as for women, they possessed none who were recognized as their very own.

"Seeing the condition they were in, our father the Sun was ashamed for them, and he decided to send one of his sons and one of his daughters from heaven to earth, in order that they might teach men to adore him and acknowledge him as their god; to obey his laws and precepts as every reasonable creature must do; to build houses and assemble together in villages; to till the soil, sow the seed, raise cattle, and enjoy the fruits of their labors like human beings.

"Our father the Sun set his two children down at a place eighty leagues from here, on Lake Titicaca, and he gave them a rod of gold, a little shorter than a man's arm and two fingers in thickness.

" 'Go where you will,' he said to them, 'and whenever you stop to eat or to sleep, plunge this rod into the earth. At the spot where, with one single thrust, it disappears entirely, there you must establish and hold your court.

And the peoples whom you will have brought under your sway shall be maintained by you in a state of justice and reason, with piety, mercy, and mildness.

" 'To the entire world,' added our father the Sun, 'I give my light and my brilliance; I give men warmth when they are cold; I cause their fields to fructify and their cattle to multiply; each day that passes I go all around the world in order to have a better knowledge of men's needs and to satisfy these needs: follow my example. Do unto all of them as a merciful father would do unto his well-beloved children; for I have sent you on earth for the good of men, that they might cease to live like wild animals. You shall be the kings and lords of all the peoples who accept our law and our rule.'

"Having thus declared his will to his two children, our father the Sun dismissed them. They then left Lake Titicaca and walked northwards, trying vainly each day to thrust their rod of gold into the earth. And so they came to a little shelter about seven or eight leagues from here. Day was breaking when they left it and that is why the Inca called this spot Caparec Tempu, which means: the Inn of Morning. Later, he filled it with people and, to this day, the inhabitants of that village take pride in this name that comes from our first king. From there, the Inca and his bride, our queen, entered into Cuzco valley which, at that time, was nothing but wild, mountainous country.

"The first halt they made in this valley," my uncle said, "was at a place called Huanacauri, a half-day's walk from here. There they tried their rod and not only did it sink into the earth, but it disappeared entirely. Then our Inca turned to his sister-bride:

" 'Our father the Sun,' he said, 'has commanded us to remain in this valley, to settle here and make it our home. You then go your way, and I shall go mine, to call together and assemble the inhabitants of these regions, in order that we might teach them good, as we have been ordered to do.'

"Now they left the hill of Huanacauri, each going his own way; and this spot being the first to have been trod on by their feet, you will understand," my uncle said, "that we built a temple there, so that our father the Sun should be perpetually adored in recognition of the signal favor he showed us on that day.[1] The prince set out for the north and the princess for the south. They explained to all whom they met that their father the Sun had sent them on earth to be the rulers and benefactors of this country, to teach them all how to live, how to clothe and feed themselves like men, instead of like animals.

"The savages to whom they spoke these promising words marveled as much at what they saw as at what they heard: for the Inca and his sister-bride were both arrayed in garments and ornaments that had been given to them by our father the Sun, and both of them had ears that were pierced and open the way we, their descendants, wear ours today. Never had the inhabitants of this region seen anything like it; therefore, they believed all that was told them, they worshiped our ancestors as the children of the Sun, and obeyed them as their kings. The news of this wonderful event began to spread from place to place and a great gathering of men and women was soon assembled about the two Incas, ready to follow them wherever they might lead.

"Our sovereigns then distributed the necessary tasks amongst this crowd of persons, ordering some to go seek food for all, whilst others, following their instructions, were to begin to build huts and houses. Thus our imperial city came into existence, and was divided into two halves: *Hanan*-Cuzco, or Upper-Cuzco, and *Hurin*-Cuzco, or Lower-Cuzco. Hanan-Cuzco was founded by our king and Hurin-Cuzco by our queen, and that is why the two parts were given these names, without the inhabitants of one possessing any superiority over those of the other, but simply to recall the fact that certain of them had been originally brought together by the king, and certain others by the queen. There existed only one single difference between them, a difference in accordance with the king's desire, and that was, that the inhabitants of Upper-Cuzco were to be considered as the elder, and those of Lower-Cuzco as the younger brothers. Indeed, it was as it is in the case of a living body, in which there always exists a difference between the right and the left hands, for the reason that those from above had been brought together by the male, and those from below by the female element. All the cities and all the villages in our Empire were subsequently divided in this way into upper and lower lineages, as well as into upper and lower districts.[2]

"While peopling the city, our Inca taught the male Indians the tasks that were to be theirs, such as selecting seeds and tilling the soil. He taught them how to make hoes, how to irrigate their fields by means of canals that connected natural streams, and even to make these same shoes that we still wear today. The queen, meanwhile, was teaching the women how to spin and weave wool and cotton, how to make clothing, as well as other domestic tasks.

"In short, our sovereigns, the Inca king, who was master of the men, and Queen Coya, who was mistress of the women, taught their subjects everything that had to do with human living.

"The first subjects of the Inca were soon well aware of the numerous benefits they derived from their new situation and they went immediately into the mountains to proclaim to all their neighbors the arrival on earth of the marvelous children of the Sun. In proof of their statements, they displayed their clothing and their foodstuffs, explaining that now they lived in houses, grouped together in villages. Soon, the savages began to marvel, too, and they came in droves to join the Inca and his sister, remaining to serve and obey them. After six or seven years, they had become so numerous that the Inca possessed armed troops for his defense and for subjugating those who did not come of their own accord. He had taught them to make bows, lances, arrows, and bludgeons.

"In order to shorten this account of the exploits of our first king, we shall say simply that he extended his rule towards the east as far as the river which we call Paucartampu, that he conquered eight leagues of land to the west, as far as the great Apurimac river, and nine leagues to the south, as far as the Quequesana. In this latter direction, he had more than one hundred villages built, the most important of which contained a hundred homes.

"Such then," my uncle concluded, "were the beginnings of our city which, today, as you can see, is rich and populous; such were those of the great, illustrious Empire that your father and his companions took from us; and such were our first Incas, our first kings, those who came here during the first centuries of the world and from whom all our other kings are descended, in the same way that all of us, all your relatives, are. I am unable to say exactly at what date the Sun sent his first children down to earth, because that demands calculation that is beyond my memory; let us say that it was at least four hundred years ago. Our Inca's name was Manco Capac and our Coya Mama, Occlo Huaco. They were brother and sister, as I explained to you before, the children of the Moon and the Sun.

"I believe now that I have answered all your questions and, in order not to make you weep, I have held back from my own eyes the tears of blood wrung from my heart by sorrow at the spectacle of our Incas' downfall and our lost Empire."

My uncle, the Inca, had told all this in his own language, which is my mother tongue, and I have tried to translate it faithfully, without, however, being able to convey all the majesty and significance of his words. I have also been obliged to omit certain phrases that might have seemed offensive. What was important, was to lose none of the real meaning of his story, and this I have made an effort to do. My uncle, the Inca, told me other things, too, when he used to come to see my mother, and I'll tell them when I come to them, in the course of this volume, naming their author, and regretting only that I did not question him further, for I had in him a valuable source of information.

After having established his capital, the Inca Manco Capac founded many other towns and villages. East of Cuzco, as far as the river called Paucartampu, and on either side of the Antisuyu royal road, he set up thirteen villages, nearly all of which were inhabited by the people call Poqués. To the west, in a space eight leagues long and nine to ten leagues wide, he founded thirteen villages, along both sides of the Cuntisuyu royal road. Three peoples contributed to this: the Mascas, the Chillquis and the Pap'ris. To the north of the city, the Mayas, the Cancus, the Chinchapuyus and the Rimactampus inhabited twenty villages. The remainder of these peoples settled in the lovely Sacsahuana valley, the very same spot where, later, Gonzalvo Pizarro was to be defeated and imprisoned.[8] The most remote of these villages was seven leagues from the city. Finally, to the south of Cuzco, he founded some thirty-eight or forty villages, eighteen of which were inhabited by Ayarmacans, and the others by five or six different tribes. Among the latter were the Cauinias, who held the following belief: their ancestors, they said, had originated in a lagoon to which the souls of the dead returned, then reappeared in the bodies of newborn infants. They had a very frightening looking idol to whom they made barbaric sacrifices, but the Inca, Manco Capac, abolished both idol and sacrifices, and orderd them to worship the Sun, as his other vassals did.

These first villages, which numbered about one hundred, were still quite sparsely populated. However, thanks to the privileges and advantages that Manco Capac granted them, they soon grew in size, and counted from four hundred to one thousand inhabitants. The great tyrant Atahualpa was jealous of these same privileges which had been, for centuries, the source of their prosperity, and he did away with a great number of them, just as he did in many other parts of the empire.

Today, in fact, nothing remains of them, since a Spanish viceroy overthrew all the former organization of Peru, making five or ten villages into one, and often with such unfortunate consequences that I prefer not to speak of it.

Having thus assembled his first subjects together, and taught them what was necessary for the maintenance of life, the Inca Manco Capac instructed them in the natural and reasonable laws that were to govern their relationships to one another.

In order that peace and concord might reign, and that neither anger nor passion should come between them, he succeeded in convincing them that each one should do unto others as he would have others do unto him, so true it is that the law must be the same for all. He particularly inculcated them with respect for women and young girls, since, until then, the lack of it had been a feature of their triumphant barbarism. Adultery, homicide, and theft were punished with death. Marriage was allowed with only one woman, who was chosen in the husband's family, in order not to alter his lineage. A married couple being required, from the moment of their union, to supply their own needs and govern their own household, it was against the law to take a wife who had not attained to her twentieth year. In the same way that the queen, Mama Occlo, had taught the Indian women to spin and weave, the king had all the animals that were wandering freely over the mountains rounded up, so that their wool could be used to clothe men and women. At the head of every village he established a *curaca,* or lord, chosen for his merits, and the others had to obey this leader, in the same way that a son obeys his father.

In all the villages the harvest was reaped in common, after which it was divided equally among all the inhabitants, pending the time when there would be sufficient arable land to permit each one to have his own plot. Divine worship was also prescribed and regulated, and temples were erected on sites chosen by the Inca, in order to make sacrifices to the Sun and thank him for his blessings. At the same time they worshiped the Moon, as being the mother of the royal couple without whom humanity would have remained in its primitive state of barbarism. Lastly, when there were enough girls of royal blood, the Inca founded a home for the brides of the Sun, that is, a convent for dedicated virgins.

And the Indians, with the simplicity that is still theirs, believed firmly in all these fables, and never doubting the divine nature of their king and queen, obeyed strictly everything that was ordered them.

Having tested for many years the love, devotion, and respect of his subjects, the Inca decided to ennoble them, in order to increase their attachment to him; and in so doing, he accorded them certain privileges of dress which, until then, had been limited to his own person, and, more especially, to his head. In this connection, it should be recalled that the Inca Manco Capac, as well as his descendants, wore his hair cut a finger's length from his skull. Being unfamiliar with scissors, they cut their hair like that with a knife, made of silex, at the cost of what effort we can imagine, which caused a young Inca classmate of mine to say one day: "If your Spanish forefathers had done nothing else than to bring us scissors, combs, and mirrors, I think we should have given them all the gold and all the silver we had in our country."

The Incas were conspicuous not only for this haircut,

but also for their ears, which, as I have already said, were pierced, and so elongated by the volume and weight of the enormous jewels they hung on them, that if the lobe became detached as a result, its distended flesh formed a strip half as wide as a man's finger and longer than his hand: which seems impossible when we see how little flesh there is ordinarily on the lower part of an ear. This Indian custom is the source of the nickname, "Ear People," that the Spaniards gave them.

For their headdress, the Incas wore a braid the width of a finger, which they called a *llautu*, made of several colors, and rolled four or five times around their skulls.

It is by these first three peculiarities, their cropped hair, their ears, and their braid, that one recognizes an Inca. The first privilege that Manco Capac granted his subjects was that of being allowed to wear this braid, on condition that it would not be of just any color, but of black only.

A little later, he permitted them to cut their hair as well, but, in order to maintain certain distinctions between the different peoples of the empire, as also between them and himself, he invented a hairdress proper to each one, according to rank and province of origin. Thus, certain of them wore their hair in the shape of a toque, that came down over the lobes of their ears and left their foreheads and temples free; while others had the right to show half their ears—but only half—and not one had the right to crop his hair the way the king did. These traditions were faithfully held to during the entire history of Peru, no one wanting to be confused today with one and tomorrow with another of his neighbors.

Still later, wishing to show his satisfaction by granting a new favor, the Inca authorized his subjects to pierce their ears. But, here too, there were regulations as to the size of the hole that was allowed, the shape and type of ornament that each one could stick in or hang on it, according to rank and province of origin. The Maya Indians, for instance, wore a little baton as thick as one's little finger, stuck through the lobe, while the Poqués decorated themselves with a tuft of white wool, as thick as one's thumb, which hung down on each side of their ears. The Muinas, Huarucs and Chillquis were given reed pendants, and the Rimactampus and their neighbors had the exclusive right to use for this purpose the soft, light wood we call *maguey*, and which, in the Peruvian language, is called *chuchàu*. The Urcos, the Y'ùcays and the Tampus, from the lower Rio Y'ùcay, had the right to pierce the biggest holes in their ears, but even these holes could not be larger than half the size of that pierced in the royal ears.

When old age was upon him and the Inca felt that he was ready to die, he summoned to him the leaders among his vassals and explained to them that the time was approaching when he was going to return to heaven and take his rest in the arms of his father the Sun; but before leaving them, he wanted to bequeath to them his own name, in memory of himself, in the same way that a father bequeaths his name to his beloved sons, in order that they should remain honored and respected by everyone. And thus it was that the first subjects of Manco Capac, and their descendants, had the right to the title of Incas. But neither their wives nor their daughters could be called *pallas*, this title remaining the exclusive privilege of women of royal blood.

The descendants of these Incas, whom from now on I shall call Incas by privilege, are those who are still most commonly to be seen in Peru, and who enjoy certain advantages granted them by the Spaniards.[4] As for the Incas of royal blood, only very few of them are left, and frequently they are wretched and unknown, as a result of the cruelty and tyranny with which Atahualpa pursued them.

For himself, and for the kings who were his descendants, the Inca Manco Capac retained only one of the marks that set him apart, and that was a colored band worn about the forehead, from one temple to the other. The king's band was red, and that of the crown prince yellow and narrower. We shall learn later how, in the course of a solemn ceremony, these bands were conferred upon them.

It is not known exactly how long Manco Capac's reign lasted: thirty years according to some, forty according to others; all we know is that it was quite a long reign. When this first Inca felt the approach of death, after calling together his most faithful subjects, as we said before, he held a second, secret, conference, in the company of his sons, to whom he transmitted his last will and testament:

"You must never forget," he said to them, "that you are the sons of the Sun. You must worship him and respect him as a god, and as a father. Be kind and merciful towards your subjects. Enlarge the Empire and draw the Indians to you by love and not by force, for men who are under constraint are never good vassals. Never say one thing, then do another, for if your actions are the opposite of your words, you will lose the confidence of your people. My father the Sun has called me, and I must go to rest in his arms. When this same moment comes for you, make the same recommendations to your sons that I am making to you today, in order that from generation unto generation, the Sun's orders may be respected. Live in peace, for I shall watch over you from above, and I shall come to your assistance every time it is necessary to do so."

This was his last will. He left, as his successor, the Crown Prince Sinchi Roca, who was the first son he had had by his sister-bride, the Coya Mama Occlo Huaca. Prince Sinchi Roca married his eldest sister, Mama Cura; and all of Manco Capac's other children also married one another, in order that there should be no alteration in the purity of this royal blood that, quite fabulously, they said was the blood of the Sun.[5]

The burial ceremonies of our first king lasted several months, during which his vassals mourned his loss with great sincerity. They offered him numerous sacrifices of sheep, lambs, ewes, domestic rabbits, birds, grain, and vegetables, as though to the real master of all this wealth which he had bequeathed to them.

And I, myself, think that this first Inca, whose name meant both the Good and the Wealthy, must have been a man of wisdom, prudence, and intelligence, who well understood the simplicity of his peoples, and who had astutely and shrewdly invented this fable about the Sun in order to make them obey him and follow the path of natural progress. Thus, and thanks to the unusual appearance he assumed (by piercing his ears in the way I have described), he succeeded in convincing them that he was not a man like other men, but actually the son of this heavenly body; which was why he could be respected, obeyed, and adored as he was. And this belief became so deep-rooted that, from then on, no Inca of royal blood, nor any other ordinary person in the whole of Peru, ever attributed any other origin to our kings.

1. The Incas held in reverence two totem stones, known as Huanacauri and Añahuarque, on two sacred hills which bore their names, at a short distance from Cuzco. Even today, at the top of the hill called Huanacauri, about ten miles from Cuzco, the foundations of a square Inca-style temple can still be seen, half-buried in the undergrowth. These two stones were believed to be two mythical ancestors, male and female, according to Krickeberg (?). The stone called Huanacauri, mentioned frequently in the present work, was, according to Cobo, the "brother" of Manco Capac, the first Inca, also represented by a stone preserved in the Temple of the Sun in Cuzco. Again according to Cobo, the Inca armies never took the field without taking with them either the Huanacauri stone or its "brother," known as Manco Capac.

2. This division into two halves, known as *hanan* and *hurin*, was common to all the Andean tribes from Ecuador to the south of Peru. Perhaps the Huanacauri and Añahuarque totems corresponded to these two matrimonial "halves." (Note 3, Book VII)

3. Gonzalvo Pizarro, a rebel against the crown, was defeated in battle on the plain of Sacsahuana and decapitated at the command of the Viceroy La Gasca, in 1548, seventeen years after the arrival of the Spanish in Peru. This event can be considered as marking the end of civil war and the beginning of the Spanish colonization of Peru.

4. Most of these Incas by privilege were named by the Inca Pachacutec in the fifteenth century. (Rowe)

5. Garcilaso believes that it was, and always had been, decreed that the Inca should marry his own sister. This belief was not shared by Cobo, who regarded Tupac Inca Yupanqui, the son of Pachacutec, as the originator of this custom:
   "This king [Tupac Yupanqui] broke the inviolable Inca law forbidding marriage with blood relations of the first degree. For in spite of this custom, to which there had never previously been an exception, he took to wife Mama Occlo, his full sister, and . . . decreed that kings, and kings alone, might marry their sisters as he had done; and, on his deathbed, he ordained that his two children, Huaina Capac and Coya Cusi Rimay, who were brother and sister, should marry; he justified this by certain dreams he had had and gave as his reason that he who was to be the Inca should be of pure, unmixed blood and that procreation by sisters gave a true line of succession." (Cobo)

BOOK TWO

Which treats of the life,
works, and conquests
of Sinchi Roca,
second king of Peru,
and of the third king,
Lloque Yupanqui;
together with the administrative
divisions of the Empire,
and the knowledge acquired
by these lords in astrology,
medicine and pharmacy,
geometry, geography,
arithmetic, music,
philosophy, and poetry

It was the duty of the priests to make sacrificial offerings. In Cuzco all the priests of the house of the Sun were Incas of royal blood, and the other attendants were Incas by privilege. The high priest was usually an uncle or brother of the king. None of these monks wore any special vestment. The priests of the other temples of the Sun—which existed in numerous provinces—were chosen in the immediate family of the provincial leaders, but the superior—the bishop, as it were—had to be an Inca, in order that the ceremonies and sacrifices everywhere should correspond to those performed in the capital. There were also numerous convents for continent nuns, some of whom remained virgins all their lives without being able to leave the convent, while others became concubines of the king. We shall explain later the situation of these women.[1]

It should be recalled that every time the Inca kings wanted to promulgate a new law, they always attributed its authorship to their ancestor Manco Capac who, they said, had promulgated certain laws during his lifetime and left others dormant in order that his successors might make them public whenever they proved to be necessary. They added that all of these laws had been taught him by his father the Sun, before he was sent to earth.

As a result of this tradition, it being impossible for us to say exactly to which Inca may be attributed this or that new decree promulgated during the course of history, we shall limit ourselves to giving an account of the laws of the Empire, beginning with the first one upon which the entire organization of the public welfare was based.[2] Then we shall recount the conquests and noble deeds of each ruler, alternating them with descriptions of the customs that were established little by little, of the temples, convents, and other sacred spots, of the festivals, the noble army, service in the royal household, and the majesty of court life, and thus, by varying our account, reduce its monotony.

The Inca kings divided the Empire into four districts, according to the cardinal points, the whole of which they called *Tahuantinsuyu,* which means the four parts of the world. The center was Cuzco which, in the Peruvian language, means the navel of the world. This name was well chosen, since Peru is long and narrow like the human body, and Cuzco is situated in the middle of its belly.

The eastern part of the Empire was called Antisuyu, from the name of the Anti, or Andes, country. Cuntisuyu took its name from the little province of Cunti, which lay west of the capital and covered the entire occidental part of the Empire. The northern part, which included the province of Chincha, was called Chinchasuyu; and the southern part, which covered the very large Colla [3] province, was called Collasuyu. The entire territory of the Empire, as far as the Inca's conquests extended, was encompassed by these four names. Thus the kingdom of Chile, although it is six hundred leagues from the province of Colla, was a part of Collasuyu and, in the same way, the province of Quito, which is separated by more than four hundred leagues from Chincha, was a part of the district of Chinchasuyu. The names of the four highways that stretch from Cuzco towards the cardinal points were also taken from this first division of the territories and kingdoms.

The first law promulgated by the Incas divided all the inhabitants of the Empire, province by province, and village by village, into groups of ten souls, each group being headed by a decurion chosen among the ten. One decurion out of five commanded the four others, and thus was in charge of fifty souls. For two decurions heading fifty souls, there was a new superior who, consequently, presided over one hundred souls. A decurion captain headed five of the latter, and, therefore, was in charge of five hundred persons. Two of these companies took orders from a general whose power, therefore, extended to a thousand souls; and there was no higher echelon among the decurions for the reason that, according to the Incas, the care of one thousand persons is quite sufficient to occupy one man alone.[4]

The ordinary decurions, or leaders of ten, had two principal responsibilities. One, more or less that of an attorney, or representative, consisted in diligently and earnestly soliciting the help of the higher authorities on behalf of those under their jurisdiction who were in any sort of difficulty. Thus they had to ask for grain if it happened to be lacking for planting or for food; or for wool to make clothes with, or perhaps the necessary materials to repair a run-down or burned-out house. Their second responsibility, which was of a juridical nature, consisted in reporting to their superiors all misdemeanors that occurred inside their group of ten. According to the seriousness of each case, punishment of these offenses fell upon one or the other of their superiors in the hierarchy, a leader of fifty, or one hundred or more, in order that the higher ranks need not intervene about peccadilloes, and, even less, the judges of the supreme court. Whoever, among these corporals, inferiors or superiors, failed to report an offense within an hour, was himself punished in proportion to its seriousness, in fact, he was doubly punished; on the one hand, for not doing his duty, and on the other, because, by keeping silent about a misdemeanor, he had assumed it as his own. And since special officials were assigned to supervise these corporals, the latter fulfilled their obligations with exactitude and diligence. For this reason there were neither vagabonds nor idlers in the Empire, application of the law being instantaneous, and punishment being so severe that it consisted, for the most part, of the death penalty, whatever the crime it was intended to punish.[5] And this is explained by the fact that not so much the seriousness of the offense itself was considered as the crime of lese majesty and, therefore, of lese divinity that it implied.

The offenses of children were punished in proportion to their age and to the degree of their innocence. The fathers of the guilty ones were often punished more severely than they themselves were, for having neglected their first duty which was to educate their children in respect of the law. And this is why children were so obedient and so well brought up that there was no difference between them and pet lambs.

Our sovereigns were always opposed in their legislation to imposing fines and confiscating property. Because, they said, if a man guilty of an offense is deprived of his property, and his life is spared, what else will he do with it, if not commit even more offenses! If a curaca[6] became rebellious (nothing was more severely punished by the Incas) or committed some other offense that incurred the death penalty, his heir was not deprived of the right to succeed him; but the accusation was transferred to the son with a detailed account of the crime, and the punishment that had been meted out to him, in order that, having thus been warned, the son would beware of falling into the same errors.

This procedure also obtained with regard to the military, so that captains who were natives of the provinces in which they levied their men of arms were never discharged; on the contrary, they were maintained in their rank, even in the case of camp commanders, and put under the leadership of princes of royal blood: and these captains, who were very proud of having become the "limbs," as they said, that is, the legs and arms of these princes, served them all the more devotedly. A judge had to apply the law to the letter, without ever attempting to arbitrate it, for the law was considered as a royal edict and therefore allowed of no appeal. We might consider, given the severity of this legal system, that it was the creation of barbarians. But if we also consider how much it benefited the nation, then we come to the conclusion that it was the creation of wise and prudent men, concerned, above all else, with eradicating evil wherever it might exist. All men naturally love life and hate death, with the result that the subjects of the Inca came to hate quite as naturally the offenses that led to death and, for this reason, there was little occasion to apply the law, from one year's end to the other, throughout the whole of this great Empire. Thus, although it was more than thirteen hundred leagues long, and comprised a great variety of peoples and tongues, ancient Peru, thanks to the uniformity of its legislation, was as simply governed as any home.

Lastly, it should be added that the divine origin which the Indians attributed to this legislation, as also to the Inca's person, helped to inspire respect and love for both. And because of this fact, he who broke the law, whatever his misdemeanor, was charged by the entire people with sacrilege and anathema. Frequently even, a delinquent, prompted merely by the pangs of his conscience, would come of his own accord to accuse himself before the court, being persuaded that his offense was at the origin of this or that calamity that had overtaken the Empire, as, for instance, an epidemic or poor harvests; and he would say that, by his death, he hoped to appease the wrath of the divinity. I believe that we may see in this custom, which, to a certain extent, is analogous to that of public confession, the source of a mistake which has been made by several Spanish chroniclers, who have stated that the Peruvian Indians practiced confession in the same way that Christians do.

There was no possibility of appeal to courts of justice, either civil or criminal. Minor proceedings were heard before a village judge who, after having listened to both sides, had to settle the matter within five days. For more serious cases, the persons involved were heard by a provincial governor without ever having to go beyond this point. And this was a wise provision on the part of the Incas whose aim was to make it impossible for poor people to lose more in costs of travel and procedure than they frequently might hope to win by going to court.

Each lunar month, the local judges reported on the cases they had handled to other judges of higher rank, and the latter to still others, up to the supreme judges, who were the governors or viceroys of the Empire. All these reports were thus transmitted to the Inca's court by means of colored cords, tied in a certain way, with each knot having its precise significance. We shall speak later, in a special chapter, of this utilization of colored knots, by means of which all the imperial archives were constituted.

Territorial disputes, that arose between the different kingdoms or provinces, were settled by special envoys of royal blood, sent from Court by the Inca to pass judgment in his name. If such a decision failed to meet favor with the sovereign, he put off its application until a voyage made it possible for him to handle the affair himself, which his vassals considered to be a very special favor.

In addition to the dual responsibilities we have already described, the decurions were obliged, each lunar month, to furnish their superiors in line of rank with a record of the births and deaths that had occurred in the territory administered by them, as also of their conscripts who had died in battle. In the army, the officers, from lieutenants to generals, fulfilled the same duties of protector and accuser, as did their counterparts in the civil administration, with the result that the same order and discipline reigned in the thick of battle as at court and in the pacified provinces. Pillaging cities was forbidden, even when they had been conquered by armed force.

Thanks to this constant census of his subjects, which was carried out kingdom by kingdom and province by province, the Inca was able to make a judicious distribution of the tasks necessary to the public welfare, such as construction and care of roads, bridges or crown properties, as well as military enlistment of both soldiers and porters. If a man came back from the war without permission, his commanding officer made this fact known to the civil authorities of his province, and he was put to death.

The Inca had a census made, not only of the inhabitants of each province, but also of all that these provinces produced annually in the way of goods of every sort. This was in order to learn what provisions would be required to come to the assistance of his vassals, if they were to suffer from shortages, or had a poor harvest, and the quantities of wool and cotton that would be needed to clothe them, as we shall explain later.[7]

The fact that the Incas took such attentive care of the welfare of their vassals explains the frequent statement made by Father Blas Valera,[8] who said that, even more than kings, they were the prudent, diligent guardians of their people.

In order to make sure that governors, judges, and other civil servants did their duty in a precise manner, inspectors or secret visitors were constantly traveling about the Empire, and they brought back reports of what they had seen to their superiors. They were called *tucuyricoc,* that is to say, the men-who-see-everything.[9] These civil servants, like all the others, from the lowest to the highest, were organized hierarchically, in order that none should neglect his duty. The penalties inflicted upon civil servants were always greater than those involving ordinary citizens, and their severity increased with increase in rank, because, it was argued, the first obligation of men who have been chosen to punish the offenses of others, is to commit none themselves.

According to the Indians, no Inca of royal blood was ever punished, at least, not in public. And indeed, the

The Author (Guaman Poma) en route to the City of Lima

doctrine of their ancestors and the example of their elders, in addition to the commonly accepted belief that they were descended from the Sun, and that their lives had no other aim than that of teaching and dispensing good among men, maintained them in conditions of such constraint that they naturally presented an example of virtue, rather than one of scandal. And how, one might ask, would these princes, whose life permitted them to gratify every desire, ever have had occasion to commit an offense? If he happened to desire some pretty woman, the Inca knew that he had only to ask her father, who not only would not refuse to let him have her, but would also consider this opportunity to give satisfaction to his sovereign as a great honor and good fortune. And the same thing was true with regard to material possessions as to women, since the entire land belonged to the Sun and to his descendants, whether they occupied public office or not; this permitted them to choose whatever they wanted, throughout the Empire, without it being possible to refuse them; nor was there any more possibility that they might kill or wound someone than that they would take something from him, since the entire people adored them, and could not offend them, however slightly, without laying themselves open to the terrible punishments provided by the law. It may be stated, in fact, that in the entire history of Peru, there is no example of an Indian having committed an offense against an Inca, either with regard to his person, his property, or his honor. Certain Spanish chroniclers have said that there existed a law according to which no Inca could be executed for a crime. In the eyes of the Indians, such a law would have constituted a scandal, since it would have seemed to encourage their kings to do evil rather than good. What does appear to be certain, however, is that had an Inca been guilty of a crime, he would have first been cast out by his peers, then punished with unprecedented harshness and severity.

At the head of each one of the four parts of the Empire, councils of war, justice, and internal affairs sat in permanent session. These councils were presided over by the viceroys who were thus able to keep their sovereign informed of all that went on in the kingdom. All four of these viceroys were of royal blood and as familiar with matters of peace as with those of war. Together with the Inca king, they formed a council of state by which all important decisions concerning the Empire were taken.

Here I shall end this first account of the laws and government of the Incas.

Manco Capac was succeeded by his son Sinchi Roca, whose name meant "The Brave," which he was, in everything except war, since he never had to make war against anyone. However, as a wrestler, runner, jumper, or discus and javelin thrower, as well as at any exercise requiring strength, he was unsurpassed.

After having presided over solemn funeral ceremonies for the departed king, this prince gathered together his principal curacas and informed them that he had decided to enlarge the Empire by convoking the neighboring nations, in order to conform to the last wishes of his father and convert additional souls to the cult of the Sun. The curacas replied that they were ready to carry out any orders he might give, even it it meant casting themselves into flames to show their love for him.

They set out in the direction of Collasuyu, and the Inca convoked the savages, immediately upon crossing his own frontiers, in order to induce them to accept the Sun's laws. The Puchinas and the Canchis listened attentively to his wise words and complied without making any difficulties. Others followed suit and thus, without striking a single blow, the Inca extended his frontiers to the village of Chuncura, twenty leagues further than Manco Capac had gone. Throughout all this new territory the Indians swore faithful allegiance to the new code, and renounced the cult of idols along with their other bad habits.

Certain persons have stated that Sinchi Roca's conquests stopped here but, according to others, he also acquired the nations that were established on the Umasuyu road, such as those formed by the Cancallas, the Cachas, the Rurucachis, the Asilus, the Asancatus and the Huancanis, as far as the place called Pucara de Umasuyu. *Pucara* means fortress, and it is said that Sinchi Roca did, in fact, build a fortress here for defense of his frontier. On the Andes side, he went as far as the Callahuya river, which furnishes a gold ore so fine and so pure, that it is over twenty-four carats in weight. Whether the conquest of these new territories was accomplished by the second or the third Inca is of little importance; what is certain is that they were acquired, not by force of arms, but by the force of conviction and promises, over several years, the exact number of which we do not know exactly, any more than we know the exact length of Sinchi Roca's reign: it is generally thought that it lasted thirty years; and the king's role, during this time, was that of a competent gardener who harvests his crops in all confidence, as a result of careful, diligent work.

When his hour was near, the Inca Sinchi Roca announced that he was going to rest in the arms of his father the Sun; then he breathed his last, leaving as his successor his legitimate son Lloque Yupanqui, born of his sister-bride, Mama Cura. His other children, both legitimate and illegitimate, were very numerous, and thus the house of the Sun's descendants continued to increase.[10]

As soon as he came into power, the Inca Lloque Yupanqui, whose name means "the left-handed," levied an army of some six to seven thousand men, in order to extend the limits of the Empire among the peoples who had not been amenable to the voice of persuasion. He chose his counselors and captains among his own relatives and named two of his uncles as camp commanders. Then, leaving the Umasuyu road which his father had followed, he took the Orcosuyu road which, with the first-mentioned, takes in the great Lake Titicaca, in the Collasuyu district.

Having crossed the frontier, the Inca entered into a province called Cana, from where he dispatched messengers to invite the Indians to join him. The Canas, after having demanded and been given detailed information about what they would have to do, replied that they would be glad to comply with the Inca's wishes, since his laws and customs appeared to be preferable to their own. Leaving the task of instructing and organizing their territory to his minister-delegates, the king forged ahead in the direction of their neighbors, the Ayauiris. But unlike all the Indians encountered thus far by the Incas, these people refused to hear what they had to say, and determined to fight to the last man rather than renounce their freedom. Now, for the first time, the Incas were obliged to use force, not because it was to their liking to do so, but because they had to defend themselves against these people, who attacked them instead of listening to them. There were killed and wounded on both sides, then the Ayauiris entrenched themselves in their capital, from where, having fortified themselves as best they could, they made deadly attacks every day against the Inca's troops. However, recalling the will of his ancestors, the Inca avoided battle each time, and conducted himself as though he were the besieged rather than the besieger, ordering his army to encircle these barbarians, if possible, without actually coming to grips with them. The Ayauiris, mistaking for cowardice what, in reality, was merely royal lenience, grew bolder instead of calmer, and even went so far as to attack the king's own headquarters, despite the losses incurred.

At this point, the Inca, fearing that this bad example might incite other nations to take up arms against him, decided to punish these die-hards as they deserved. He called up fresh troops, not because the war made this necessary, but in order to make the enemy aware of his power, and encircled the besieged troops so effectively that, being confined to their fortress, they were soon reduced to a state of famine. Finally, out of despair, they tried to leave in a body. The result was a fierce battle that lasted a whole day and left many dead and wounded in both camps; however, the Ayauiris found themselves in such a sorry plight that they made no further attempts to come forth from their fortress. Indeed, the Inca could have massacred them all. Instead, they preferred to tighten their hold until the Ayauiris would be obliged to surrender, which, finally, they did. The king did not take advantage of their defeat, but was content with making them see how great an offense they had committed in refusing to listen to the Sun's envoy. Then he pardoned them and gave orders that they should be well treated. Following upon which, after naming minister-delegates to instruct them and make a census of all assets in their land that would become the property of the Sun and of the crown, he continued his march as far as the village we today call Pucara, which he was obliged to take by force, and on the site of which he had a fortress erected to mount guard over his new frontier. After accomplishing all this, he returned to Cuzco, where he was received with much feasting and rejoicing.

A few years after these military exploits, the Inca Lloque Yupanqui returned to the fortress of Pucara with some eight or nine thousand fighting men, determined to succeed in making new conquests. In order to satisfy his ambitions, he alleged as pretext, as all the Incas did, that he had received orders from the Sun. From Pucara, he sent messengers to the cities of Paucarcolla and Hatuncolla, from which the name of the Collasuyu is derived. This is a vast province that groups numerous different peoples under a single name.

After having listened to the imperial messengers, the Collas decided that the resistance of the Ayauiris having brought divine punishment upon them, it would be better not to follow their example but, on the contrary, to comply, without further ado, to the will of this son of the Sun. They therefore came out to meet him, dressed in gala array, acclaimed him with songs suitable to the occasion, and led him into their city with great pomp, assuring him that nothing could give them greater happiness than to be his vassals, adore the Sun, and obey his laws.

The Inca was very pleased and applauded them; among other favors, he distributed his own garments among them, which they took as a very special honor. Since that time, these two cities, particularly Hatuncolla, have always been in high favor with the Incas, and obtained important distinctions from them; tall, handsome edifices were constructed there, among which are a Sun temple and a convent for nuns, that are still famous throughout the Empire.

The numerous peoples who composed the Collas claimed to have strange origins. There were those who said that their ancestors had sprung from the great Lake Titicaca: they considered this lake as their mother, and before the arrival of the Incas, they used to offer up sacrifices on its shores. Others claimed to come from a spring, and others still believed that they were the children of a series of rocks in which were numerous grottoes and natural crevices; they even went there at periodic intervals and carried out sacrificial rites, out of filial gratitude. There were some, too, who said they descended from a river, which they held to be so sacred that they would have considered it a heinous crime to fish in it, for the reason, they said, that all such fish are our brothers.

One sees the many fables they invented. Nor were their gods less varied than their pretended origins. There was one god, however, which was common to all their nations, and which they set above all the others: this was a white lamb, for these people owned countless flocks of sheep. The first lamb, they said, lived in the world above (meaning the sky) and he must have loved the Collas more than any other people, since he had given them such numerous flocks. And true it is, that nowhere in Peru can one see so many herds. Every year they sacrificed lambs and sheep to this god.

In addition to these extravagant goings on, there existed among the Collas a custom that was far more shameful and infamous, which was, that their women, before they married, could live as licentiously as they wanted; the more dissolute their habits, the easier it would be to find a husband, as though their bad conduct had been a virtue. The Inca kings reformed all that, and especially was it forbidden in the country of the Collas to worship any other god than the Sun.[11]

Once this conquest had been assured, the Inca returned to Cuzco. In doing this, he acted wisely, and his successors have done the same, knowing that it is better to win over men and peoples little by little, than to appear to be tyrannical, ambitious, jealous, and scandalous, by trying to subdue too many nations at one time.

After having reigned several years in peace, without leaving Cuzco, the king decided to undertake an exhaustive visit of the Empire, both in order to give his subjects the pleasure of welcoming him in person on their estates—which was an immense pleasure to them—and to inspect the work of his ministers.

On returning from this voyage he levied ten thousand fighting men and started a new campaign. Passing through Hatuncolla, he went as far as Chuquitu, a province that is so renowned and so densely populated that the Spanish, when they divided Peru among themselves, reserved this part for the Emperor. The inhabitants of Chuquitu were powerful, and their ancestors had subdued numerous peoples. They nevertheless surrendered, without hesitating, to the Inca.

This rapid success incited the king to continue. He therefore sent ambassadors to other nations, as far as the outlet of Lake Titicaca, and the Hillauis, the Chullis, the Pumatas and the Cipitas surrendered without resisting any more than had the Chuquitus.

The Inca, Lloque Yupanqui, insisted upon presiding in person over the setting up of his administration in these new provinces, which were destined to play an important role in the life of his Empire. In order to give greater evidence of the confidence he had in his new subjects, he dismissed the army, except for his personal guard. And thus he passed yet another entire winter in Collasuyu, which filled the curacas and the people with gratitude towards him. He flattered them continually, showering them daily with marks of attention and presents. For Lloque Yupanqui knew well how powerful an asset is the art of making oneself liked, for him who seeks to bring foreigners under his sway. And indeed he was so successful that people went about singing his praises everywhere, insisting that he really was the son of the Sun.

Meanwhile he had sent orders to Cuzco to raise a new army of ten thousand men, and when spring came, he put his own brother in charge of it, with four camp commanders to assist him. Then, having explained to them that they should show their strength, but not use it, he ordered them to march westward, towards the province of Hurin Pacasa.

And this new campaign took place according to the Inca's wishes. Along the twenty leagues that led to the spot where the cordillera descends to the coast, forming a natural frontier, all the Indians they encountered fell in with his rule. It was not hard to interest them, nor to convince them, for these people at that time were so wretched that they lived like animals, without order or reason. A large number of them approached the prince-general of their own accord, attracted by his reputation and by the wonderful things people told about this son of the Sun. Nevertheless the campaign lasted three years, for it took a long time, not to subjugate these rustics, but to make them understand their new duties as men and citizens.

However, the Inca visited his Empire and worked to increase its prosperity, constructing canals, granaries, bridges, and roads. Finally, the army came back home again, and was given the rewards it deserved, after which the Inca decided to return to his court and make an end to his conquests, which had been considerable, since he had extended his frontiers more than forty leagues, from north to south, and twenty, from east to west.

He therefore returned to Cuzco, where he was welcomed like a beloved father, and he was able to spend the rest of his days in peace and quiet, devoting himself entirely to the welfare of his subjects and the maintenance of justice. Twice he sent his son and heir, Maïta Capac, accompanied by older, experienced advisers, to visit his kingdoms, in order that these travels might prepare the prince for the heavy responsibilities soon to fall upon his shoulders.

Lloque Yupanqui died in peace, leaving numerous children born to his concubines, but only one legitimate heir, his sister-bride having borne him only one son and two or three daughters. His virtues had made him beloved by all, and he was long mourned in all of his kingdoms.

In order not to weary the reader by accounts of war and conquest, which are always more or less the same, I shall now tell of the scientific knowledge that was acquired by the Incas.

Not knowing how to write, the Incas had little knowledge of astronomy and of natural history. There were of course among them enlightened minds capable of philosophizing about subtle things, but since they were unable to write anything down, their discoveries disappeared with them. That they possessed a moral philosophy, however, is evident from their laws and customs; but the philosophy of nature was entirely absent from their thinking, their lives being so simple that there was no incentive to reflect on the secrets of nature. They were able to recognize the qualities of the elements, such as cold and dryness of the earth, or heat and dryness of fire, but this they learned from everyday experience, not from either science or philosophy. Having little leaning towards speculation, they gave no thought to what they could not touch with their hands.

They took greater interest in astronomy, to which they were naturally inclined by the very manner in which their lives were organized. They made observations of the Sun, the Moon, and the planet Venus, and knew the apparent movements of these heavenly bodies.

Admiring effects without seeking to discover their causes, they were not the least interested to know whether there are several skies or only one, and it never occurred to them that there might exist others than those they could see. At the same time, they knew nothing about the Moon's phases, or the movements of the planets, with only three of which, the Sun, the Moon, and Venus, they were familiar. Indeed, they simply did not see the four others. They called the Sun *Inti*, the Moon *Quilla*, and Venus *Chasca*, meaning hirsute, because of its rays. If they so much as noticed the Pleiades, it was merely because this constellation of closely related stars may be easily distinguished from the others.[12]

Despite their primitiveness, the Incas understood the annual movement of the Sun, which they called *huata*, a word that, when used as a noun, means "year," and when used as verb, means "to attach." Most people, however, counted the years by their harvests.

They also knew about summer and winter solstices, and they left very visible evidence of this by building eight towers on either side of the city of Cuzco, four of which faced the rising, and four the setting Sun. Each one of these groups of constructions comprised two small towers, about three stades[13] in height, surrounded by two other, much higher towers. All these towers were separated regularly about eighteen to twenty feet one from the other. The tall ones, which were much higher than the watchtowers to be seen on the Spanish coast, served to indicate the smaller ones, between which the Sun rose and set at the time of the solstice.

In order to confirm the solstice, an Inca would take up his stand at both twilights, in a spot from which he watched the sun rise and set between the two towers. Pedro de Cieza de Leon and Father Acosta have both mentioned this invention of the Incas.[14] Since they counted the months by Moons, and since, too, the solar year was longer by twelve days than the lunar year, it was thanks to this observation of the solstices that they restored order to their calendar, according to the true, or solar, year, the importance of which they had understood for reckoning when to sow their crops. These astronomical towers were still standing in the year 1560, and unless they have been destroyed since then, it would be possible, by watching the solstice, to find out from where the Inca confirmed it, whether from one of the towers of a Sun temple, or from elsewhere.

They were also familiar with the equinoxes, which were the occasion for important ceremonies. At the March equinox, they cut corn in Cuzco, particularly in the fields about Colcampata, which was dedicated to the Sun. Then, at the September equinox, they celebrated one of the four great Sun festivals, called *Citua Raïmi,* meaning, the most important festival: it will be described later. They verified the equinoxes by means of a very richly carved stone column, which stood in the middle of the parvis of each of the Sun temples. When the equinoctial season was at hand, the priests made daily observations of the shadow cast by this column. A wide circle was drawn about the entire space of which this column constituted the center, and across the middle of this circle they drew a line from east to west, between two points which long experience had taught them how to locate. They could thus note the approaching equinox by observing the shadow of the tower on this line, and once this shadow was reduced by half, from sunrise to sunset, and at noon the column was entirely lighted up, without there being any shade, then they proclaimed that this day was the day of the equinox. The columns were immediately decorated with flowers and sweet-smelling herbs, and they set up a throne on the spot, for the Sun to come and sit in, as they said, "in all its light." On that day this heavenly body was adored with very special display, and it was also the recipient of gorgeous presents of gold, silver, precious stones, and other objects of great worth. With regard to this custom, it should be specified that the Inca kings, and the amautas—who were their philosophers—at the time that they were extending their provinces, noticed that the shadow of these columns diminished in the direction of the equator, and, for this reason, the nearer the columns came to Quito,[15] the more they revered them. Over and above all the others, however, they honored those they erected in and about the city itself, in the direction of the seashore, for now the Sun was "in plumb," as carpenters say, noon there being absolutely shadeless. They said therefore that these particular columns were those preferred by the Sun, who sat there quite erect, and not to one side as it did on the others.[16]

These people's astronomy was filled with such naïve notions as these, for the reason that their imagination was unable to grasp anything beyond what they saw materially with their eyes. The governor of Belalcazar destroyed all of the columns in the Quito region, because they encouraged idolatrous practices among the Indians. And the other Spanish captains did the same in the entire kingdom, for the same reasons.

They gave names to the months, which they counted by moons, as I explained before. They also counted the half-months (fortnights) and the weeks, by the waxing and waning and four quarters of the Moon, but they did not give names to the different days of the week. They knew, too, about the different eclipses of the Moon and the Sun, without, however, suspecting their causes. For them, when the Sun was in an eclipse, some misdemeanor committed in the kingdom had irritated it, since, at that moment, its countenance had the disturbed look of a man in anger, and they predicted, as astrologists do, the imminence of some severe chastisement. During an eclipse of the Moon, when they saw it darken, they said that it was ill, and that if it continued in this state, it would die and fall down to earth; that it would crush them all under the weight of its body, and that this event would be the end of the world. At this thought, they were seized with such fright that they began to play on horns and trumpets, timpani and drums, and all the noisiest instruments they could find; and, in the same manner, they would tie up their dogs, both large and small, and beat them hard to make them bark and bay at the Moon, for, they said, at one time, dogs had rendered great service to the Moon, and ever since then it had had special affection for them; for this reason, they thought, if the Moon heard them baying for her, she would awaken from the dream in which illness held her a prisoner.[17]

They told another, even more childish fable, with regard to the spots on the Moon. A fox, they said, having fallen in love with her, had leapt up into the sky in order to seize hold of her. The Moon held out her arms to him, and they embraced each other so closely that she remained all spotted, as one can see. In her periods of eclipse, they also assembled all their children together and made them cry and call the Moon loudly, begging her not to die, that they might be spared. The adults, both men and women, also mingled their voices with this concert of supplications and all together, it made an indescribable noise and confusion.

They diagnosed the condition of the Moon by the size of the eclipse; saying that if the eclipse was total, this meant that she was dead, and that the end of the world was at hand. It is easy to imagine what terror reigned then among the Indians. Later, when the Moon became a little clearer, they said that Pachacamac, the father of the universe, had hastened to her assistance, in order that her passing should not be followed by that of the entire world. Then, when she had finally recovered all her clarity, they would thank her and congratulate her on her fortunate return to health. They called the day *punchau*, the night *tuta*, and dawn *pacari*. They also had special words for other parts of day and night, such as noon and midnight.

Thunder and lightning together were called by the simple word *illapa;* they were not adored as gods, but were looked up to as attendants of the Sun, and they were believed to live in the air, but not in the sky. They also respected the rainbow, whose beautiful colors they admired, and which the Inca kings used on their coats of arms.[18] Each one of these phenomena had its altar in the Temple of the Sun, as we shall see later. They discerned in certain black spots near the Milky Way the face of an ewe suckling her young. It was often shown me when I was a child. "Look," people would say, "this is its head, arms, and legs." And yet I never succeeded in seeing anything but spots.

Although they did observe the sky, they made no prognostications by the Sun, the Moon, and the comets, except in rare cases, as, for instance, on the death of a king, or the destruction of a kingdom or a province; we shall speak later of certain comets, if we reach that point.[19] In everyday life, the only interpretations they made were of their dreams and their sacrifices; and, in fact, the predictions they deduced from their dreams were so frightening that, in order not to scandalize the average person, I shall refrain from telling what I know about the subject. As for the star of Venus, having observed that it appeared either in the evening, or in the morning, they concluded that it was the favorite of the Sun, who liked to see it moving along with him, now leading, now following him.

When the Sun set and they saw it disappear behind the sea, they said that it entered the sea, dried up a great amount of its waters and, like a very clever swimmer, dove under the earth and came out on the other side, which implies that the earth rests on the surface of the sea. They said nothing about the setting of the Moon or of any other stars. Such then was Inca astronomy, and naïve it was. We shall say no more about it, but speak now of their medical practices.

They considered bleeding and purges to be beneficial. They bled both arms and legs, not from the vein that was most likely to be effective in the case of this or that illness, but from the one that seemed to them to be nearest the point of the patient's suffering. When they had a headache, they bled their foreheads, at the spot where the eyebrows meet. Their lancet was made of a silex blade, fastened in the fork of a small, split stick, the tip of which they placed over the vein, then struck the other end of the stick with a flick of the finger.

They purged themselves usually when they felt heavy or low-spirited, even though at the time they were more often not really sick, but in good health. For this they took certain white roots, rather like turnips,[20] among which they distinguished two varieties, that they called male and female. They would crush about two ounces of one or the other, then mix it with a drink. After having swallowed it, they lay down in the Sun to allow the heat to hasten the effect of the medicine. After an hour or so, they would feel so prostrate that they could no longer sit up. It was like an attack of seasickness: their heads were reeling, and they felt as though ants were racing through their veins, their nerves, their arms, their legs, and indeed their entire bodies. Finally came the moment of evacuation, which took place both from above and from below. At that moment, they were so limp that it looked as though they were passing out. All the different humors that they might have had in their bodies escaped at one time, without their being able to either eat or drink, and they could be seen to vomit white worms, and others that were red, like earthworms. But the effect of this purge was no sooner over than they were once more full of life and so starved that they would devour everything that was offered them. I was able to note the effects of this purge in my own case, having had it given to me twice in my youth to cure a stomach ache. These bleedings and purges were carried out by persons of long experience, often by old women, who also acted as midwives, or else by well-known herb doctors, who were both renowned and numerous under the Incas. They handed down their science and knowledge of medicinal herbs from father to son, and were the appointed doctors to the king, to all persons of royal blood and to the curacas and their families: the ordinary run of humanity took care of one another, according to their limited knowledge of medicine. If a nursing infant was seized with some illness, and particularly with fever, he was washed with urine in the early morning, then swaddled in covers to protect him from the cold. Sometimes, too, he was given his own urine to drink. When a child was born, the umbilical cord was not cut close to the belly, but a piece about as long as one's finger was left hanging. Then when this little gut became detached, it was carefully preserved and given to the child to suck, in case of some illness. In order to judge of the child's condition, they opened his mouth and looked at his tongue. If it was coated, they concluded that he was ill and immediately gave him the little gut to suck. But it had to be a piece of his own umbilical cord, as otherwise, they said, this remedy would be of no effect.

I did not ask to be told all these things, but saw them done with my own eyes. The Incas did not know how to count the pulse beats or analyze urine, and they only recognized a state of fever by the heat of the body.

They knew the virtues of milk as well as of the resin of a tree they called *mulli,* and which the Spanish call *mollé.*[21] Its effect on wounds is so remarkable that it appears to be almost supernatural. The herb they call *chilca*[22] is marvelous for setting dislocated joints, and is even used for horses. A root rather like that of the dandelion, only larger and with thicker, smaller nodes, was used for invigorating the teeth and gums. They heated it until it was burning hot, then split it in two with their teeth, applying the halves to the gums where they left it until it had cooled. Apparently, the patient suffered during the entire operation, as though he had held his mouth in the fire. If this treatment is applied at night, the next morning the gums are as white as boiled meat, and for two or three days the patient, being unable to chew at all, must be fed with a spoon. Later, however, the burned flesh falls away of itself, and underneath, other quite red, quite healthy flesh has replaced it. I have often seen the Indians renew their gums in this way, and I wanted to try it on myself, but the pain was so violent that I didn't have the courage to pursue the experiment till the end.

Tobacco, which they called *sairi,* had many uses for them, one of which was as snuff to clear the head. The virtues of this plant are well known today in Spain where it has been called a "holy weed." Another plant, which they called *matecclu,*[23] is remarkable for curing diseases of the eyes. This plant grows in brooks, is only one foot high, and on the end of the stem has but one single, perfectly round leaf. It looks like the "abbot's ear," a plant that grows on the roofs of Spanish houses in winter. The plant is first chewed and the paste that results is applied to the eyes overnight. I once had occasion to test the efficiency of this treatment on a child whose eye was bulging and so inflamed that it was red all over, like a piece of raw meat, so that the iris could not be distinguished from the cornea. After the first night's application, the child's eye had returned to its socket and, after the second, it was quite cured. I have seen this child since, in Spain, and he told me that he could see better today with that eye than with the other. I had heard about this plant from a Spaniard who swore to me that, after having been totally blind, he had recovered the use of his eyes in two days, thanks to its curative properties. Every time he discovered a specimen of it, he would take it in his hands and kiss it with great feeling, then apply it to his eyes and head, while thanking our Lord Jesus Christ for the miracle He had accomplished in restoring his sight through this plant. My Indian relatives used many other herbs, but I do not remember their names.

This, then, was their notion of medicine, and it was based principally on the use of healing herbs. Since they have been in Peru, the Spanish have become acquainted with several of these plants, particularly, however, have they been impressed with the remarkable curative properties of corn, which is not only the principal article of food in America, but is also of great benefit in the treatment of affections of the kidneys and bladder, among which are calculus and retention of the urine. And the best proof I can give of this is that the Indians, whose usual drink is made of corn, are afflicted with none of these diseases.

They had an excellent knowledge of geometry, which they had to have in order to survey and portion out the land; this knowledge, however, was merely empirical, not speculative, and they made their calculations and allotments by means of pieces of cord and little stones. But I shall not go into this further, for fear of not being able to make myself understood. As for geography, they knew enough about it to be able to draw, construct, and paint models of their towns and provinces, and I saw a model of Cuzco and the surrounding country, that was made of clay, small stones and little sticks. It was constructed to scale, showing both the large and small open spaces of Cuzco, both its principal and less important streets, its different districts, its suburbs and all its houses—down to the very humblest—its three brooks and the starting points of the four great highways that cross the empire; it was really a pleasure to look at it. All the neighboring countryside was also marvelously reproduced, with its hills and mountains, its plains and valleys, its rivers and streams, including all their bends; indeed, the best cosmographer in the world could not have done better. The Indians carried out this model for an inspector named Damian de la Bandera, who had been entrusted by the Royal Chancery with the task of taking a census of the villages and population of the Cuzco district.[24]

The Incas also had an excellent knowledge of arithmetic, and the way they counted was quite remarkable. Throughout the Empire, all levies and taxes, both exemptions and claims, were recorded by means of knots made in colored cords. They could add, subtract, and multiply with these knots, and in order to determine what was owed to each village, made their allotments on the basis of little pebbles and grains of corn, in such a way that there could be no mistakes in their calculations. Special bookkeepers were appointed for each section, whether it had to do with war or peace, such as taking a census of the vassals, or of levies, herds, laws, and ceremonies, and they were able to give an accounting at any moment, their collections of cords and knots being as clear and exact for them as any books. The head accountants, who were in charge of several things at a time, worked with these same means, quite as easily as the others. We shall have occasion to speak again of these cords and knots.[25]

The Colla Indians and all those in their district had a certain knowledge of music. They played reed or cane instruments, made by joining four or five tubes together, each one of which furnished a higher or lower note than the preceding one, as in the case of organ pipes. There existed four such instruments, each one keyed to a higher or lower scale, in the same way as the four human voices: soprano, tenor, contralto, and bass. When one Indian played, a second answered him, shall we say, in fifths, then a third on another harmony, and the fourth on still another, each one in time.[26] They were unfamiliar with diminished chords, their instruments being tuned by whole tones, and the tempo always the same. These were professional musicians, who practiced in order to give concerts for the king and nobles of the Empire. They also had flutes with four or five holes, like those played by shepherds. But since these were never played on in concerts, each player carved his own in his own manner, according to what suited him best. With this flute he accompanied his love songs, which recounted, in even meters, the favors or disfavors of his ladylove.

Each one of these songs had its own melody and no two of them could have been set to the same tune. Thus it was possible for the suitor, when he played his flute in the evening, by the manner in which he played it, to convey his joy or his pain to his lady, and to everyone else, according to whether she had granted or refused her favors; one might say, in short, that they conversed with these flutes. The story is told of a Spaniard who, one evening, upon meeting an Indian girl of his acquaintance on a Cuzco street, urged her to come home with him. "Señor," she replied, "kindly let me go my way. The flute you hear is calling me with such tenderness and passion that I can't resist it. Leave me, for your own life's sake; my love is calling me and I must answer him, that he may be my husband and I his wife."[27]

The songs they composed on the themes of war and of their great deeds, were not played on the flute, since they did not concern woman. They were only sung during the festivals, or on occasions of victory and triumph. In the year 1560, when I left Peru, there were five Indians in Cuzco who played the flute so well that they could interpret any piece of organ music you put before them; and today, in 1562, I am told there still exists a considerable number of excellent musicians.

The amautas, or philosophers, were quite clever at composing tragedies and comedies that were played before the king and the lords of his court, on high feast days. The actors were not yokels, but Incas or nobles, curacas, captains, and even camp commanders: each one, in fact, being obliged to possess in real life the quality, or occupy the function, of the rôle he interpreted. The themes of the tragedies were always taken from history, and usually related the triumphs and valorous acts of one of the early kings, or some other hero of the Empire. As for the comedies, they treated of rustic or family life. When the performance was over each one returned to the position that was his, according to his station or occupation. The interludes, too, were never unseemly, cheap, or base; and all, on the contrary, treated of subjects that were extremely serious, moral and sententious. The best actors were rewarded with gifts of great value.[28]

The verses were composed in different meters, some short and others long. In addition to the love poems I have already mentioned, there were others that, being handed down from generation to generation, made it possible to keep alive the memory of the kings, the lords and all who had accomplished remarkable feats in the history of the Empire.

These verses were very short, in order that they might be easily memorized; but they were as terse and precise as mathematics. There was no assonance, each verse being free. In fact, they often resemble the natural form of composition that, in Spanish, is called *redondilla.*[29] I recall a love song, composed of four lines, from which may be judged the austerity of these terse compositions I spoke of; here it is, with the translation:

Caylla llapi	To this tune
Puñunqui	you will sleep
Chaupituta	At midnight
Samusac	I shall come.

An Indian poet, called a *harauec*, that is, an inventor, composed quantities of other verses of all kinds. I found some in Father Blas Valera's papers, which he calls spondaics; they all have four syllables, unlike the preceding ones, that may have either four or three. He noted them down in the Peruvian language and in Latin; their subject matter is astronomy. The Indian poet who composed them speaks, like a philosopher, of the secondary causes that made God create, in the air, thunder and lightning, as also hail, snow, and rain. They were based on an Indian fable which goes as follows: The Creator, they say, took care to set a girl of royal blood in the sky, to whom he entrusted a vase full of water that she is supposed to pour on the earth whenever it is needed. Sometimes, it so happens that one of the brothers of this girl breaks the vase, and this is the source of thunder and lightning. It can easily be seen that this is a man's doing, since thunder and lightning are fierce the way a man's nature is, and not tender, like the nature of a woman. On the other hand, they add, it is the girl who sends hail, snow, and rain, these being soft, tender things that are beneficial, just as the feminine nature is beneficial.

Father Blas Valera said that he had discovered this tale in a very old *quipu* and that, having been surprised and amazed by its beauty, he had recalled it and written it down from memory. I remember having heard it myself when I was a child, among the countless things my relatives told me, but I was too young to look for its meaning or to ask it, and they didn't tell it to me. For the benefit of those who understand neither the language of the Indians nor the Latin in which Father Blas Valera transcribed these verses, I have ventured to translate them into Spanish, basing myself more on the first of these two languages, which I learned at my mother's knee, than on the second, which remains foreign to me, for the reason that the little I know of it was taught me in the heat of battle over my native land, in among weapons and horses, gunpowder and harquebus firing, all of which I am more familiar with than I am with Latin. Here, then, is the poem and the translation of it:

Camasunqui	Beautiful princess
Sumac Niusta	Your brother
Toralaiquim	Has broken
Puinuy quita	Your vase,

Paquir cayan	And that is why
Hina mantara	It thunders, why lightning flashes
Cucununun	And thunderbolts roll.
Illapantac	But you, princess,
Camri Niusta	Mistress of the rain,
Unuiquita	You will give us water,
Para munqui	And, at other times,
Mai nimpiri	Your hand will scatter hail,
Chichi munqui	Or snow.
Riti munqui	Pachacamac,
Pacha rurac	Creator of the world,
Pacha camac	And our god Viracocha
Vira cocha	Have given you a soul
Cai hinapac	And a body
Churasunqui	For this sole purpose.

I have recalled these verses in order to enrich my poor tale, for it is only fair to say that everything Father Blas Valera wrote is as though it were embroidered with pearls and precious stones, and that my native land had not deserved such an honor.

I have been told that today the half-breeds work diligently at composing these verses in the Indian language, as well as others of different sorts, sometimes on secular, sometimes on sacred themes. May God grant them His grace, that they might be of service in all things! [30]

1. See Note 2, Book IV.

2. Most of the laws mentioned by Garcilaso are not as old as he claims: they date back chiefly to the reign of the Inca Pachacutec, known as "The Reformer" (1438-1471).

3. For convenience sake, we have placed the explanatory notes on these tribes that gave their names to the four great divisions of the Inca Empire, with the chapters in which Garcilaso speaks of their conquest. (Note 8, Book IV; Note 11, Book II; Note 20, Book VI)

4. I do not know why Garcilaso denies the existence of the chief of the ten thousand, or chief of the *ayllu*, directly subordinate to the governor of the province. These provincial officials were divided into two separate categories:
1. the curacas, in charge of ten thousand, one thousand, five hundred, or one hundred, whose posts were hereditary.
2. the "subalterns," in charge of fifty or ten. Their posts were

not hereditary; they were appointed and paid by their curaca.

This hierarchy, as explained by Rowe, has been established from the evidence of numerous chroniclers, including Cieza de Leon, Acosta, Cobo, etc. (Note 6, Book II and Note 3, Book VII)

5. Those condemned to death were stoned, hung by the feet, thrown over cliffs, or beaten with clubs. In cases of high treason or of particularly serious political crimes, the condemned man was not executed but shut up in a dungeon with snakes and carnivorous animals. He had accordingly little chance of survival. This is the only case in which Inca law provided for imprisonment. Crimes which did not incur the death penalty were punished by exile to the coca plantations (in hot regions)—a particularly harsh punishment for those who came from the puna, or high valleys of the Andes—loss of post (a punishment worse than death for an Inca by blood or privilege), torture, or *hiwaya*. The punishment of *hiwaya* consisted in dropping a very heavy stone on the victim's back from a height of about three feet. It frequently caused death by fracture of the spinal column. (Rowe)

6. After the Incas by blood (that is, belonging to the Inca *ayllus* proper) and the Incas by privilege, the curacas formed a third class in the *Tahuantinsuyu* social hierarchy. The word curaca is said to derive from the Quechua word *koraka*, or official. Generally chosen from among the chiefs and from dignitaries of the conquered tribes or of the tribes joining the Empire of their own free will, they fulfilled for the most part administrative functions (Note 4, Book II) but they could sometimes be military leaders. Whatever their functions, they were always under the authority of an Inca official. In ordinary parlance, the word curaca is a synonym for cacique.

7. These accounts were kept by means of the quipus. (Book II and Book VI)

8. Garcilaso often refers to this author, whose manuscript has been lost. (Book IV and Note 11, Book IV)

9. See, in this work, the *tutuy-ricoc* depicted by Guaman Poma in the collection, "The Great Officials of the Empire."

10. Of the first two Incas, Manco Capac and Sinchi Roca: "Most of the Spanish chroniclers, including Garcilaso, call the first ruler Manko Kapak and the second Sinchi Roka. According to Montesinos and Acosta, the Inkas date back to a later ruler called Inka-Roka. Where does the truth lie? After a most brilliant period of the Tiahuanaco civilization, it suffered a long eclipse. It was then that the *Sinchis* took over the leadership of the tribes. These *Sinchis* were temporary leaders nominated by primitive groups of people (*ayllu*) for hunting, fishing, or warfare. No doubt they became perma-

nent chiefs and were the first rulers. This explains the tendency today to regard Manko-Kapak and Sinchi-Roka not as two individuals but as two dynasties, as mythical beings. The legendary character of the former in the writings of the chroniclers confirms this supposition." (Baudin)

11. The Collas, often confused with the Aimaras, were in early Inca times a much more important tribe than the Incas, to the south of whose territory they lived, near Lake Titicaca. They are regarded by some authors as the heirs of the last Tiahuanaco civilization. The absence of supporting documents makes any hypothesis as to their origin subject to the greatest caution. In early historic times, that is to say, when the Inca expansion began in the fourteenth century, the Collas were conquered, together with Umasuyu, by King Pachacutec and his General Capac Yupanqui, not by Lloque Yupanqui, as Garcilaso claims. (Rowe) It should be remembered that all the military campaigns and stories of conquests in Garcilaso's first three books are more legendary than historic. Indeed nothing certain is known of the reigns of the first six Incas. (Notes to Books IV, V, VI)

12. See Book III, and Note 14, Book III.

13. Old Spanish measure of height. It represented the average height of a man standing with his arms raised. It was equivalent to seven Castilian feet, or about six and a half of our feet, the Castilian foot measuring about eleven inches. The small towers referred to were accordingly about twenty-six feet high, if Garcilaso is to be believed.

14. Pedro de Cieza de Leon, Part I, Chapter 92: "On the hill at Carmenca there were certain small round towers used to observe the movements of the sun, to which they [the Incas] attached great importance."

    Cieza de Leon is one of the most important chroniclers of the conquest. He was born in 1518 and died in 1560, making a military career for himself in Peru, where he arrived at the age of thirteen.

    Father Acosta, Book VI, Chapter III. Father Acosta, 1539-1600, arrived in Peru in 1572, twelve years after Garcilaso had left for Spain. He spent fifteen years there. At once a naturalist, philosopher and poet, he earned the name bestowed upon him by Humboldt two hundred and fifty years later, of "Pliny of the New World." His work is of the greatest significance even today.

15. It will be recalled that the equator passes close to Quito, the capital of the present Republic of Ecuador.

16. Garcilaso is the only chronicler who asserts that the Incas observed the equinoxes, and the first to speak of them observing the solstices. Both these statements are regarded as doubtful by Rowe: in the first place because the solstices and equinoxes do not appear in the ritual calendar of the Incas, and secondly because such observations would imply a system of lunar months. It is to the famous historian of

America, Erland Nordenskiöld, that we owe unprecedented discoveries concerning the astronomical knowledge of the ancient Peruvians. Nordenskiöld succeeded in deciphering a collection of quipus, preserved in various European museums, which were probably used for astronomical calculations. His deductions show that the Incas probably had an amazingly accurate knowledge not only of the revolutions of the Sun and the Moon, but even of the synodic revolutions of the planets Jupiter, Mercury, and Venus. These are the figures that Nordenskiöld was able to "read" from the quipus:
Lunar revolution (or month): 29 and a half or 30 days.
Year: 365 days.
Synodic revolution of Jupiter: 397 days (instead of 398).
Synodic revolution of Mercury: 116 days.
Synodic revolution of Venus: 584 days (like the Mayas).

The Inca year probably had twelve months of thirty days each, plus five additional days.

As will be seen, the sensational revelations of Nordenskiöld are far in advance of Garcilaso's statements which, for once, minimize the knowledge of the Incas. As in Central America, says Nordenskiöld, the intimate details of the calendar were kept secret by the astronomer-priests, which explains the very superficial note of the chroniclers on the subject. Montesinos is the only author to assert that the Incas had a year of 365 days. He relates that an Inca named Yahuar Huquiz, who was a great astrologer, was endeavoring to determine how many days should be added to 365 every four years. True, says Nordenskiöld, Montesinos' statements should be treated with caution. Another Inca, according to Montesinos, introduced the system of dividing the year into weeks of ten days, with five days only in the last week. Nordenskiöld also quotes Molina, according to whom the quipus were used traditionally to count the years and the months until the reign of the Inca Yupanqui, who introduced the system of counting by winters and summers.

As Nordenskiöld remarks, such a degree of scientific knowledge on the part of people who had no form of writing, even hieroglyphics, is one of the most original features of the Peruvian civilization. (Nordenskiöld, Volume 6)

17. It was not a disease which threatened the Moon, but a lion or a serpent which was seeking to devour it, which explains why it was important to make as much noise as possible to frighten it away. According to Rowe, this custom persists in Cuzco even today.

18. See the description of the Temple of the Sun, Book III, and Note 15, Book III.

19. See Book IX, the death of Huaina Capac and Book X, the death of Atahualpa.

20. This plant, the name of which Garcilaso does not mention, is called *cuacancha* by Cobo. It is the *euphorbia huachanhana* of d'Harcourt. Garcilaso, on the other hand, omits to mention the use of the enema; on a *mochica* vase a witch-

doctor is to be seen blowing through a small tube, held by an assistant, into the patient's anus. Velez reports this in *El clister en el antiguo Perú,* a report presented to the twenty-third session of the International Congress of Americanists, London, 1913. (d'Harcourt)

Let us add, lastly, to what Garcilaso says of Inca medicine, that the ancient Peruvians also had a knowledge of surgery, and that they practiced trephining, as is proved by remains found in many cemeteries, both in the mountains and in the coastal plain.

21. *Mulli, mollé,* or *cullash: Schinus molle L.,* or peppercorn; an anacardiaceous plant.

"The dried latex derived from this resin was used as a plaster and helped wounds to heal. Dissolved in water, it was used as a purgative. According to Cobo, the same resin was used for embalming, but there is no proof of this. It was also used in the form of suppositories to treat intestinal worms." (Valdizán and Maldonado)

22. According to Father Cobo, the Indians used this plant grilled with cinnamon and then dissolved the mixture in an alcoholic liquid. It cured flatulence, acute indigestion, and headaches when applied to the forehead. Mixed with *mollé* and a large quantity of salt, it was a cure for gout. According to Pagador, it was also used to stimulate the circulation.

23. *Matecclu* or *Matecclo:* Hydrocotyl SP. (Maldonado) Family of umbellifera. The leaves were used at Arequipa as a poultice for toothache; for diseases of the eyes in the Huancayo region; as an infusion for bathing wounds at Ayacucho and Lima, etc. (Valdizán and Maldonado)

24. Garcilaso is probably referring to the famous relief map of Cuzco prepared at the instigation of the Inca Pachacutec when he was rebuilding his capital. See Book VI.

25. This is the quipu, the appearance and uses of which are described in Book VI. According to Guaman Poma, "the Empire was governed by quipus." Henry Wassén, a disciple of Nordenskiöld, discovered in a drawing by Guaman Poma that the Incas used in counting not only the quipu but also the abacus. One of these is to be seen quite clearly, at the feet of the "grand treasurer," in the illustrations of officials. In the light of the part played at one time—and probably still—by abacuses of all kinds in Asia and particularly in Russia, this discovery by Wassén goes to swell the evidence of the kinship of the Asian and American civilizations.

26. "There is only one thing to be learned from this statement," writes d'Harcourt, "and that is that the syrinx [Panpipe] was already being made in the sixteenth century in a series of different sizes, and it is natural to suppose that, as today, they differed by an octave, since they were played together: this would not necessarily entail even the most elementary

form of polyphony." This statement of d'Harcourt is disputed today. The same author adds, at the beginning of his chapter on the Panpipes: "It is probably on the shores of the Pacific and in the high mountains of Bolivia that the syrinx attained its greatest perfection of form . . . the extreme care devoted to fashioning this instrument is remarkable . . . Today, although the syrinx has almost entirely disappeared from the Peruvian coast, the Sierra remains faithful to it . . . and it is in Bolivia, near Lake Titicaca, that it still lives on and flourishes."

The Panpipe is indeed one of the most characteristic instruments of South America, especially of the Western regions. The ancient Peruvian civilizations produced syrinxes not only of reeds but also of terra cotta (those of the coastal civilizations, especially of Nazca, are sometimes real works of art) and even carved in stone, chiefly among the Araucans. Today Panpipes are still very widespread, not only in the Sierra of Peru but also in the *llanos* and forests of the Amazon. I have myself come upon and recorded groups of two or three playing in unison among the Guahibos of the Orinoco *llanos*. Further information can be found in the work of Izikowitz and the recordings published by the Musée de l'Homme, in particular the album of the Orinoco-Amazon expedition: *"Musiques primitives indiennes."*

27. The Peruvian flute—or *kena*—is so famous that it has given rise to abundant literature, often of a naïvely romantic variety. The truth remains that, as d'Harcourt points out, it has always been *par excellence* the instrument of contemplation and of love. To this celebrated anecdote of Garcilaso might be added the reflections of another author of the end of the sixteenth century, Gutierrez de Santa Clara.

"These Indians play on small flutes with two holes at the top and one at the bottom. With these they sing their romances and express everything they have to say. At night they use them to call the women and girls shut up in their houses or in their masters' houses; the latter understand immediately, from the sound of the instruments, what the musician is trying to say, and they escape in secret to go to him."

28. We can imagine what the court drama of the Incas was like from the play *Ollantay,* which is presumed to have been written in Quechua before Garcilaso wrote *Comentarios.* Among the characters of this play, which was translated from Quechua into French before being published in Spanish, are King Tupac Yupanqui and General Ruminaui.

29. Octosyllabic quatrain rhyming a b b a.

30. Elegiac poetry was certainly well developed in ancient Peru. There are many examples, such as this love poem, so remarkably pure and concise, used by Sarmiento. It is traditionally believed to be the epitaph of the great Inca Pachacutec, the "Reformer":

Born like a lily in the garden
I grew like a lily
And when the time came,
I withered
And died.

Guaman Poma quotes numerous poems and popular verses in Quechua, as for example this refrain accompanying a drawing of dancers:

Murmur, shade!
Murmur, shade!
Secretly, shade!
Why are you here, rose in bloom?
Why are you here, flower of the thrush?
Why are you here, tiny lily?

and this complaint of a pair of lovers, hung by the hair and condemned to die so:

Father Condor, take me,
Brother Falcon, take me,
Tell my little mother I am coming,
For five days I have not eaten, or drunk a drop,
Father messenger, bearer of signs, swift messenger,
Carry me off, I beg you: little mouth, little heart,
Tell my little father and my little mother, I beg you, that
I am coming.

Much less anxious than Garcilaso to idealize the Incas, Guaman Poma does not hesitate to give examples of the crueler side of their civilization, as shown in this war song quoted by Means:

We will drink from his skull,
We will adorn ourselves with his teeth,
With his bones we will make flutes
And we will dance to the sound of a drum made of his
skin.
(Note 19, Book VI)

BOOK THREE

Which treats of the life,
works, and conquests of Maïta Capac,
fourth king of the Incas,
and of Capac Yupanqui,
their fifth king,
with the description of a famous bridge
on the Apurimac river;
and that of the very famous temples
of Cuzco and Titicaca

The Inca Maïta Capac, having succeeded his father to the throne, undertook, first of all, a general visit of the kingdom. Then, once back at Court, he collected twelve thousand fighting men and decided to invade the territory of the Collas, which, being perfectly flat, seemed to him to be particularly easy of conquest. When he reached the shores of Lake Titicaca, he had a number of large rafts built, on which his army crossed. The first villages he came to surrendered without resistance, and thus, the city of Tiahuanaco [1] became a part of the Empire. It is fitting, therefore, that we should speak here of the large, unbelievable monuments that it contained. One of the most remarkable is an artificial mound of great height, the foundations of which are large stone slabs cemented together, in order that this enormous mass of earth, piled there by the hands of men, should not be threatened with collapse. In another part of the city, quite far from this spot, are to be seen two giants carved in stone, wearing caps on their heads and their bodies covered by long garments that come down to the ground. All of these monuments were very worn with time and must have dated back to very early antiquity. There was also an immense wall, made of stones that were so large in size that one wondered how they could have been transported that far, especially in view of the fact that the country surrounding Tiahuanaco is flat, as I said before, and neither stone nor quarries exist there. There were many other astonishing edifices, the most remarkable of which were undoubtedly a series of gigantic gates, scattered about the city. Most of them were made of a single block of stone, and were based on stones certain of which were thirty feet long, fifteen feet wide, and six feet high. How, and with the use of what tools or implements, massive works of such size could be achieved, are questions which we are unable to answer.

According to the natives of Tiahuanaco, these marvelous constructions were carried out long before the time of the Incas, and their creators left them unfinished. All of this has been recounted by Pedro de Cieza de Leon in his accounts. But I should like to add to it what a childhood friend of mine wrote me, a friend who was like a brother to me, since we were born in the same house and went to school together. His name is Diego de Alcobasa, and he is now a priest. Here is what he wrote me about Tiahuanaco:

"In amongst these vast edifices there exists a square patio fifteen spans wide and enclosed by a wall two stades high. One side of this patio opens into a large hall measuring forty-five by twenty-two feet. The floor and walls, the hall and stone roof, imitating the straw that generally covers Indian houses, the gates and doors of both the patio and the hall, are all made of a single piece of stone hewn from one immense block, and the walls of the patio are nearly three feet thick. The natives say that these constructions were dedicated to the creator of the universe. There is also in this town a great number of stones, sculptured in human form, so naturally that they might be alive. Certain of them are seated, others are standing, others are crossing a brook, and still others are drinking, with glasses in their hands: some of them represent women with their children perched on their backs, clinging to their skirts, or accompanying them in a thousand other poses. The Indians say that all these statues were formerly living beings whom God changed into stone because they had thrown rocks at a traveler."

We may believe what Diego de Alcobasa says, for he has traveled considerably in Peru, and being a native half-breed of Cuzco, knows the Indian language better than those who are born elsewhere.[2]

To return to the subject of the Inca Maïta Capac, one might say that he conquered in this manner, without meeting with any resistance, the greater part of the province, called Hatunpacasa, which extends leftward from the Desaguadero [3] canal of Lake Titicaca. The imperial army then reached the frontiers of the Cac-Yauiri country, the inhabitants of which were living in small scattered groups under the reign of petty kings. As soon as they heard of the Inca's arrival they assembled together on an isolated hill that stands out like a sugar loaf in the middle of these flat lands, which was also a hill they revered, and on which they offered up sacrifices. Very rapidly they built a stone enclosure, roofed over with earth and grass, in which they shut themselves up with their wives and children, their old people, and all the provisions they had been able to collect. When envoys of the king came to beg them to surrender, they told them to go their way and leave them in peace, inasmuch as they had their own gods and their own customs, and desired no others. The Inca was obliged to lay siege to them, which he did by dividing his army into four parts which he stationed around their fortress.

The siege was long, for Maïta Capac was loath to use force, and his only intention was to conquer them by virtue of patience and hunger. There was nevertheless a heated struggle to end with, after which they were obliged to surrender. According to one legend, their own army turned against them, with the result that they had only themselves to blame for their many dead and wounded. The Incas were quick to seize upon this tale and, each time it seemed useful to do so, they spread it abroad, in order to impress other peoples who attempted to resist.

What is certain, however, is that when the inhabitants of Cac-Yauiri decided to surrender, they sent out first the women, the aged, and the children, with the request that no harm be done them since they were in no way responsible for the resistance that had been opposed; the last to leave were the curacas who, having decided to pay with their own heads for the safety of their people, came as a group to kneel before the Inca, who was waiting for them on his throne. They walked barefoot, a cord about their necks and their hands tied together, as a sign of humility, and in order to show that they accepted death for having dared to take up arms against the sons of the Sun.

But the Inca, after having heard them, commanded that their thongs be unbound, and told them that they could return to their homes and would suffer no harm, provided that henceforth they respected his law, and worshiped the Sun. In conclusion, he allowed them to approach him and kiss his right knee, in order that, having had the honor of touching his august person, they would understand that from now on, they belonged to his people.

The news of this signal leniency on the part of the king, as well as the fable according to which the Collas' army had turned against them, spread so rapidly among the nations bordering upon Hatunpacasa, that numerous peoples came of their own accord to surrender to the authority of Maïta Capac. Thus without striking a blow, he won the very rich and powerful provinces of Cauquicura, Mallama, and Huarina, which possessed fine herds and countless fighting men. He then decided to return to Cuzco, leaving his troops to his four camp commanders whom he had ordered to march westward in order to capture the provinces that extended to the sea, on the slopes of the cordillera. This campaign got under way slowly and with difficulty, because the army was obliged to cross thirty leagues of wilderness, with no roads, and carrying all its supplies, in order to reach the western slope. They finally arrived in a province called Cuchuna, where the natives immediately took refuge in a fort that they were obliged to surround. This new siege lasted more than fifty days, during which the besieged, harassed by famine, let their children leave in order to save their lives. The camp commanders, acting in accordance with the Inca's policy, took these children in charge and sent them back to their parents with provisions and encouraging words, with the result that the parents finally decided to surrender. No harm was done them and the camp commanders hastened to inform them of their real intentions, explaining that the Inca, who was the son of the Sun, did not desire to conquer new territory for the purpose of tyrannizing their inhabitants, but, on the contrary, to help them, as his father the Sun had ordered him to do.

The land in this province appeared to them to be fertile and capable of feeding a more numerous population. The captains therefore sent messengers to the Inca to inform him of their conquest and to ask him to send vassals to found two new cities. One of these was established at the foot of the mountain on which the Indians had built their fortress and it took the name of Cuchuna; the other was called Moquehua. Five leagues separated these two cities which today have given their names to the provinces surrounding them.

Now it so happened that, while the captains were working to establish these new cities, they learned that certain of the Indians in this country made use of a poison against their enemies, not so much in order to kill them —only the undernourished succumbed to it—but rather to weaken them, to leave them deprived of all their physical and moral strength, reduced to a state of inner and outer wrecks for the rest of their lives and longer, since their issue were also affected by it: the result being that, in a way, this poison was more to be feared than death itself. The captains reported this discovery immediately to the Inca who replied by ordering them to burn alive any Indian convicted of using this poison, even if he had only done so once. The entire population of the province applauded the king's sentence which was carried out immediately. And not only did they burn alive the poisoners, but at the same time they burned all their property, including their cattle and the trees they had planted. Even their houses were razed to the ground.

The severity of this punishment had a salutary effect, and from that time until the arrival of the Spaniards, one heard nothing more of such things in Peru.

The Inca's ambition was growing from day to day, with the result that it was not long before he undertook a fresh campaign. Having raised a considerable army, he left for Pucara de Umasuyu, where his fathers had halted their conquests in the east, as we have already related. Continuing his eastward march, he reached a province called Llaricassa, which surrendered without striking a blow, as did another called Sancauan. These two territories cover a space that is more than fifty leagues long and twenty to thirty leagues wide. Their population is dense and they possess an abundant number of cattle. A third province, called Pacasa, soon surrendered peacefully, as the two others had done. It will be recalled that a part of this province, which is very extensive, had been conquered earlier by the Inca Lloque Yupanqui.

After these fortunate events, the army reached the Umasuyu royal road, near an important village that today is called Huaichu. The king then learned that a numerous band of armed warring Indians had assembled farther on in order to bar his way. He continued his march in their direction and met the enemy after crossing a river called Huichu. They were faced with some thirteen or fourteen thousand warriors from various tribes, which may be called by the name of Colla. Once again, the Inca sought to give evidence of his peaceful intentions, but the enemy refused to receive his messengers and in the end, he was obliged to fight them. The combat was a terrible one and it lasted an entire day; the Inca himself entered the fray among his people, while the Collas continued to attack, with insane courage, but in such disorder that over six thousand of them are said to have perished in this affair, whereas the losses of the royal armies were not more than five hundred. When night fell, the Collas, exhausted, decided to surrender. Their captains went to the Inca's camp barefoot, with uncovered heads and their hands tied, not to beg for mercy, but for punishment. The king, with great magnanimity, sent back an answer to the effect that he would forgive them, and their lives would be spared, on condition that they would henceforth serve him faithfully. Then they were given clothes and presents, their wounded were treated, and they returned home deeply ashamed of their rebellion and grateful for the Inca's mercy.

The news of this battle won over numerous towns to the Inca's sway, throughout the thirty leagues that separate Huaichu from Cajamarca, farther south, on the Charca road. The king continued his march twenty-four leagues beyond this latter town, as far as the lagoon of Paria and, as he advanced, he received offers of surrender from all the peoples he encountered. From the lagoon of Paria, he turned toward the east, through the Anti country, and arrived in the valley that today is called Chuquiapu. The climate here being excellent and propitious for growing corn, the Inca had transplanted into this valley numerous villages that had been settled on less fertile land. Then he continued eastward as far as the grand cordillera of the Andes, which is more than thirty leagues from the Umasuyu royal road.

Establishment of these new towns and their governments took three years, at the end of which the Inca returned to Cuzco. He was greeted with magnificent festivities and was now finally able to consider taking a rest. But three years had not passed before this indefatigable conqueror began to raise fresh troops. This time his covetousness was aroused by the numerous, rich lands that lay west of Cuzco, in the Cuntisuyu district. In order to reach them, he was obliged to cross the Apurimac with all his men, and this is why he had the idea of having a reed bridge[4] constructed across this great river, which was the first of its kind in the history of the Incas. Writers on the subject of Peru have often mentioned these braided bridges, but since they have never explained how they were made, I shall do so now. First of all, the Indians collected a vast amount of Peruvian reed, which is thinner and more pliable than Spanish reed. Three shoots braided together make a first strand. Then three of these strands braided together make another one that now contains nine shoots. With three strands of nine shoots they make one with twenty-seven and, by repeating the same operation several times, they finally obtain a rope as thick as a man's body, and calculated to be as long as the bridge they are building. Then, on either side of the river, just opposite each other, they set up two stirrup supports made of hewn stone, or solid rock, with the opening toward the ground, and thick, very strong sides. They next lay across these supports five joists as thick as an ox, to which are attached the ends of the five ropes. In order to cross the river with these very heavy ropes, the workers either swim or take a raft, dragging behind them one cord to the end of which is tied an Indian hemp cable as big as your arm. This cable tows the rope, while a group of men join forces to haul it from one bank to the other.

Three of these ropes constitute the roadbed of the bridge and the other two are suspended a little higher up, to the left and to the right of the first ones, to serve as ramps. Then planks laid across the first ropes are covered with branches to allow the pack animals to walk on them without slipping. Finally, fastened between the edges of these planks and the ropes that serve as ramps, a closely woven fabric of willow and other branches serves as a parapet. The Apurimac bridge, which is the longest in Peru, is at least two hundred feet long and two feet wide. However great the effort made to stretch the ropes taut, such bridges remain nevertheless a bit swayed and curved between their two points of attachment, and the whole thing starts to swing as soon as the wind blows a bit hard. For this reason, it may seem rather precarious to cross these bridges on foot, and even more so on horseback. And yet I have seen the Spaniards cross them at a gallop. These works were indeed quite marvelous, incredible even, when one considers the frailness of the raw materials of which they were constructed. At the time of the Incas, they were watched over and rebuilt every year with contributions from the peoples who lived nearest the rivers and therefore used the bridges more than the others.[5]

And so twelve thousand men of war crossed the Apurimac, under the command of the Inca. Maïta Capac first set armed detachments to watch over the bridge, for fear that his enemies might set fire to it. But the fame of this extraordinary construction, so far from exciting the jealousy of the Indians, brought such credit to the Inca that it sufficed to attract new peoples under his sway, peoples who, in the face of such an exploit, had no further doubt but that they were actually in the presence of the son of the Sun, descended on earth for their benefit. Such is the simple nature of the Indians, for whom everything new is marvelous, and all marvels are convincing. The Incas owed their prestige more to such inventions as these than to feats of arms, and to their prestige they owed their empire. Later, the same was true of the Spaniards whom the Indians considered as gods because of their horses and their harquebuses.

Thus, the Inca's army, thanks to this bridge, was able to win over, without striking a blow, magnificent territories such as the Chumpiuilca province, which is twenty leagues long and more than ten leagues wide. The only ones to attempt any resistance were the inhabitants of a village called Uillilli, who shut themselves up in a fortress. But even they surrendered after twelve days, and the Inca pardoned them, as was his custom.

After these first conquests the imperial troops were obliged to cross the Cuntisuyu desert which is sixteen leagues wide. When they reached the middle of it they encountered swamp land three leagues wide which appeared to present an insuperable difficulty. But the Inca had numerous stones of all sizes collected and, setting to work himself in the midst of his men, in a few days he constructed a fine road that was no less than eighteen feet wide and six feet high. This road still exists and the Indians who live on the edges of these marshes keep it in excellent repair, as much out of respect for the Inca, who worked on it with his own hands, as on account of the precious benefits it has never ceased to yield them.

Once beyond these swamps, one encounters the steep slopes of the Alca mountains, to cross which, even in time of peace, is most hazardous. Numerous warriors had assembled here to halt the Inca's advance, and despite his deep desire for peace, Maïta Capac was consequently obliged to give fight, since the situation was a dangerous one. But he was naturally so prudent, so reasonable, and so versed in the arts of war, that he demolished his enemies after two months of struggle and suffering, during which many Indians, on both sides, perished. The entire province of Alca then surrendered, and the Inca entered the capital as its lord and master. He later won other fine provinces, such as Taurisma, Cotahuaci, Pumatampu, and Parihuana Cocha. Pumatampu means "lion reservation," from *puma* meaning lion, and *tampu,* which means yard, or reservation: no doubt at one time lions had been kept there. Parihuana Cocha means "flamingo lake," from *cocha,* which applies to the sea, lakes, or any large stretch of water, and *parihuana,* which means "flamingo." The Spanish, by means of an ellipsis, reduced this name to Parinacocha.

After crossing the Coropuna desert, the king reached the provinces of Aruni and Colluhua, from where he went down into the Arequipa valley, which was at that time deserted. All of these provinces surrendered of their own free will, and the Inca, finding the Arequipa valley particularly healthy, decided to populate it. He sent three thousand families to live there, dividing them between three or four villages, the most important of which were Chimpa and Sucahuaya.[6] These conquests and public works occupied him for three years and increased his empire by ninety leagues in length and twelve to fifteen in width, according to location. All of this land was in one piece and contiguous to our former borders.

The Inca Maïta Capac then returned to Cuzco where, having decided that his conquests were sufficient, he ended his days in peace and quiet, devoting himself especially to the poor, and to widows and orphans. He died after a reign that is estimated to have lasted about thirty years, and mourning for him was observed in the entire Empire, for a whole year, as is customary. He left as his heir his first-born, Capac Yupanqui, the son of his sister-bride Mama Cuca.

The Inca Capac Yupanqui began his reign by a visit to the Empire that lasted two years. When he returned to Cuzco, he ordered that an army twenty thousand men strong be levied for the following spring. It being his intention to seek conquest through the Cuntisuyu district, west of Apurimac, he had a second bridge built over this river, larger than the preceding one, eight leagues away from Cuzco.

These preparations were finished on schedule, and the imperial army, having crossed the river, entered into a large, rich province, all the inhabitants of which—men, women, children, and old people—came out with great festivities to meet the Inca and tender him their surrender. This was the Yanahuara province, which measures twenty by fifteen leagues and today is the site of more than thirty villages. The Inca insisted on visiting it in detail, in person, in order to express his satisfaction to his new subjects. From there he went to the Aimara country, which is separated from this province[7] by a desert fifteen leagues long. The Aimara province is thirty leagues long by fifteen wide, and it is very rich, not only in men and cattle, but also in gold, silver, and lead mines. Its inhabitants, in order to resist the Inca, entrenched themselves on a mountain called Mucunsa which marks the gateway to this country, on the edge of the desert. The Inca was obliged to besiege them for over a month, while waiting for hunger to force them to lay down their arms. They finally sent a deputation to him to offer their surrender on condition that the imperial army help them to conquer their neighbors of the Umasuyu province, a bellicose tyrannical people who made them suffer all sorts of harassments.

The Inca replied through one of his captains that he accepted their surrender but not their terms; that he had come to force all men, without distinction, to listen to the voice of reason; that if disturbances and disorders existed anywhere, it was his duty alone to judge them and put an end to them; that, in short, it was not their place to dictate laws to him, but their duty to submit to his law, and that for the rest, his father, the Sun God, would tell him what to do.

The ambassadors returned with this answer and, the following day, all the Indians who had entrenched themselves on the mountain came down to the royal camp. It was a considerable crowd, composed of more than twelve thousand warriors and thirty thousand women, children and old people. They advanced by groups through the towns and villages and all came to kneel before the king, bearing in their hands gold, silver, and lead, to be presented to him as tokens of tribute and tokens of surrender.

Since they were half-starved, the Inca ordered supplies distributed, before sending them home with peaceful words.

Then the Inca settled in a village in the same province, called Huaquirca, from where he sent messengers to the Umasuyu caciques. "You must stop attacking your neighbors like wild animals over questions of pasturage," he told them, "because there is enough good land here to permit your herds and theirs to graze in peace. I shall expect you all to come to Huaquirca where I shall settle your differences with the Aimaras, and teach you the laws of wisdom and reason to which my father the Sun has ordered me to subject all mankind."

The curacas of Umasuyu met together to study this message and finally replied to the Inca's envoys that they had no need to go to Huaquirca; that if the Inca wanted to see them he had only to come to where they were and that they were waiting for him with drawn swords; that they had their own gods and cared neither for the Sun, nor for the Inca, whether or not he was its son; that if he wanted to make any changes in their mode of life, he would have to use force; and that if this reply was not sufficient they were ready to give him another, on the battlefield.

Capac Yupanqui, who was determined to show his strength without using it, however, decided to win these men over by surprise. He therefore called up immediately eight thousand of his best warriors, and himself taking the lead, left on a forced march for the province of Umasuyu. No one expected him to arrive there before a month had elapsed; but he reached there in a few days, after marching night and day, and the curacas, who were disconcerted by the rapidity of his reply, and knowing that the bulk of his army would soon overtake him, did not dare to persist in their stubbornness and came to beg him humbly to pardon their impudence. They expected that they would be slaughtered; but they had only to listen to a talk on religion and morality, after which they all hastened to recognize the divinity of the Sun and the majesty of the Inca, their lord and master.

The king next visited one of their towns called Chirirqui where, after having examined the question of the pasture lands, he had boundary stones placed between the lands of the Aimaras and those of the Umasuyus, to the great satisfaction of both sides. These boundary stones have been preserved and cared for with gratitude, for they were the first in Peru, and they still exist today.

The Inca then returned to Cuzco where he made a triumphal entry. His captains marched round about his golden litter which the princes and curacas of the three new provinces carried on their shoulders. The army led the way, grouped according to seniority, and the proximity of the men to their leader was in proportion to the length of time their province had been a part of the Empire. The entire city came out to meet them, and there was singing and dancing, as usual.

The Inca remained four years in Cuzco, in order to take charge of the government of the Empire. However, convinced as he was that the affairs of peace should not exclude all military activity, in the very year of his return, he ordered that an army of five thousand men, together with abundant provisions, be levied for the following spring.

Command was conferred upon the Inca Auqui Titu, the king's brother, who was seconded by four of his close relatives, all men of age and experience.

On the day set, the king explained their mission to them, which was to continue the conquest of the Cuntisuyu district, and he himself went with them as far as the Huacachaca bridge, where he left them, after having given them his final instructions.

Hardly had they entered Quechua [8] territory when the Inca general and his camp commanders saw coming towards them the princes of the two first provinces of this nation, Cotapampa and Cotanera, accompanied by numerous followers in festive array:

"General," they said, "we welcome you to our land. Please believe that it is an honor as well as a pleasure for us to take our places, with all our people, under the authority of the son of the Sun, and that we worship you with him, since you are his own brother and have been so kind as to come this far in person. Please believe, too, that, had you not done this, we ourselves would soon have gone to the imperial city of Cuzco, to beg your brother the king to admit us into his Empire, for your fame has long been known to us, and we have desired for many years to be counted among your subjects. In addition, only your august king can free us from the tyranny and cruelty that we have suffered, for several generations, from forays into our territory by our neighbors the Chancas, the Hancohuallus, and others still. May your father the Sun watch over you and give you long life, because your presence here is a realization of our most cherished desire."

Thus the imperial troops watched these first two Quechua provinces surrender of their own accord, and there were others that did the same, among them Huamampalpa. All this land is very rich in gold and cattle.

Having completed the conquest of the Quechuas, General Auqui Titu reached the Huallaripa mountain, which is famous for its gold mines, and, after a march of thirty-five leagues across this desert region, went down to the seacoast. These low lands are covered with sand and are therefore uninhabitable, except for the rich green valleys that open on to them here and there, along the slope of the range.

The first valley they came to was the Hacari valley, which is both wide and rich and once had a population of twenty-five thousand persons. Its inhabitants surrendered with no difficulty, as did also their neighbors in the Uuinia, Camana, Carauilli, Picta, Quelca valleys, and in all those that follow one another southward, covering a tract of land sixty leagues long. Thus the army joined up with that part of the coast that had already surrendered to the Inca, with the result that it was obliged to end its conquests at this point.

General Auqui Titu then sent messengers to his brother the king, to inform him of these new conquests and describe to him the particularities of these regions and the religion of their inhabitants, who worshiped no other gods except the fish in the sea. Having made serious inquiries with regard to their rites and secret customs, he had discovered that many of these Indians, not whole valleys of them, but scattered here and there among the different valleys, indulged secretly in the foul vice of sodomy, and of this he also apprized the king.

The Inca was very pleased with these new gains, which had been obtained quickly and without bloodshed. He told his brother to return to Cuzco, but he ordered that, before he did so, all the Indians, not only those who were convicted, but even those who were suspected of sodomy, should be burned alive on the public square, their houses razed to the ground, their fields decimated and their trees pulled up by the roots, so that the very memory of these heinous practices should disappear from Peru for all time.

The sentence pronounced by the Inca was carried out in detail, to the great satisfaction of the Indians in these valleys, and this foul vice was thenceforth so despised throughout the Empire that people did not dare pronounce the name.[9]

The general and his troops then returned to Cuzco where they were received with honor and gratitude.

A few years after these conquests, the Inca Capac Yupanqui decided to undertake a new campaign, in the direction of Collasuyu. While an army of twenty thousand men was being assembled and equipped for this purpose, he divided among his relatives the principal duties of government. His brother, General Auqui Titu, and his four camp commanders received general interim direction of Empire affairs, while four other Incas of noble blood were chosen to accompany him as camp commanders.

After crossing the Paria lagoon, where his father's conquests in this direction had ended, without encountering any resistance, the Inca learned that a war was raging not far from there between two important captains, the heirs of two princely houses that had conquered considerable territory in these parts well before the time of the Incas, and had finally turned against each other.

This war had lasted for several generations, and threatened to continue until the extermination of both sides, since they were practically equal in strength and in courage. And so these two princes, whose names—like those of their fathers—were Cari and Chipana, when they heard of the advance of the very famous and powerful Inca, resolved, after deliberating with their advisors, to submit their dispute to him, and to abide by his arbitration. They therefore dispatched messengers to him, to beg him to receive and hear them. The Inca had a reply sent to them to the effect that his father the Sun assisted him in all things, and that he would succeed in finding a fair solution to their dispute, in order that their war should end and that they should become friends again.

They therefore both came to the royal camp and, together, they kissed the king's hand, neither wanting to take advantage over the other. Prince Cari, whose territory was nearer that of the Inca, spoke first and explained at length their history and the causes of their disagreement. The Inca listened attentively, then called two captains of his own blood, and ordered each of them to take one of the princes with him, to show him how the army was organized, and teach him the laws, all of which were based on natural law, that governed the kingdom and maintained it in peace. At the same time he sent two other Incas to inquire about the lands that belonged to these two princes, in order to obtain a better understanding of their rivalry.

When these envoys had submitted the conclusions of their inquiry, the Inca, after deliberating privately with his advisors, summoned the two princes to him and said:

"The Sun, my father, has commanded that, in order for peace and concord to dwell amongst you, you must, from now on, observe the laws that have been taught you by the Incas, and watch over the health and increase of your subjects; for you have nothing to gain, neither the one nor the other, and everything to lose, in this war. And if it were to be pursued, you would become so weakened that you would be at the mercy of any other curaca who could then, without effort, make you disappear from this world, even to the very memory of the glorious conquests of your fathers. You will therefore set up boundary stones in such and such places to delimit your territory. And should you transgress the orders of the Sun that I have just communicated to you, you will be severely punished, inasmuch as He it is whom you have made judge of your dispute."

The curacas replied that they would obey everything His Majesty had ordered and that, in accordance with his desire, they would, from now on, comport themselves as real friends. And they really did their utmost to apply the laws of the Inca to the affairs of their courts and in their governments. But, above all, they had both been extremely struck by Capac Yupanqui's mild manners, his sense of justice, and the way he had made equitable division of their territories. With the result that, after having given much thought to it, and deliberated upon the matter with their counselors, they both decided to seek his protection and to become his subjects. No doubt the Inca's strength, and the proximity of his territory played a part in their decision, for they well realized that they could not hope to resist him should he decide to invade them. Indeed it was to their advantage to willingly take their places among his vassals, which, fortunately for them, is what they did. The Inca did not fail to thank them, extended them many privileges, and even went so far as to divide his own garments among them, which they accepted as an exceptional favor.

Thus it was that the Inca subjugated to his Empire the numerous provinces that belonged to the two caciques from the Collasuyu district. These included all the territories that extended eastward, as far as the Andes mountains, among which were the provinces of Pocoata, Murumuru, Maccha, and Caracara, as well as the great desert of Tapacari which covers more than thirty leagues of barren land; this desert is remarkable as much for its innumerable herds of wild and domestic cattle as for its springs, some of cold, delicious water and others of warm sulphur water, that, together, form the Cochapampa river.

Beyond this great desert, the road leads down hill for seven leagues until it comes to the low lands of the Tapacri province, which was the first granted to his lordship Garcilaso de la Vega. It is very fertile and populous, rich in cattle, and is more than twenty leagues long by twelve leagues wide. Eight leagues farther on we come to another beautiful province called Cochapampa. It stretches across a valley thirty leagues long and four leagues wide, on either side of a wide river. These two provinces were also part of the assets that the curacas Cari and Chipana brought to the Empire.

The Inca entrusted the organization of these new territories to his camp commanders, and returned to Cuzco, taking the two captains with him, that they might become acquainted with his court. He was pleased, beyond all expectations, at the results of this campaign which had not lasted more than a year. The two caciques spent some time in the imperial city, where people took pains to treat them with great consideration, as the king had expressly requested they should do. They finally returned to their own lands, after having taken leave of the Inca who asked them to hold themselves in readiness for his visit the following year, since he was planning to undertake conquest of the territories situated on the other side of their provinces.

The Inca Capac Yupanqui was very proud of the bridge he had had built over the Apurimac river. In order to facilitate the movements of his troops in the Collasuyu district, he decided to construct another one, of a different type, across the river the Spaniards call Desaguadero,[10] because it flows out of Lake Titicaca toward the south.

All of the bridges in Peru are made of reed. This one, however, was constructed with two other plants: cattails and rattan palm, both of which grow in abundance on the shores of Lake Titicaca. It was not suspended in the air, as reed bridges are, but rested on the surface of the water, the way the boat-bridge in Seville does.

One of the chosen plants was gathered in large bunches, as thick as a steer, to be used as floaters, instead of boats. With the other plant, they plaited four cables as big as a man's thigh, then stretched them from one bank to the other at water level, gripping the mass of the floaters between them. The roadbed, as usual, was made of planks, grass and branches. One can imagine the enormous quantities of grass and plants that had to be collected, if I say that the bridge is thirteen to fourteen feet wide, more than three feet high, and one hundred and fifty feet long. Every six months it has to be entirely made over, since these materials could not resist any longer the process of putrefaction that results from their long stay in the water.

When this work was finished, the Inca went without stopping to the furthermost provinces of the caciques Cari and Chipana, which are called Tapacri and Cochapampa, as has already been told. He took with him his young son and heir, in order to let him learn from experience about war and politics. The two caciques Cari and Chipana joined him, on the way, with their troops. From Cochapampa they all went as far as the entrance to Chayanta, where the Inca sent his ambassadors, as was customary.

The Chayanta caciques remained undecided for a long time. Certain of them were in favor of resistance and others of surrender. They finally came to an agreement, however, and answered the ambassadors as follows: The Inca and his troops should come to their territory and settle there; then he should explain clearly in detail the laws and obligations to which they would be expected to submit, should they become his vassals; if these terms suited them, the Inca could reside in their land, as their lord and master; if not, he could return home with his army.

The Inca accepted this proposal, insisting nevertheless that he did so out of pure kindness of heart and in order to remain faithful to his father the Sun who had ordered him to use gentleness and love in all things, rather than violence; for otherwise, he added, I could easily have subjugated you to my will by the force of my arms.

The imperial troops then entered the province of Chayanta, and the king's counselors, who were men of a certain age and experience, met together with the caciques of this province to explain the laws of the Empire to them. The crown prince took part in this discussion, which lasted several days. After the curacas had heard and meditated upon this teaching, they declared that the Sun and the Incas, its sons, really deserved to be worshiped and treated as gods and lords of all the earth, their ordinances and their laws being just and profitable for all. Having thus confirmed their sentiments, they bowed down before the crown prince and adored him in the place of the Sun and his father the Inca Capac Yupanqui; then they gave orders that their former idols should be overthrown, and that the new order of things should hold sway throughout their entire land.

The admission to the Empire of this new province, which is no less than twenty leagues square, was celebrated by feasts and dances and songs improvised in praise of the Inca, in a style that was quite new to him.

Having spoken of the two sorts of bridges that the Incas had built, it is right that we should explain, too, the various other means that the Indians invented for crossing rivers; for bridge construction was too long and too costly to be envisaged elsewhere than on the royal roads, and, since the mountains of Peru are divided by an infinite number of rivers, it was necessary for the Indians to think up a quantity of other expedients for crossing them.

The only tall trees in Peru being of a hard wood that is

as heavy as iron, they did not carve out canoes as is done elsewhere in America, but constructed rafts principally, made of a tree very commonly found in the mountains, that is no thicker than a man's thigh and as light as a fig tree. These rafts were usually built of five or seven tree trunks tied together and cut in such a manner that, on either side of the central trunk, which was the longest of all, they gradually became equally shorter. Thus, in front as well as in back, these rafts had the same pointed shape. They were connected with the banks by two ropes which, when pulled, made it possible to cross over.

The Indians also made little boats with bundles of the reed we call cattail. These bundles, which were the size of an ox, were tightly fastened in such a way that they were higher in front and broader and lower behind. One Indian alone steered these little skiffs. With his chest resting on the back of the boat and the rest of his body in the water, he guided it with his hands and feet, which served as oars; meanwhile, the load was carried in front. In order to take a passenger across, he was stretched out face downward, with his head toward the back, and told to keep still, to press his chest against the reeds and, above all, not to raise his head or open his eyes during the crossing. I understood quite well the importance of these instructions after having myself been set across a very swift river in this manner. I was a child at the time, and with the curiosity that is natural to this age, I could not resist the temptation to open my eyes and look about me during the crossing, expecting to see some marvel from the other world. But what I saw of the torrent raging on a level with my face so terrified me that I quickly closed my eyes tight, having understood a bit late that my ferryman's instructions were very reasonable.

The Indians also make other kinds of rafts with giant gourds squeezed into a net and securely bound together, forming a surface of one meter or a meter and a half square, according to their needs. An Indian jumps in the water and sticking his head through a loop attached to the front of the raft—like a horse's bridle—he pulls the raft on his back across the river. When the load is very heavy, or the current particularly swift, two more Indians help him by pushing the raft from the back.

They also tie ropes to trees or high rocky peaks, above the rivers that cannot be crossed in rafts. A wicker basket is attached to this rope by a wooden handle, and two cords connect it with the banks. Three or four persons at a time may sit in this basket. But since these ropes curve considerably, one of the ferrymen has to hold the basket back while it follows, through its own weight, the first, downward, lap of its course. Then, the second ferryman hauls it by hand to the other bank. Often, too, there are no ferrymen, and the passenger is obliged to accomplish these two gestures for himself, standing up in the basket. By this same means, small cattle may be sent across, but not the big ones from Spain which are too heavy. This vehicle is not to be found on the royal roads, but only on paths that connect the Indian villages to one another. It is called *uruya.*

Along the entirc coast of Peru, the Indians go fishing in the little reed boats we have described, and the sea being very calm, they can venture four to five leagues from shore [11] in these light skiffs. But to carry heavier loads they always use rafts.

The fishermen, in their little reed barks, remain on their knees, using as a crude rudder a piece of bamboo split lengthwise, which thus ends naturally in the form of a shovel. They row, first on one side then on the other, so skillfully in fact that they may attain to astonishing rapidity. They fish with harpoons, on a cord thirty to forty spans long, the end of which is tied to their boat. When their harpoon gets caught in a big catch, they loosen the cord and maintain their equilibrium by putting both hands in the water, until the fish wearies of towing them and they can pull it on board.

These tiny little barks are too unstable for it to be possible to rig up a sail, but, on the other hand, they do put sails on their rafts when they go out to sea.

Having described these things, I shall now return to the conquests of the Inca Capac Yupanqui.

After leaving Chayanta, the Inca went into the region of Charca, which groups a great number of provinces and nations speaking different languages, in the Collasuyu district. The principal of these are the Tuturas, the Sipisipis, the Chaquis, and, farther east, toward the Andes, the Chamurus and the Sacacas. All of these nations knew what had happened in Chayanta, and they surrendered of their own accord, without making any difficulties. This campaign took two or three years, after which the Inca

The Inca speaking to the huacas

The Inca praying in Cuzco

Idols and huacas *of the Chinchasuyus*

Idols and huacas *of the Antisuyus*

Idols and huacas *of the Collasuyus*

Idols and huacas *of the Cuntisuyus*

The high priest and the Inca

Three sorcerer-priests

The soothsayers

Ritual sacrifice of the llama

and his son separated, returning to Cuzco by different roads, in order that a greater number of villages should be honored with a princely visit.

At the end of this campaign, the Cuzco Empire covered the following territories: toward the South, as far as Tutura and Chaqui, covering one hundred and eighty leagues; toward the West, as far as the seacoast, which is sixty or eighty leagues from Cuzco, depending on the place; toward the East, as far as the Paucartampu river, covering thirteen leagues; toward the southeast, as far as Callauaya, covering forty leagues.

This enlargement of the Empire seemed to the Inca to be great enough to allow him to devote several years to matters of government. Thus it was that, among other tasks, he undertook to embellish the Temple of the Sun in Cuzco, which had been founded by the first Inca, Manco Capac, as well as the convent of the virgins and numerous other public edifices. He also had a number of new constructions built throughout the Empire, such as bridges, canals, and roads.

Six or seven years later, the Inca Capac Yupanqui again raised an army of twenty thousand men, command of which he entrusted to his son and heir, Inca Roca, with the mission to conquer new territory in the direction of Chinchasuyu, to the north of the kingdom; for the frontier in these parts was the same as had been established by Manco Capac, that is to say, at Rimactampu, only seven leagues from Cuzco. The Prince crossed the Apurimac river on large rafts built for the occasion and, encountering only depopulated lands, continued his way as far as Carahuaci and Amansay, eighteen leagues from the imperial city. From the province of Amansay, he turned left off the royal road that goes from Cuzco to Rimac, crossed twenty-two leagues of the Cochacasa desert, and reached the province of Sura, which is densely populated, as well as rich in gold and cattle, and where he was received without difficulty. In the same way, he won over the two neighboring provinces of Rucana and Hatun-Rucana, or greater Rucana.[12] All of these provinces, and those that follow, were at war with one another, and for this reason, he had no trouble subjugating them. He next went down toward the coast where he conquered all the valleys that stretch from Nanasca (which the Spaniards pronounce Lanasca) as far as Arequipa, covering more than eighty leagues of coast and fourteen or fifteen toward the interior. The most important of these valleys were Hacari and Camata, which counted a population of some twenty thousand persons.[13]

Shortly after the arrival of the Spaniards, a curaca from the Hacari valley, being jealous of another curaca, invited him to drink with him from a cup that contained poison. The man, who knew many a wile, replied: "Our drinks would give us even greater pleasure if we exchanged cups." The curaca was obliged to accept and thus it was that he died, both from the poison he had intended for another, and from fury at having been foiled.

On the royal road that leads from Cuzco to Rimac, there is a region which is so hot that the mountain Indians, who are accustomed to cold, cannot live there. The Inca took advantage of Prince Inca Roca's recent conquests in the coastal areas to people this region with natives from the Nanasca province, who were accustomed to intense heat. Thus very profitable gardens were laid out, only a short distance from Cuzco, on the banks of the Apurimac river.

The Inca Capac Yupanqui lived in peace several years longer, and died after having embellished considerably the city of Cuzco. He deserved this name of Capac, which had remained in high favor with the Indians, for he was a very valorous ruler. He was greatly mourned for a long time, and his body was embalmed and laid beside those of his ancestors, as was the custom. His son Inca Roca, who was born of the Colla Mama Curilipay, succeeded him. He is said to have had eighty, or one hundred, or even two or three hundred, other children, both legitimate and illegitimate.

In the whole of old Peru, there was undoubtedly no place that was as deeply revered as the imperial city of Cuzco, which is where all the Inca kings held court and established the seat of government. When two Indians met on a road leading to this city, the one who was going there immediately greeted the one coming from there as his superior, and in all the kingdom there was neither vegetable, grain, nor other produce, of however superior quality, to compare with those from Cuzco. All the Incas enriched this city and, among its countless monuments, the Temple of the Sun remained the principal object of their attention. They vied with one another in ornamenting it with incredible wealth, each Inca seeking to surpass his predecessor. Indeed, the splendors of this temple were such that I should not venture to describe them, had not all Spanish historians of Peru done the same. But nothing that they have written, nor anything that I might add, could ever depict it as it really was. This temple is usually associated with the name of the Inca Yupanqui, the grandfather of Huaina Capac, not because he built it—for it went back to the first Inca—but because it was he who completed its ornamentation and conferred upon it the luster and splendor that it had when the Spaniards first saw it.

The Temple of the Sun was located on the site that today is occupied by the Church of San Dominique, and its walls, which are made of highly polished stone, still exist.

What we shall call the high altar, although this expression did not exist among the Indians, was to the east, and the roof, which was very high, was of wood, covered with straw. The four walls were hung with plaques of gold, from top to bottom, and a likeness of the Sun topped the high altar. This likeness was made of a gold plaque twice as thick as those that paneled the walls, and was composed of a round face, prolonged by rays and flames, the way the Spanish painters represent it; the whole thing was so immense that it occupied the entire back of the temple, from one wall to the other. There was no other idol in this temple, nor in any other, for the Sun was the only god of the Incas, whatever people may say on this subject.

When the Spaniards entered Cuzco, this likeness of the Sun, as the result of a division of property, fell into the hands of one of the early conquistadors, who was a man of noble birth by the name of Mancio Serra de Leguisamo, whom I knew very well before I came to Spain. He was a great gambler and he had no sooner acquired this treasure than he gambled and lost it in one night; and we might even say, echoing Father Acosta, that this is the origin of the expression "to gamble the Sun before it rises."

On either side of this Sun, were kept the numerous mummies of former Inca kings, which were so well preserved that they seemed to be alive. They were seated on their golden thrones resting on plaques of this same metal, and they looked directly at the visitor. Alone among them, Huaina Capac's body had assumed a peculiar pose, facing the Sun, as though from childhood, he had been its favorite son who deserved to be adored for his unusual virtues. The Indians hid these bodies along with other treasures that have not yet come to light. In 1559, the scholar Polo discovered five of them, including three kings and two queens.

The main door of the temple opened to the north, as it does today, and there were several others, of less importance, which were used for services in the temple. All of these doors were covered with plaques of gold and the walls of the building were crowned on the outside with a gold band, three feet wide, that went all around it.

The temple was prolonged by a square cloister with an adjoining wall, and crowned by a gold band like the one we have just described. The Spaniards replaced this by a plaster band of the same width that could be seen on the walls, which were still standing, when I left Peru. The three other sides of the cloister gave on to five large square rooms, that had no communication between them, and were roofed over in the form of a pyramid.

The first of these rooms was dedicated to the Moon, the bride of the Sun, and for this reason it was nearest to the main building. It was entirely paneled with silver, and a likeness of the Moon, with the face of a woman, decorated it in the same way that the Sun decorated the larger building. The Indians offered no sacrifices to her, but they came to visit her and begged her intercession, as to the sister-bride of the Sun and to the mother of all the Incas. They called her Mamaquilla, which means our mother the Moon. The bodies of queens were laid away in this Temple, just as those of the kings were kept in the other. Mama Occlo, the mother of Huaina Capac, occupied the place of honor, before the likeness of the Moon, because she had given birth to such a son.

The room nearest that of the Moon was devoted to Venus, to the Pleiades and to all the stars. As we said before, Venus was honored as the Sun's page, who accompanies him on his way, now following him, now preceding him. The Indians considered the other stars as servants of the Moon, and this was why they were represented near her. The constellation of the Pleiades was particularly revered because of the regularity and perfection of its well-grouped design.[14]

This room was hung with silver, like that of the Moon, and the ceiling was dotted with stars, like the firmament. The next room was dedicated to lightning, and to thunder, which were both expressed by the single name, *illapa*. If they said: "Did you hear illapa?," it was understood as "thunder." And if they said: "Did you see illapa?" or "illapa struck there," this meant "lightning."

Both were respected as servants of the Sun, just as the gentiles used to consider lightning as Jupiter's own weapon. This room was entirely covered with gold, but neither lightning nor thunder were represented there, because they would not have known how to go about it.[15]

The fourth room was devoted to the rainbow, which they said had descended from the Sun, and which figured on the scutcheon of the Inca kings. It was entirely covered with gold and the rainbow was painted, in beautiful colors, across the entire surface of one of the walls. They called the rainbow *cuichu* and revered it very specially. When it appeared, they immediately put their hands over their mouths through fear, they said, that it might make their teeth decay. I can't say why.

The fifth and last room was reserved for the high priest and his assistants, who were all of royal blood. They did not live there but met there in council, either to give hearings, or to decide upon the sacrifices and all that had to be done in connection with the service of the temple. This parlor was paneled with gold, in the same way as the others.

The name of the high priest was *uilac-umu,* which the Spaniards have made into *vilaoma*. This name means "he who speaks of divine matters," from the verb *uilla,* to speak, and *umu,* the divine. It was he who communicated to the people the decisions of the supreme god, the Sun, as well as his own interpretations of dreams and all the signs in which he believed he could read the divine will.

In my youth, I recall having seen three of these five rooms, still almost intact, all that was missing being the silver and gold paneling. Nothing remained, however, of the two others, those of the Moon and the stars. Outside these rooms, four recesses had been hollowed out in the thickness of the walls, on each of the three sides of the cloister that they enclosed. These recesses were covered with carving on their entire surface and lined with gold plaques incrusted with emeralds and turquoises, that espoused the relief of the sculptures. During the Sun festivals the Inca sat in one of them, on one or the other side of the cloister, according to the feast day being celebrated.

The twelve doors of the sacred rooms that opened on to the cloister were paneled in gold, with the exception of those of the Moon and the stars, which were in silver.

There were many more, smaller rooms in the enclosure of the Sun temple, which were used to lodge the priests and servants of these sacred precincts. All of these men were chosen from among the Incas, some of royal blood, others merely privileged, and access to these premises was forbidden to men who were not of Inca blood, and to all women, without consideration of rank or birth: even the wives and daughters of the king were denied entrance here. The priests succeeded one another in the service of the temple, according to the quarters of the Moon. During that time, they could have nothing to do with their wives, nor could they even leave the temple, by day or by night.

The servants of the temple, such as porters, cleaners, cooks, cup-bearers, lackeys, jewelers, weavers, or others, were chosen from the same villages as were those in the service of the king, and these posts were considered to be obligatory responsibilities incumbent upon the villages in question. For the service of these two houses, that of the king and that of the Sun, were equal in all things, like that of father and son, with this single difference, that no sacrifices were offered in the king's house, and there were no women among the servants of the Sun. In everything else, the two houses were equal in grandeur and in majesty.

Sacrifices were offered up in different spots, that varied according to their importance and solemnity. The grand area of the temple, however, was reserved for the richest of them all, called *Raïmi,* which took place during the principal Sun festival. Sacrifices were also offered up on the parvis, on the occasion of other festivals to which the provinces and different nations of the empire sent delegations to bear offerings and dance in the capital.

It was forbidden to enter the grand area, or the temple itself, without first having removed one's shoes.

The main square of Cuzco was connected with the Temple of the Sun by three principal streets that ran north and south. One of these streets followed the river that divides the city; the second was called, in my time, Prison Street, because of a jail the Spaniards had built there; and the third was the one that runs from a corner of the square in the same direction. Lastly, it was possible to reach the temple by taking a fourth street that lay to the east of the three others; today this street is called Saint Augustine.

The most important of these four streets used to be Prison Street, which was called then the Street of the Sun. All processions, as well as the delegations that came to present offerings to the Sun and to the Inca, took this street both to accede to the temple and to come down from it.

Mention should also be made of a cross street, running east and west, that cut across the four roads to the temple at one particular point, beyond which it was forbidden to continue with one's shoes on. From this point to the entrance of the temple properly speaking, there remained about two hundred steps to be taken.

The temple was decorated with five fountains that were fed from five different sources. Their pipes were of solid gold and their stone pillars were covered with either gold or silver, for the sacrifices were washed in these waters. I remember the last of these fountains which was used to water the garden of the convent that the Spaniards established on this sacred ground. One day it stopped working, to the great despair of the Indians who, not knowing where the water came from, were unable to repair it; and the garden dried up, in spite of their desire and their efforts to save it. This only shows how quickly the Indians lost their traditions, since, in the space of forty-two years, there was not one left who could say from whence came the waters that circulated throughout the temple of their god the Sun.

In the time of the Incas, this garden, in which today the convent brothers cultivate their vegetables, was entirely made of gold and silver; and there were similar gardens about all the royal mansions. Here could be seen all sorts of plants, flowers, trees, animals, both small and large, wild and tame, tiny, crawling creatures such as snakes, lizards, and snails, as well as butterflies and birds of every size; each one of these marvels being placed at the spot that best suited the nature of what it represented.

There were a tall corn stalk and another stalk from the grain they call *quinoa,* as well as other vegetables and fruit trees, the fruits of which were all very faithfully reproduced in gold and silver. There were also, in the house of the Sun, as well as in that of the king, piles of wool made of gold and silver, and large statues of men, women, and children made of the same materials, in addition to storerooms and recipients for storing the grain they called *pirua,* all of which, together, tended to lend greater splendor and majesty to the house of their god the Sun. All of these valuable works were made by the goldsmiths attached to the Temple, from the tribute of gold and silver that arrived every year from all the provinces of the Empire, and which was so great that the most modest utensils used in the temple, such as pots and pans, or pitchers, were also made of precious metals. For this reason, the temple and its service quarters were called Coricancha, which means the place of gold.

All the other temples in the kingdom were patterned on this one, as were also the convents for virgin women, that have been so well described by Pedro de Cieza de Leon, in his accounts of Peru, in which he gives a detailed picture of the provinces, one after the other, that compose this vast Empire.

The priests for these numerous temples of the Sun were chosen from among the nearest relatives of the curacas. The superior, however, who was, so to speak, the bishop of his province, had to be an Inca of royal blood, in order to assure that the sacrifices should be carried out everywhere in the same manner as in Cuzco, and that the barbarian rites and ceremonies that the Incas had forbidden, such as human sacrifice and the custom of later eating the human flesh of the victims, should not reappear. There were also other horrible things that had existed formerly, but we shall tell of these when we come to them.[16]

One of the most famous temples of the Sun, which easily

rivaled that of Cuzco, was located on an island in Lake Titicaca, at two harquebus lengths from the shore. It took five or six thousand steps to go around it and, according to Inca tradition, it marked the spot where the Sun had left his two children whose mission it was to teach humanity. The Indians complemented this fable with another, according to which the rays of the sun were supposed to have touched this island before any other spot on earth, after the flood, a belief that was current before the first Incas. Manco Capac took advantage of this legend, and it was because the Indians already considered this lake and this island as sacred ground that he claimed it as the place of the miraculous origin he had invented for himself. The Indians from this region who were transferred to Copacabana, told Father Blas Valera that there was everything that was needed there to build a second temple, quite as large, of gold and silver alone, without using any other materials. They also said that the attendants of the temple, when they heard that the Spaniards had arrived, had thrown everything in the water that they could not carry away with them in their flight.

I remember another, similar tale; it had to do with a small lake, about one-half league around, but very deep, and surrounded by high mountains, some six leagues south of Cuzco. It is well known that, on the arrival of the Spaniards, the Indians threw a great part of the treasures from the Cuzco temple into this lake, among other things, the famous gold chain that Huaina Copac had had made, and about which we shall speak later. Some twelve or thirteen Spanish inhabitants of Cuzco having learned this fact, formed a company among themselves to dry up this lake, and thus retrieve these treasures. After having sounded it, they decided that it was about twenty-three to twenty-four fathoms deep, without counting the added depth of ooze. That seemed a great deal, so they decided to dig a tunnel east of it through which the water could find outlet. They started working in 1557 and, after having dug a gallery more than fifty steps long, encountered rock as hard as silex, from which they got nothing but sparks, with the result that they became discouraged and abandoned their project. I have seen the gallery they dug and have even been inside it several times. There are numerous other places, in the mountains, the lakes and the caves, where the Indians are supposed to have hidden treasures that can never be recovered.

In addition to the temple, the Inca kings did much to make this island in Lake Titicaca more beautiful. They first leveled it, which was very laborious, for it was entirely of rock, and they dug roads which they filled with earth brought from elsewhere. They even succeeded in growing corn, which was a rare achievement in this cold country where nothing grows. The ears of this corn were carefully conserved, as sacred objects, and taken to the king who, in turn, divided them between the temples of the Sun and the convents for virgin women, throughout the Empire, so that all should receive their share of this miraculous grain, which seemed to have come from heaven.

1. The origin of the name of this city is unknown. It is perhaps the most important pre-Columbian site of Peru. It may be assumed, however, that the name is a recent one, dating from some centuries later than the most ancient structures of this renowned site of pre-Columbian days.
   Clements R. Markham, in his *History of Peru,* relates in this connection an anecdote which has at least the merit of charm, although some may regard it as inaccurate: An Inca prince visiting the ancient city once received a message brought by a runner. Struck by the speed and the pleasant appearance of the young messenger, the prince is said to have invited him to rest before leaving, saying: "Tia, huanaco!" or "Rest, guanaco!"—the guanaco being, of all the American camelidae, the most reputed for its speed.

2. According to Wendell C. Bennett in *Ancient Arts of the Andes,* the combination of styles of Tiahuanaco dominates the fourth archaeological period of ancient Peru, between the years 1000 and 1300 of our era. The main structures of the site may therefore be assumed to date from that period, when the pre-Inca civilization of Tiahuanaco was exerting its influence not only on the highlands of Lake Titicaca, but over all Peru, including the coastal populations. The style known as "Ancient Tiahuanaco" dates from the third Peruvian period, or "classical period," between 400 and 1000 A.D. This period is chiefly characterized by the Nazca, Mochica, Recuay, and Pucara cultures.
   Garcilaso, of course, knew nothing of all the pre-Inca Peruvian civilizations. See, in the Appendix, the chronological table of Peruvian civilizations, according to Henri Lehmann.
   It should be added that the great monolithic gateway, called "The Sun Door," measures 12.59 feet in width, 8.95 feet in height, and is 19.7 inches thick.

3. Stream joining Lake Titicaca to Lake Poopo, into which it overflows.

4. It was not reed but plaited agave fiber—or "cabuya"—which is still in constant use for all handicrafts in the Andes. See the position of this bridge on the map of the Cuzco region. According to Bennett (*Handbook* V), the supporting cables of this bridge were 17.7 inches in diameter.

5. In spite of its instability, since it swayed constantly in the wind, and the fact that it had to be rebuilt every year, this famous Apurimac bridge, which measured more than 230 feet in length, was so useful and so cleverly built from materials available on the spot, that it remained in service until the end of the nineteenth century, that is to say for more than four hundred years.

6. It seems in fact that the valley of Arequipa was decimated by a volcanic eruption in the time of the Inca Pachacutec, and repopulated later by people from the highlands, speaking Aimara and Quechua. This explains its name, half Quechua and half Aimara, which means behind the peak, from the Aimara word *ari* meaning needle or peak, and the Quechua word *quipa*, meaning behind. (Rowe)

7. The Aimara tribe should not be confused with the Aimara language. The question as to whether the two were related has never been settled. According to Markham, the Aimaras spoke Quechua and their name was given to the Aimara tongue by the Jesuits of Juli in the late sixteenth century. This is a rather questionable hypothesis. It has never really been proved that the Aimaras spoke Quechua. It is possible, and even probable, that in the fifteenth century they spoke an Aimara dialect. Unfortunately, the language situation in this region was not dealt with by any of the chroniclers and the problem remains insoluble. (Rowe)

8. A distinction must be made between the Quechua region, tribe, and language: this confusion is one of the most common causes of error in the history of the Andes. The Quechua tribe lived between Curahuasi and Abancay, in a semi-tropical climate, which explains their name, that seems to mean: temperate valley, and is said to have been given them by their neighbors the Incas. In the early fifteenth century, they formed one of the large and powerful tribes of this part of the Andes. Situated between the Chancas and the Incas, they no doubt possessed at that time the province later called Chanca and that of Cotapampa (and Cotanera), which explains why Garcilaso speaks of the Quechua generals, Cotapampa and Cotanera. It was no doubt at this time that the Incas gave the name of this tribe to the dialect which was to become the official language of the whole Empire. The leadership of the Quechua-speaking peoples was taken over by the Incas after the invasion of the Quechua territory by the Chanca tribe, who, by weakening all the other tribes, made possible the remarkable rise to supremacy of the Incas. (Rowe) They were made Incas by privilege by Pachacutec. The original language of the people of Cotapampa and Cotanera is unknown. (Note 7, Book IV)

9. The punishment of sodomy. Garcilaso seemed to think that no law had ever been passed against this vice before that of the Incas. It is known, however, that the Chimu tribe, forming the chief sovereign state of the coastal area, considered sodomy, long before the Incas, as a crime warranting burning at the stake. (Book VI)

10. See Note 3, Book III.

11. The Spanish leagues measured 6,092 yards, and so, if Garcilaso is to be believed, these small skiffs ventured as far as 15 to 20 miles from the coast.

12. The territory of Rucana (probably *rok'ana:* finger) was divided into three parts: Upper Rucana, or Greater Rucana, Lower or Lesser Rucana, and Anta-Marka. According to Rowe, the people of Rucana paid tribute to the Emperor in the person of young porters. Garcilaso discusses this matter in Book VI.

13. It must be remembered that, with our present knowledge of the history of Inca expansion, all these conquests related by Garcilaso must be regarded as legend rather than fact. It is indeed most unlikely that the Incas reached the Pacific coast before the reign of the Inca Pachacutec in the fifteenth century.

14. The Pleiades were regarded as divinities watching over the sowing of seed and indicating certain agricultural seasons. (Rowe)

15. Illapa lived in the heavens and was identified with a constellation. He was the god of seasons and was invoked to bring rain. He was represented in the form of a man dressed in rich and gleaming garments, holding a club in one hand and in the other a sling. Thunder was the sound made by the sling, and lightning the reflection from his garments when he moved; thunderbolts were the missiles he hurled from his sling. (Rowe)

16. Baudin has stated: "The most reputed and efficacious sacrifices were human ones. Here we turn a dark page in Inca history which Garcilaso, in his loyalty to his race, would have liked to efface. There is no doubt however, that, on great occasions, and, it must be admitted, in exceptional circumstances, children and young people were put to death. The most beautiful were chosen; they were fed well, intoxicated with *chicha* or anaesthetized by the absorption of massive doses of coco, then made to turn three times round the idol, like llamas, before being strangled. Such sacrifices took place, for example, when the Inca fell ill or when a powerful nation declared war." Thus wrote Baudin, in 1928. The following is the opinion of Rowe, twenty years later: ". . . Human sacrifices, regarded as the most efficacious, were only offered to deities of the greatest importance on

the most solemn occasions, such as in times of epidemics, famine, military defeats, and for the coronation of a new Emperor (when two hundred children were sacrificed).

"The victims were of three kinds. When a new province was captured, some of the finest looking of the inhabitants were chosen to be brought to Cuzco and offered to the Sun in thanksgiving for the victory. All the other victims were boys and girls from among those regularly given in tribute by the provinces or offered by their parents in cases of extreme need. They had to be perfect physical specimens, aged ten in the case of boys, and from ten to fifteen for girls. The latter were chosen from among the virgins in the convents. When they had been strangled with a rope, their throats were cut, or else their hearts were cut out, still beating, and offered to the deity. With the blood of the victim, the priest drew a line across the mummy or effigy of the god, from ear to ear, across the nose. Sometimes the blood was spilled on the ground and sometimes on the figure of the god." Rowe's work was based on that of Cobo, Molina de Cuzco, Morúa, Cieza de Leon, and Polo. In addition, see Note 2, Book IV.

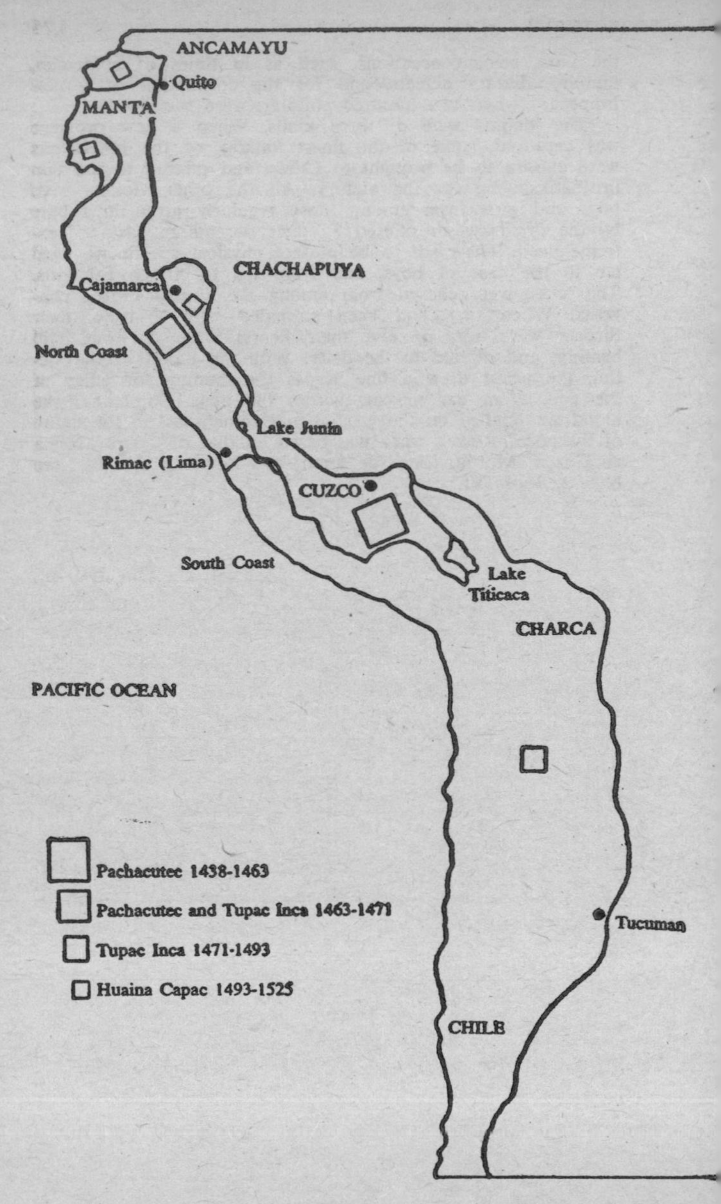

Extension of the Inca Empire between 1438 and 1525.

BOOK FOUR

*Which treats of the life, works,
and conquests of Inca Roca,
sixth king of Peru, and of his successor,
Yahuar Huacac, seventh king.
With the life and status of the virgins
dedicated to the Sun; and the customs
relative to marriage,
birth, family life, and
child education. Also the disgrace
of the crown prince,
the vision that comes to him, and
the revolt of the Chancas*

In spite of their ignorance of real religion, the Inca kings accomplished some great things, that are worthy of note, one of which was the vow of celibacy observed by certain chosen women, in the houses of reclusion built for them throughout the Empire by these kings. All the Spanish historians who have approached this question have passed over it "like a cat on hot bricks," as they say. For this reason, therefore, we shall give a detailed description, in order to make clear what these women were, what their vows consisted of, and how they observed the rules of monastic life.[1]

In Cuzco their convent was built in the neighborhood of the Temple of the Sun, and not inside the enclosure of the temple itself, as those who have written on the subject have erroneously asserted. An essential consideration in the choice of the women—a choice based on beauty and lineage—was that they should be virgins; they were therefore designated before they had attained to their eighth birthday.

Since, too, they were considered to be the wives of the Sun, they had all to be of royal blood, free of all taint. There were usually about fifteen hundred of them, although no limit was set to their number.

Those who had reached maturity assumed the title of *mamacunas,* or matrons, and fulfilled the duties of abbesses, either teaching the younger virgins the rules of the divine order, or else undertaking certain manual labors such as spinning, weaving, and sewing. They also occupied many other posts, such as that of porter or bursar, and in general, watched over all the needs of the convent. The Temple of the Sun maintained them in a situation of abundance, which was as it should be, since they were the brides of the Sun.

They passed their entire lives in a confinement that was as strict as was their own celibacy, and indeed, there was no parlor or other place in their convent where they could have come in contact with anyone from the outside, either man or woman. The Inca himself did not dare to see them, although being their king, he had the right to do so. The Coya only—that is, the queen—together with her daughters, went occasionally to visit them, to report to the king on their general condition, and what, if anything, needed to be done for them.

When the Spaniards arrived, the Indians set fire to the entire city of Cuzco, with the exception of the king's mansion, the Temple of the Sun, and this convent for virgins, which explains why I was able to see it in my youth. A corridor just wide enough for two persons to stand side by side, separated this building in two parts, in its entire length. To the left and right of this corridor, following upon one another, were the lodgings of the women who were engaged to work at the convent. The virgins themselves, however, who were also the wives of the Sun, lived farther away, in the very end of the building, where no one was allowed to enter. The main door of the convent was opened only to the queen, or to new postulants, who would never in their lives cross its threshold again.

At the service entrance, which was located at the beginning of the corridor, twenty ordinary porters were stationed to receive and transport to the second door everything that came into the convent. They were forbidden to go beyond the second door, under penalty of death.

Five hundred young girls, also virgins, who had been chosen among the families that were Incas by privilege, were employed in the service of the nuns and to care for their house. Like the nuns themselves, they obeyed their own *mamacunas,* who were designated among the older members of their group. At the time of the redistribution that followed the fall of Cuzco, the Spaniards divided this convent into two parts. Pedro del Barco—of whom we shall speak again later—received the front or servants' quarters, and the other part was given to the scholar de la Gama, then later, to Diego Ortiz de Guzman, a gentleman from Seville. I knew them both, and Diego de Guzman was still living when I left Peru.

The principal occupation of the wives of the Sun was spinning, weaving, and sewing the garments of the king and queen, as also those that were offered up to the Sun during sacrificial rites.

The king wore a tress called *llautu* wrapped four or five

times about his head, and a scarlet bandeau that stretched from one temple to the other. In addition to this sort of crown, his costume was composed of a shirt, called an *uncu,* which came down to his knees, and a square-cut mantle or cape, called *yacolla.* The nuns also made the little purse called *chuspa,* which was for his personal use, and which he wore slung from his left shoulder to his right side, to keep his coca leaves in. The use of coca was nothing like so widespread then as it is today, but was the exclusive privilege of the king who, occasionally, offered a few leaves, as a mark of favor, to this or that prince or curaca in his immediate circle.

The virgins also wove the red and yellow bandeaux worn on the right temples by princes of the royal line.

The Inca king received all these works made by the recluse brides of the Sun as sacred objects, which he surrounded with the greatest veneration, and he could give them to no one who was not of royal birth.

The recluse virgins also made the special bread, called *sancu,* that was sacrificed during the two principal Sun festivals, that of *Raïmi* and that of *Citua;* as well as the beverage designated by the name of *asa* that was drunk by the Inca and his relatives on the occasion of these ceremonies. All the table service in their convent, as well as that in the Temple of the Sun, was either of gold or silver. They also had the privileges of a garden of precious metals, similar to that of the temple; for, being the wives of the Sun, it was required that they be given the same treatment, in every particular.

A special law provided for sanctions to be taken should one of the nuns fail to keep her vow of chastity: she was to be buried alive and her accomplice hanged; he, his wife, his children, his servants and all his close relations; and, in order that the punishment should be complete, his cattle were also to be put to death, his fields destroyed, his house razed to the ground, and the entire place was to be strewn with stones, so that nothing could grow there again.

Such was the law, but I do not believe that the occasion ever arose to enforce it, for the Indians had deep respect for their duty, particularly for those duties that touched upon religious beliefs.

In each one of the principal provinces there was a convent similar to the one in Cuzco. The inmates of these convents were chosen not only among the families of royal blood, but also among those we call bastard, that is to say, those that are cross-bred with foreign blood, or even with that of women of the people, provided they were sufficiently beautiful. These virgins were destined, not for the Sun however, but for the king, whose concubines, as it were, they became.

The organization of their convents was based on that of the Cuzco convent. They also spun and wove for the Inca, and he distributed what they made among the lords, the captains and all those whom he wished to favor or reward.

When the Inca desired to possess one or the other of these women, he had her summoned and she was brought to wherever he happened to be. Their transgressions were punished quite as severely as those of the virgins of the Sun but we may infer that there was no more occasion to enforce the law with them than with the others, thanks to the deep respect in which the subjects of the Empire held their duties.

Those who had once had relations with the king could not go back into the convent. They were brought to the royal palace, where they served as attendants or as ladies-in-waiting to the queen, until the day when they were sent back home to their own provinces, richly endowed with land and other benefits. There they ended their days in the esteem and veneration of their neighbors, for it was a great honor for them all that a woman from their country should have been singled out by the king and have become his bride. Those who had never had relations with the Inca remained in the convent until an advanced age, then returned to their own country, unless they preferred to remain cloistered until they died.

When a king had just died, these virgins were given the title of *mamacuna,* and were regarded as the mothers of his successor. Each convent had a governor who had to belong to the Inca class, and who was surrounded by a majordomo and numerous other assistants. The tableware in all these convents was also of gold and silver. In fact, it might be stated that all the precious metal that was dug in the imperial mines served no other purpose than that of decorating the temples, convents, and royal palaces;

for the princes and owners of vassals used none of it in their houses, since the only things in gold or silver they could acquire were a few cups to drink from, which the Inca granted them according to a scale of numbers and forms that was reckoned by the importance of the privileges they enjoyed. Some was used too on the clothing and ornaments required for the celebration of the principal festivals.

Certain writers have stated that the Inca offered dedicated virgins to his captains; but they could not have understood their informers correctly. For these virgins, having been considered once and for all as brides of the Inca, could not become again like other women. Otherwise people could have said: "That woman you see there was the Inca's bride," and that would have been to profane what was most sacred in Peru. The Indians paid the same scrupulous attention to all that, because the Incas, as I have already explained, were considered not only as kings, but as gods.[2]

It is nevertheless true that the Inca did confer gifts of women, with his own hand, upon his captains, or any others who had rendered him distinguished service, but in these cases the women were either the daughters of other captains or of curacas.

In exceptional circumstances, he also occasionally gave illegitimate daughters of his own blood to certain eminent vassals and lords of important provinces, this being a means by which he could be even more assured of the loyalty of these princes. The fact that these bastard women, who were of mixed blood, had, as it were, fallen from the divine estate which was that of the king and his family, authorized this custom, without in any way weakening the unalterable principle that separates the family of the Sun from those of other men, in the same way that what is sacred must be kept separate from what is profane.

Other women of royal blood lived in the palace, and observed the vow of perpetual celibacy, without, however, adding to it that of confinement. Occasionally, they would go to visit close female relatives, if the latter were ill or with child, or if someone entered orders, or there was a name to be chosen for a first-born child.

They were called *occlos,* and were treated with the greatest consideration. Nor was their chastity feigned. On the contrary, it was very real, and they would have risked death if they had broken their vows. I knew one of these women in my youth; she was quite old, and came to see my mother from time to time; I believe that she was her great-aunt. She was always given the place of honor, and I remember quite well the respect my mother showed her.

Widows, too, lived perfectly virtuous lives. They refrained from going out and saw no one during the entire first year of their mourning. They also rarely remarried, and then only if their first marriage had been childless. Indeed, their virtue was so generally acknowledged that their land was the first to be ploughed, before that of the curacas, and even before that of the Inca; nor was this their only privilege.

These, then, are the most important things I have to tell as regards virgins, virtuous women, and widows.

Every year, or every two years, the Inca gathered together in Cuzco all the young people of his line, both girls and boys, who were at an age to be married. The girls had to be between eighteen and twenty years old, and the boys had to have celebrated their twenty-fourth birthdays. They were forbidden to marry at an earlier age.

The Inca took his place among them, then, having looked attentively at them, he joined them together, two by two, and returned them like this to their parents who led them to the house of the young man's father, where the marriage was celebrated a few days later. The women chosen in this way were the legitimate wives referred to in their language as the *wife received from the hand of the king.* The Inca's ministers joined in the same fashion all the other young people of Cuzco, with respect for the division of the two basic parts of the city, Upper Cuzco and Lower Cuzco, which we described, with their particular features, at the beginning of this book.

The houses of the newly married couples of royal blood were constructed by the men of such and such a province, according to the distribution of the various imperial tasks, which was exact in the least important details. The parents of one or the other of the young people agreed to furnish the house according to their taste, in furniture and household utensils, and there were no other ceremonies or sacrificial rites. Spanish authors have frequently gone astray on this point, having identified the local customs of such and such a nation in the Empire with what was specifically Inca in nature.

The governors married the young people of their provinces with the assent and actual presence of their curacas, and it was the curaca's duty to consecrate these unions, in order that the natural rights of each nation should be respected, as the Incas always wanted them to be. The governor, in other words, as the representative of the king, only recorded marriages that had been freely decided upon by the curacas, without interfering with their choice.

With regard to the young married couples among the common people, it was the duty of their village councilors to procure a roof for them, while their parents were responsible for their furniture and other household goods. Young people from different provinces, or even from different villages, were never joined together, it being essential that both nations and lineages, even the humblest, should remain free from all taint, as was the case among the tribes of Israel. In the same way, families were not allowed to move from one province to another, or even from one village to another, or from one neighborhood to another, to avoid making changes in the order of the decuries.[3]

The law ordaining that the Inca king should marry his eldest sister, born in wedlock, was always respected, and the first-born of this union had the right of succession to his father, on the latter's death. The origin of this law came from the Sun, of which they said that the Moon was both its sister and its bride, and from the first Inca who, according to tradition, was the brother of his bride Mama Occlo. If they had no legitimate sister, they married their nearest female relative, either cousin, niece or aunt, and if they had no male heir, she could succeed the king, as is the case in Spain.

If the crown prince had no male heir by his first sister, he married the second, then the third, until he obtained one. Thus the blood of the Sun was not mixed with human blood, which was the blood of all the rest of mankind, but not of the Incas.

They said, too, in order to explain this custom, that if the queen were not of divine blood, there would be no reason to adore and revere her more than any other woman as gifted or more gifted than she.

In addition to his legitimate wife, the king had many concubines, some of whom were outsiders, and the rest related up to the fourth degree. The children of the latter were considered to be legitimate, since they were of pure blood. The others, however, were considered to be bastards, and although, as sons of the king, they were respected, they were neither flattered nor adored as the former were. Thus the king had three sorts of sons: those by his wife, who had legitimate rights of succession to the Empire; those by female relatives, who were legitimate as regarded their blood; and the bastards, who were the sons of outsiders.

The oldest legitimate son of royal blood could inherit the kingdom, in case the queen did not leave a son, but under no circumstances could a bastard son pretend to the throne. If there was not a single legitimate son, the crown devolved upon the nearest male relative of the same blood. This is why the bastard Atahualpa did away with all the Incas of royal blood, for fear that they would take the throne he had usurped. This law of succession was strictly observed by the twelve Incas who reigned until the arrival of the Spaniards.

Among the curacas, who were the leaders of nations that had become vassals, the laws of succession varied from one state to the other. In certain provinces, the right to the title passed to the eldest son, whereas in others, it went to his most preferred subject, which meant succession by election rather than by inheritance. This was a good law because it made it impossible for a tyrant to take the place of a virtuous man.

In other provinces, the office passed to all the sons, in the order of seniority: that is to say, that at the death of the father, his eldest son succeeded him, then the second, then the third, and so forth . . . then, when all the brothers had died, the inheritance passed to the sons of the first, then to the second, and so on. A Spanish historian, having heard a description of this custom, attributed it erroneously to the Incas, saying that the king's brothers and sons succeeded him, which is not true, as we have just seen.

These three modes of succession which were met with in the different regions of Peru, were part of the traditions peculiar to each one, prior to their attachment to the Empire. The Incas being desirous of maintaining everything that constituted the originality of their numerous peoples, had taken pains not to interfere with these traditions, in the same way that they had never dispossessed any leader of a newly conquered nation or province.

The crown prince was weaned only at the end of his second year. This was the occasion of a great feast, at which all the king's relatives assembled together at court. The child's hair was then cut for the first time, and a name was chosen for him.[4] One of the relatives, who had been designated as godfather, was the first to use the scissors—or rather, the knife, since the Indians, in their ignorance of scissors, used knives made of silex. Then each member of the family cut a lock of the child's hair, taking turns, according to his age or rank. They then announced the prince's name, and all the guests gave him presents, such as clothes, cattle, arms, or gold or silver vases.

In celebration of this event, they drank and sang for days, and the same ceremony took place in honor of the weaning of all the royal princes. However, the godfather of the first-born, who was heir to the Empire, was always the high priest of Cuzco, whereas any blood Inca could be godfather to the other children. All the curacas of the kingdom came to Cuzco especially to attend the crown prince's tonsure, and then the feast could last as long as twenty days, or more.

The same custom was observed throughout the Empire, in all strata of society, so true it is that we all want to do what is done at the top.

Children were brought up very severely, not only among the Incas, but among simple people as well. From birth, they were washed in cold water every morning, then wrapped in swaddling covers. However, really tender, attentive mothers took the water in their mouths before washing their babies. This custom of a cold dip was said to strengthen the child's legs and arms and give him greater resistance to the severe mountain climate. His arms were kept tightly bound until the age of four months. Indeed, during the entire first cycle, he remained attached night and day to a netting that was as hard as wood, and which was stretched across a chest with only three legs, to make it rock like a cradle.[5]

In order to nurse her child, the mother leaned down to him, without ever untying him or taking him up in her arms. He was fed the breast three times a day, morning, noon, and night, and never at other hours, even if he cried and called his mother. The women always nursed their own children, no matter what their rank; they abstained from all relations with their husbands as long as they were nursing, and until the child was weaned, it received no other food than its mother's milk. When the time came to take the child out of its cradle, in order not to have to take it into their arms, the mothers put it in a hole, dug in the ground, which was as deep as the child's chest.

When he reached the age where he could walk on his hands and feet, he nursed kneeling, and walked around his mother to change breasts, without her giving him any help whatsoever. At the birth of the baby, the mothers took less care of themselves than they did of their children: after having given birth, either in their homes, or beside a river, and having washed the newborn baby, they washed themselves and went back to work as though nothing had happened. There were no midwives, properly speaking, and those women who served in this function were more like witches than anything else.

This was the common custom among all the Indians in Peru, whether rich or poor, nobles or commoners.

Married women were generally dedicated to the care of their homes; they knew how to spin and weave wool or cotton, according to whether they lived in cold or hot regions. They did little sewing however, for there was hardly any needed, Indian garments, both masculine and feminine, being generally woven in one piece in the proper length and width.

There were neither shoemakers, nor cobblers, nor men's tailors in Peru. And, indeed, how many things that seem so necessary to us they did without, not knowing that they even existed! Although the care of clothing was incumbent upon women, that of shoes was left to the men. I have already spoken of the fact that, in order to be dubbed knights, the nobles had to know how to make their own sandals; to which I shall add that the princes and even the king, although they had servants specialized in these matters, did not disdain, on occasion, to make a pair of sandals, or any other object, with their own hands.

All the men and all the women worked together in the fields. In a few distant provinces that were not as submissive as others to all the details of the Inca laws, the women worked in the fields while the men stayed at home to do the spinning and weaving. But that sort of thing was both barbarous and unusual, so that we can pass it over. Everywhere else, in fact, the women were so accustomed to spinning that they brought their spindles out into the streets or on the highroads when they were on their way to see a friend, and they kept on working after they reached her house, while they were chatting together.[6] This was true of the women of the people; as for the pallas, although they did not actually spin on the street, it was nevertheless their custom to have themselves accompanied by a slave who kept at their work, which they themselves took up again once they were settled with their friends. Their spindles were made of cane and had a spring balance, but the point was not hollowed out. To spin, they pulled out a strand of wool or cotton that was as long as possible, and they adjusted it to the spindle with the first two fingers of the left hand. Meanwhile they held the distaff, which was about a foot long, with the other fingers of the same hand, and then let go of the spindle in order to twist the thread and roll it around.

The women who went to visit the pallas did not take their handwork with them. However, once they had exchanged greetings, they asked if there was nothing for them to do, thus making it understood that they did not pay them visits as one does to an equal, but that they had come to serve, as is meet on the part of an inferior to a superior. The palla, to honor her visitor and show her that she did not identify her with her servants, would then give her something that had been started by her own hands, or by those of one of her daughters, and it was the greatest favor she could have granted.

Spanish women in Peru imitated this wise custom of visiting one another frequently, without forgetting to bring some handwork, until Don Francisco Hernandez Giron's tyranny put an end to this tradition, just as, with his government, it put an end to all honesty and virtue. I have forgotten to say how the simple people repaired their clothes, and I must make amends for this negligence. To tell the truth, they did not repair them, in the sense that we understand this word, but darned the snags by re-weaving the torn stuff, thread by thread, with a thorn which they used instead of a needle. I should specify, too, that the Indians did their cooking on earthenware stoves, which they lighted through a lateral opening, and the top part of which was pierced with circular holes, over which they set their pots. They were very careful about fires, and economical in their use of wood, so that the waste of wood by the Spaniards never ceased to shock and surprise them.

I have yet to speak of the prostitutes, whose activities were authorized by the Incas in order to avoid worse catastrophes. They lived in the country in wretched thatched huts, each one separately, and they were forbidden to enter the towns and villages in order that no virtuous women should ever encounter them. They were called *pampairuna,* a word containing both the place and the occupation, since *pampa* means any level place or country, and *runa* means people.

The men treated these women with great contempt, and the women never spoke to them, under penalty of having their hair shorn in public, or of being repudiated by their husbands and treated like the others. The latter were never designated by their own names, but always by the common name of *pampairuna.*

Three years after he had started to wear the scarlet bandeau, which was the badge of royalty, Inca Roca assembled an army of twenty thousand men, in order to extend his conquests north of Cuzco, through the Chinchasuyu district.

After crossing the Apurimac river over a new bridge built for the occasion, the Inca reached the Amansay valley, from where he turned right, in the direction of the grand cordillera, or Sierra Nevada. As he advanced, he subjugated the occasional villages he encountered on the

Tacmara, Quiniualla, Cochacassa and Curampa territories. He finally arrived in the province of Antahuailla, the inhabitants of which were wealthy and very bellicose. These people were called Chancas and they claimed to be descended from a lion, which at that time, they adored as their god. On the occasion of their principal festival, twelve of them dressed themselves in lion skins, like Hercules. I remember seeing them in this getup during the feasts of the Holy Sacrament in Cuzco.

Various nations are grouped together under this name of Chanca, among them the Hancohuallus, the Utunsullas, the Uramarcas, the Uillcas, and others still. They claimed all sorts of imaginary ancestors, such as a spring, a lake, or a very high mountain pass, and each one offered up sacrifices to its so-called father. In reality, the ancestors of these peoples had come from a great distance and had conquered vast stretches of land, principally from the Quechuas, whom they drove back to the far end of their provinces, after having subdued and tyrannized them. Today the Chancas still pride themselves on these exploits and on their ancestors, in whom they glory.[7] The King Inca Roca was entirely familiar with their history when he arrived in their country and sent his messengers to them. They met together to decide on their reply, and it turned out that they were very divided in their opinions. Some advocated surrender, and others—the so-called Sons of the Lion—were of the opinion that the armies should have the last word as to which was the stronger, the Lion or the Sun.

Several days passed without their being able to reach an agreement. The Inca Roca, who was informed of this situation by his spies, decided to wait no longer, but to charge against them, in order to frighten the more valorous among them and strengthen the hand of those who wanted to surrender without fighting. At the same time that he gave orders to his camp commanders to immediately get under way, he sent more messengers to the Chancas, informing them that he was about to arrive, and that he demanded immediate surrender from them, as soon as they should have received his message, otherwise they had only to prepare their throats for the knife, since he would not leave a single person alive, should they persist in their impertinent attitude.

In the face of such language, the Chancas resigned themselves to accepting the Inca's yoke, not out of love for his laws, but much more out of fear of his strength, as also of the vengeance of the Quechuas, many of whom were serving in the imperial army. But although they seemed to abandon their arrogance, it was replaced by a stubborn resentment that they were not soon to forget, as we shall see later.

The Inca left certain of his ministers with them and continued his advance toward the province of Uramarca, which was also peopled by Chanca Indians. After brief resistance, this province surrendered, despite the fact that its inhabitants were numerous, cruel, and very accustomed to war. Indeed, if the Inca Roca had not disposed of an advantage in numbers, these conquests would not have been made without violent combat, for these opponents were of a very different stature from those he had encountered in the Cuntisuyu and Collasuyu districts. Still facing the same odds, he nevertheless conquered, as well, the provinces of Hancohuallu and Uillca (which the Spaniards call Vilca), which were also peopled by warlike, tyrannical, ambitious Chancas, all of whom surrendered with the same deep-rooted resentment. In these two provinces, they were accustomed to sacrifice children during their festivals. When the Inca heard this, he let it be known that if a single child were killed from then on, he would have them all slaughtered and send other peoples to inhabit their lands.

From Uillca he turned westward and arrived in one of the two very large provinces that are called by the common name of Sulla; that is to say, in Utum-Sulla. There were more than forty thousand persons of various nationalities in this province, and the Inca took a long time to subjugate them without using force. It has even been said that it took him three years to break down their resistance. After these victories he returned to Cuzco. It should be noted that only thirty-two years ago several silver and mercury mines were discovered in the two provinces of Sulla.

Several years after these events, the King Inca Roca decided to send his son, the Crown Prince Yahuar Huacac to conquer certain Antisuyu territory, east of Cuzco. The Empire frontiers had not advanced in this district since the death of the first Inca, Manco Capac, and they were quite near the city.

Before going any further, I should like to explain this name, Yahuar Huacac, which had been given the prince because, people said, he had wept tears of blood at the age of three or four. He may perhaps have had a disease that made his eyelids bleed, or he may even have been born with a few drops of his mother's blood in his eyes, because there were others who said that this event had taken place when he was born. Be that as it may, his name comes from that, and it means, not "tears of blood," as certain historians have asserted, but "he who weeps blood," which the Indians, superstitious as they have always been, interpreted as an evil omen that meant that the reign of this king would be marked by some catastrophe, caused by his father the Sun's anger, as they said.

This story of an omen makes me think of another superstition of the Indians regarding their eyes. They considered, for instance, that palpitation of the upper lid of the left eye was a good omen, and that of the same lid of the right eye as even more auspicious; whereas, on the contrary, palpitation of the lower lids was maleficent, that of the right eye meaning tears and sorrow, and that of the left eye worse still. Indeed they believed this so firmly, that if one of their lower lids began to twitch, they began immediately to weep and moan, as though they had been really overwhelmed by great misfortune; and in order not to die of an ailment they had not yet seen, they resorted to a remedy that was as ridiculous as the ailment itself: they took a piece of straw and having moistened it with their saliva, applied it to the baleful lid, saying that, in this way, the tears could flow no longer and the evil fate would be averted. I can assure my readers that I have not invented this and that what I have just told, I have often witnessed.

And so the King Inca Roca, having decided to send his son campaigning, levied fifteen thousand fighting men and three camp commanders. The prince had no difficulty in crossing the frontier, which was set at the Paucartampu river, and he entered the region of Challpampa, where the rather sparse number of inhabitants surrendered without resistance. He pushed on to Pillcupata, where he settled the populations of four villages, who had been uprooted elsewhere. From Pillcupata he went to Huaisca and to Tunu, where the Incas had laid out their first coca plantations. The government of Huaisca was later entrusted to my father, Garcilaso de la Vega, and he, in turn, donated it to me for all my life, but I lost the benefit of this gift when I left Peru.

The Antis [8] adored tigers and certain large snakes called *amarus;* the latter being bigger than a man's thigh, twenty-five to thirty feet long, but harmless, in spite of their monstrous size. According to the Antis, these snakes were once very ferocious, and the reason they have become gentle and somewhat stupid today is that a magician cast a spell [9] over them. The Antis also worshiped a plant called *cuca* or, as the Spaniards say, *coca.* On this expedition Prince Yahuar Huacac won thirty leagues of new, very sparsely populated land. He advanced no farther into this mountainous region, which is marshy and unhealthy, and which forms the border of the Anti province, properly speaking, in the Antisuyu district.

The prince then returned to Cuzco, and the king, his father, decided to undertake no more conquests for the moment. At that time the Empire extended more than one hundred leagues from west to east on the latitude of Cuzco, and from north to south, two hundred. Throughout all this vast area, there were royal palaces, gardens, baths, houses of recreation for the Inca, and, all along the royal roads, warehouses in which were kept reserves of weapons, equipment, and all sorts of provisions for the royal armies.

After several years of peace, the king decided to finish subjugating the Charcas in the Collasuyu district, a task that had been begun by his father the Inca Capac Yupanqui. For this expedition, which promised to be an important one, he raised an army of thirty thousand men: never before had an Inca king assembled so many troops. He chose six camp commanders, and, after having handed over the government of the kingdom to his son, Prince Yahuar Huacac, who was assisted by four Inca counselors, he got under way.

The first non-subject provinces that he encountered were those of Chuncuri, Pucuna, and Muyumuyu. Their chiefs, who were young and bellicose, gave the royal envoys a cold welcome, and decided to fight to the death, rather than renounce their customs and traditions, and surrender to those of a foreigner.

But the old people of these provinces, realizing all the benefits their neighbors had derived from their surrender to the Inca, the fairness of the laws he gave his vassals, and the considerable strength of his army, thought it best not to resist him, and succeeded in convincing the younger generation to this effect. They therefore went all together to present themselves to the Inca. The old people made him gifts of the fruits of their estates, to show him that thenceforth they were his own; while the younger men came with their arms and asked to serve in the imperial army as faithful vassals, ready to devote all their strength to its future conquests.

The Inca welcomed them with great good nature. To the old people he distributed garments from his personal wardrobe, and he chose five hundred warriors among the young men, taking care to have them draw lots, in order that there should be no jealousy among them. Thus all of them, both young and old, were satisfied, and they acclaimed the king unanimously.

The army continued its march toward the provinces of Misqui, Sacaca, Machaca, Caracara, and all those that extended as far as Chuquisaca, which, today, is called the "silver city." Here one finds different tongues and nations, all of which stem from the Charcas. They surrendered, as the first had done, with no exceptions, and thus the empire was increased without striking a blow by more than fifty square leagues. This campaign was to be King Inca Roca's last and, once back in his capital, he spent the rest of his days there, devoting himself to the good of his subjects, as his predecessors had done. He founded schools in which the amautas taught their various sciences, promulgated new laws, and was universally mourned when he died. After his death he was embalmed, according to tradition. He left as his heir Yahuar Huacac, son of his sister-bride Mama Micay. The number of his other children, both legitimate and illegitimate, was very great.

Father Blas Valera, who is so versed in everything concerning the Incas, says that the prince reigned fifty years, and that he was responsible for numerous reforms and codifications of Inca customs. Their principal characteristics were the following:

The study of science was the exclusive right of the sons

of noblemen, and the children of the common people had to be content with learning the same trade as their father. Robbery, adultery, homicide, and willful arson were punishable with death by hanging. Male children were bound to work for their fathers until they were twenty-five years old, after which they entered the service of the state.

Again, according to Father Blas Valera, Inca Roca was the first Peruvian king to open state schools in the city of Cuzco, for the education of young nobles. The subjects taught them by the amautas included the rites, precepts, and ceremonies of their false religion, the foundations of their laws, their numbers and the art of equitably interpreting them, the military arts and those of government, how to keep account of the years and of history by means of quipus, oratory, child education, the precepts of domestic life, poetry, music, philosophy, and astronomy.

Father Blas Valera said too that this king, contemplating the grandeur and beauty of the sky, had many times exclaimed that Pachacamac—that is to say, God—must needs be a great and powerful lord, to possess a dwelling place of such splendor.[10] "If I had to worship someone here below," he would add, "I should most assuredly choose the wise, discreet man who causes all the good things of this earth to fructify. But he who is born and grows only to die; who yesterday had a beginning and tomorrow will have an end; who can neither free himself from death nor recover the life of which death has robbed him; such a being could never be adored." [11]

The Inca Yahuar Huacac, having donned the scarlet bandeau, applied himself with justice, devotion, and mildness to governing the Empire. The fatal sign attached to his name made him refrain from undertaking any new conquests, out of fear that the divine punishment with which he believed he was threatened might be hastened. Thus, nine or ten years passed without his leaving Cuzco, except to visit his vassals, throughout the Empire, which he did two or three times. He was torn, nevertheless, between the wrath of God and the judgment of his fellow man, with the result that, not wishing to appear either cowardly and pusillanimous in the eyes of his contemporaries, or unworthy of the tradition of conquest that was the pride of his line, he finally decided to organize a campaign, without, however, taking the risk of leading it himself. He then assembled twenty thousand men, naming as their leader his brother the Inca Maïta who, thenceforth, was never called otherwise than Apumaïta, which means "Commander-general Maïta."

The army descended the mountains to the southwest of Cuzco and subjugated with no difficulty the entire coast from Arequipa to Tacama, which is where Peru ends today. This region is so long and narrow, and so sparsely populated that it took Apumaïta longer to traverse it than to conquer it.

However, this first success decided the king to take personal command of important campaigns in the rich provinces of Caranca, Ullaca, Llipi, Chicha, and Ampara, all of which are in the Collasuyu district.

While he was away on these conquests, the Inca, who was still torn between the fear of his fate and the hope of having averted it, was preoccupied by matters concerning his own household, his eldest son, the heir to the kingdom, having caused him great sorrow and anguish, by his naturally violent disposition. Already, as a child, the boy had mistreated his playmates and, in all his actions, given proof of an obdurate, cruel nature. The Inca had tried every means to bring him to adopt the habits of gentleness, kindness, and mildness that were the rule in the royal family, but nothing, neither punishment, nor persuasion, nor example, seemed to succeed in breaking down the resistance of this savage heart, for which all remedies were transformed into poisons.

The prince was nineteen years old and his grievous tendencies were becoming worse every day. Yahuar Huacac decided to punish him severely. He gave orders that he was to be banished from the palace and the court, and taken to a spot more than a league outside the imperial city, in the extensive, rich fields of Chita, where large herds dedicated to the Sun were grazing. There, among the shepherds, and himself a shepherd, the young prince would perhaps learn to correct his bad tendencies; otherwise, he would be definitely cast out, repudiated, and disinherited.

The prince lived there for three years in silence and oblivion, where we shall leave him, until such time as he himself returns and forces us to tell about his exploits, if we are capable of doing so.

This very grave decision, and the perspective of the even more unheard-of decision that he might have to resign himself to making, should the young prince not mend his ways, discouraged the Inca from undertaking any further conquests or voyages which, by leading him too far from his exiled son, would make it impossible for him to watch over him as constantly and as diligently as such an exceptional case required.

In consequence, Yahuar Huacac remained in Cuzco, but he was so anxious and stricken by the persistence of his evil fate that he could find no respite from it. Three years passed, during which the only event of any importance was the dispatch of a mission of inspection, composed of four Incas, to all parts of the kingdom. This tour had just ended when, one day, shortly after noon, the exiled prince suddenly appeared, alone and unescorted, at the palace gate, in the garb of a man who had fallen into complete disrepute. He asked to see his father immediately, saying that he brought him certain tidings. The Inca sent back harsh word to the effect that he should return immediately to the place of residence assigned to him, if he wanted to avoid capital punishment for his disobedience. But the prince insisted, saying that he had not come to avoid compliance wih the king's orders, but in obedience to the orders of another, as great and powerful an Inca as his father himself was.

At last, he insisted so much that Yahuar Huacac decided to grant him audience, in order to learn what extraordinary news lay beneath these words, and to punish him as he deserved. When he had been brought into the presence of the king, the prince made the following declaration:

"Know you, oh my only lord, that today at noon, as I lay stretched out under one of the rocks in Chita, a man with a strange face—I am unable to say whether he was asleep or awake—appeared before me. His beard was as long as the palm of my hand,[12] and he wore a loose garment that came down to the ground. Beside him was an unfamiliar animal which he held by a leash attached about the animal's neck. 'My nephew,' he said to me, 'I am a son of the Sun, and a brother of the Inca Manco Capac and of the Coya Mama Occlo Huaco, who were the founders of your line; I am therefore a brother to all of you and also to your father; my name is Viracocha Inca; the Sun, our father, has sent me to tell you, so that you might repeat it to the Inca, that the greater part of the provinces of Chinchasuyu, which are now subject to the Empire, as well as those that are not yet imperial subjects, are in rebellion; that a large number of people have joined with them; and that they are raising a powerful army to come and depose the king from his throne and destroy our imperial capital of Cuzco. Go, therefore, to see my brother, the Inca, repeat to him what I have just said, and tell him to be on his guard, and to make ready to answer these rebels as they deserve. As for yourself, I want you to know that, whatever adversity may befall you, I shall always be beside you, ready to help you as one of my own flesh and blood; that you must never yield to fear, but seek to do great deeds, worthy of the majesty of your blood and the grandeur of your Empire; for I shall protect you always, and, in all circumstances, I shall seek the help that you will need.' Having spoken these words," concluded the prince, "the Inca Viracocha disappeared, and I did not see him again. I then set out to report to you what he had ordered me to tell you." [13]

The Inca Yahuar Huacac was so angry that he did not want to believe his son; he called him mad and pretentious, and said that he was trying to pass off for revelations what in reality were merely the extravagances of his imagination; he should return to Chita immediately and not leave there again if he did not want to feel the fire of his wrath upon him. And the prince went back to his herds, more discredited than ever, in the eyes of his father. But the highest lords of the court, the uncles and brothers of the king, who had been present at the discussion, took the matter very differently.

"If the Inca Viracocha is your brother and a son of the Sun," they said to the king, "you have no right to ignore his message; and it would be a sacrilege to imagine that the prince, who is of our blood, would invent such a story or dare to tell it to you, who are his king and his father! What we should do is to examine his words one by one, make sacrifices to the Sun, and consult the oracles, so as not to risk being taken unawares by so serious a hazard. To comport oneself otherwise would be an insult to the majesty of the Sun, and only increase still more the state of error in which we are perhaps already."

But the Inca felt such hatred for his son that he was deaf to all pleas.

"He is a madman," was his reply, "and we have not to listen to him. He invented this nonsense to try to impress us, and to regain my favor. He only deserves to be definitely disinherited, as I shall do as soon as possible; and I shall name in his place one of his brothers who has more right than he to the name of son of the Sun, of which his madness and cruelty have made him unworthy. And I command you," he said in conclusion, "to forget all he told us, or else I shall have his head cut off immediately for having disobeyed me by coming to court without my having summoned him."

The Incas grew silent, but their hearts were filled with fear and dark forebodings, so great was their faith in dreams, and particularly in the dreams of the king and his family.

Three months after Prince Viracocha's dream (for that is how it was referred to thenceforth) the news, still uncertain, of an uprising in the Chinchasuyu provinces reached the capital. According to this rumor, which was passed about by word of mouth, the insurgents were assembled in the province of Antahuailla, just forty leagues north of Cuzco. Although there was in this news a strange echo of what his son had predicted—or perhaps because of this fact—the king refused to heed these rumors. A few days later, they became more precise, and it was whispered that the enemy had blocked the roads in order that nothing should be known of their uprising until they had reached the gates of Cuzco. It soon became evident, however, that this uprising was only too real, and that there were numerous nations participating in it, among them the Chancas, the Uramarcas, the Uillcas, the Utunsullas, the Hancohuallus, and others. It was said that, in all these provinces, the Inca's governors and ministers had been exterminated, and that an army of forty thousand men was marching on the capital.

These were the nations that we saw surrender to the Inca Roca more from fear than from love, and as we said before, their rancor and hatred toward the Inca were still smoldering in them. In short, their surrender had been nothing but the mask behind which they awaited an opportunity to avenge themselves. Despite all the efforts of the King Yahuar Huacac, Prince Viracocha's dream had gone beyond the palace gates and had been repeated even in the provinces. Knowing, too, what a real distaste this king had for all the ordeals of war, on account of the evil fate attached to his name, these unregenerate peoples had seized the right moment to act against him. Their army was very powerful; it was made up, in reality, of more than thirty thousand men, and they marched against Cuzco, under the leadership of three great curacas one of whom, aged twenty-six, was called Hancohuallu, the second, Tumay Huaraca, and the third, Astu Huaraca; the two latter were brothers, and relatives of the first who, because of his great valor, had been named commander-general of the insurgents. [14]

Perceiving his blindness too late, the Inca Yahuar Huacac remained confused. The enemy was too close for him to have the time to raise an army, and he did not even possess a fortress within which to entrench himself, while waiting for help. He therefore decided to abandon the capital and seek refuge in the province of Collasuyu, where the loyalty of the people constituted an assurance that at least he would not lose his life, even though he should lose everything else.

Thus the imperial city, deprived of its leader, fell into a state of affliction and distress. People had but one idea, which was to flee.

The news of these unhappy events reached the ears of Viracocha Inca, who was deeply upset by his father's conduct. He immediately gathered together the handful of men about him and dispatched messengers to all the Indians able to bear arms, to arm themselves as best they could and hasten to join the king. He himself set out for Collasuyu by a roundabout way, in order to elude the enemy, and advanced so rapidly that he caught up with the royal escorts in the Muina pass, before they had had time to emerge from it.

The prince, who was covered with sweat and dust, holding aloft a lance he had picked up on the road, suddenly appeared before his father, and in a tone of sadness and gravity, spoke to him as follows:

"Inca, how is it possible that the news, true or false, of an uprising on the part of a handful of men, could suffice to make you abandon your palace and the court, and turn your back to the enemy, before you had even seen him? How could you have abandoned the temple of our father the Sun, and allowed barbarians to defile its sacred soil with their sandals and set up human sacrifice again as well as all the other abominable practices that were combated by your ancestors? What will become of the virgins dedicated to the Sun whom you left defenseless and at the mercy of these barbarians? What will it gain us to have saved our own lives, in exchange for so many sacrilegious horrors? As for myself, I prefer to die rather than see Cuzco vanquished and all evidence of our past grandeur lost as a result of our present cowardice! Let all who will, follow me, and I shall lead them to an honorable end that, alone, can save us from disgrace."

Having spoken thus, in a tone filled with emotion and suffering, he started back to Cuzco, without even waiting to be given food and drink. All the Incas and their retinues, who numbered about four thousand persons, followed him, while the king remained behind with only the aged and infirm. Soon the prince encountered numerous groups of fugitives; but he firmly reminded them of their duty, and throughout the land, the news of his determination having spread by word of mouth, he rallied to him all those who were more tempted by a glorious death than by a life of misery.

He re-entered the city and gave orders that all its inhabitants should be immediately recruited and equipped, and sent to face the enemy. Then, taking the lead, he himself left without further ado.

As we shall see later, this was the end of Inca Yahuar Huacac's reign; and in order not to confuse the achievements of the father with those of the son, we shall return to questions of Empire government, in order to give variety to our tale and not weary the reader. Then, later, we shall come back to an account of the Inca Viracocha's exploits, which were great and memorable.

1. See following notes in which everything relating to this famous subject has been collected.

2. This, according to Rowe, is how the convents, described rather inaccurately by Garcilaso, were organized: "Every year a special official visited the villages of each province

and the girls of ten years of age were presented to him. He took away with him to the convent of the capital of the province those whom he thought the most beautiful and the most gifted. There, these girls, called *oklla-kona,* or the chosen girls, followed a four-year course during which they were taught spinning, weaving, cooking, the preparation of *chicha* and all other women's tasks. After this first course, they were divided into two groups: 1. Some were given to the nobles and the military leaders. 2. The others, known as *mamacunas,* entered the king's service as concubines, or in the service of the Sun. In the latter case, they had indeed to pronounce vows of chastity.

"At the time of the initial selection of ten-year-old girls, some were set aside to be offered as sacrifices at ceremonies of exceptional importance requiring human sacrifices." (Note 16, Book III)

3. Trial marriage. In connection with marriage customs, mention should be made of the tradition of trial marriage, or *tincunapuspata,* whereby an Indian could choose a girl freely and take her to live with him for a few months without committing himself in any way. During this trial period of conjugal life, each of the partners tried to convince the other of his or her domestic virtues, after which, if no understanding was reached, the girl returned home to her parents and no blame attached to her. Garcilaso refers to this custom when speaking, in another chapter, of corrupt tribes in which women were the more highly prized the more men they had known. But he adds that the Incas had suppressed this custom, which greatly shocked him as a good Christian. However, it was a deeply rooted custom among the inhabitants of the Sierra and is still practiced to this day, after four hundred years of Christianity. This is reported by d'Harcourt, from his personal observations, and by Arriaga and Villagomez, for the Inca period; by Valdizán and Maldonado, for the contemporary period.

4. This name, which was only a provisional one, was the "childhood name" and was replaced by a final adult name at the ceremony of initiation to puberty. (Book VI, and Note 32, Book VI)

5. Cobo explains that this cradle was surmounted by two flexible arches at the head and foot, so that a blanket could be placed over it and the child isolated. The women never took their children from this bed, to which they were permanently tied, in order to carry them on their backs. See drawings by Guaman Poma in the present work, "The Ages of Man" and "The Ages of Woman."

6. We have explained how "chosen girls" learned spinning and weaving from the age of ten in all the convents and educational establishments of the Empire. (Book IV and Note 2, Book IV)

7. The Chanca tribe. Here we come to one of the greatest

sources of Garcilaso's mistakes. In the reign of Inca Roca (early fourteenth century), the Incas possessed only a small stretch of territory adjacent to that of the much more powerful Quechua tribe, who occupied the province later called Chanca, with its capital Antahuailla. It was not until the reign of Viracocha Inca, the grandson of Inca Roca, that the Chanca tribe attacked the Quechuas, captured Antahuailla, and gave their name to the whole region. Garcilaso is thus anticipating history by two generations. It should be added that even after the wars between the Quechua and Chanca tribes, the Incas did not conquer the latter. They were not incorporated in the Empire until they had first attacked the Incas—this Garcilaso wrongly refers to as their "rebellion"—and were defeated. The great expansion of the Incas began then, after their two great rivals, the Quechua and Chanca tribes, had been weakened, leaving them free to assume the leadership of the mountain peoples. (Books IV, V, VI)

8. The Andeans, from Anti: Andes.

9. It seems strange that Garcilaso should speak of this *amaru,* which is none other than the python, the anaconda of Brazil, or the boa constrictor in the Andes. These snakes are known to prefer a hot climate. This is not so improbable when we remember that the author applies the name of *anti* not only to the crest of the cordillera but also to the whole hinterland, that is to say, the eastern slopes right down to the hot Amazon basin, as will be observed several times in the present work.

10. See Note 36, Book VI.

11. Father Blas Valera. Baudin's excellent bibliography gives the following information concerning Father Blas Valera, who is one of Garcilaso's main references:

"The manuscript of Father Blas Valera was lost during the siege of Cadiz by the English, in 1596. Father Maldonado de Saavedra, Professor of Theology at Cordoba, had given a few pages of it to Garcilaso. Blas Valera was a member of the Juli mission to the shores of Lake Titicaca. Part of his work was also used by Montesinos; he wrote between 1586 and 1591."

It should be added that Blas Valera was half-Inca, like Garcilaso. His father was the conquistador Luis de Valera and his mother was from the court of Atahualpa.

12. The Indians were almost beardless. See Garcilaso's reflections on this dream, Book V.

13. "Viracocha, the Creator, was the theoretical source of all power. But the Indians believed that he had delegated the administration of his creation to a multitude of supernatural beings, who were his assistants, and who had accordingly a more direct influence on human affairs. He lived in heaven and appeared to men in times of crisis. He was also a cul-

tural hero, since it was believed that after the creation he traveled on earth to teach men how to live and to perform miracles. His travels took him to Manta (Ecuador) from where he crossed the Pacific Ocean, walking on the water." (Rowe) To respect the phonetics of the Quechua language, which has neither b nor v, many modern authors write "Huiracocha" instead of Viracocha.

14. The Chanca rebellion. As has been explained above, the provinces which, in Garcilaso's day, were called Chanca, were formerly inhabited by the Quechua tribe. It was in the time of Viracocha Inca, and not of Yahuar Huacac, that the Chanca tribe attacked the Quechuas, allies of the Incas, and seized their capital Antahuailla. This spelled the downfall of the Quechuas who, until then, had been more powerful than the Incas. The Chancas crossed their provinces, eventually threatening Cuzco. Garcilaso wrongly calls this the Chanca "rebellion." In all the events he recounts, he anticipates by a generation. The prince we are to see rising to the defense of Cuzco is not Viracocha, son of Yahuar Huacac, but Yupanqui, son of Viracocha. (Rowe) See the end of this affair in Book V, and also Note 14, Book V. This king was not as passive as Garcilaso makes out (speaking of him as Yahuar Huacac): in the face of the Chanca menace and the collapse of the Quechuas, he straightway formed an alliance with the Anta tribe, by marrying the chief's daughter. This tribe occupied the plain and the large town bearing their name. (Rowe)

BOOK FIVE

Which treats of the life,
works, and conquests of
the Inca Viracocha,
eighth king of Peru.
With the laws and customs of
the Incas concerning land division
and their manner of tillage;
taxes, benefits, and statute labor;
rules and regulations
covering public
and private estates;
the Inca Viracocha's great victory,
and how he predicted
the coming of the Spaniards

When the Inca had conquered a new province he immediately sent engineers there, who were specialized in building canals for irrigation, in order to increase the corn acreage, which otherwise could not flourish in these torrid lands. In the same way, he irrigated the prairie lands, as may be seen today from the evidences of canals that still subsist all over Peru. On the mountain sides, on the peaks and on all rocky surfaces, they built terraces, sustained by stone walls, which they filled with light soil brought from elsewhere. These terraces grew wider from the top to the bottom of the slope, where they occasionally attained to as much as two hundred and forty acres in size. These were arduous undertakings, but they made it possible to give the maximum development to the tiniest plots of barren land. Indeed, it often happened that they would build canalizations fifteen to twenty leagues long, to irrigate only a few acres of land.[1]

Community records of landholdings were carefully kept up to date in all the provinces and villages, and arable land was divided into three parts: that belonging to the Sun, that of the Inca, and that of his vassals. This latter part was calculated to permit each village to provide for its own needs and, in case there was an increase in population, the Inca reduced the surface of his own holdings. Thus it may be said that he kept for himself only that part that, without him, would have remained uncultivated. The major part of the terrace crops belonged to the king and to the Sun, which was only normal, inasmuch as it was the Inca who had had the terraces built. Other cereals and vegetables were raised, such as potatoes, *oca,* and *anius*, on other land which, not being irrigated and fertilized the way the corn lands were, did not yield an annual crop. *Quinoa,* which is a sort of rice, was also cultivated in the cold climates.

Tilling and sowing were always done according to the

same order. The Sun's land was the first to be ploughed, then came that of the widows and orphans, as well as of all those who had been reduced to helplessness by sickness or old age. Deputies called *llamactus* went up at night on towers specially built for this purpose, and after calling the population together by blowing on a conch horn, they specified which fields were to be ploughed the following day. Each worker who went to work in the field of a widow or an orphan was obliged to take his own food with him, since, they argued, the burden of their own wretchedness was all these poor people could bear, and they should not be charged with the care of others. When a man went off to war, his wife had the same rights as a widow, in that her land was worked by her neighbors.

After the fields belonging to the poor, they ploughed their own, always in common, then those of the curaca, and finally, the last of all, those of the king. For this occasion, they wore their festival dress, ornamented with gold and silver, and on their heads, crowns of large bouquets of feathers. They sang praises to the Inca while working, and this labor was thus transformed into a festival, by virtue of their great love for their god and king.

The first field dedicated to the Sun was located inside the Cuzco enclosure, near the fortress, and was referred to as Collcampata. No one had the right to touch it except the pallas or Incas themselves. When this field was ploughed it was the occasion of a very sumptuous festival that was attended by all the Incas, dressed in their finest array.[2]

They ploughed with a stick that was about a span in length, four fingers thick, flat on top and rounded underneath. About eighteen inches from the end, two more sticks, well fastened to the first one, formed a sort of stirrup, in which the man ploughing placed his foot, in order to plunge this spade-like object, that served as a plough, into the ground. They all worked together, in groups of seven or eight, and it was marvelous to see the amount of work they accomplished with such poor implements, singing the while, without ever losing the rhythm. The women walked beside the men, pulling up the weeds with their hands. When I was three years old, I witnessed in Cuzco this ploughing festival of the Collcampata, which served as a model for all similar festivals celebrated elsewhere. It had already lost most of its past splendor, and yet it was still quite marvelous to watch.

For this occasion, in the year 1551 or 1552, the choirmaster of the Cuzco cathedral had revived some of the poems that were usually sung at this event, for the festival of the Holy Sacrament. Eight half-breeds, who were classmates of mine, sang them to an organ accompaniment. They were dressed the way the Indians used to dress, and carried plough sticks in their hands during the entire procession. A large chorus repeated the verses of the song, and the Spaniards were very pleased. As for the Indians, nothing could have given them greater delight than to see their most cherished traditions revived in honor of this supreme God of ours, whom they called by the name of Pachacamac,[3] that is to say, the creator of the universe.

Each Indian received one *tupu,*[4] which corresponds roughly to one *fanega*[5] and a half, of corn acreage, for himself and his wife. For each son, he had the right to an additional tupu, and to one half a tupu for each daughter. When the son married, he kept for himself the tupu that his father had been given to provide him with food. The daughters, on the contrary, were not allowed to keep their share when they married: it either remained the property of the father, if he needed it, or reverted to the community to be allocated to someone else. Under no conditions, however, could a plot of land be bought or sold.

The land intended for vegetable growing was distributed according to the same principle.

The nobles, such as the curacas, for instance, were given land in proportion to the size of their households, that is to say, according to whether they had wives or concubines, sons, or slaves of both sexes. This law also applied to the Incas, who thus had their own personal land holdings, in addition to those they received from the domains of both the king and the Sun, since they were all considered to be the brothers of one and the sons of the other.

The fertilizers they used differed, according to the region. In the Cuzco valley and in its environs, the corn fields were fertilized with human manure, which the Indians considered to be matchless for cultivating this particular plant. They collected it carefully throughout the year, dried it and then kept it in powdered form. In the *collao,*[6] where it is too cold to grow corn, the potato fields, which extended over more than one hundred and fifty leagues of land, were enriched with animal manure.[7]

Along the entire coast, from Arequipa to Taracapa, which is a distance of over two hundred and fifty leagues, the only fertilizer used was that of seagulls,[8] unbelievably numerous flocks of which were to be found there. These birds, both large and small, live on islands not far from the shore, which are covered with such quantities of their droppings that they look like mountains of snow. Under Inca rule, the birds were protected by very severe laws: it was forbidden to kill a single one of them, or even to approach their islands during the laying season, under penalty of death.

The development of the valuable wealth of these islands was also subject to regulation, each one being assigned, according to its size, to one, two, or three specified provinces. In the latter case, the zones reserved for each province were separated by rows of boundary stones which no one who had not the right to do so was allowed to cross, under penalty of death. Lastly, it should be stated that no one could take more fertilizer than was needed for his own fields from the island or plot allotted to him, under penalty of severe punishment for wastefulness. This, alas, is no longer the case today.

In other coastal provinces, such as Atica, Uillacori, Malla, and Chillca, the fields were manured with the heads of sardines. These regions are very poor, covered with sand, and subject to total drought: there is not a single river in the area, it never rains during the entire year, and indeed, the same situation obtains over a stretch of more than seven hundred leagues of land. The inhabitants of these disinherited areas usually establish their villages near the sea, in order to breathe a little cool air, and if they want to grow anything, they are obliged to dig deep down under the sand to reach real soil. They have been known to dig several meters under the sandy surface, which explains the name of "basin" that the Spaniards gave to their mode of cultivating the soil; certain of these tilled areas covered only a few hundred square meters but others were several acres[9] in size. They used to dig holes with the end of a stick, then put a sardine head and two or three grains of corn in each one.

Divine Providence, which is generous in all things, takes equal care to provide for the needs of both these men and these birds; for the sea furnishes sardines for them both so regularly and so generously, that after all have fed on them, and after the men have fertilized their fields with them, there are still enough to load whole boats full of them, if any come that far.

These basins I have just described denote a very inventive mind; but who first thought of them, no one knows: necessity is no doubt the mother of invention, another proof being the terraced corn planting I spoke of.

The Indians, as we have seen, ploughed and harvested the Inca's lands, as well as those of the Sun. They picked the fruit that grew on these lands—the principal one being the *uchu,* which the Spaniards call *aji,*[10] or pimento—and stored them both in their granaries and in the royal warehouses. It may be said that this was the principal tribute received by the Inca, since his subjects kept the whole of their harvests for themselves, as Father Acosta has attested, in the fifteenth chapter of the sixth book of his work.

Their granaries, which they called *pirua,* were built of earth and straw. They were high, narrow constructions, square in form and varied in size; certain of them containing two hundred and seventy-five bushels, and others five or six times that amount. They were built in a row, one next to the other, and between them was left a narrow alleyway by which one could fill or empty them. For this purpose, square gratings, about two fingers wide, were cut in one of the sides. There was nothing accidental about these constructions; on the contrary, they were carefully calculated in order that it might always be known what quantity of grain there was in reserve. I saw many such granaries in my childhood, the finest of all, in fact, for they had been built to store the grain intended for the virgin-brides of the Sun, in Cuzco. The Inca's harvests, and those of the Sun were stored separately, but in the same way as those of the rest of the people.

In addition to the tribute already described, the Inca's subjects were obliged to furnish the clothes, shoes, and necessary weapons for the army, as well as for all other needy persons such as widows, orphans, and invalids. In the mountains, these clothes were made from the wool of the countless herds that belonged to the king and the Sun. Whereas on the coast, where wool cannot be worn on account of the intense heat, they spun and wove the cotton grown on the king's plantations and on those of the Sun.

There were three kinds of wool materials. The roughest, which they called *auasca,* was woven by the women for the common people. The second, which was of a closer weave, was called *compi.* It was made of two-ply yarn, like Flemish broadcloth, and they dyed it in all colors, to be used by the captains, curacas, and other nobles. The third, which was the finest of all, was reserved for the nobles of royal blood. These two latter materials were woven by men, not by women, for the reason that they required vertical looms. It has even been said that the Incas themselves also wove. The significance of this fact will be seen later in the chapter that treats of the manner in which the young nobles were knighted.

In the richer provinces, shoes were made out of a vegetable raw material derived from agave plants. In the same way, weapons came from different regions, according to the various materials that entered into their making. One province furnished bows and arrows, and another lances, javelins, hatchets and bludgeons, or perhaps, slings and shields. These were all the arms used by the Indians.

In short, it may be said that each province furnished what it could produce without its inhabitants being obliged to travel about; and, thanks to this system, the Indians fulfilled the levies made upon them without leaving home, which was in line with the first principle of Inca government: namely, that each man should live in one spot, and never move from it, since vagrancy makes ne'er-do-wells and disturbs the peace.

Thus the Inca's vassals furnished him with four types of statute labor: they tilled his land, spun and wove his wool and cotton, and manufactured shoes and weapons for his troops.

We shall add to these the special tribute that, every year, the poor and disinherited paid to the governors of the territory they lived in; which consisted of a tube filled with lice.

The Incas said that this token tribute was intended to show that everyone, no matter what his station, owed something to the State, in exchange for the benefits he received from it. They added, however, that this custom owed its existence to the vigilance of their kings and to their love for the poor: because, in this way, these wretched people were obliged to get rid of their vermin which, in their great indigence, they might otherwise have died of. This example suffices to explain why the Inca kings were generally called the *friends of the poor.*

Nobles of royal blood were exempt from all levies or task duties. The same was true of priests, ministers, curacas, camp commanders and army officers, governors, judges and administrators as long as they were in office, soldiers in active service, young men under twenty-five, or who had been married for less than a year, old men over fifty, and all women, of whatever age or station. Sick persons enjoyed the same exemptions, until they were quite well again, as did the blind, the halt, the stiff-jointed, and those who had only one arm. On the other hand, deaf and dumb persons were exempt from nothing, for the reason that they could work like everybody else and that, in the minds of the Incas, the work of each individual, when all was said and done, was the source and end of all law.

Since, as everyone knows, the Incas possessed great quantities of gold, silver, and precious stones, it might be thought that it all came to them through compulsory tribute, which was not at all the case.

Nothing could be bought or sold in their kingdom, where there was neither gold nor silver coin, and these metals could not be considered otherwise than as superfluous, since they could not be eaten, nor could one buy anything to eat with them. Indeed, they were esteemed only for their beauty and brilliance, as being suitable for enhancing that of royal palaces, Sun temples and convents for virgins.

The result was that when the Indians brought gold and silver to the Inca, it was not at all by way of tribute, but as a gift, for it would not have occurred to them to pay a visit to a superior without bringing him a present, even if it were only a little basket of fruit, as was often the case.

The curacas and all the noble lords made it a point, therefore, to bring gifts of the finest and rarest products of their estates, when they visited their king. These consisted of gold, silver, precious stones, rare woods, strange, wild or magnificent animals, such as tigers, bears, lions, monkeys, macaws, ostriches, condors, enormous snakes, big toads, and, along the coast, seals and the oversized lizards called *caïmans*. In other words, there was nothing that was remarkable for its ferociousness, its size, or its beauty that they did not bring to the Inca, in order to show him that he was not only lord of all these things, but of those who gave them to him. The subjects of the curacas collected these presents in their leisure moments, their only intention being to give pleasure to the king and to the Sun, whom they considered to be their gods.

There were three kinds of warehouses in the Empire. Some of them, intended to give emergency help to the populations in case of scarcity, were built inside the villages, while the others, which contained the harvests and the tribute paid to the king and to the Sun, were located both in the villages and along the royal highroads, the warehouses spaced three leagues apart: the Spaniards transformed these warehouses into inns.

In all the royal district, which extended fifty leagues all round the city of Cuzco, the harvests belonging to the Sun and to the Inca were used for court expenditures, with the exception of a part of the Sun's revenues, which were left in the village warehouses for the vassals.

Elsewhere, throughout the Empire, the royal harvests went into royal warehouses situated in the villages, and from there to the nearest roadside warehouses, where were also kept provisions of clothing, weapons, and shoes intended for the army. These latter reserves were so abundant that, as Agustín de Zarate [11] has remarked, an army of twenty to thirty thousand men could be entirely clothed, armed, and provided with supplies. For this reason, the soldiers did not have the right to help themselves to anything whatsoever in the villages, under penalty of death, a statement that is confirmed by Pedro de Cieza de Leon.[12]

When a war entailed unusual expenditures, to cover which the king's granaries alone were insufficient, recourse was had to those of the Sun, and all provisions that were left over after the war were once more divided between the three kinds of warehouses we have just described.

The Sun's revenues covered the upkeep of the priests during the time of their service in the temples. The expenses entailed, however, were not so great but that there remained large quantities of provisions at the disposal of the Inca to cover his own needs.

The Inca's reserves did not serve to clothe only the soldiers, but the entire population of the Empire as well. Indeed, every two years, under supervision of the decurions, the wool from the royal herds was distributed in every village, in order that each person should be decently clothed during his entire life. It should be recalled that the Indians of the people, and even the curacas, possessed only very few cattle, whereas the Inca's and the Sun's herds were so numerous that, according to some, they no longer knew where to send them to graze by the time the Spaniards arrived in Peru. In hot climates, cotton from the royal plantations replaced wool. Thus, everyone was always provided with clothing, shoes, food, and all that is necessary in life, and it may be said that there was not a single poor man or beggar throughout the Empire. But while there were no poor, there were no rich either, since everyone had what was necessary without ever living in superfluous luxury. Father Acosta has expressed agreement with me on this subject, in the fifteenth chapter of his sixth book.

No one ever begged for alms in Peru, and things were still like that when I left my country in 1560. The only person I ever saw begging was an old woman in Cuzco, named Isabel; and at that, she only went to the homes of Spaniards, because the Indians, both men and women, became so angry when they met her, that they spat on the ground out of disgust.

Nor had the Incas forgotten, in their republic, to look out for the needs of travelers, for whom there existed, all along the royal roads, inns called *corpahuaci,* in which they could obtain a meal as well as provisions to take with them, and receive treatment, should they have met with an accident or fallen sick. It is true, of course, that they traveled neither on their own business nor for pleasure, but by order of the king, of their curaca, of a captain or of a minister of peace or war. Anyone who moved about without being ordered to do so, was punished for vagrancy.

Strange birds, large and small, snakes, and wild animals were kept and fed in certain provinces that still bear their name, as also at court. When I left Cuzco, their traces could be seen in the names of certain neighborhoods, such as Amarucancha, which means the place where there were pythons or boas, or Pumacurcu and Pumachupan, the lions' quarter. Birds were kept outside the city, to which fact, for instance, may be traced the name of Surihualla, or ostrich field,[13] that is still the name of a place about one league south of Cuzco.

Such wild animals as tigers, lions, snakes, and toads were kept for punishment of evildoers.

The first gesture of the Inca, after he had conquered a province, was to take its principal idol as a hostage and have it transported to Cuzco, until such time as the cacique and his Indians had understood the vanity of their false gods and surrendered to the cult of the Sun. The head cacique and his elder sons were also brought to Cuzco, so that they could become familiar with court life and learn not only about the laws and customs that governed the Empire, but also the new rites, ceremonies, and superstitions that they would have to observe. The curaca was then reintegrated into his former dignity and governed his people like a king.

In order that vanquished soldiers and their victors should become reconciled and forget the past, magnificent banquets were organized to which the blind, the lame, the deaf-mutes, and all those who were afflicted, were invited to share in the king's generosity. On these occasions, there were dancing contests, games of skill, and military exercises, in which girls, boys, and adult men participated. Each one was given an award and, at the same time, the king made generous dispensations of gold, silver, and feathers, so that the festival might be as complete and as splendid as possible.

To come back to the Inca Viracocha, whom we left marching toward the enemy and determined to die rather than see him enter the imperial city, we should first say that he made a halt on a vast plain situated about half a league from Cuzco, where he planned to wait for those he had left in the capital, and retrieve a few more fugitives, before establishing contact with the enemy.

More than eight thousand fighting men, all of them Incas and determined to die with their prince, had already joined him, when he learned that the insurgent army was crossing the Apurimac, only nine or ten leagues away.

The next day he received other news, that made the first less awkward for him: an army corps of twenty thousand men had collected in the Cuntisuyu district and was marching to his assistance: these were Quechuas, Cotapampas, Cotaneras, Aimaras, and other peoples from the provinces that bordered on those of the insurgents.

The deep hatred that has always existed between the Quechuas and the Chancas is well-known. It should be recalled, too, that all of these nations that came of their own free will to help the prince, had earlier surrendered without coercion to the Inca Capac Yupanqui, as we have already recounted. It may therefore be said that hatred of the Chancas and love of the Incas played equal parts in impelling these people to fight on the side of the prince.

But the Inca Viracocha and all of those about him were inclined rather to see in this unexpected assistance, the intercession of their divine ancestor, as well as further confirmation of all the young prince had heard in his dream.

After holding council, they decided to change their plan, taking this important news into consideration. Instead of advancing to meet the enemy in the high passes he would have to take after having crossed the Apurimac, they decided to stay where they were until reinforcements arrived. They also thought that, given the strength of the forces that they would soon have assembled, it would be preferable for them not to go too far from the city, which constituted their only source of supplies.

Reinforcements consisting of twelve thousand men arrived. Prince Viracocha welcomed them as best he could, praising their exemplary loyalty, and to each one he promised a generous reward. The curacas in command of these reinforcements told him that five thousand more men were marching at a two days' pace behind them, but that they had felt it was better not to wait for them, since they knew the imminent danger that threatened the prince.

After consulting together, the Inca Viracocha decided to remain in the plain with his army, while the five thousand men who had come to his assistance would go and lie in ambush on the heights to which the road from the Apurimac leads. They would let the enemy join battle on the plain then attack him, without warning, from the rear.

Two days later the advance guard of the enemy's troops emerged on the Rimactampu ridge, five leagues away from the position occupied by the Inca, where they halted to wait for the bulk of the army and their rear guards, before advancing farther. The following day they continued, in full force, for a league and a half, as far as Sacsahuana, where later Gonzalvo Pizarro was to fight de la Gasca. There was now a distance of only three leagues and one half between the Inca and his opponents. The Inca Viracocha immediately dispatched messengers to Sacsahuana, to offer the rebels peace and pardon for their offense; but the Chancas had heard of Yahuar Huacac's flight, and they were so convinced that, having beaten the father without striking a blow, they could easily succeed in breaking down the son's resistance, that they refused to listen to the prince's envoys. At dawn the next day they set out, in formation for battle. But despite their haste, by nightfall they had not yet established contact, and were, consequently, obliged to pitch camp a quarter of a league from the imperial troops.

All night long, the two armies remained facing each other, on the alert. When day broke, the conch horns, timpani, and trumpets began to sound, and they marched toward each other, with loud shouting. Leading his troops, the Inca Viracocha struck the first blow and, in no time, there was a terrible struggle. The Chancas had sworn to win, and the Incas to avenge their king's honor, with the result that both fought with equal courage. Neither side had succeeded in seizing the initiative, however, until at noon, the five thousand men who had been hiding in ambush, swept down suddenly upon the enemy's right flank, in the midst of such an outcry, and with such violence that, at first, the Chancas were obliged to retreat several feet. But, by virtue of mutual encouragement, little by little they recaptured the ground they had lost, and they fought on with a doggedness that was all the greater for the fact that time was passing and they were still far from having achieved the victory they had counted on. The fighting continued two more long hours, with the same intensity and without either side having obtained advantage over the other; after which, the Chancas began to show signs of weakening, when they saw that fresh enemy forces kept arriving to join in the conflict. And the fact is that, from every side, the fugitives of the preceding days, and peasants from the surrounding villages had grouped together at news of the battle, and were hastening to join the fighting, in groups of fifty and one hundred. They gave such shouts and bestirred themselves in such a manner that one would have thought they were ten times more numerous than they actually were, and it was this trick that made the Chancas weaken: whereas earlier they had fought to win, now they were fighting to die. The Incas, ever inclined to embellish their history and invent fables and false evidence at every turn in honor of the Sun, did not let this opportunity pass to enhance their legend. They began by proclaiming, on every side, that the very stones and grass on the battlefield had been transformed into warriors come to help the prince, at Viracocha's and the Sun's orders. And this surely added greatly to the discouragement of the Chancas, who were credulous and simple-minded, like all Indians.

"When victory became assured," wrote Father Acosta, "the Prince told his soldiers, that it was not they whose force had been decisive, but a number of bearded men, invisible to all but himself, whom Viracocha had sent to help them, and who, later, had changed into stones. 'You must look for them,' he added, 'for I would recognize them.' And they collected quantities of stones on the mountains, which they adored and to which they offered up sacrifices. After that, when they started out to war, they never failed to take with them some of these stones, being convinced that they would bring them victory."

When the Incas saw that the enemy was weakening, their ardor increased twofold, and they kept invoking the name of Viracocha, as the prince had ordered them to do. They killed a large number of Chancas, and those that remained lost their grip and turned and fled in complete bewilderment: victory was now won, and the prince had all his troops assembled in order to put an end to the useless slaughter. He himself inspected the battlefield in its entire length and breadth and ordered the wounded to be brought in and the dead buried. He freed the prisoners, and after having pardoned them, sent them back to their homes. The fighting had lasted over eight hours and had been so violent that a dry brook which passed through there ran with streams of blood all that day, according to the Indians, who since then, have called this plain *Yahuarpampa,* which means "blood-soaked plain." More than thirty thousand men died there, eight thousand of whom were on the Inca side.

General Hancohuallu and his two camp commanders were made prisoners. The prince kept them for the feast of triumph he planned to organize later, and he even had the general given special care, despite the fact that he was not seriously wounded. Several days after the battle, an uncle of the prince reprimanded them very severely for having dared to attack the sons of the Sun. He explained to them that the Incas were invincible, since, at the Sun's command, trees and stones became transformed into men sent to help them, as they had seen in this battle, and as they would see again every time they might be inclined to put the matter to the test. Then he told them a lot of other fables on the subject of the Incas and, in closing, he bade them give thanks to the Sun: because it was to the Sun that they owed preservation of their estates, their lives, as well as those of their curacas, when in reality they had all deserved the cruelest of ends for having dared to rebel. He then dismissed them, bidding them henceforth to remain good vassals, unless they wanted the Sun to punish them by ordering the earth to open up and swallow them. The curacas thanked the Sun with extreme humility and promised, in the future, to remain his faithful servitors always.

After this great victory, the Inca Viracocha dispatched abroad three messengers. One went to announce the victory to the Sun, as though it had not witnessed it! But all the Incas were like that: at the same time that they considered the Sun as a god, they nevertheless always treated it as a person. In Cuzco, for instance, they gave it to drink in a golden vase which they set on the parvis of the temple; and, when evening came, they said that the Sun had really taken a drink, since the vase, which had been full that morning, was now only half full; which was not entirely false reasoning, since it was the heat that had evaporated the liquid. They also gave it platters of meat to eat. And, in the case of a great victory, sent a messenger to tell the news, as Prince Viracocha had just done.

His second message was addressed to the cloistered virgins whose prayers had contributed to the success of the undertaking; and the third sought out the Inca, father of the prince, to inform him of the victory, and urge him not to move from where he was until the prince's return.

After the messengers had left, the prince disbanded all his

troops, except for six thousand picked soldiers, whom he kept with him. He named two of his uncles camp commanders and, two days after the battle, left with these troops in pursuit of the remainder of the Chanca army, not to maltreat them, but to give them personal assurance of his good will. He therefore had all those he met on the way cared for and refreshed, and even sent some of them as scouts into their own provinces to proclaim in advance that the Inca extended his pardon to them all. Thus he arrived in the nearest of the insurgent provinces, which was Antahuailla. There, a procession of women and children waving green branches, came out to meet him, with acclamations, and repeating: "Oh Lord, thou who art a friend of the poor, have pity on us, and forgive us!"

The prince gave them a kindly welcome, and had them told that only their fathers and husbands were guilty, but that he had forgiven them, and that he had come there in order that all might hear these words from his own lips. He gave orders that all the needs of these people should be satisfied, and that the widows and orphans of those who had died in the battle of Yahuarpampa be given special care.

Thus he traveled through all the provinces that had rebelled, in so short a time that he was back in Cuzco one Moon after he had left it. All of the Indians, the loyal ones as well as the others, were dumbfounded by the mildness and generosity of this prince; because after his victory and what was known of his past, everybody had expected that there would be terrible slaughter.

They concluded from this that the Sun-god had changed him in order that he might be worthy in all things of his forefathers. But it would appear rather that fame and glory have so powerful an attraction for a generous spirit that they permit it to completely transform its worst natural tendencies, as happened in the case of this prince, who was to leave behind him such a great reputation.

The Inca Viracocha entered Cuzco on foot, thus espousing the conduct of a soldier rather than that of a king. He was flanked by his two uncles, surrounded by all his soldiers, and the prisoners brought up the rear. The entire population welcomed him with demonstrations of joy and such acclamations as were never heard. The older Incas came out to meet him and worshiped him as the son of the Sun. They then took their places in his retinue, in order to share his triumph, showing in this way that they would have liked to be young again in order to have the honor of serving under his command. His mother, the Coya Mama Chic'ya, and her closest relatives, sisters, aunts, and cousins, also came out amidst a crowd of other pallas, to acclaim and honor him: some embraced him, others brushed the dust off his garments or wiped the sweat from his brow, while still others strewed flowers and scented herbs at his feet. Thus he walked as far as the Temple of the Sun, into which he entered, after having removed his shoes, as was customary, to thank the sacred orb for the victory it had granted him. He next paid a visit to the cloistered virgins, then, finally, left the city once more to take the mountain pass for Muina, where his father awaited him.

The Inca Yahuar Huacac did not welcome his son with the joy and pride one might have expected, after this glorious exploit and this unhoped-for victory, but, on the contrary, with a serious and melancholy mien, in which could be read more sadness than pleasure. What was it, exactly? Was it envy, shame, or fear that dictated his conduct? It would be hard to say, and, indeed, it might well have been all three of them at once.

After having exchanged a few words in public, the king and the prince retired in order to be able to speak more at length by themselves. It was then, no doubt, that they discussed the fate of the crown. Finally, the king decided not to return to Cuzco, since he had abandoned his capital. Then, in order to avoid either scandal or civil war—and because he could not do otherwise—he agreed to yield to any decisions his son might make. Thus the crown changed heads,[14] which decision corresponded with the secret wishes of the entire court. A plan was drawn up for a palace near the Muina pass,[15] to have vast numbers of orchards, gardens, hunting and fishing preserves, and countless other refinements suitable for a royal dwelling place. From now on, this is where Yahuar Huacac was to live.

The Inca Viracocha then returned to Cuzco, where he exchanged his yellow bandeau for the scarlet one, without consenting, however, that his father should cease to wear his, which he retained till the end of his days. But why cling to the outward insignia of power, if it cannot really be wielded! The Inca Yahuar Huacac ended his life in opulence, but also in the solitude of exile, with only animals for company, as though fate had turned against him the punishment he had originally inflicted upon his son. And so ends the story of the Inca Weep-Blood.

As we have already seen, the name Viracocha was given to the prince after his dream, which everybody considered to be premonitory. He had specified that the ghost who had appeared before him wore a thick beard—whereas the Indians are clean-shaven—and that his robe came down to the ground—while that of the Incas came only to their knees: this is why the Peruvian people called the Spaniards "Viracochas," the minute they saw them. And this belief in their sacred origin, as soon as they set foot on land, was only strengthened when these same Spaniards killed Atahualpa, the usurper-tyrant, who had just seized power unjustly from the legitimate heir to the throne, Huascar Inca, and put him to death. For, in the simple minds of the Indians, only the same messenger from God could have manifested himself in this way twice in their history to save Cuzco and the dynasty; the first time from the Chancas, and the second from Atahualpa.

Therefore, the Indians had no difficulty in believing that the Spaniards were all the sons of God, and that is why they adored them and did not dream of taking up arms against them. If, at that time, the Spaniards had taken advantage of this situation, to explain that the only real God had sent them to free all peoples, not from the tyranny of Atahualpa, but from that of the demon, which is a thousand times worse, and if they had taught the New Testament right away through example, as Christian doctrine teaches us to do, there is no doubt but that they would have greatly benefited by it. But everything happened quite differently, as all the chroniclers have recognized; and I shall accept what they have told us, not being in a position to discourse any longer on this subject myself, for, were I to do so, people would not fail to remind me of my Indian origin and they would say that I am blinded by passion.

This unexpected victory, coming as it did after the dream, brought such prestige to the Inca Viracocha that he was adored during his lifetime as none of his predecessors had been, although he always tried to divert this excessive homage in favor of his uncle, the ghost, but in vain, since the people, in their naïve credulity, confessed them one with the other. As we shall see later, the Inca Viracocha had a temple built in honor of this uncle and, perhaps too, the better to ensure his own personal fame.

No doubt it was the demon who inspired this dream of the prince's, in order to consolidate the idolatry of the Incas which, indeed, had never been so deep-rooted in the past as it became after these extraordinary events. The credit and authority of the Inca Viracocha became such that he was considered to be an oracle, and anything that he took it into his head to order was obeyed as divine word. One should not, however, fall into the error that was common to many Spaniards, who insisted that Viracocha was Peru's principal god, and that he was adored even more than the Sun. Because there was never in the Empire any other recognized god than the Sun, and Pachacamac, the invisible God.

In the village of Cacha, sixteen leagues south of Cuzco, the Inca Viracocha had a temple built in honor of his uncle, and to perpetuate the memory of these events. It was the king's desire that this edifice, in its plan and general arrangement, should recall the spot at which the ghost had appeared to him. One floor, therefore, was built in the form of an entirely open, unroofed terrace, to resemble the plain on which he had been exiled by his father, and on it there was a small stone chapel that recalled the cave in which the prince had seen the ghost. It was unlike anything that has ever been built in Peru, either before or since, because never, except this time, did an Indian dream of building a storied house.

The temple was one hundred and twenty feet long, by eighty feet wide, and was built entirely of extremely well-carved stones. Four doors, located at the four points of the compass, were to be seen in outline on the walls. But only the one that looked eastward was used to come in and out, the others being merely for ornament. Since the Indians knew nothing about real arches, they built a series of parallel walls inside this enclosure, oriented north and south, three feet thick and spaced in groups of seven. These walls supported the terrace more securely than wooden beams, and they served to mark out twelve alleyways inside the temple through all of which visitors had to pass in order to reach the stairway that led to the terrace. The floor of the ground level was made of stones ten feet square and a foot and a half thick, that were perfectly flat on all sides. Once inside the temple door, one turned to the right and took the first alleyway as far as the north wall, after which one retraced one's footsteps, and turned leftward along the second alleyway, as far as the south wall. Here one turned right again along the third alleyway, and so on, until one reached the back wall, through the twelfth alleyway, which finished at the foot of the stairway leading to the terrace.

The north and south walls had a dozen openings for skylights, which sufficed to light the twelve alleyways. In order not to block the passages, the attendants remained seated all day long in recesses hollowed out under these skylights. The stairway was a double one and opened on to the high altar. The terrace floor was of gleaming jet-black flagstones, that had been brought from a great distance. What I shall continue to call the high altar was located in a sort of chapel, twelve feet square, capped by a four-faced pyramid, made of these same black flagstones fitted one into the other: this was the masterpiece of the entire edifice. Viracocha's statue was kept in a tabernacle carved directly in the temple wall, at the back of this chapel. The four walls rose about nine or ten feet above the terrace and there was no opening in them. They were topped by a cornice that was finely wrought and ran about the entire perimeter.

Viracocha was represented as a tall well-built man, wearing a beard as long as your hand; he was dressed in a tunic that came down to his feet, and he was holding on leash, at the end of a chain, a strange animal with paws that looked like lion's claws. There was something about this statue that reminded one of the likenesses of our holy apostles, and especially of his honor Saint Bartholomew, who is always shown with the Devil tied to his feet. When the Spaniards discovered this temple and the statue of Viracocha, they said that Saint Bartholomew had perhaps been in Peru to teach the word of God to the gentiles. And more recently—thirty years ago—the Cuzco half-breeds founded a brotherhood under the patronage of this saint, the rules of which forbade Spaniards to join it. With the result that the latter, being jealous of the luxury and extravagance that marked the festivals of this brotherhood, whispered that it was perhaps less the apostle than the Inca Viracocha they revered.

Why did the Inca want to build his temple on this site rather than on the exact spot where the ghost had appeared to him, or on the Yahuarpampa plain, which was the scene of his victory over the Chancas? No doubt he had some good, secret reason, for it is certain, in any case, that the site for the temple was chosen on his orders. Today, nothing remains of this admirable edifice. The Spaniards destroyed it, despite the fact that it was unique of its kind, in the same way that they destroyed all of Peru's most beautiful monuments; whereas, in their own interests, they ought to have preserved and, at their own expense, kept up all these marvelous things, which would have borne witness for centuries and centuries to the grandeur of this Empire that they had succeeded in conquering, and consequently, to their own strength and good fortune.

But they preferred to raze everything, out of cupidity, because they could not believe that the Indians had built such monuments as these, unless it was for the purpose of hiding important treasures. In the case in question, they began by pulling down Viracocha's statue, in the idea that it contained piles of gold. Then they destroyed and excavated the entire edifice to its very foundations, without finding anything. A few years ago, this disfigured statue was still lying in the grass, near the ruins of the temple. Then, one fine day, they broke it in pieces, to be used for cobblestones.[16]

Not content with having built this temple, the Inca Viracocha discovered yet another means of distinguishing himself for future generations, in a manner that was as flattering to himself as it was caustic with regard to his father. On a very high, rocky peak, near the spot where the latter had retired after fleeing Cuzco, he had two condors painted: one had his back turned to Cuzco, with his head hanging and his wings closed, in the position that all birds assume, whatever their pride, when they want to hide; the other, who was looking toward the city, had, on the contrary, his wings wide open and a fierce expression, as though he were about to swoop down on his prey. The first of these birds was said to represent Yahuar Huacac, and the second the Inca Viracocha. This painting was still in excellent condition in 1580. In 1595, however, I asked a Creole priest who had come from Peru if he had seen it, and he said that there was almost nothing left of it, so great had been the damage caused by exposure and neglect.

In order to express his gratitude to the vassals who had rushed to his aid, and especially to the Quechuas named Cotapampa and Cotanera, the Inca Viracocha authorized these people to shave their heads and pierce their ears like the Incas, down to a certain length, the way the Inca Manco Capac, founder of the dynasty, had allowed his companions to do. He spent several years visiting the Empire, then returned to Cuzco, and decided to resume conquest of the great provinces of Caranca, Ullaca, Llipi, and Chicha, a task his father had abandoned before it was completed, as we have already written. He therefore levied thirty thousand fighting men in the Cuntisuyu and Collasuyu districts, entrusting command of them to his brother, Maïta Inca, whose name means "he who flies," for the reason that he was the swiftest runner of his time.

The Chicha and Ampara provinces adored the Sierra Nevada on account of the rivers that flowed down the slopes of these mountains to water their fields. But in spite of their reputation for being courageous soldiers and proud of their independence, the inhabitants of these provinces surrendered almost without resistance, so great was the Inca Viracocha's reputation. Nevertheless, it took three years to conquer and organize them properly.

After these last conquests had been achieved, the Empire stretched eastward to the snowy peaks of the Andes, westward to the sea, and southward as far as the deserts that separate Peru from Chile, more than two hundred leagues from Cuzco; in consequence, it could only grow now toward the north. The Inca Viracocha, being insatiable, as all kings are, decided, therefore, to himself lead an expedition in this direction, that is to say, through the Chinchasuyu district; to do this, he collected thirty thousand men and engaged six Incas as camp commanders. Having left the government of the city in the hands of his brother, the Inca Pahuac Maïta, he took command of his troops and marched to the province of Antahuailla, where the Chanca language is spoken. These repentant rebels—who had retained the nickname *Auca,* meaning traitor—welcomed him with such good grace as people afflicted as they were could muster. The Inca behaved very generously toward them and visited all their provinces, after which he assembled his army and marched against those that had not yet surrendered. They all had the wisdom to capitulate without attempting resistance, which allowed the Inca to disband his troops and devote his time to organizing these new territories. He had numerous public works undertaken, among which was a canal twelve feet deep and more than one hundred and twenty leagues long, which irrigated a strip of land eighteen leagues wide that ran the whole length of the region.

In the Cuntisuyu district, there is another canal of almost equal size, which runs as far as the Quechua territory and measures more than one hundred and fifty leagues from one extremity to the other. I could name many other magnificent canals, all of which give proof of the greatness of our former kings. They may be compared favorably with the most famous achievements of the Old World, if, indeed, they are not superior to them, when one considers with what primitive means they were carried out and across what terrible mountains; for it is well known that the Indians had no knowledge of the uses of iron; and it should be added, for instance, that more than once, in order to obtain passage for these canals, they were obliged to divert the course of entire rivers, from the very source, by blocking the beds with stones.

All these canals were bordered on both banks with cemented flagstones, from one to two meters long by one meter high, which were sustained on the outside by embankments of earth, to keep the cattle from damaging them when they crossed from one side to the other.

Unfortunately, the Spaniards did not understand the useful purposes of these valuable works, which are now in ruins.

After having drawn the plan of the canal and finished attending to the various matters that had kept him in these provinces, the Inca Viracocha, instead of returning to Cuzco, decided to make another tour of the Empire, visiting all its cities and provinces. He went first to the Cuntisuyu district, where the Quechuas welcomed him with splendid festivals, after which, returning to the seacoast, he went from there to the Collasuyu district. As he traveled from place to place, he investigated and inspected the work of his ministers and governors, and he punished very severely those who had been guilty of the slightest negligence in the accomplishment of their duties.

While crossing the Charca province, ambassadors from a kingdom called Tucma, out of which the Spaniards made the name Tucuman,[18] requested an audience.

"The fame of your ancestors," they told him, "has come all this way. We know how humane are your laws, how honest your judgments, the benefits that each one of your subjects derives from your government, the excellence of your religion, and the great miracles that your father the Sun has just accomplished in your favor. The curacas of the kingdom of Tucma have sent us to beg you to welcome us into your Empire, to make us your vassals, and to send Incas of royal blood to our land, who will show us how to emerge from our barbarian state, and teach us your laws and your religion. Permit us, therefore, to worship you in the name of our entire kingdom, and to acknowledge you as our lord and king; in witness whereof we make you a gift of our persons, as well as of the fruits of our land."

After having thus spoken, they knelt down before the Inca and put into his hands cotton garments, honey, and all sorts of grains and vegetables that they had brought from their country. They gave him neither gold nor silver, however, since there was none in Tucma, nor has any yet been discovered there.

The Inca accepted these presents very graciously and ordered his relatives to serve wine to the ambassadors, which was granting them a rare favor. He also had the finest woolen cloth brought for them and even went so far as to give them some of his own sacred garments that had been woven by the Cuzco virgins. A few days later, the ambassadors left for their own country, and Inca relatives of the king accompanied them, as they had requested, to teach and organize their new kingdom, according to the laws and customs of the Empire.

The Inca pursued his travels in the Collasuyu district where he was welcomed, as he had been elsewhere, amidst such feasts and acclamations as were never seen. For Viracocha's dream and the victory of Yahuarpampa had made of this prince a sort of new god, whom all were eager to worship: even today, the rock underneath which he was lying when his uncle appeared to him, is an object greatly revered by all the Indians, despite the fact that they are all Christians, and are therefore not prompted by a spirit of idolatry, but by loyalty to the memory of one of their former princes.

From Collasuyu, Viracocha went to the district of Antisuyu, where he was surrounded with less pomp, not because he was less beloved there than elsewhere, but because this district is the poorest in Peru. They nevertheless built triumphal wooden arches along his way, according to Indian custom, and strewed his path with flowers and green branches.

The Inca Viracocha visited twice more the totality of his kingdoms and provinces. During the second of these voyages, while he was visiting the Chicha province, in the extreme southern part of Peru, the news reached him that Hancohuallu, the brave king of the Chancas, had fled, and the Inca was both pained and annoyed.

Ten years had passed since the battle of Yahuarpampa, and all during this time the brave Hancohuallu, whose offenses had been forgiven, at the same time that he had been returned to his throne, had enjoyed the privileges in keeping with his rank, under the mild tutelage of the Incas. But his proud and generous spirit, accustomed as it was to wield absolute authority, and being heir to a long tradition of sovereignty and conquest, could not adapt itself to the weight of a yoke, however light. It is hard to accept as equals those whom we have long held to be inferiors, and such was the case of this prideful prince when he saw his overlord, the Inca, heaping favors and privileges upon his neighbors, the Quechuas, whom he himself had once conquered and made his vassals. In consequence, mere liberty seemed to him to be preferable to the fortunate conditions in which, nevertheless, he felt himself to be constantly reduced in station and, with each passing day, a little more dispossessed of the honor that, for him, constituted the supreme possession. He assembled a few of his own Indians and poured out his heart to them, telling them that he had decided to abandon his throne and his country, and go outside the Inca Empire, to win a new kingdom or to die, but in any case, to free himself, in one manner or another, from this tutelage that had become unbearable to him. He asked them to secretly inform all his people of his decision, in order that they might get under way, with their wives and children, in small groups and as quietly as possible, so as not to rouse suspicion among the imperial ministers and inspectors. He furnished them with papers justifying their journey and promised to join them beyond the frontier, in as short a time as possible. "This," he concluded, "is the only chance left us to recover our freedom. For it would be mad, vain and criminal for us to rise up in revolt again against the Inca: mad and vain, because we know that he is infinitely more powerful than we are, and criminal because given his magnanimous, generous conduct, I am honor bound not to undertake to oppose him."

These resolute, generous words convinced the prince's hearers. They persuaded others who, in turn, spoke to others still, to such good purpose that, shortly after that, more than eight thousand Chancas, all of them fighting men, without counting their wives, children and servants, joined their brave king, Hancohuallu, in the provinces of Tarma and Pumpu, which lie sixty leagues from their own. It would have been easy for them to subjugate these nations and settle on their land, but Hancohuallu preferred to go farther still from the Empire of the Incas, so as not to risk having them lay hands on him one day, as a result of further conquests. They pressed on, therefore, till they reached the cordillera of the Andes, where they disappeared. Some say that they crossed it and settled in the east, beside a river that watered rich, fertile lands, and that there they founded a kingdom, more than two hundred leagues from their point of departure. The last Chancas in Peru still tell fabulous tales of Hancohuallu's heroic adventures. All of these, however, are more legend than history, although there is no doubt that so valorous a man as he must have accomplished other great feats.[19]

Although this event had upset his plans, the Inca Viracocha was unwilling to interrupt his journey. He therefore sent messengers at once to his brother Pahuac Maïta, who was in charge of the Cuzco government during his absence, and to two other members of the imperial council, asking them to go immediately into Chanca territory, with sufficient escort, to quell the uneasiness that the prince's disappearance must have given rise to.

The three Incas did as they were told and restored people's confidence as best they could. They visited the two famous fortresses of Challcumarca and Suramarca, where Hancohuallu had dwelt before his departure. It was said, in fact, that he had been so attached to these two buildings that it had cost him more to leave them than to leave his entire kingdom. Finally, the Inca Viracocha came back from his journey, and decided to stay several years in his court, attending to his government, until such time as these two mutinies on the part of the Chancas would have been completely forgotten.

He began, therefore, by promulgating new laws especially intended to prevent the recurrence of similar disturbances in the Empire. Then he transferred ten thousand persons, chosen from the most peace-loving provinces, to the Chanca territories, under the authority of Incas by privilege. Once this was done, he undertook to embellish the Empire, particularly the Y'ùcay valley and the Tampu [20] region, with magnificent new buildings. The Y'ùcay valley is undoubtedly the most beautiful in Peru, and all the Incas, from Manco Capac on, were accustomed to come there to seek repose from the responsibilities of government. It lies hardly four leagues southeast of Cuzco and is really an enchanting spot: the air is cool and soft, the water is crystal clear, it has a temperate climate that is always the same, with neither intense cold nor excessive heat, and there are no flies, mosquitoes, or other pests. It is bordered by two mountains chains, one of which is the Great Sierra Nevada, extending beyond it toward the east. Numerous streams flow down from perpetually snow-capped peaks, thus making it possible to irrigate the fields and pastures. On the mountain slopes, troops of wild animals may be seen grazing on vast natural prairies, which also contain an abundance of roe deer, deer, guanacos, vicuñas, partridge, and many other birds of every species, although Spanish negligence has considerably reduced these game resources. The bottom lands of the valley are dotted with orchards and magnificent gardens, in which are grown grapevines and all kinds of fruit trees, as well as sugar cane brought there by the Spaniards.

The mountain that borders on the west side of the valley is not high, although it takes an hour to climb it. At the foot of this mountain, the beautiful Y'ùcay river flows gently and calmly by. This river, which is filled with fish, is also the habitat of quantities of waders, ducks and other waterfowl. For all of these reasons, the inhabitants of Cuzco are accustomed to come and stay in this valley, to recuperate from illness, and today there is not a Spaniard in the city with any claim to distinction, who hasn't striven to acquire a bit of land in this region.

The first-born son of the Inca Viracocha and his sister-bride, Coya Mama Runtu, was first called Titu Manco Capac, but his father had expressed the wish in his last will and testament that this name should be changed to Pachacutec, which means, he-who-changes-the-face-of-the-world. To tell the truth, Viracocha himself should have been the one to receive this name, since, in reality, he had changed the face of the world, from bad to good, through the victory of Yahuarpampa, after his own father had brought it from good to bad, as a result of his conduct at the time of the Chanca uprising. But the entire Empire having called him Viracocha because of his prophetic dream, he wanted to give this name of Pachacutec to his heir, in order that memory of the father's exploits might be perpetuated through the son.[21] Let me add, for the sake of those who are curious about linguistic matters, and may those who aren't excuse me, that the name of Mama Runtu means the mother-egg, and that it was given to the Inca's bride because of the fact that her skin was unusually white, so when they said Mama Runtu, it was as though they said *she who is as white as an egg*.

The Inca Viracocha is also credited with having been the first of the Incas to foresee the coming of the Spaniards. The Indians say that after events had proven the exactness of his first dream, the amautas, the high priest and the elders of the Cuzco temple, who fulfilled the duties of soothsayers, acquired the habit of questioning the Inca Viracocha regularly on the subject of his dreams. They interpreted them by observing the comets in the sky, in addition to earthly auguries taken from birds and animals offered up in sacrifice. It was on the occasion of one of these collective consultations that a dream dreamt by the Inca Viracocha warned them that, one day, unknown bearded men would land in Peru and overthrow both the religion and the Empire of the Incas. This message was transmitted traditionally by each king to his successor, without anything being known by the people, in order that the dignity of the Incas and their supposed supernatural origin should risk no perturbation as a result of this prediction. For this reason, not a word was spoken about it until the Inca Huaina Capac, as we shall see later, made these divinatory words public, as he lay dying. Some historians, having had wind of this story, attribute it to an Indian they call Ticci Viracocha. What I myself tell, however, was told me by the old Inca, my mother's uncle, who taught me many things.

When the Spaniards conquered Peru and abolished Sun worship, which they replaced by the Catholic faith of our Holy Roman Church, the Indians, recalling this dream, concluded from it that these new men must be the sons and envoys of the god Viracocha, which is why they called them quite naturally Viracochas.

The Inca Viracocha died at the apex of his power and majesty. He was universally mourned throughout the Empire, and many sacrifices were offered up to him. He had conquered eleven provinces, four of which stretched toward the south and seven to the north of Cuzco. It is estimated that his reign lasted over fifty years, which would appear to be correct, judging by his body, which I saw in the beginning of the year 1560, when I went to bid adieu to the scholar Polo de Ondegardo, Chief Justice of Cuzco, before leaving Peru for Spain.[22]

"Since you are going to Spain," he said to me, "come in this room, where you will see some of your relatives, whom I disinterred, and about whom you may want to speak over there."

There were five bodies in there, three of whom were Inca kings and two, Inca queens, and it was thought that one of them was the Inca Viracocha. He had undoubtedly died when he was very old, because his head was as white as snow. The second was the great Tupac Inca Yupanqui, great grandson of Viracocha; and the third, Huaina Capac, son of Tupac Inca Yupanqui, great-great grandson of Viracocha. These latter two must have died when they were younger, for, although they too had some white hair, there was much less of it. One of the women was Mama Runtu, the sister-bride of Viracocha, and the other was Coya Mama Occlo, the mother of Huaina Capac. It appeared likely that the Indians had found them in couples, united in death as they were in life.

All these bodies were so well preserved that not a hair, not an eyebrow, not even a lash was missing. They were dressed in their royal garments and were seated Indian fashion, with their hands crossed on their breasts, the right hand reposing on the left, and their eyelids all but closed, as though they were looking at the ground. Father Acosta, who saw these bodies, mentioned how perfectly they had been preserved. I did not succeed in finding out how they went about the embalming, nor with what ingredients: the Indians hid this from me, just as they did from the Spaniards, or maybe they themselves had all of them already forgotten these things when I questioned them.

I remember that I touched one of Huaina Capac's fingers, and found it as hard as wood. The bodies were so light that the Indians carried them in their arms with no difficulty, from one house to the other, to show them to the gentlemen who wanted to see them. In the street, they covered them with a white sheet; and all the Indians who saw them pass knelt down immediately and bowed, sobbing, their faces bathed in tears. Many Spaniards too, took off their hats in the presence of the bodies of these kings, which touched the Indians so much that they did not know how to express their feeling.

This then, is what I know of the Inca Viracocha's noble deeds and exploits. It is to be regretted that the Incas had no writing, for all the rest of what they knew disappeared with them, and the memory of so gallant a man as this would have deserved to be kept alive in greater detail.

1. Below are Baudin's remarks on the subject:

"Doubtless this method of cultivation (terracing) was in existence before the Inca period, since it is to be found in the Polynesian and Melanesian countries and in America itself, in regions where the rulers of Cuzco never penetrated, and where it appears to have existed since very ancient times: but the Inca terraces are better constructed than any others. This construction, on steep slopes, requires great skill . . . Even today the traveler is amazed to see how the best use is made of every tiny morsel of land and also what gigantic works were sometimes carried out to bring water to the diminutive strips of land.

"To have the land is not enough; water must be brought to make it fertile. The importance of hydraulic works will be understood when it is remembered that to water the upper terraces on the slopes of steep mountains, water had to be brought from great distances in jars which men carried on their backs.

"The irrigation works carried out by the Indians appear fantastic to us. The channels, some of them more than 62 miles long, are hollowed out of the rock, pass through tunnels and cross valleys by means of aqueducts sometimes 50 to 65 feet long. They are often fed by reservoirs, such as that of Nepeña, formed by a stone dike built across a gorge, and measuring 3936 feet long and 2624 feet wide.

"Well before the Incas, the Indians had begun to irrigate. The Kalchaki and Kara Indians seem to have been most expert at this, as well as the Chimu, since the Incas, to subdue them, were obliged to cut some of their aqueducts."

2. This ceremony, which Garcilaso calls Cusquieraïmi, is characteristic of agrarian civilization. It was still celebrated long after the conquest. D'Harcourt quotes Cobo describing it fifty years after Garcilaso: "It is a real pleasure to see the Indians ploughing after their fashion, as I have seen them many times. Their singing is very pleasant and can be heard more than half a league away." In ancient China, too, the Emperor in person turned the first earth in a sacred field.

3. See Note 36, Book VI.

4. Aimara word meaning measure. (Baudin)

5. A somewhat elastic measurement, representing the amount of land that can be sown with a quintal of corn. The *fanega* was originally a measure of capacity, of Arab origin. As a measure of area it was variable, even in Spain. As an indication, a Castilian *fanega* represented about two-thirds of a hectare. It is worthy of note that the measure of area in the Andes is today called a *fanegada,* and not *fanega.*

6. Territory of the Colla tribe.

7. Corn was grown to an altitude of 11,500 feet, quinoa and potatoes up to 14,000 feet.

8. This is *guano,* the basis of the Chilean nitrates, that were to be found even in the islands off the Peruvian coast several centuries ago.

9. Literally, from a half, to three or four *fanegas.*

10. This word, now used throughout Latin America (except in Mexico) for pimentos, was borrowed by the Spaniards from the Arawaks of the West Indies.

11. ". . . Guaynacava (Huaina Capac) had built along the mountain road, day by day, great palaces with many apartments, in which he could lodge himself, his suite and all his army. He had similar ones built in the plain . . . these buildings were called *tambos* and the Indians of the region took care to stock them with all the provisions required by the army of this prince, not only in food but in all kinds of supplies and arms, so that from each of these *tambos* twenty-five to thirty thousand persons could be clothed and armed, if need be." (Zarate)

Zarate went to Peru with the first Viceroy Blasco Nuñez

Vela. His work is a valuable source of information on the history of the conquest proper. He dedicated it to the Emperor Charles V who thanked him by making him Grand Treasurer of Flanders. He was secretary of the Royal Council of Castile when he left for Peru as Treasurer-General to His Majesty. See Book IX.

12. Pedro de Cieza de Leon, Part I, Chapter 60: ". . . for the Incas were so greatly feared by their subjects that they would never have dared to neglect to stock any of these storehouses lest they suffer a terrible punishment if the least thing were found lacking." (Cieza de Leon, Chapter 60)

13. This refers to the American ostrich, or Rhea americana. (Gilmore) It weighs between fifty and one hundred pounds and is to be found chiefly in Bolivia and Chile.

14. After he had defeated the Chancas, and thus saved Cuzco and the Incas, Prince Yupanqui—not Viracocha—was crowned in place of his brother Urcon and received the title of Pachacutec, in 1438. This is the earliest date in Inca history of which we are certain. It is most surprising that Garcilaso should have been so mistaken on this decisive moment in the history of the *Tahuantinsuyu,* which marks the beginning of the tremendous expansion of the Inca Empire. Garcilaso does not seem to know the name of Urcon, who is mentioned, however, by other chroniclers, e.g. Cieza de Leon (Part II, Chapters 44 to 47). This is no doubt because he is relating the official history of the Incas (when his memory does not deceive him): it is said that Pachacutec deleted his brother's name from the list of Incas. These corrections are based on Rowe (Handbook II).

15. According to Cesar García Rosell, Muina, or Muyna, is today the name of an archaeological site on the banks of the river of the same name (more commonly known as Mohina). The site covers .39 square miles. It is surrounded by a wall of large blocks of granite, still standing in places. Squier, who visited it about one hundred years ago, reported that this wall was more than twenty-five feet high. At that time, it was possible to distinguish the outlines of numerous buildings, some square, some circular or triangular, built of curiously cut red stone. Muina was certainly a town, which was already abandoned in the time of Cieza. It is also said to have possessed a sanctuary and an oracle.

16. The ruins of this temple have been studied by L. A. Pardo. According to this author, it was probably a pre-Inca sanctuary, perhaps recent Tiahuanaco (?). This assumption must be treated with great caution. There remains, says Pardo, a great wall of volcanic stone topped with *adobe,* measuring three hundred feet long, forty feet high and almost seven feet thick: the author concludes that there must have been three stories (?). The temple is said to have formed a T-shape, with the traces of twenty-four columns, only one of which is still standing. It measures five feet eight inches in

diameter at its base; it is made of *adobe* on a foundation of volcanic stone, like the wall. There are numerous traces of subsidiary structures, not mentioned by Garcilaso. Pardo's study is cited by Cesar García Rosell.

17. For all these campaigns and the journey of Viracocha across the Empire, see Note 19, Book V.

18. Tucuman, which today forms one of the northwest provinces of Argentina, was at that time peopled by the Diaguita and Chalchaqui tribes, of whose origin little is known. These peoples lost their cultural characteristics when the Inca Viracocha invaded Tucuman, early in the fifteenth century. (Krickeberg)

19. It is difficult to distinguish in this account, half legend, half history, by Garcilaso, which conquests are to be attributed to Viracocha and which to his son Yupanqui, crowned, as has been explained, under the name of Pachacutec, after his victory over the Chancas. It is quite simple, on the other hand, to establish the facts with regard to the flight of Hancohuallu. On assuming power, Pachacutec sent one of his generals, Capac Yupanqui, to conquer new territories. A Chanca contingent, led by Hancohuallu, formed part of the army of Capac Yupanqui, who had received detailed instructions from the king to pursue his conquests to the north to a point beyond which he was not to go on any pretext. But the ambition of Capac Yupanqui made him forget, on the way, the limits fixed by Pachacutec. Having conquered in succession Aimara, Umasuyu, Cotapampa and Chilque, he went ahead, disobeying the royal command. It was then that the Chanca contingent, commanded by Hancohuallu, deserted and fled into the forest, above Huanco. On his return, General Capac Yupanqui was executed for disobedience. (Rowe)

    Pachacutec then reassumed personal command of the army and led a campaign into the Lake Titicaca basin. He quelled the revolt of the Avaviris and conquered the Lupacas.

20. Tampu or Tambo, today Ollantaitambo. "The Incas," says Cieza, "had built at Tambo the strongest fortress of all their Empire. It was placed on inaccessible rocks and could thus be defended by a few men against great numbers. The Incas had adorned the whole valley, where they came to make merry and hold festivities in their palaces, especially Viracocha Inga, who was the ancestor of Topa Inga Yupanqui. The ruins of numerous edifices are to be seen there, chiefly in Tambo, three leagues south of Yùcay, between two high mountains." (Cieza, Part I, Chapter 94) The remains of palaces, defensive walls, baths, and oratories are still to be seen in Y'ùcay.

21. Garcilaso gets out of his contradictions elegantly, since it was indeed on the conqueror of the Chancas that the title of Pachacutec was conferred, as explained in Note 14, Book V.

22. The *corregidor* (officer of justice) Polo de Ondegardo, a cultivated man most interested in Peruvian civilization, was one of the first Spanish scholars sent to Peru, no doubt to counterbalance the uncouthness of the first conquistadors. He left a valuable memorandum, drawn up on the instructions of the viceroy, the Count of Neiva, on the advantages of taxing the Indian commands and divisions, and the manner of doing so. See J. Cassou.

BOOK SIX

Which treats of the life,
works, and conquests of the Inca Pachacutec,
ninth king of Peru.
With a description of the royal mansions;
of the funeral ceremonies of the kings;
of the hunting season; posts and messengers;
Empire archives and accounts kept with
cords called quipus;
the great Sun festival; divinatory
sacrifices and ceremonies;
the manner in which the young
Incas were knighted;
schools; and subjugation of
the great Chimu

The royal mansions of the Incas were second to none in the grandeur, opulence, and majesty of everything that pertained to the service of these princes, and one might even say that certain of them, as we shall see later, outshone all the royal and imperial palaces in the world. The walls of these mansions, like those of the temples, baths and gardens, were made of very perfectly carved stones that fitted so well into one another that the Spaniards frequently thought that they had been assembled without mortar. There was one mansion, however, made of the red earth they called *llancac allpa,* or "earth that sticks." Often, too, they poured molten lead, or gold or silver, between the stones, as Pedro de Cieza de Leon has told in the ninety-fourth chapter of his book,[1] and this is why nearly all of these palaces and temples, which had been built to resist the ravages of the centuries, were destroyed in a few years by the Spaniards. The temples and royal chambers, throughout the Empire, were lined with gold, and, in preparing the stone, they left niches and empty spaces in which to put all sorts of human or animal figures: birds, or wild beasts, such as tigers, bears, lions, wolves, dogs and wildcats, deer, guanacos, vicuñas and even domestic ewes,[2] all of which were made of gold and silver. Pedro de Cieza de Leon tells about this in detail in his forty-fourth chapter.[3]

Imitation of nature was so consummate that they even reproduced the leaves and little plants that grow on walls; they also scattered here and there, gold or silver lizards, butterflies, mice and snakes, which were so well made and so cunningly placed, that one had the impression of seeing them run about in all directions. The Inca usually sat on a solid gold seat one foot high, without either arms or back, that rested on a square dais of the same metal. All the tableware in the house, whether for the kitchen or for the dining hall, was of solid gold, and all the royal mansions in the Empire were abundantly furnished in tableware, so that the king need take nothing with him when he traveled or went to war. These mansions and the warehouses along the royal roads were also well stocked with robes and other garments, which were always new, since the Inca only wore a costume once, after which he gave it to someone in his entourage. The use of mattresses was unknown and the king slept between two sheets made of vicuña wool, which is so fine and so much in demand, that the Spaniards brought some to King Philip II for his bedchamber.

The royal table was abundantly served, because it had to supply the king's entire retinue, which was very numerous, as well as the Incas of royal blood, at their discretion. Usually two meals were served, at court as among the common people, the first between eight and nine in the morning, and the second, which only consisted of light refreshments, at the end of the day. But then they drank until nightfall, so it might be said that the Incas were at once small eaters and heavy drinkers. This was only true, however, of the nobles, for we have seen that the people, although they lacked for nothing, disposed of only what was necessary. They went early to bed and rose at dawn, to start their work.

In all the royal mansions there were gardens and orchards given over to the Inca's moments of relaxation. Here were planted the finest trees and the most beautiful flowers and sweet-smelling herbs in the kingdom, while quantities of others were reproduced in gold and silver, at every stage of their growth, from the sprout that hardly shows above the earth, to the full-blown plant, in complete maturity. There were also fields of corn with silver stalks and gold ears, on which the leaves, grains, and even the corn silk were shown.

In addition to all this, there were all kinds of gold and silver animals in these gardens, such as rabbits, mice, lizards, snakes, butterflies, foxes, and wildcats (there being no domestic cats). Then there were birds set in the trees, as though they were about to sing, and others bent over the flowers, breathing in their nectar. There were roe deer and deer, lions and tigers, all the animals in creation, in fact, each placed just where it should be.

Each one of these mansions had its bathing suite, with large gold and silver basins into which the water flowed through pipes made of the same metals. And the warm springs in which the Incas went to bathe were also ornamented with very finely wrought gold trimmings.

When the Indians saw how greatly the Spaniards were attracted to gold and silver, they hid the greater part of these treasures so well that, today, it is no longer known where they are, and, indeed, there is very little hope that they will ever be found, even in part, unless it be by chance. And the reason for this was that no Indian would have agreed to let someone else use what was reserved for his king. Pedro de Cieza de Leon and Agustín de Zarate have both mentioned these lost treasures:

"When I was in Cuzco," Pedro de Cieza wrote, "I was told that the Inca Paul and other princes, too, had said that if a collection were made of all the treasures that had been dispersed among the temples in all the provinces of the Empire, the amount that the Spaniards had taken away from Peru would be but a drop in the bucket in comparison. And, taking up a handful of corn in one of the granaries, they added: 'Here is what the Spaniards got, and, as for the rest, we ourselves do not know where it is!' "

This Inca, whom Pedro de Cieza called Paul, was named Paüllu, and all the Spanish historians have mentioned him. He was one of Huaina Capac's numerous sons, and he served the Spanish faithfully in the Peruvian wars. My lord and father Garcilaso de la Vega stood as godfather at his baptism, and I knew him very well.

The servants in the royal mansions were furnished, as a levy, by certain villages designated to supply them. Thus, one village sent sweepers, another water carriers, another cooks for state meals (the Inca's own cooking being done by his concubines), another porters, or gardeners, or valets, or jewel bearers, etc.

Since, in the entire Empire, there was no greater favor than to be able to approach the Inca's sacred person, one can imagine in what esteem the villages bound by this special obligation were held. This was more than a tribute, it was a privilege, and it had always devolved upon the first villages that had been founded by Manco Capac, in a perimeter of six to seven leagues around Cuzco, when he laid the bases of his Empire. As we explained at the beginning of this account, the inhabitants of these regions were the first Incas by privilege, and they retained for all time the exclusive right to serve the king. The men who carried the gold litters on which the Inca moved about were chosen from the two neighboring provinces called Rucana and Hatun-Rucana, or Grand-Rucana. The population numbered more than fifteen thousand inhabitants, all of whom, from the age of twenty, received special training in carrying the litters without jolts or jars, in the absolutely uniform, regular manner befitting royal majesty. A historian tells that if one of these porters fell, he was put to death, and that some twenty-five substitutes always followed the royal litter, should it be necessary to replace a porter on duty. This office, like the above-mentioned, was greatly prized because it allowed those who filled it to approach the Inca's sacred person.

The royal kitchens used great quantities of different meats, but the flesh of roe deer, deer, guanacos or vicuñas was never included, being reserved for hunting; bird meat was the only exception. Incredible quantities of drinks were also consumed, all the curacas and other visitors to the king having the right to be served.

The funeral ceremonies for the Inca kings were extremely solemn. The body of the deceased was embalmed, as we said before, after which his internal organs were taken to be buried in the Tampu[4] temple, less than five leagues from Cuzco, on the banks of the Y'ùcay river.

The women he had cherished most and the servants closest to the king, allowed themselves to be killed, or buried alive, so that they could accompany their master into the next life. However, nobody obliged them to sacrifice themselves in this manner, as certain chroniclers have lyingly stated; on the contrary, in many cases, the palace officers intervened to keep too many of these unhappy persons from taking their own lives.

We have also explained how the bodies of the kings were kept in the Temple of the Sun, in Cuzco. During the entire month following upon the king's death, he was mourned every day, with great feeling and sincerity, by all the inhabitants of the imperial city: each neighborhood formed in a procession and went out into the country, wearing the insignia of the deceased king, and singing out loud an account of his feats of arms and all the benefits he had granted them during his lifetime. This same ceremony was repeated every fortnight, during the entire year. These rites were not observed by the common people only, but also by all the Inca princes, with pomp and solemnity, and they were performed, as well, in all the provinces of the Empire. People even made pilgrimages to all the places where the king had distinguished himself during his lifetime by some notable exploit or benefaction, which was recalled to the minds of all, in order that his memory should endure. Similar ceremonies, although less solemn, took place when a cacique or an important vassal died, and I still remember with what emotion I watched the people mourning, when I was young, for a Quechua cacique named Huamampallpa.[5]

Every year the Inca kings organized a great ceremonial hunt called *chacu,* which means *stop,* the method they employed being to group, then stop, their game.

In order really to understand this custom, it must be remembered that, throughout the Empire, hunting was ordinarily forbidden, except in the case of certain birds, that were to be served on the tables of governors and curacas; and that even this minor form of hunting required both an order and a license. The result was that no one dared, without permission, to kill so much as a single bird, through fear of being killed himself for having broken the Inca's law, which had not been formulated to be flouted.

Indeed, thanks to the severity of this ordinance, game proliferated in such quantities that sometimes the creatures actually went into people's houses. But the Inca, whose aim was to keep game for his vassals, not vassals for game, allowed his subjects to hunt the deer and other animals that came on their plantations.

The great annual royal hunt took place shortly after the mating season. In the province chosen for that year, the Inca first assembled some twenty to thirty thousand Indians. He then divided them in two groups whose duty it was to walk in circular formation across the fields and prairies, rivers and mountains, over a tract of land about twenty to thirty leagues long. As they advanced, these men headed off all the animals they came upon, forcing them back toward the middle of the circle with shouts and clapping of hands. Then the circle of beaters began to close in on the creatures who, by now, were imprisoned as though between four walls of human bodies, so that it soon became possible to catch them by hand. Included among them were lions, bears, foxes, the species of lynx they call *ozcollo,*[6] and all kinds of other harmful beasts, which they killed right away, in order to rid nature of these low breeds. I have not mentioned tigers,[7] which one scarcely ever encounters in Peru, except in the wild Andes mountains. But roe deer, deer, and the big game animals called guanacos and vicuñas were caught in vast quantities: indeed, there were sometimes as many as thirty to forty thousand head of them, and one can imagine what a magnificent spectacle they presented, huddled together that way. Yes, that is how things were then. But today, what remains of this great natural wealth has been so decimated by use of the harquebus that one hardly sees a single guanaco or vicuña in the whole of Peru!

The game collected in this manner was sorted, and the females of an age to bear young were freed, along with the finest specimens among the males, while old or ungainly animals were killed and their meat divided among the ordinary people. The guanacos and vicuñas, however, were sheared before they were set free. Meanwhile, a complete census of all this game was taken, according to sex and species, and the figures were noted down by means of quipus.

All the guanaco wool, which is coarse in quality, was distributed among the people; while that of the vicuñas, which, as we explained elsewhere, is the finest in the world, was sent to the royal stores, and only the Inca, or those to whom he expressly granted this favor, had the right to wear it. Indeed, any infraction of this law was punishable by death. But the meat of the guanacos and vicuñas that were killed was also divided among the people.

These hunts took place in each district every four years, in order to give the game time to reproduce and also to allow the vicuñas and guanacos time to grow new wool.

The organization of these hunts, which benefited the entire Empire, gives evidence of the order and wisdom, applied to the slightest details, with which the Incas administered their Empire. The bezoar [8] stone, for instance, was taken from the intestines of these wild animals, and it was said to vary in quality according to the species.

The Inca viceroys and governors hunted in the same manner, on the estates under their administration, taking personal part in the *battues,* as much for the pleasure they derived as to supervise the distribution of wool and meat among the people.

With the exception of the Collas, the Peruvians were poor in cattle and, therefore, short of meat, which is why these big hunts constituted such a valuable resource for the inhabitants of the villages. Each one dried his own ration of meat, and it was sparingly consumed, in order to make it last all year.

The Indians also dried numerous nourishing plants which they picked wild. Nor did they neglect to collect with care the spawn of fish, which they dried and kept to be used as meat. This does not mean that they never ate any fresh food, such as lettuce or radishes, but they were unfamiliar with the art of preparing salads.

The messengers stationed on the royal roads for the purpose of rapidly conveying the Inca's orders and delivering reports to him from his kingdoms and provinces, were called *chasquis* and they lived in groups of four or six in two thatched huts, located a quarter of a league apart along these roads. They were all young men who were especially good runners, and it was their duty to keep permanent watch of the road, in both directions, in order to catch sight of messengers from the other relays, and hurry out to meet them, before they had even covered the distance assigned to them. For this reason, these huts were built on high ground, in sight of one another.[9]

The word *chasqui* has three meanings: exchange, give, and take, and it was a very suitable name for these men since they exchanged, received, and gave messages, from post to post. The messages transmitted in this manner were always oral, for the reason that the Incas had no written language. They were composed, therefore, of a few simple, precise words, in order that the messengers should not risk changing their meaning or forgetting some of them. When a messenger arrived in view of the next hut, he began to call out, the way our outriders blow their horns, to warn the one who was running out to meet him, as we said before, and he repeated the message three or four times, before continuing his way alone.

The Incas also used a form of messages that might almost be said to have been written: these were made of cords and knots called quipus, concerning which we have already had occasion to speak, and which I shall soon describe in detail. When circumstances required it, the number of *chasquis* stationed at the relay points along a certain road could be increased to include ten or twelve men.

But they also had yet another means of transmitting important news, which consisted in lighting fires on the hills, from place to place. These fires gave smoke in the daytime and light at night, which is why the *chasquis* had to remain constantly on the alert, at all hours of the day and night. This latter system of sending messages by fire was only used, however, in exceptional circumstances, such as an uprising in one of the kingdoms, or in some large province. The Inca could then be informed of the fact, within two or three hours, even if he were five or six hundred leagues away.

The word *quipu* means both *knot* or *to knot;* it was also used for accounts, because they were kept by means of the knots tied in a number of cords of different thicknesses and colors, each one of which had a special significance. Thus, gold was represented by a gold cord, silver by a white one, and fighting men by a red cord.

When their accounts had to do with things that have no color—such as grain and vegetables—they were classified by categories, and, in each category, by order of diminishing size. Thus, to furnish an example, if they had had to count the various types of agricultural production in Spain, they would have started with wheat, then rye, then peas, then beans, and so forth. In the same way, in order to make an inventory of the arms of the imperial army, they first counted the arms that were considered to belong in a superior category, such as lances, then javelins, bows and arrows, hatchets and maces, and lastly, slings, and any other arms that were used. In order to ascertain the number of vassals in the Empire, they started with each village, then with each province: the first cord showed a census of men over sixty, the second, those between fifty and sixty, the third, those from forty to fifty, and so on, by decades, down to the babes at the breast.

Occasionally other, thinner, cords of the same color, could be seen among one of these series, as though they represented an exception to the rule; thus, for instance, among the figures that concerned the men of such and such an age, all of whom were considered to be married, the thinner cords indicated the number of widowers of the same age, for the year in question: because, as I explained before, population figures, together with those of all the other resources of the Empire, were brought up to date every year.

According to their position, the knots signified units, tens, hundreds, thousands, ten thousands and, exceptionally, hundred thousands, and they were all as well aligned on their different cords as the figures that an accountant sets down, column by column, in his ledger. Indeed, those men, called *quipucamayus,* who were in charge of the quipus, were exactly that, imperial accountants.

The number of quipucamayus scattered throughout the Empire, was proportional to the size of each place. Thus the smallest villages numbered four, and others twenty, or even thirty. The Incas preferred this arrangement, even in places where one accountant would have sufficed, the idea being that, if several of them kept the same accounts, there was less risk that they would make mistakes.

Every year, an inventory of all the Inca's possessions was made. Nor was there a single birth or death, a single departure or return of a soldier, in all the Empire, that was not noted on the quipus. And indeed, it may be said that everything that could be counted, was counted in this way, even to battles, diplomatic missions, and royal speeches. But since it was only possible to record numbers in this manner, and not words, the quipucamayus assigned to record ambassadorial missions and speeches, learned them by heart, at the same time that they noted down the numbers, places and dates on their quipus; and thus, from father to son, they transmitted this information to their successors. The speeches exchanged between the Incas and their vassals on important occasions, such as the surrender of a new province, were also transmitted to posterity by the amautas, or philosophers, who summarized them in simple, clear fables, in order that they might be implanted by word of mouth in the memories of all the people, from those at court to the inhabitants of the most remote hamlets. The *harauicus,* or poets, also composed poems based on diplomatic records and royal speeches. These poems were recited for a great victory or festival, and every time a new Inca was knighted.

When the curacas and dignitaries of a province wanted to know some historical detail concerning their predecessors, they asked these quipucamayus, who were, in other words, not only the accountants, but also the historians of each nation. The result was that the quipucamayus never let their quipus out of their hands, and they kept passing their cords and knots through their fingers so as not to forget the tradition behind all these accounts. In fact, their responsibility was so great and so absorbing, that they were exempted from all tribute as well as from all other kinds of service.

All laws, ordinances, rites, and ceremonies throughout the Empire were recorded by these same means.

When my father's Indians came to town on Midsummer's Day to pay their tribute, they brought me the quipus; and the curacas asked my mother to take note of their stories, for they mistrusted the Spaniards, and feared that they would not understand them. I was able to reassure them by re-reading what I had noted down under their dictation, and they used to follow my reading, holding on to their quipus, to be certain of my exactness; this was how I succeeded in learning many things quite as perfectly as did the Indians.[10]

After having succeeded his father, the Inca Viracocha, to the throne, the Inca Pachacutec spent three entire years in his capital. Then, for three more years, he visited the Empire in detail, as tradition demanded he should do. Finally, after his return to Cuzco, he decided to undertake a military campaign in the Chinchasuyu district. He therefore raised an army of thirty thousand men and, with his brother Capac Yupanqui, who was a brave prince in every way worthy of the name, he set out. When he reached Uillca, which marks the imperial frontier in this direction, the Inca Pachacutec placed his brother in supreme command and returned to his capital.

And so Capac Yupanqui and his army entered the large and beautiful province of Sausa, which at that time counted more than thirty thousand inhabitants, all speaking the language and belonging to the nation of the Huancas.[11] These people claimed to descend from a man and a woman born of a spring. In any case, they were quite bellicose, and skinned alive all those they captured in combat. Sometimes they filled the skins with ashes and stood them up in a temple, as war trophies; sometimes they covered drums with them, in order, as they said, to frighten and put their enemies to flight with the sound of their brothers' skins. All of their villages were fortified, for the reason that they were constantly quarreling among themselves over questions of land and pasturage, despite the fact that they formed a single nation.

These Huancas were especially well-known for their strange cult of a dog, which was represented in all their temples. Indeed, they had such an immoderate passion for dog meat that they would have ruined themselves to obtain it, and we are told that we must look in one of these facts for the explanation of the other, that is to say, that their gluttony is at the origin of their religion. There was no feast more important for them than a dog banquet. And in their dances and peaceful festivals, as well as when they went to war, they blew on horns made of dogs' heads, which, they said, "gave us, who were worshipers of the Dog-god, as much pleasure, as it gave fright to our enemies, who were unaware of him." Even today, in speaking of the Huancas, they are called "dog-eaters," on account of their well-known passion. After he had subjugated them, not by the force of arms, but through diplomacy, General Capac Yupanqui forbade this cult of their idol by the Huancas, but authorized them to make horns out of deer or doe heads, to play at their festivals, as they had been accustomed to do with the heads of dogs.[12]

In order that their territorial quarrels should cease definitively, he ordered division of their land into three provinces, which were named Sausa, Marcauillca and Llacsapallanca. Then, in order to differentiate the inhabitants of these three provinces, he decreed that their headdress, which was the same throughout the entire Huanca nation, should be of a different color in each of the three provinces, at the same time that the form remained unchanged.[13]

Capac Yupanqui conquered several other provinces in the Chinchasuyu, to the right and left of the royal road that crosses this district. The most important were those of Tarma and Pumpu, which the Spaniards call Bombon. There were a few skirmishes here and there, because all of these people were courageous, competent soldiers, but these were only minor incidents in comparison with what could have happened if General Capac Yupanqui had not succeeded in cleverly winning over both populations and leaders to his cause through gifts and friendly words. Among the natives of these provinces, it was customary for a fiancé to kiss the forehead or cheek of his promised bride, before taking her for his wife; widows shaved their heads and were not allowed to marry for a year; the men observed periods of very severe fasting during which they could eat neither meat, nor salt, nor pepper, nor could they have intercourse with their wives; and the most superstitious among them, who were, in a way, their priests, often fasted for the salvation of the others.

After having subjugated these two provinces, the Inca Capac Yupanqui continued his conquests toward the east, as far as the cordillera of the Andes. This region was peopled with savages who lived like animals, without order or law, godless and homeless, scattered about in the mountains and forests, killing each other when they met, without rhyme or reason. They occupied a territory that was at least thirty square leagues in size. However, they surrendered to the Inca without resistance and, simple-minded as they were, gathered together where they were told to go. Thus, for the first time in their history, they founded villages in which they were taught the Inca laws. Continuing his advance, the Inca Capac Yupanqui finally reached the Chucurpu territory, which was occupied by a very fierce people whose idol, in conformity with their own nature, was a tiger.

The Inca had difficulty in getting such people as these to listen to the voice of reason, and because of this fact, he only succeeded in subjugating them after several battles, which are said to have cost the lives of four thousand Indians, on both sides. But when they had understood the Inca's mildness, for he could easily have killed them all had he wanted to, but was content to defend himself from their attacks, the Chucurpu people surrendered unconditionally.

Crossing over to the other side of the Chinchasuyu royal road, Capac Yupanqui conquered two more well-populated provinces; one called Ancara[14] and the other Huaillas. In this latter place, the abominable vice of sodomy was rife, although this was the first time the Incas had met it outside the coastal regions, where we have already noted its existence.[15] The sodomites were punished with the greatest severity, after which, the Inca, considering that these conquests sufficed, left for Cuzco.

This campaign had lasted three years, during which the

confines of the Empire had been extended so far that it now took in more than sixty leagues of new land, running north and south, between the western plains and the crest of the Andes.

The Inca Pachacutec welcomed his brother with all the pomp he deserved, and the victory festivals lasted one entire lunar month, since the Indians as we explained earlier, count time by the Moon.

The army was finally disbanded, after all the camp commanders, captains, and soldiers had received from their king the gifts and decorations they deserved. The Inca Pachacutec then undertook an extensive visit of the Empire, during which he had built new Sun temples and new convents for virgins, the one always accompanied by the other. They also built fortresses on the new borders, and royal mansions along the roads and in places where the landscape was most beautiful. The Inca promulgated several new laws, intended to maintain in the newly conquered territory all the traditional features that gave no offense to the precepts of the sons of the Sun.

All of this took three years, after which he returned to his court and, at a meeting with his advisory council and his brother—who was like his second self [16]—he discussed the advisability of undertaking further conquests. A decision was taken to organize another campaign in the Chinchasuyu district, and it was understood that the Crown Prince Inca Yupanqui, who had just turned sixteen, would be given his first taste of war at this time. An army of fifty thousand fighting men was raised and the two Incas, the uncle and the nephew, leading the first third of these forces, marched as far as the province of Chucurpu, which is where the Empire ends.

From there, ambassadors were sent to the natives of a non-subject province called Pincu, where the inhabitants having understood that it was not to their interest to resist, immediately fell in with the laws of the Empire. However, the troops continued their march and entered three more provinces, named Huaras, Piscopampa and Cunchucu. But the people of these territories, so far from following the example of their neighbors, forgot the quarrels that divided them among themselves, and united to combat the Inca. They sent back word to him by his ambassadors that they could not be hoodwinked, as others

January

February

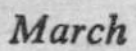

March

April

May

June

July

August

September *October*

November *December*

THE MONTHS AND THEIR OCCUPATIONS

January: Work in the potato fields; a man and woman are seen with hoes in their hands.
February: The foxes and deer come into the fields; drums are beaten to frighten them away.
March: Birds attack the crops; the guardian of the crops comes with his sling and stick hung with bells.
April: The month of the Moon; the corn, potatoes, and fruits are ripe; opposite the llama, in the corn field, a thief may be seen.
May: The corn harvest.
June: The potatoes are dug with spades.
July: The grain and leguminous crops are carried into the state granaries.
August: Month of tilling. The Inca and his brothers are represented turning the first sod with a spade in the sacred field of the Sun, while a woman offers them goblets of *chicha*.
September: The corn is sown; this is the month of female deities.
October: The guardian of the crops watches over the young corn shoots.
November: Month of drought; the crops must be constantly irrigated.
December: The potatoes and *quinoa* are planted. The illustration shows a peasant being helped by a woman to make a hole in the earth with a spade driven in by a mallet, while a second woman is preparing to place a potato in it.

had been, by his so-called religious zealotry. After which, being unwilling to risk combat in the open country, they shut themselves up in their fortresses with ample provisions, destroyed the roads that lay in back of them, and set up defenses at all the weak points.

The arrogance and impudence of these people had no effect on the determined attitude of General Capac Yupanqui, whose spirit was sufficiently well-tempered for him to receive both bad and good news with the same equanimity. As soon as he heard of the enemy plan, he decided to divide his armies into four corps of ten thousand men, which independently, would each encircle one of the principal rebel fortresses, and, without establishing contact, force it to surrender, as a result of hunger. Then, since this siege risked being a long one, the Indians having shut themselves in with very ample provisions, he immediately asked his brother the Inca to send him from the interior of the Empire twice as many supplies as had been originally estimated for this campaign.

But the general's precautions, and his desire to avoid useless fighting, did not keep the war from being a long and a cruel one. On the contrary, the besieged enemy, having guessed his intentions, made countless raids, and provoked the imperial troops with the zeal and courage of desperation. There were many dead on both sides and, in all these useless encounters, it seemed as though the three provinces were vying with one another in pride and bravery.

The imperial troops sought to avoid combat every time, however, and when they met wretched groups of women and children sent out by the besieged army to spare them the horrors of the siege, they always tried to console them, caring for them and feeding them as best they could, before sending them back to their relatives. They did this in order to make them understand that the Inca's intentions toward them were of the best; also, it was easier for them to resist when they were alone among men, than with these additional, useless mouths to feed; and the tears and wailing of all these women and children would surely have an effect on the proud soldiers, whose resolve, otherwise, might never weaken.

And yet, with the passing days, it seemed as though the tenacity of the besieged only increased.

This state of affairs lasted for five or six months, until the effects of famine began to be felt amongst them. Then, when they saw their women and children die, they were obliged to envisage what their own death would not have permitted them to accept, and the day came when they finally resigned themselves to sending ambassadors to the Inca. They came, in fact, with great humility, imploring forgiveness, and promised that, in the future, their peoples would be submissive and obedient.

The Inca's clemency was the same as it had always been on similar occasions. The past was forgotten and the former rebels, who had now become loyal vassals, returned to their villages, in accordance with the orders that were given them. The additional supplies that General Capac Yupanqui had had collected were used to feed them all and to keep them from suffering further shortages for an entire year, this long siege having made them lose the fruits of all the seeds they had previously sown.

Continuing their campaign, the inperial armies reached the frontiers of the great Huamachucu province, over which reigned a prince by the same name, who was famous for his wisdom and perspicacity. Nevertheless, this nation had some very barbarous, cruel traditions: they worshiped the mottled stones that they picked up in streams, and sacrificed human flesh and blood to them. Also, there were neither cities nor villages, the people being scattered about like animals in the out-of-doors. The worthy Huamachucu would have liked to remedy this state of affairs, but he did not dare to undertake the necessary reforms, for fear of being killed by his own subjects, so strong was their attachment to their evil ways. He consequently received the Inca's ambassadors like long awaited friends: "I envy your regime and the honesty of your laws," he told them, "and if my territory were not separated from yours by an enemy province, I should have long since come myself to beg you to let me be one of you."

Thus the Prince Yupanqui and his uncle the general entered Huamachucu territory without striking a blow, and this worthy lord came in person to welcome them and throw himself at their feet. The general returned his courtesies in the name of his brother, the Inca, and the prince gave him garments that had belonged to his father, to convince him of the esteem in which they held him. Since then, this province has never ceased to derive benefits from the felicitous manner in which it came voluntarily to join the Empire, thanks to the worthy Huamachucu's intelligence.

After this event had been celebrated with great feasting, the great curaca of Huamachucu explained to the general all these wicked customs that he had not been able to root out of the habits of his subjects, and he begged the general to help him in this undertaking, which was quickly done. The scattered huts were reassembled in places that were more propitious to the founding of villages, the painted stones they had adored until then were thrown out into the streets, and soon, together with all the other inhabitants of the Inca Empire, they revered only the Sun-god.

When this affair was settled, the Incas, both uncle and nephew, continued their march until they reached the frontiers of Cajamarca, since made famous by Pizarro's capture of Atahualpa, and which, for that time, was a rich, very fertile province, peopled with the most bellicose [17] of nations.

Already, for a long time, the inhabitants of Cajamarca had been observing the movements of the imperial armies and, accustomed as they were to war, they had laid in supplies in their fortresses and everything was ready to block the roads and resist their possible aggressors. The result was that the arrival of the Inca ambassadors did not catch them unawares. They replied with great arrogance that they did not need either new gods or a foreign lord, and that they had inherited a sufficient number of laws from their ancestors not to desire any new ones: the Incas, they concluded, should be content with those who had already agreed to obey them, or seek elsewhere if they wanted more subjects, because none here was willing to hear them.

The Inca general immediately ordered his troops to march, and they entered the Cajamarca province. But, from the very first, despite the general's peaceful intentions, they were obliged to fight, since otherwise it was impossible to advance. There were even a few battles on open terrain, and many men were killed. But the Inca power was such that the people in Cajamarca were soon obliged to withdraw into their fortresses, from where they made frequent raids, that were costly both for them and for the imperial troops. This state of affairs lasted four months.

During this entire time the Incas never ceased to bear in mind the fate of their enemies. They were quite content to do nothing more than repulse their attacks, and all prisoners were returned to their curacas with kind words and many blandishments. They also took care of the sick and wounded, and in general, gave every possible evidence that the sons of the Sun were neither tyrants nor cruel enemies.

These attentions gave results. The Cajamarca fighters began to weaken and, among themselves, they said that it would perhaps not be a bad thing to surrender to such kind, generous princes, rather than for all of them to die of hunger, which they felt was what threatened them sooner or later.

And thus it was that they finally sent ambassadors to the general and to his nephew, the prince, imploring forgiveness, acknowledging that the Incas' virtues were such that they deserved to rule the entire world, and tendering a profession of humble allegiance.

These ambassadors had hardly left, when the grand curaca of Cajamarca, together with his captains, decided that it would perhaps be wiser if they themselves went to offer their surrender.

General Capac Yupanqui welcomed them with great friendliness and assured them, in the name of his brother and his nephew, that they had been forgiven, which was a source of great joy to them: "You really deserve to be called the sons of the Sun," said the grand curaca, speaking for all the others, "and it is a great good fortune for us to be able to surrender to such lords as yourselves." After which the new vassals took leave of the general and returned to their homes.

It did not take long for this beautiful province to become one of the most famous of all Peru, one that could soon boast of possessing a Sun temple and a convent for dedicated virgins, in addition to numerous other public edifices.[18]

General Capac Yupanqui then took the road back to Cuzco, not forgetting, on the way, however, to subjugate a tract of land that he had passed by, when he had come there. Although it was difficult of access, and inhabited by a very warlike people, it seemed to him that twelve thousand men would suffice to conquer it, so he disbanded the rest of his troops.

The population of Yauyu, after some hesitation with regard to the reply to be given the imperial ambassadors, finally came over to the side of the wisest among them, who saw nothing to gain and everything to lose, if they were to offer resistance to the all-powerful Incas. They therefore welcomed the general and his suite with all the pomp and ceremony worthy of these great lords, and the general responded to their warm greeting with his usual gracious kindliness.

The two Incas, the uncle and the nephew, then resumed their journey to Cuzco, leaving ministers and administrators in the new province. The Inca Pachacutec came out to meet them in person and, on his order, they entered the imperial city on litters carried by the natives of the provinces they had just conquered. Their triumph was in keeping with their exploits: representatives of all the nations in the Empire paraded through the city, acclaiming their noble deeds and their glory, followed by the army, corps by corps, each with its weapons and its bands playing. Lastly, the Incas of royal blood, also fully armed, walked in procession beside the gold litters of the general, the prince and the Inca Pachacutec, their king. They all marched in this order as far as the bounds of the Temple of the Sun, where all, except the king, removed their shoes. There they worshiped their god, thanking him for all the victories he had given his sons, after which they returned to the main square of the city, where a festival awaited them, with drinking and singing and dancing worthy of so great a day. Each one of the Empire peoples, in the order of seniority, came to dance before the king, after which they watched the rest of the spectacle, quaffing many a cup the while. The feast was not limited to one day, but lasted an entire lunar month. This triumph of General Capac Yupanqui's was the grandest that had ever been celebrated in all the history of the Incas.[19]

Three years of peace and repose had passed since these days of feasting, when the Incas decided to undertake subjugation of the still unconquered plains on the other side of Nanasca. These were lowlands, and not only unhealthy but dangerous as well for persons accustomed to a mountain climate. In consequence, the war council decided to equip two armies of thirty thousand men, that would relieve each other every two months, during the entire campaign.

The second army pitched camp in the foothills of the mountains, while the first moved on down toward the plain, with the king, his son the prince, and his brother the general. The king wanted to settle in a place that would permit him to follow developments of operations as closely as possible, without being cut off entirely from the interior affairs of the Empire. He therefore chose to remain in the provinces of Rucana and Hatun-Rucana, leaving his brother and nephew to continue alone with their troops as far as Nanasca, on the northern frontier. When they reached there, the prince and the general made a halt and sent their ambassadors into the first unconquered valley, which was called Ica. The Ica people, as well as those from the neighboring valley called Pisco, being aware of the disproportion that existed between their forces and those of the Incas, understood that it was to their interest to surrender without resistance, which is what they did.

Since that time, the Ica valley, which is naturally very fertile, has been further endowed by the Inca kings with a magnificent canal for irrigation purposes, that very artfully collects the water of a torrent that originally ran down the mountain in a northerly direction. They diverted it toward the south, and thus made up for the shortage of rain that keeps the land in this valley from producing as much as it otherwise could. The acreage of arable land was considerably increased as a result of this clever achievement, and the prestige of the Incas in this region, among the unconquered peoples as well as among those who had rallied to the Empire, grew proportionately greater, thanks to this fine canal. The natives of this coast, along the five hundred leagues—or thereabouts—that separate Trujillo from Tarapaca, shared a common cult of the sea, which they called *mamacocha,* or our mother the sea, because the fish it furnished them were so abundant that one might really have said that it fed them like a mother; and we have already seen how, in certain of these coastal regions, they went so far as to fertilize their fields with the heads of sardines.

These people practiced as well the cult of certain fish, in particular, of whales, the size and monstrosity of which struck their imaginations. Such then, briefly summarized, were the principal superstitions of the inhabitants of this coast, before the Incas had brought them under their laws.

Beyond the Ica and Pisco valleys, stretched the great and very powerful valley of the Chinchas, from which the Chinchasuyu district takes its name. Here it was that the Incas sent their messengers, after they had finished organizing these two new imperial territories.[20]

The Chinchas were so confident in the strength of their arms that they decided to defy the Inca. "We want neither your God nor your king," they replied to the messengers. "The sea is a much bigger thing than the sun, as anyone can see; and it benefits us greatly, whereas the sun only prostrates us with its burning rays; it is natural for you, who live in the mountains, to adore it, because it gives you warmth. But it is also quite as natural that we should prefer the sea, which is our mother. Tell your general, therefore, to return home and not to pick a quarrel with the king of the Chinchas, who is a very powerful lord. Otherwise, he will not have to look long for us, for we shall come and show him how we defend our freedom, our lord, and our faith."

As soon as they had been brought this reply, the Incas started out for Chincha. The enemy leader—who himself was called Chincha—came out from his territory to keep them from entering it. There were numerous skirmishes between the Incas and the Yuncas,[21] but no really serious fighting, the sandy terrain on which these operations took place making all maneuvering very awkward for both sides. Finally, the Yuncas were forced to retreat toward the mouth of their valley, which they made vain attempts to defend. But the Incas overran them, and the war immediately took on a savage, dogged character. There were dead and wounded on both sides: on the one hand, men were fighting to defend their country from invasion, and on the other, to enhance their Empire and their glory.

Two months passed without the Yuncas having shown the slightest sign of weakening. The moment had come, therefore, when, according to the Inca's plan, the second army was to relieve the first one. This operation was carried out punctually. The excessive heat in the lowlands presenting a risk that, after a while, endangered the young prince's life, the general took advantage of this occasion to send him back to the mountains with the first army. He also asked that a third army be raised immediately, to relay the second, in case the war should last more than two months.

With these fresh reserves, they continued to beleaguer the Chincha country. Finally, General Capac Yupanqui encircled the enemy troops and, on every side, had their harvests and crops destroyed, in order that through hunger, quite as surely as through the force of arms, they would be forced to surrender. With this same intention, he also had all the irrigation canals blocked, and indeed this was the worst blow of all for the Yuncas, because the earth is so dry in their country that it becomes barren again, if it is not irrigated at least every three days.

But the courage of the Yuncas did not falter, although they had lost all hope of seeing the Incas put to flight by the hardships of their climate. They continued fighting for two months longer, refusing to listen to the peace offers that General Capac Yupanqui sent them every week, and they now put all their hopes in their god Chincha Càmac, whom they considered to be their father. Indeed, the women prayed to him every day, with tears and sacrifices, imploring him to deliver them from the Incas.

This idol had the same importance among them as the invisible god Pachacamac, whom the Incas considered to be the creator of the universe, as we have already explained. The Chinchas having learned that the inhabitants of another big valley, about which we shall speak later, adored this same Pachacamac, and had constructed a magnificent temple in his honor, had concluded from this that if this god was in charge of the whole universe, he could not also take care of the Chinchas in the way they required. For this reason, they had had the idea of inventing another god, who would devote himself solely to their land, and this was the one they called Chincha Càmac.

And yet the Inca Capac Yupanqui began to consider that he was wasting his time and his reputation. He had certainly shown enough patience to conform with the traditions of gentleness and pity that were the rule among those of his line. He even became convinced that the mildness with which he had handled the enemy was being repaid by cruelty toward his own men, since this cruel climate constituted a greater threat to his soldiers every day. Finally, as a result of these reflections, he sent a message to General Chincha, informing him that he should surrender during the week that followed, and that if he did not do so, his entire people would have their heads cut off and new populations would occupy his land. The messengers who delivered this ultimatum were given orders to return without waiting for a reply.

Now the Yuncas grew frightened. For they had understood that the Inca was more than right, that he had exercised great patience, and had endured their obstinacy with great tolerance. They also realized that already, long ago, he could have brought the war to a bloody issue, instead of showing them such leniency; so they discussed all this among themselves, and came to the conclusion that it would be best not to irritate him further, but to surrender without delay. Upon which, they sent their ambassadors to beg Capac Yupanqui to pardon them and to welcome them among the Empire's vassals. They then promised that they would serve him henceforth as obstinately as they had fought him. The following day their curaca went in person, accompanied by all his lieutenants and his lords, to kiss the hands of General Capac Yupanqui.

The Inca general was very relieved to see the end of this war, which had caused him such great concern. The result was that he gave the Chincha curaca a hearty welcome. He told him to forget the past, which his brother the king had already banished from his memory. And, in order that this lord should understand that he was entirely forgiven, he gave him a quantity of presents, both for himself and for his people, on behalf of his brother the king. Thus, all the Yunca leaders returned home happy and confident.

These Chincha Indians still pride themselves today on the strong resistance with which their ancestors opposed the Incas, and, interpreting in their own manner the story of the two armies that relieved each other, they tell that it took two successive campaigns to conquer them. They are not the first, of course, to boast like this, after the worst is over.

They tell, too, that they were so powerful before they were integrated into the Empire, that they carried out frequent campaigns far from their own frontiers; that the mountain people held them in awe, and that more than once, they had advanced as far as the interior of the Colla province. All of this is untrue and will not bear scrutiny, because the Yuncas have always been so indolent that they could never have made the two hundred, or so, league journey, through more extensive, more densely populated provinces than their own, that separates their country from that of Colla. And what proves better than anything else that it is all nothing but idle bragging, is the fact that the Yuncas, who are accustomed to a dry, hot climate, entirely free of storms, are thrown into a panic when, if they happen to have ventured into the mountains, they suddenly hear the roll of thunder. Then, not knowing where to seek refuge, their only thought is to hasten back to their own homeland.

While the Chincha government was being organized, General Capac Yupanqui informed his brother of his victory and asked him to send him another army as soon as possible, in order that he might pursue his conquest of the Yuncas.

This, then, was how the Incas subjugated the Chincha valley, which their kings were to enhance so greatly. General Capac Yupanqui was severe only with the sodomites, who, alas, were very numerous there: he had them all assembled and burned alive, after which he had their houses razed to the ground, their fields destroyed, and the very trees they had planted dug up by the roots. Had it not been inhuman to do so, General Capac Yupanqui would have had their wives and children burned at the stake as well, so that no memory of this vice should remain; because the Incas held it in such abomination that merely to mention it was enough to make them forget their usual pity and generosity. They later, however, built a Sun temple and a convent for virgins, that housed more than thirty thousand persons and indeed, in all Peru, there undoubtedly exist few such marvelous valleys as this one. But in order not to weary my readers by continued accounts of Pachacutec's conquests—which were very numerous—I shall interrupt myself here to speak of the two principal feasts that these gentiles celebrated in honor of their god the Sun.

For the Indians, the word *Raïmi* had the same ring that

the word Easter has for us. Of the four solemn feasts that the Inca kings celebrated in Cuzco, which was another Rome, the most important was the one that was celebrated in June, and which they called *Inti Raïmi*. It was more generally referred to as *Raïmi*, and it took place at the time of the summer solstice.

This was the great feast of the heavenly body which they adored as the only universal god, whose light and virtue cause all things on earth to grow and to flourish.

Since the Sun was the natural father of the first Inca, as also of his sister-bride and the entire line of these rulers, said to have come down on earth for the good of mankind, this feast was more solemnly celebrated than any other.

All the curacas, all the lords, and all the great captains of the Empire met together at this time, not because they were obliged by law to do so, but because it was both a pleasure and an honor for them to participate in this great feast, and to adore their god at the same time that they worshiped their prince: and indeed, none failed to be present. If old age, illness, distance, or important government business kept a curaca from coming, he would delegate his brothers, his sons, and the most distinguished lords among his associates to go in his name.

The king always went in person, unless a war or some long journey kept him from doing so.

He himself accomplished the first rites, before the high priest, even though the latter was of his blood and his close relative, for the reason that it was meet and right that the king, who was the head of the dynasty, should be the first to pay homage to the father of all the Incas.

The curacas came to the ceremony in their finest array, with garments and headdresses richly ornamented with gold and silver.

Others, who claimed to descend from a lion, appeared, like Hercules himself, wearing the skin of this animal on their backs and on their heads, its head.

Others still, came got up as one imagines angels, with the great wings of the bird called condor, which they considered to be their original ancestor.[22] This bird is black and white in color, so large that the span of its wings can attain to fourteen or fifteen feet, and so strong that many a Spaniard met death in contest with it.

Others wore masks that gave them the most horrible faces imaginable, and naturally these were the Yuncas, who came to the feast with the heads and gestures of madmen or idiots. To complete the picture, they carried appropriate musical instruments, such as out-of-tune flutes and drums, with which they accompanied their antics.

All the curacas in the region came, too, decorated or made up to symbolize their armorial bearings. Each nation presented its weapons: bows and arrows, lances, darts, slings, maces and hatchets, both short and long, according to whether they used them with one hand or two.

They also carried paintings, representing feats they had accomplished in the service of the Sun and of the Inca, and a whole retinue of musicians played on the timpani and trumpets they had brought with them. In other words, it may be said that each nation came to the feast with everything that could serve to enhance its renown and distinction, and, if possible, its precedence over the others.

The Sun Raïmi was preceded by very strict fasting that lasted three days: water was the only drink permitted, and the only food was uncooked corn and a few handfuls of the plant they called *chucam.*[23] No fires were lighted in the entire city during this period, and the men abstained from all intercourse with their wives.

At the end of the fast, on the eve of the feast day, the Inca priests in charge of sacrificial rites were brought the rams and sheep, as well as all the food and drink that were to be offered up to the Sun. The curacas and ambassadors of the various nations participating were not the only ones responsible for these gifts, but also their relatives, their vassals, and all their subjects, because, in reality, all Peru was one people during this feast.

The wives of the Sun worked all night preparing great quantities of a sort of corn bread called *sancu,* which was in the form of little paste-balls the size of an apple. I should perhaps say, too, that the Indians only ate their wheat—or rather, their corn—in bread form on this occasion, and for another feast called *Citua.* At that, however, they only took two or three mouthfuls at the beginning of the meal and, ordinarily, they ate nothing but boiled or roasted corn, either in the grain, or in meal form.

The chosen virgins, or brides of the Sun, prepared the meal for this bread themselves, as well as all the meats that were to be presented to the Sun and to the Inca on that day. For they believed that it was the Sun who gave the banquet for his sons, and not the contrary. It was therefore the duty of his wives to prepare it.

A vast number of other women, chosen for this task, prepared the bread and other foods to be eaten by the people. But bread being a sacred thing, that could not be eaten except on this feast day, which was the greatest of all the feasts, only pure young girls could grind the meal for it.

The following day, which was the feast day, the Inca went out at dawn, accompanied by all his relatives, each one of whom was placed according to his age and rank. The procession walked in this order to the main square of the city, called Haucaipata, where they all took their shoes off and, turning to face the east, waited for the Sun to rise. As soon as this heavenly body appeared, they squatted down on their haunches—just as we go down on our knees—and worshiped him, with outspread arms and their hands lifted to their faces, blowing kisses into the air with warm marks of affection.

Since the curacas were not of royal blood, they gathered on another square, adjoining the first one, called *Cussipata,* where they adored the Sun with the same gestures. The king then rose, while the others remained crouching, and took in his hands two large bowls of *chicha,*[24] called *aquilla.*

It is a frequent custom to invite friends for a drink in Peru, and our lords themselves often offered a drink to their visitors, as a sign of approbation. Thus, the Inca, in the Sun's name, began by pouring the contents of the bowl he held in his right hand, into a gold basin connected directly with the house of the Sun by extremely well-made underground pipes; with the result that the liquid that had been poured into it disappeared as though the god-star had really drunk it. Then the Inca himself drank a draught from the other bowl, after which he divided the rest among the gold goblets being held out to him by his relatives. In this manner, this first beverage, which had been blessed, communicated its virtues to the prince and to all those of his blood. The curacas crouching on the other square were also given drinks, but their *chicha,* although it too came from the wives of the Sun, was not blessed like the first, which only the Incas had the right to drink.

The procession next headed for the house of the Sun and, at two hundred steps from this building, they all took their shoes off, except the king, who only took his sandals off at the temple door. He then passed through it, with those of his blood, and began to worship the image of the star. The curacas, who were considered to be unworthy to enter into so sacred a place, since they were not among the progeny of the god-star, remained on the outside, on a square that can still be seen today.

The king tendered the gold bowls that had been used during the first ceremony with his own hands; then the other Incas handed their goblets to the priests of royal blood who were assigned to the Sun's service, and they, in turn, presented them in the name of their relatives, before returning to the door of the temple, where all the curacas came, by order of seniority, to present their offerings. These did not consist only of gold and silver bowls and goblets, but also of a quantity of animals made of precious metals, such as ewes, lambs, toads, lizards, snakes, foxes, tigers, lions, and all sorts of birds, which represented, one might say, all that was typical in the different provinces.

Once the offerings had been made, each one returned to his place. Then the Inca priests brought in the animals to be sacrificed, which were lambs, rams and sterile ewes, chosen from the Sun's herds, the coats of which were as varied as those of Spanish horses.

The first animal sacrificed was always either a black or a dark brown lamb, these coats being considered as the only ones that were entirely pure and unmixed, and therefore preferred by the gods. Thus, they said, a white lamb that might well be considered to be without imperfections, is not so, since its muzzle is black. And that is also why the Inca kings so frequently wore dark garments.

They looked for omens and predicted the success of the feast by examining the heart and lungs of this lamb, as they did in all important circumstances, whether of peace or war, now with a lamb, now with a sheep, or with a sterile ewe.

Three or four men held the animal, with its head turned toward the east, without its having to be tied. They then slit it open on its left flank while it was still alive, and the priest, thrusting his hand into its body, took out the heart, lungs and all the interior organs, taking care that they should be whole and all in one piece, without being torn.[25]

If the lungs were still palpitating in broad daylight, there could be no better omen, and they looked no further for others: why continue, they said, since even if all the others were to indicate the contrary, all of them together would not suffice to destroy all the good fortune contained in the first one.

In order to continue their prophesying, they would blow air into the viscera; then, holding the end tight between their fingers, watch the way the air filled the lungs even to the tiniest vessels, and the more they blew, the better that omen became. There were many others, however, which I am unable to describe, since I did not take note of them.

The details given here were furnished me by two private sacrifices that I witnessed when I was quite young, among some unbaptized old Indians who, because I was a child, were not on their guard. It was already a long time since the feast of Raïmi had been celebrated, but the manner of interpreting omens being the same, whether the ceremony be public or private, what I was able to observe in this case, applies quite as well to the others.

If the animal broke away from those who were holding it, and stood up while it was being cut open, this incident was supposed to be a very bad omen. It was also considered to be bad when the viscera and lungs did not come out whole, which I remember well hearing said by the old Indians whom I watched performing these rites.

But to come back to the Raïmi, it should be added that sacrifice of the lamb, if it didn't give good omens, was followed by that of the sheep and, lastly, of a sterile ewe. Then, if this consultation was no more fortunate than the others, they celebrated the feast, none the less, only in sorrow and affliction, believing that the Sun was angry as the result of some mistake or negligence that may have been committed in its service, unwittingly; and all the Indians were fearful lest it should be followed by a hard war, or an epidemic that would decimate their herds, or a drought that would injure their crops.

After this consultation of omens, great sacrificial offerings were made, during which a quantity of lambs, sheep, and ewes were slaughtered. The blood, heart, and entrails of all these creatures were offered up to the Sun and, to this end, burned until nothing remained of them but ashes.

The fire used for this sacrifice had to be fresh or, as they said, given to them by the hand of the Sun. For this, they took a large bracelet, belonging to the high priest, and similar in form to that usually worn on their left wrists by the Incas. The central motif of this bracelet was a very carefully polished concavity as big as half an orange. They turned this to the Sun to capture its rays, which they then concentrated on a small wisp of very dry, fluffy cotton, that caught fire instantly.[26] This, then, was the origin of the fresh fire which, as I said before, served to burn the sacrifices offered to the Sun and to roast all the meats consumed on this feast day. They used it, too, to relight the fires both in the Temple of the Sun and in the convent for virgins, where the sacred flame was carefully tended throughout the year. If the sky was gray on the eve of the sacrifice, when they were making their preparations, the fire was lighted by means of two little sticks the size of one's little finger, which they rubbed against each other. These little sticks, called *u'yaca,* were to be found in every house, as well as in every traveler's bag, the way, in Spain, one finds pieces of flint and steel.

The flesh of the sacrificed animals was roasted in the open, on the two public squares, then divided among those who had been present at the ceremony, from the Incas right on down to the people, both of whom were given their share of meat and the piece of sancu bread we described earlier. This was the first course of their great feast and the beginning of their solemn banquet. Then came a quantity of other dishes which were eaten without any sort of beverage, as is the custom in Peru.

It is doubtless because of this that certain Spaniards have felt it their duty to affirm that the Incas and their vassals celebrated Holy Communion as Christians do: and certainly, every one has the right to understand and interpret in his own way the facts we have just described.

Later, when they had finished eating, drinks were served, because the Indians drank in the most incredible manner: indeed, drunkenness was certainly their commonest vice, although today, thanks to God's mercy and to the good examples furnished them by the Spaniards in this respect, there are no Indians left in Peru who get drunk, without their being put to shame, as though it were a great disgrace; and I shall add that if the same good example had been given them as regards all vices, today all the Indians would be apostles and would be preaching the Gospel.

Seated on his solid gold throne, raised on a dais of the same metal, the Inca sent his relatives from Hanan-Cuzco and Hurin-Cuzco to the principal representatives of the other Empire nations, to invite them to drink, in his name. He first invited all the captains who had distinguished themselves in recent wars, and even if they were not lords or vassals, on this occasion, they had precedence over the curacas. The curacas in the vicinity of Cuzco, who had received their power from the first Inca Manco Capac, were the next to be invited; it will be recalled that they had the title of Inca by privilege, and that their nation was preferred to all others.

In order to understand how this rite was observed, it should be pointed out that all the Indians in Peru had, and still have, drinking goblets that go in pairs, both of them absolutely identical in every respect, whether they are made of gold or silver, or simply of wood, and this was so that there should always be equality between the drinkers.[27]

If they wanted to invite someone, they took their two goblets, one in each hand, and handed the guest either the right or the left one, according to his rank, keeping the other for themselves; and, together, they drank equal quantities of the beverage served.

During the Raïmi feast, the Incas representing the king, addressed their guests as follows: "The king has invited you, and I have come in his name to drink with you."

The captain or the curaca who was the recipient of this honor, lifted his eyes toward the Sun, without a word, as though to thank the heavenly body for his good fortune, and drank the cup that was handed him, after having made a deep bow as he took hold of it.

It should be pointed out that the king invited all the captains to drink, in his own name, but not all the curacas, among whom only those who had served the people they administered with particular devotion were honored with this favor. The others also drank with certain Incas, but in this case these princes acted in their own name, not in that of the king.

Invitations to drink were returned by their recipients in the order in which they had been received, and those who had been invited by the king approached his throne, goblets in hand, to invite him, in their turn, without daring, however, to address a word to him. The king received them graciously, taking in his hand the goblets they held out to him. Raising them to his lips, he sometimes took a draught that was in proportion to his desire to honor his guest. He then handed the goblets, more than often still full, to one of the attendants to the throne, Incas by privilege, who drank in his name.

These goblets that had been touched by the hand and lips of the Inca, were considered, from that moment on, as sacred objects. Their fortunate possessors never used them again but kept them as idols, through which they worshiped him whose imprint the objects retained. All of which is proof that the love and veneration these Indians bore their prince was as deep-rooted as it was apparent.

After each guest had returned to his place, these first invitations to drink being ended, the entertainment began. The performances were composed of alternating songs and dances, each nation presenting, in contest, its most original features, while the public continued to extend invitations to drink among friends.

This feast lasted nine consecutive days, at the close of which the curacas, with the king's permission,[28] returned to their homelands, filled with joy and gratitude.

The Peruvian word *huaracu* corresponds exactly to our verb to *knight*, and it was applied, in fact, to the ceremony during which young men of royal blood received the insignia of virility without which they were not entitled to participate in either military or civilian life: until that time in other words, to borrow the language of chivalry and romance, they had been mere pages incapable of bearing arms.

The ceremony was preceded by an extremely severe novitiate, during which time these young men had to learn all the exercises and necessities of war, whether the fortunes of combat should be foul or fair. The day they were put to the test was a festive occasion, as much for the people as for the blooded nobility, and the honor or disgrace that awaited each novice was shared by his entire family; there was, consequently, not a single Inca who was not interested in it.

The novices, who had to have passed their sixteenth birthday, were gathered together every year, or every two years, in a special building, located in the Collcampata quarter, where older Incas, very well versed in the arts of peace and war, were in permanent residence as instructors. The tests began with a very strict fast that lasted six consecutive days, during which the novices lived on a small quantity of water and fresh herbs, with no condiments, and neither salt nor pepper. Except for the huaracu, such severe fasting as this was never authorized for more than three successive days and, if exceptionally, this period was doubled on this occasion, it was in order to be sure that these young men had really become men capable of facing all the ordeals that may result from the hazards of war. The father, brothers, and close relatives of each novice also fasted, albeit less strictly, and they prayed the Sun-god to help their kin, and to give him a stout heart. If any showed the slightest sign of weakening in the course of this test, or if he complained, or asked for food, he was immediately expelled from the novitiate.

The running test succeeded the fasting test, and, once they had taken nourishment again, the novices had to run from the mountain called Huanacauri (which was holy ground) to the Cuzco fortress, which meant running about a league and a half. The victor in the race was named captain of the novices, and the following nine also received an award of honor. During the entire period relatives, massed on either side of the road, encouraged their boys out loud, telling them it were better to drop dead at the end of the race than to faint on the way.

Another time they were divided into two camps, the first of which took up quarters in the fortress, while the second tried to dislodge them from it. The struggle lasted all one day, and started again on the following day, with the roles reversed, that is to say, the attackers becoming the defenders and the defenders, the attackers; in this way, each group could show its good qualities in both situations. Although they were given special weapons, less dangerous than those used in actual war, there was no lack of wounded, and, sometimes, even dead, during these exercises, so ardently and determinedly did these young men compete for victory.

They were also made to wrestle with each other, after being matched according to age, and practiced as well jumping, discus throwing, lancing, and the use of all propulsive weapons. They shot at a target with bows and arrows, or with slings, for which tests of range succeeded those of aim. In other words, they were examined in the manipulation of all the weapons of war. They had to do ten to twelve consecutive nights of sentinel duty, to show their capacity to resist falling asleep, and if one of them was caught, during the most dubious hours of the night, with drooping eyelids while he was on guard, he was harshly scolded and told that he was a boy who was not worthy of the virile insignia. They were beaten hard on the arms and legs, with cane whips, to test their resistance to pain, and a boy who manifested the slightest sign of suffering was pitilessly banished: "How will you resist the enemy's relentless weapons," he was told, "if you are incapable of standing the caress of this gentle switch!" Indeed, they were obliged to appear totally without feeling.

At other times, they were stood side by side on a street along which the fencing captain was advancing toward them, carrying a sort of two-handed sword called a *macana*,[29] or pike. This man, who was an artist in the use of his weapon, would then begin to cut and thrust about him, twirling it between them, in such a way that it looked as though he must inevitably put out one man's eye, cut off another's head, or break somebody's leg. And if one of the young men gave the slightest sign of apprehension, either by blinking an eye or moving a leg, he was banished from the contest, on the theory that a man who is afraid of what he knows to be only a feint will never be capable of facing a real threat. They were, therefore, obliged to submit to this test without flinching, remaining quite motionless, like rocks in the ocean under the onslaught of wind and wave.

They were also obliged to know how to make their offensive weapons with their own hands, in any case, those which, like bows and arrows, wood or stone lances, or slings, did not demand the help of a smithy. As regards defensive arms, they were only familiar with one, the shield, which they called *huallcanca,* manufacture of which they also had to master. Lastly, they learned to make their own shoes, called *usuta,* which were made of a leather or string sole, tied to the ankle by a little cord, like Spanish sandals or, better still, like the open shoes worn by Franciscan monks.

Every day, one of the captains or teachers in this school

lectured to the novices. He reminded them of the history of the Incas and of the exploits of their ancestors, explaining to them the amount of courage and tenacity that must needs mark all wars fought to enlarge the Empire; the patience, generosity, clemency, and mildness required to administer all matters and especially those that concerned either the poor, or newly conquered populations; the uprightness without which there can be no justice; the liberality and magnificence toward all that the descendants of the Sun owed to themselves as well as to their forefathers. In short, he taught them everything in the way of moral philosophy that a people who believe themselves to be of divine essence, descended from heaven, can have attained to. The novices were obliged to sleep on the bare ground, eat little and poorly, and walk barefoot, as any good soldier must be able to do.

The crown prince passed all of these tests, like all the other Incas, when he reached the required age. He was treated just as strictly as the others, and there was no work from which his rank exempted him; indeed, the only privilege that distinguished him was the fact that, after the running contest, he received the flag that the winner was given at the entrance to the fortress, it being considered that this flag devolved upon him by divine right, in the same way as the throne. Except for this detail, the crown prince was treated with the same severity as the others, if not more harshly still, because, it was felt, if he was to be the greatest of all, he should become that in all things.

The novitiate lasted one entire lunar month, and during this time, the prince was dressed only in rags, like the poorest inhabitant of the Empire, and he even appeared in public like that every time his work obliged him to do so. Thus, it was said, when, later, he would be accompanied by all the pomp of royalty, he would not feel contempt for wretched people, recalling that he himself had once worn their mean attire: also he would deserve the genial title of *huachacuyac,* or friend to the poor, that was given the Inca kings.

At the end of their novitiate, the young men were given their virile insignia and the title of true Inca, descended from the Sun. Their mothers and sisters then came to tie on their new sandals, which denoted that they had met with success the hard tests of the novitiate.

The king then came and made them a short speech in which he exhorted them to understand that the title they had now acquired did not exempt them from persevering in their efforts, or continuing on the path of virtue; on the contrary. When he had finished his speech, the novices knelt down before him, one after the other, to receive from his hand the first and principal mark of their rank, which was to have their ears pierced. And, in fact, the Inca pierced their lobes himself, at the point where, in Spain, earrings are fixed to the ears, with big gold needles, that were left there some time, so that the wounds might heal without closing and the lobes grow longer, which they did, in the most incredible manner.

The young man then rose, kissed the hand of the king who had so honored him, then passed on to another Inca, either a brother or uncle of the king, and the highest dignitary after him. The latter untied his novice's sandals and put finer ones on him, made of soft wool, like those worn by the king and the other Incas. Concerning this detail of the ceremony, one might say that it is similar to the awarding of spurs in European chivalry. After having taken off the young man's shoes, the Inca kissed his right shoulder, saying, "The son of the Sun, who gave such proof of his worth, deserves to be adored"; because to kiss, to adore, and to pay obeisance were, for them, the same thing. Then the novice went into an enclosure where other dignitaries invested his nakedness with the *huara,* which was the sign of virility that he had not yet worn. This was a three-pointed piece of cloth or linen, one point of which hung over the belly, to hide the shameful parts, while the other two were fixed to a cord that went round the hips and was tied in a knot in the small of the back. The first point was then passed between the thighs, and knotted in the back to the two others, in such a way that, if the Inca undressed, he remained, nevertheless decently and sufficiently clad.

If ear-piercing, being a royal attribute, was the first sign, the *huara,* which denoted virility, was the second, and the rest was less important, being composed in reality merely of prizes that had no direct significance as regards either honor or quality. It should, moreover, be stated that the word *huarasca* comes from *huara,* which is sufficient indication of the importance the question of puberty plays in this tradition.

The new Incas were next crowned with very lovely

yellow and red flowers, of two species, called *cantut* and *chihuaihua*,[30] use of which was strictly reserved for men of royal blood. Their hair was also decorated with a green leaf, called the *uinay huaina*,[31] which means "forever young." It has the shape of a lily leaf, and stays green, even after it has been dried.

The crown prince received the same insignia as his companions of the novitiate. Later, his brow was encircled, from one temple to the other, with the yellow bandeau made of fringe about four fingers long, which was the sign of his caste. Lastly, he was given a battle-axe with a very long handle, called *champi*. This was a sort of halberd, finished on one side with a sharp point and on the other by a keen-edged blade. As it was handed him, the word "*Aucacunapac*" was spoken, which, in its dative form, meant: against tyrants, traitors, cruel men, and all that is meant by the word *auca*. The prince's uncles and brothers, then all those of his blood, next came to kneel before him and worship him as their future king. It was at this moment that he was given the yellow bandeau which consecrated definitively his titles and prerogatives. Thus ended the solemn feast during which the Incas dubbed their new knights.[32]

I told in my first book how the first royal insignia was a bandeau, not yellow, like the crown prince's, but scarlet. I shall add that the Inca had on his head another ornament that was peculiar to him, which consisted of two feathers from the wing of a bird called in Peru *corequenque*.[33] These feathers were mixed black and white, and resembled in size the feathers of a swallow hawk. In fact, they had to be twin feathers, that is, one had to come from one wing, and one from the other. I saw them worn by the Inca Sairi Tupac. These birds may be found in the Ulicanuta desert, thirty-two leagues from Cuzco, on a small lagoon that exists at the foot of the inaccessible Sierra Nevada, and it is said that no one has ever seen more than one couple of them. Nor does anyone know where they come from, or where they lay, or raise their young. It seems to me that this bird must be like the phoenix, although I don't know who has ever seen a phoenix, whereas people really have seen swallow hawks.

The rarity of these birds was what gave their great value to the two feathers and the Incas considered them as sacred, for the reason that like their own ancestors, the first two Incas, they formed a unique couple that one might well believe had come down from heaven. They therefore wore the feathers of one of these couples in order to honor and recall the memory of the other. As for myself, I think there must exist somewhere other specimens of these birds, because such singularity is impossible. However, so much for the phoenix.

Many Indians today wear these *corequenque* feathers, pretending to be descendants of the Incas. And this makes me laugh, because I have every reason to know that the royal line is extinct. But the foreign example of flourish and ostentation has been so frequent in Peru that, today, nearly everybody is supposed to be of either Inca or palla descent.

Our kings, then, wore these two feathers above their scarlet bandeaux, the two quills together at the base, and the ends spread apart at the top. When a new Inca came into power, an expedition was organized to obtain these two feathers for him, because he could not use those of his predecessors, since the dead kings were embalmed with all their personal insignia, including the two feathers they had worn during their entire reign. All of these details will perhaps seem quite futile to persons in Spain, but I make a point of telling them, because they are necessary in order to understand our former kings and their majesty.

But to finish with the ceremony during which the young Incas were knighted, I should add that, after the award of their insignia, they went in their new garb to the main square of the city, and there was carousing, both there and in private houses, for several days, with much singing and dancing, in celebration of their success. The most eager to honor them were the members of their own families, the same who, the day before, had been their drillmasters and their most merciless critics during the tests that had made of them real fighters and men worthy of the name.

It should be recalled, returning to the history of Inca Pachacutec's reign and conquests, that his brother, General Capac Yupanqui, after having subjugated the great curaca Chincha, had asked the king for a new army, in order to make his way towards other valleys. The Prince Inca

Yupanqui, who had a real taste for the military profession, returned with very well equipped new troops and abundant supplies. The general then decided to conquer the beautiful valley of Runahuanac, which was very populous, as was also the Huarcu valley that prolongs it toward the north; indeed, there were, at that time, thirty thousand inhabitants in this region which, today, is nothing but desert.

These two valleys, as well as the Malla and Chilca valleys, that are situated farther north, were united under the authority of a lord named Chuquimancu,[34] whose conduct was that of a king, and who was convinced that he was feared and dreaded by all his neighbors, even though they were not his vassals. When he learned of the Inca's approach, he collected as many men as he could and advanced to the very swift river that protects the entrance to his kingdom, in order—as he said—to prevent access to it. There were several encounters, with losses in human life on both sides, but the Incas ended by crossing the river on rafts. On this occasion Chuquimancu did not put up as great a resistance as he might have, in the idea that he would do better to attack the imperial forces farher down in the Huarcu valley. He had cause to rue this decision, however, for, less than a month later, the Incas having conquered the whole beautiful Runahuanac valley, came and attacked him in Huarcu, where the fighting became exceedingly cruel, Chuquimancu having assembled at this point all his forces, amounting to more than twenty thousand men. The struggle lasted more than eight months, and the Incas were obliged to renew their armies three times, if not four, as some people say. In order to make it clear to the enemy that they considered themselves to be on their own territory and would not leave until they had conquered it, the Incas called their general headquarters by the name of Cuzco and their other positions by the names of the principal suburbs of the capital. This explains why Pedro de Cieza de Leon, who obtained his information from the Yuncas, tells in his sixty-third chapter that the Incas founded a second Cuzco there, and that they continued to fight for more than four years. The persons who told him this story arranged it in favor of their camp, and the four years they talk of were, in reality, the four Inca armies that succeeded one another in these parts until victory was achieved.

After eight months of fighting, the Yuncas began to feel

the pangs of the cruelest sort of hunger, an ordeal that breaks down even the most tenacious of resolutions. For a long time already, Chuquimancu's subjects had been urging him to surrender, before the Incas should take all their land and possessions to give to the Chinchas—who were their hereditary enemies—to punish them for their obstinacy.

These two reasons, and fear lest his subjects should abandon him and join the Inca camp, finally weakened Chuquimancu's will. He therefore consulted his captains and decided, in agreement with them, not to send a mission to the Inca, but to go himself with his counselors.

The Incas, both uncle and nephew, received the surrender of this lord and his vassals with their traditional graciousness, gave them immediate assurance of their forgiveness, and made them numerous presents which completely reassured them, with the result that Chuquimancu and his men returned home quite delighted.

In order to perpetuate the memory of this important conquest, the Incas had a large fortress built on a small site in the Huarcu valley, which was marvelous both in design and execution. The waters of the sea dashed against the foot of the walls, and it really deserved to last forever. I saw it in 1560, when it still had such a proud look that one could only be moved to sorrow to see it so abandoned.

The Inca army decided to pursue its campaign in the direction of six beautiful valleys, among them the Pachamac, Rimac, Chancay, and Huaman valleys, all of which belonged to one very powerful lord named Cuismancu who, like Chuquimancu, had assumed the title of king.[35]

It should be pointed out, as regards these valleys, that the word *Rimac,* corrupted by the Spaniards, has become the name *Lima.*

I have already said that the Incas, according to the lights God had granted them, were not ignorant of the fact that there existed a universal creator, whom they called Pachacamac.[36] Indeed it was because they had understood that this supreme God is invisible and does not desire to be seen, that they never edified a temple to him, as they did to the Sun, but were content to adore him in the secret recesses of their hearts. This belief spread rapidly through all Peru, among the non-subject peoples as well as among those who had accepted the laws of the Empire, and was particularly deep-rooted in the big valleys by the sea, among the predecessors of Cuismancu; which explains why the principal territory belonging to this lord, at the time of my tale, was called Pachacamac. It supported a very large temple, built in honor of this supreme God, and in which the Yuncas had erected their customary idols: the fox and the fish. I shall speak further on of Pachacamac, but I only want to say that, in this temple, which was the only one in Peru dedicated to him, and one of the most famous in the entire country before the conquest of this valley by the Incas, numerous sacrifices, both animal and human, were offered.

The Rimac [37] valley lies four leagues north of Pachacamac, and the word *rimac* means "he who speaks." In this valley there was an idol with a human face which was said to reply to the questions asked it, like the Delphic oracle, and from this the valley took its name. After the Incas conquered the valley, they continued to respect this idol, which was deeply revered by the Yuncas. Thus, it was here that the Spaniards founded the capital city of Lima, which they called the City of Kings, because it was founded on the day of our Lord's appearance.[38] In other words, Rimac, Lima and the City of Kings are one and the same place; its shield bears three crowns and a star.

The temple of this idol was very magnificent (although it was in no way equal to the Pachacamac temple) and all the lords in Peru sent messengers to consult it about their fates. Spanish historians, however, have confused these two temples, and say that there was an oracle at Pachacamac. This may be explained by their slight knowledge of the Peruvian language.[39]

But to return to this campaign, we shall mention that General Capac Yupanqui sent messengers to King Cuismancu before entering his territory, calling on him to surrender to the laws of the Empire and not to attempt to resist him.

The great lord Cuismancu, having been warned of the Inca advance, received their ambassadors, surrounded by his court and his captains, all of whom were on a war footing. He rejected their summons, saying that he worshiped Pachacamac, creator of all things, and consequently, greatly superior in divinity to the Sun; that no one could point to a more fervent, more respectful cult than the one they practiced toward this supreme God, to whom no one dared raise his eyes inside the temple, and to whom animals, men, women and children were frequently offered up in sacrifice; that he also worshiped the all-powerful oracle of Rimac whom people from all Peru came to consult. And the fox, whose wiles are proverbial. And *mamacocha,* the ocean mother, who fed all her people with her fish. And that, lastly, neither he nor any of his followers had any need to worship the Sun, which only gave them excessive, pitiless heat. That, therefore, he begged the Inca to leave them free, him and his peoples, because they wanted none of his Empire and his laws.

The Incas were very happy to learn that the Yuncas adored the great God Pachacamac whom, in their hearts, they too revered. So they decided to attract them through reason and fair promises, without using force, unless it should become indispensable. They therefore entered into the Pachacamac valley[40] and King Cuismancu went forth to meet them with his army, determined to drive them out of his territory. But General Capac Yupanqui immediately sent fresh emissaries who explained to him that the Incas had been very happy to learn that the Yuncas revered the great God Pachacamac for whom they themselves had such respect that they dared not speak his name; that they also respected the Rimac oracle, and that they were ready to worship and revere it as the Yuncas did, if only the Yuncas would accept, in exchange, to worship the Sun, which, because of its light and resplendent beauty, deserved this much more than a fox, a fish, or any other animal. Lastly, as a token of peace and friendship, the general asked Cuismancu to obey the Inca, his lord and brother, son of the Sun, and God's vicar on earth. Extolling the kindness, the gentleness, and the innumerable merits of their king, whom so many peoples obeyed already, to the happiness of them all, the ambassadors concluded by praying the great lord Cuismancu and his captains to give calm, dispassionate consideration to all that, and to make the reply that their reason dictated, when they so desired.

There was a truce of several days, and King Cuismancu and his followers, yielding to the persuasiveness of the Incas, decided to accept what had been proposed to them. Peace was therefore concluded on the following terms:

The Yuncas would worship the Sun as the Incas did.

The palace mayor in Hanan Cuzco

The grand alguazil in Hurin Cuzco

The provincial corregidor

The provincial administrator

The royal courier (Hatun Chasqui)

Those-who-mark-the-frontiers

The inspector of the roads

The inspector of the bridges

The secretary of the Inca

The grand treasurer, keeper of accounts

The traveling inspector of the Empire

The Tahuantinsuyu supreme council

They would build a temple and make sacrifices to it, without ever, however, offering up human beings, which is against the law of nature. They would destroy all the idols of the Pachacamac temple, since their very presence reduced the majesty of this supreme God who should only be worshiped in the secrecy of each man's heart.

They would build a convent for virgins in the Pachacamac valley. King Cuismancu would retain his government, while acknowledging himself to be the Inca's vassal in the same way as all the other Empire princes. He would obey his laws and customs and, on the other hand, the Incas would esteem and revere the Rimac oracle, and order it to be respected and revered in all their kingdoms.

Once these agreements had been concluded and garrisons had been established to watch over the new conquests, General Capac Yupanqui decided to return to Cuzco with the prince his nephew and King Cuismancu, in order that the king his brother should meet this new ally and thank him in person, since he was a friend who had freely joined the Empire, and not a conquered prince. Cuismancu was delighted to kiss the hand of the Inca and to visit the famous city of Cuzco, so they set forth.

King Pachacutec, who had been back in his capital for some time, came out in person from Cuzco to meet his brother and his son, with all desirable pomp. There was a moment of particular triumph when the king ordered Cuismancu to walk in procession among the Incas of royal blood, because, like themselves, he worshiped Pachacamac; and this was such an exceptional favor that this lord was an object of jealousy on the part of all the other curacas in the Empire. He then returned to his own country, with all the members of his suite, who, from that moment on, did not cease to praise the great merits of the Inca.

THE GREAT OFFICIALS OF THE EMPIRE

(See pages 235-237)

The mayor of the palace, or alcalde *of the court: "This is a great lord chosen among the Incas of Hanan-Cuzco or Hurin-Cuzco, or among the leading caciques . . . he carries out the orders of the royal council of the Inca."*

The grand alguazil, a Hurin-Cuzco Inca: "He is called Uauatay-

camayoc; he is always chosen among the loyal Hanan-Cuzco, Hurin-Cuzco, Anta, or Quilliscancha Incas, or from the sons of the lords of the province of Huanacu, and never from anywhere else." When he goes on a mission, he takes as his insignia the Inca's coca pouch.

The provincial corregidor: *He is chosen from among those "with the pierced ears."*

The provincial administrator: "They were the sons of the great lords of these kingdoms; they were given responsibilities so that they would learn how to work, to keep accounts and to take command, and govern upon their father's death; this is why no man of lowly birth was ever appointed to such a post."

The greater and lesser couriers, or hatun *and* hurin chasqui: *"They were the sons of curacas; each one had a headdress of white feathers to enable the next chasqui to see him from a distance, and a trumpet known as* putoto *to call him, so that he would be ready; he ate at the Inca's depots."*

Those-who-marked-the-frontiers: "They put up boundary stones all around the Empire, from the seashore to the cordillera, by order of Tupac Inca Yupanqui."

The inspector or governor of the royal roads: "In Inca days, there were six royal roads, each governed by an Inca." (Note 13, Book IX)

The inspector or governor of the bridges: "All the bridges were governed by a chief Inca throughout the kingdom."

The secretary of the Inca in his royal council: The Inca had his secretary and so did the council, "and also His Excellency the viceroy, second to the Inca."

The grand treasurer, keeper of accounts: "He was a captain's son; his skill at counting with the quipu or with quinoa *seeds was greater than it would have been with paper and ink. He counted by hundreds of thousands, thousands, hundreds, tens, and units: everything that went on in the kingdom—feasts, holy days, months, years, and every Indian town and village." (Note 25, Book II)*

The traveling inspector of the Empire: "They were employed to inspect all the tambos *in the kingdom, the* acllacona *convents, the storehouses and all public property." They were known as "those-who-see-everything."*

The supreme council of the kingdom: the illustration shows the Inca surrounded by the governors of the four divisions of the Tahuantinsuyu. "There were two Hanan-Cuzco Incas, two Hurin-Cuzco Incas and four great Chinchasuyu lords, two Antisuyu lords, four Collasuyu lords, and two Cuntisuyu lords. These were the lords of the royal council and when one of them could not attend he sent his son or his brother. Poor men or men other than of the ruling caste were never elected to the council."

But the temple of Pachacamac was no sooner rid of the idols it had been cluttered with, than the demon entered there. He began to talk to the high priests, in every nook and corner of the temple, telling them that he was the invisible, supreme God, that the idol of Rimac was his subject, that it was he, Pachacamac, whom henceforth they must consult on all important matters, and that, meanwhile, in the future, he was going to order his slave, Rimac, to answer the questions put to him by the common people only. And that is why, since that time, such has been the situation, as has been noted by Father Blas Valera.

The Inca Pachacutec decided to grant his people a little rest, after they had successfully achieved these numerous conquests, so there followed a few years of peace, during which the king and his suite did nothing but enhance the beauty of the Empire and improve its laws, for the well-being of all. Then it was that the walls of the temple were paneled with gold plaques, in addition to all its altars and a small cloister that still exists today, and which, after having been covered with gold and precious stones, has attained to the greatest of all riches, which is not material but spiritual; it being here that, today, the Holy Sacrament is exposed, and also that our processions and other sacred feasts take place. Glory be to God and to His Eternal Majesty, for all His mercies! This is the Convent of San Dominique.[41]

Six years of peace had gone by when King Pachacutec, seeing his subjects prosperous and rested, assembled thirty thousand fighting men to go to subdue the valleys that separated the most recently conquered coastal provinces from Cajamarca, where the Empire finished then, with the cordillera of the Andes. He gave command of the army to his son, Prince Yupanqui, who had acquired sufficient knowledge of the arts of war under his uncle Capac Yupanqui's schooling to be in a position to accept this important office, with the addition of six experienced camp commanders. As for Capac Yupanqui, whom his brother esteemed so highly that he called him his right hand, he remained in Cuzco, with the title of king's lieutenant and such great powers that, after the king, he was the highest ranking man in the Empire.

The prince went first to the province of Yauyu, near the City of Kings, accompanied by one third of his army. Then, after all his forces had joined him, he continued his march as far as Rimac. The great curacas Chuquimancu and Cuismancu came out to meet him with troops they had levied, like good vassals, to help him with his campaign. He thanked them, heaped gifts upon them, and visited the Pachacamac temple, then the Sun temple, where abundant sacrifices of gold and silver were being offered up. Respectful of their peace conditions, the prince next went to visit the idol of Rimac to which he offered sacrifices. He had it consulted on the subject of his campaign and, the oracle having given a favorable reply, he continued his way as far as the Huamam valley, which the Spaniards call La Barranca. It was from there that he sent his ambassadors to the lord of Chimu, who reigned over numerous valleys, from La Barranca to the city of Trujillo. In addition to the Chimu valley, properly speaking, there were the Parmunca, Huallmi, Santa, and Huanapu valleys, all of them extremely rich and populous, without counting others of lesser importance.[42]

The great Chimu replied to the Inca's messengers that he would defend his kingdom arms in hand, and that he wanted neither new laws nor new gods. This meant war. And despite all the efforts of the Yuncas, the imperial army forced its way into the province of Parmunca and settled there.[43] Prince Yupanqui immediately sent a messenger to his father, asking for reinforcements of twenty thousand men, in order that the sight of a greater mass of troops should weaken the resistance of the enemy, who appeared to be bolder and more arrogant than all those they had fought thus far.

The war was a very bloody one. The lords of Pachacamac and Runahuanac had not forgotten all the cruelty they had once suffered at the hands of the great Chimu, before they had gone over to the side of the Incas, with the result that they attacked him with great doggedness. The Yuncas were obliged to abandon successively the Parmunca and Huallmi valleys, in order to retrench themselves in the Santa valley, which was perhaps the most beautiful on the entire coast at that time, whereas today it is nothing but a desert.

The inhabitants of Santa were particularly brave, and

they fought with such ardor that they won the respect of their own adversaries. Their lord, the great Chimu, was so elated and hopeful as a result that he persuaded himself that Prince Yupanqui would be the first to grow weary of this cruel war and would soon return to the comforts of his court life, with the result that he refused to listen to the peace proposals that the Incas continued to make to him. On the contrary, he levied fresh troops in the other valleys of his kingdom, and the war became more and more pitiless; each one saw no other end than his own victory; there were quantities of dead on both sides; and indeed, it was the most costly campaign the Incas had yet conducted.

Just as the war was becoming more and more terrible, the twenty thousand relief troops arrived at Prince Yupanqui's camp. This was a cruel disillusionment for the great Chimu, and his arrogance began to change into melancholy when he realized that the sight of these reinforcements had discouraged his men. At the same time, a deputation of his relatives came to see him to urge him to conclude peace before the Incas had led away into slavery all their women and children, as they had started to do, and before, indeed, there should not be a man left alive in their valleys.

Our brave Chimu, being unwilling to accept the arguments of his relatives, merely felt that he was being abandoned by his own people at a time when the enemy had never been so powerful. He decided, therefore, that he was lost, and, in his own heart, made up his mind that he would accept the first proposals the Inca made him, without, however, going so far as to, himself, beg for peace, which seemed to him to be contrary to his honor.

Hiding his decision from his relatives, he replied that he lacked neither strength nor courage, and that he would eventually succeed in repulsing the invader. "The fortunes of war are subject to change," he added, "and the loss of a battle can well precede victory. If the enemy carries off your women, think of all those you yourselves have taken away in our former campaigns. The enemy has always seen you proud, bold and courageous: act in such a way that this may still be so, and let not your spirits be prey to discouragement; go now in peace, and know that the fate of my subjects is of greater concern to me than my own fate."

But all that was more words than fact, and our great Chimu remained deeply distressed, for he had no more hope. He put on as good a face as he could, however, and pursued the war until new envoys of the Inca came to propose peace, pardon, and friendship on the part of their master.

Here again, he put on a bold face, and replied haughtily that, as for himself, there could be no question of his agreeing to any discussion, but that, for the welfare of his people, he would consult his advisers before giving his reply. He immediately called together his captains and his relatives and transmitted to them the Inca's proposal, adding that he was willing to accept it if they were satisfied, although it was not in accordance with his will.

The captains, who were happy to see their lord's inflexible will finally yield, dared to reply resolutely that one was obliged to obey and acknowledge as one's lord so magnanimous and lenient a prince as the Inca, who offered his friendship at a moment when they were at his mercy.

Having understood from their tone that his advisers had now abandoned the humility of vassals for the audacity of free men, the powerful Chimu sent his ambassadors to Prince Yupanqui, to beg for pardon and mercy, adding that he felt confident that His Highness, who so prized his fair name of friend and benefactor to the poor, would surely not reject his plea, and, even more surely, pardon his subjects who were less to blame than he, since they had merely obeyed the orders that had been dictated by his own mad obstinacy.

The prince gave a kindly welcome to Chimu's ambassadors, and sent back a reply to the effect that they should go and fetch their lord, in order that he might receive from the Inca's own hand and mouth the pardon he had sued for.

Casting all pride aside, our worthy Chimu threw himself on the ground and implored the prince with as much humility and submissiveness as his ambassadors had shown. In order to relieve the great distress in which he saw Chimu plunged, the prince spoke to him in the gentlest of manners and ordered that he should be helped to his feet by two of his captains. He forgave him all the past, spared him his land, and assured him that he would retain authority over it, to the extent that he would banish his idols of fish and animals, worship the Sun and serve the Inca, his father.

Having found comfort in these words, Chimu began to worship the Inca, and replied that the only thing he would regret all his life was not to have listened earlier to the words of this lord; that, for the rest, he would thenceforth do as the Inca ordered him in all things, not with sorrow, but with love.

And so peace was concluded. The prince visited his new provinces and had them enriched by new irrigation canals, similar to those that existed in other parts of the Empire. He was especially solicitous about the Parmunca valley, where he built a fortress in memory of this violent war, that was to remain unforgettable.

He then returned to Cuzco, leaving the great Chimu very satisfied with his fate. The prince was welcomed back in the capital with great pomp, and his victory was celebrated for an entire month.

At this point, the Inca Pachacutec being aware of advancing age, decided to put a halt to his conquests. He had enlarged his Empire more than one hundred leagues from north to south, and from east to west, along the sixty or seventy leagues that separate, according to the place, the coast from the cordillera of the Andes. He therefore devoted himself to ratifying the laws of his ancestors and promulgating new ones for the well-being of his subjects.

He also transplanted numerous populations to found villages on erstwhile fallow land that he had rendered fertile through irrigation.

He constructed Sun temples and convents for virgins like those in Cuzco, and he increased the number of warehouses for stocking arms, equipment, and supplies, on all the roads in the Empire.

One might say, in fact, that he renewed his Empire in every respect, improving the habits and customs of his vassals, and abolishing many abuses and barbarous customs that the Indians had retained from their past life.

He reformed the army and created new honors for those who had distinguished themselves in battle. But he particularly enhanced the beauty of the great city of Cuzco, where he had a new palace built for his own use, near the schools founded by his great-grandfather, Inca Roca. The result of all this was that he was adored like a latter-day Jupiter. His reign, according to some, lasted more than fifty years, and more than sixty, according to others. And when he came to die, he was universally mourned throughout the Empire, and his body was embalmed, as was the custom. The entire Empire was in mourning for him for a whole year.

He left as his heir and successor, a son, Inca Yupanqui, born of Colla Anahuarque, his sister and legitimate bride. Tradition adds that he had more than four hundred children, both legitimate and bastard—which is not many, say the Indians, for such a man.

Speaking of this Inca's reign, Father Blas Valera has the following to say:

"He passed many laws, all of which were ratified by our Catholic kings, except for those having to do with idolatry and illicit marriage. He took particular interest in enhancing and enlarging the schools that the Inca King Roca had founded in Cuzco and ordered not only that all the inhabitants of the Empire, whatever their estate, should know the language spoken in Cuzco, but also that none should be allowed to occupy a position of importance who did not speak it very fluently. He appointed teachers for the sons of princes and noblemen, in Cuzco, as well as in all the provinces, in order that this language should be taught everywhere in the same manner. Thus, in this way, the entire kingdom of Peru spoke one and the same language: which, as a result of our negligence, is no longer the case today, to the great detriment of the spread of the gospel. And all the Indians who, till this day, have retained this teaching, are more capable and more courteous than the others.

"He forbade anyone, with the exception of the princes and their sons, to wear gold and silver, precious stones, the feathers of certain birds, or garments made of vicuña wool. He also forbade people to wear any but their everyday clothes, except on feast days and on the days of the new Moon. Overeating was forbidden, and he appointed special judges for the repression of vagrancy and idleness. It was his wish that no one in the entire Empire should remain unoccupied and that even little children, from the age of five or six years, should work at something; the same thing applied to the blind, the halt, and the dumb. As for the aged, they were fed from state warehouses, on condition that they drive the birds from the fields in which seed had been sown.[44] However, in order that the people should not be overtired, he ordered that there should be three days of rest and feasting every month, and every nine days he organized fairs to encourage the peasants to come to the city and thus learn what had been ordered by the king or by his council.

"He legislated against blasphemy, parricide, fratricide, homicide; cases of treason, adultery, kidnaping, rape; against those who dared touch the virgins in the convents, against robbery, arson, and linear incest. He enacted a quantity of other laws as well, all of which were very reasonable. Indeed, the admiration of the Indians for this king was such that, even today, they have not forgotten him."

In other of Father Blas Valera's papers, I have found a few sayings of the Inca Pachacutec,[45] such as the following:

Envy is a worm that gnaws and consumes the entrails of ambitious men.

To envy or to be envied is a source of two-fold torment.

If others envy you, it is because you are good; if you envy others, it is because you are bad.

He who envies the happiness of others derives from it only evil, like the spider which, from a flower, derives poison.

Drunkenness, anger, and madness go together; but the first two are a matter of will and may therefore be changed; whereas the last is for all time.

He who attacks the life of another without authority or just cause, condemns himself to death.

A noble, courageous man is recognizable by the patience he shows in adversity.

Impatience is the sign of a mean, low heart, that is underbred and full of bad habits.

Judges who allow a plaintiff to visit them in secret must be considered as thieves and punished with death.

Governors must never forget that he who is unable to run his own house and family, is still less competent to be entrusted with public matters.

He who pretends to be counting the stars, when he doesn't know how to count the knots of a quipu, deserves to be jeered at.

Such, then, were a few of Inca Pachacutec's sayings.

1. According to Cieza de Leon: ". . . Moreover, they say that in this building known as *tambo,* and in others of the same name, for it is not the only one to be so called, in certain parts of the king's palace, or of the Temple of the Sun, molten gold has been found in place of mortar, mixed with bitumen to hold the stones together." (Cieza, Part I, Chapter 94)

   This rumor has never yet been scientifically confirmed. It must be regarded as a legend unless some new archaeological discovery confirms it.

   With regard to Cieza's remark concerning the word *tambo,* it should be remembered that it applies to the state storehouses, situated at intervals along the roads of Tahuantinsuyu.

2. As was the custom of his day, Garcilaso normally spoke of the llamas of Peru as sheep, ewes, and lambs, just as he calls pumas lions, and jaguars tigers. We have observed this custom which is common to all the writers of the period.

3. "The walls of the royal palaces and also of the Sun temples were plated on the inside with fine gold, engraved with innumerable figures, all very delicately embossed in gold. . . . Inside the houses were sheaves of gold filaments and, on the walls, ewes, sheep, birds, and all kinds of things of the same metal. All I could say of the royal palaces of the Incas would not be enough if I wished to make them appear more marvelous than they were." (Cieza, Part I, Chapter 44)

4. See Note 20, Book V.

5. "In the case of a high dignitary, the songs of lamentation went on for one week, and the higher the rank of the official during his lifetime the more he had to be mourned and the more chicha had to be absorbed." (d'Harcourt) The same author relates that these lamentations were accompanied by dancing to tambourines (tinya).

6. Probably the ocelot, or tiger-cat.

7. See Note 2, Book VI.

8. A hard mass of hair and vegetable debris occasionally found in the stomach of certain ruminants. The *bezoard,* a magical remedy, was long regarded as a panacea for poisons and venom of all kinds. "Occidental bezoard is that found in the fourth stomach of the wild Peruvian goat." (Littré) By wild goat, Littré means the vicuña.

9. These chasquis were so rapid and the relays so well organized that a dispatch could be sent fifty leagues, or about

155 miles, in one day. Cobo relates that he had known a courier to leave Lima and arrive in Cuzco three days later, although one hundred and forty leagues of very bad roads separated the two capitals. In the middle of the seventeenth century, the Spanish horse post took twelve or thirteen days to cover the same distance. (Rowe) See the drawings and commentaries of Guaman Poma, "Officials of the Empire."

10. See Note 16, Book II. Nordenskiöld's discovery concerning the use of the quipu for astronomical calculations is of great importance. It is certain that Garcilaso exaggerates slightly when he asserts that the quipu was used to record texts. It was first and foremost an instrument for keeping accounts, simple at first, but later developed to a remarkable extent by the Incas. The use of the quipu in its most rudimentary form, consisting of a string in which knots were tied, was and still is widespread in numerous parts of America, both North and South. Nordenskiöld has made a chart of its occurrence (vol. 8) which shows that it was known on the Pacific coast from Chile to the North of California, as well as in the *llanos* of the Orinoco (where it is reported by Gumilla in the eighteenth century) and on the Guiana Coast. In most cases, says Nordenskiöld, the knots served to mark days, sometimes months, and the dates of feast days, etc. They were frequently used as invitation cards. Nowhere else, however, did they reach the perfection to which they were carried in ancient Peru.

11. It was during this campaign, led by General Capac Yupanqui, that Hancohuallu deserted and fled across the frontiers of the Empire with his Chanca contingent. (Note 19, Book V)

12. These trumpets, made from the heads of deer, are still commonly used by several tribes. We have ourselves heard them played by the Guahibos of the Orinoco *llanos*. They are normally called *cachovenado*. As will be seen from Note 1, Book IX, they were introduced at the imperial court in Cuzco. This instrument is depicted in the present work in Guaman Poma's drawing of the "Feast of Chinchasuyu."

13. Each of the three provinces had its own language. According to Rowe, *Huanca* is probably derived from the Quechua word *wanka* which means "guardian of the crops."

14. The people of this province were of a very warlike nature. The Incas settled there colonies of people from Cajamarca, Chanca, Huaro (from Huarochiri), and Quehuar (from Cuzco). (Rowe)

15. See Book III.

16. Far from considering him as a "second self," it will be recalled that the Inca Pachacutec had had this brother, General Capac Yupanqui, executed after he had exceeded his orders and thus allowed the Chancas to escape.

17. Cajamarca, with its city of the same name, was at that time a powerful province, allied to the Chimu tribe. This conquest, with that of Chimu and the central valleys, was the work of the Crown Prince Tupac Yupanqui, after his father Pachacutec had placed him in command of the armies in 1468.

18. Scarcely anything remains today of ancient Cajamarca where the destiny of the Incas was to be fulfilled on that celebrated day of November 16, 1532 (Book X). But all the chroniclers speak of this province, and above all of its capital, which some say was the largest city of ancient Peru. "In the center of the city," says Francisco de Jerez, "there was a square surrounded by walls and houses. It was larger than any Spanish square, with two gateways leading to the streets of the town. There were two fountains at the entrance. The houses were more than two hundred paces long with walls to the height of three stories, etc." (Note 17, Book VI)

19. Careful as ever to depict the Incas as favorably as possible in the light of Christian morality, Garcilaso gives us a highly idealized picture of this triumph. Below, in contrast, is a description of a similar celebration, by the chronicler Montesinos:

"The trumpeters lead the procession, followed by two thousand soldiers in battle array, the leaders wearing multicolored headdresses and gold plates on their shoulders and chests, the men covered with silver plates captured from the enemy. Some of them beat drums in human shape, six in number, made with the skins of the vanquished chiefs. Then come soldiers, prisoners with their hands tied behind their backs, more soldiers, with six more drums like the first, then the enemy ruler, lying naked on a litter surrounded by drums made of the skins of members of his family. Behind him come a group of criers, some announcing how the Incas treat those who rebel against them and others telling of the crimes of the vanquished. Three thousand *orejones* follow, richly dressed, and adorned with feathers, chanting a hymn of victory. Behind them come five hundred girls of the noblest families of the Empire, dancing and singing, with garlands on their heads, branches in their hands, and bells attached to their legs. A group of important personages follows, some removing the stones and wisps of straw along the way and others strewing flowers. Immediately behind them comes the Inca on a gold throne carried by eight *orejones*. The god in human form is protected by two feather parasols, forming a canopy, adorned with tiny leaves of fine gold and emeralds; in his right hand he holds a lance-thrower made of gold, and in the other, a staff of the same metal, which he is said to have received from the Sun. On his forehead, he wears the red wool bandeau and a richly wrought gold crown. Members of the royal family and the council, princesses adorned from head to foot, all carried in litters, complete the procession."

There is indeed no doubt that the Incas, like the other

peoples of Peru, used human trophies. According to Alfred Metraux, they sometimes stuffed the bodies of their prisoners of war with ashes or straw and made drums of their stomachs; to add to the insult, the dead man's hands were so arranged that he appeared to be beating the drum on his own stomach and a flute was placed in his mouth. The reader will recall Guaman Poma's war song. (Note 30, Book II) The existence of flutes carved out of the long leg bones of captives has been confirmed. As for cups made from skulls, at least one famous example exists in the history of the conquest: several chroniclers relate that Atahualpa drank from a skull adorned with silver, in the presence of the companions of Pizarro during his captivity at Cajamarca. He explained to them that it was the skull of one of his enemies. Shortly afterwards, Atahualpa's own brother, sent to Quito by the captive king, was to be made into a drum. (Note 21, Book X)

The war song quoted by Guaman Poma also evokes the necklaces of human teeth: "We will adorn ourselves with his teeth." This was a custom in many parts of South America and remained so for a long time. But, says Metraux, such trophies did not exist in Peru. It should be added that in the triumphal processions, Inca soldiers often carried human heads on their pikes, as is related by Cobo, on the return of Tupac Yupanqui after subduing the Colla rebellion: "He had two great nobles skinned, and two drums were made of their skins; he made a triumphal appearance in his court with these drums and the heads of the nobles fixed on pikes, and numerous prisoners destined to be sacrificed to the Sun." (Cobo, Book XII, Chapter 14)

20. The chief of the Chincha valley was a powerful ruler. According to Rowe, in Inca times the population of the valley was fifty thousand. As has been explained, all the central valleys were conquered in the reign of Pachacutec (who died in 1471) by his son, the future Inca Tupac Yupanqui. It would be irrelevant here to enter into the history of the coastal civilizations of ancient Peru, except to say that all these valleys, and those of which we are soon to speak, had known—and in some cases still possessed—brilliant civilizations which, artistically, at least, have left us works far eclipsing Inca art. Chimu and Chancay were still flourishing; Nazca had disappeared several centuries earlier; Inca was on the decline.

21. The name of Yunca applied to all the inhabitants of the Peruvian coast, from Tumbez to south of Arequipa. Unlike the mountain peoples, the Colla, Aimara, and Quechua tribes, the Yunca tribe were of a passionate disposition with a lively imagination and many talents: their temperament explains their tendency to individualism, which in turn explains why, in spite of their numbers and advanced degree of civilization, they formed a patchwork of small states which never united (any more than did the few valleys of the Chimu kingdom).

22. We can suggest an interesting linguistic distinction here. *Condor* can also be pronounced *cuntur* in Quechua, just as *Cuntisuyu* may be pronounced *Condesuyu.* It is therefore quite possible that the people of Cuntisuyu are those whom Garcilaso describes as being "as we imagine the angels," disguised as condors, this bird being their "mythical father," since their name derives from the same root. We advance this hypothesis unsupported by any text.

23. Small, vigorous, and hardy leguminous plant (trifolium amabile H.B.K.). It was regarded, in Inca times, as a tonic and a fortifier. It was chewed with raw maize, not only to help withstand the most rigorous fasts but also in battle. (Yacovleff and Herrera)

24. Kind of corn beer. This drink, which is characteristic of the Andean civilizations, is still current in many parts of Latin America, although it has been forbidden by the health authorities in various places because it is brewed privately. This nourishing drink, which is at the same time rich in ferments and yeast, can be compared to *yaraké,* the beer made from tapioca by the Amazon tribes, or *pombé,* the banana beer of the East African Chamites.

25. See Guaman Poma's drawing of this sacrifice.

26. Archaeology has not yet confirmed the existence of a bracelet such as that described by Garcilaso, and only by him.

27. See these goblets as depicted by Guaman Poma.

28. The Feast of Inti-Raïmi or Feast of the Sun has been described by several other chroniclers. According to Betanzos, it was introduced by the Inca Yupanqui, who himself established the rites. Molina stresses the sacrifice of numerous llamas, not only to the Sun, but also to the Moon, the stars, the lightning, and all the other deities of the Cuzco temple. According to the same author, the festivities lasted much longer than the nine days referred to by Garcilaso. Although prohibited by the Spaniards when they settled in Cuzco, the Feast of Inti-Raïmi continued to be celebrated: Cieza de Leon attended it in 1550. Restored officially in Peru, in 1930, under the name of "Indian Fiesta," it is celebrated every year, and is regarded as a particularly solemn occasion in Cuzco, where it partakes more of religious drama than of a simple popular festivity, as Louis Baudin points out in his study, *La vie quotidienne au temps des Incas.*

29. Long club of hardwood, flat, with a double edge. The *macana* or flat club is characteristic of Amerindian civilizations.

30. Inca flower (*Inca Pancarra*). A bright red or yellow flower, in the shape of a bell. The Inca flower is a frequent motif on Peruvian pottery of the Inca period, and symbolizes submission. It still has a special place in Peruvian folklore, especially in funeral rites. The great Bolivian Congress made

the *cantut* the national emblem. (Yacovleff and Herrera) In modern Peru it is more familiarly called the *cantuta.*

31. Small herbaceous plant whose leaves retain their bright color. It is associated, as a symbol of eternal youth, with all birth festivals and ceremonies in Cuzco.
 Scientifically speaking, two plants are confused under the same name: Spring's *Lycopodium complanatum var. tropicum* and *Epidendrum ybaguense H.B.K.*, the latter of the orchid family. (Yacovleff and Herrera)

32. This ceremony is on the same lines as the initiation ceremonies still held by numerous Indian tribes to mark the puberty of young boys. Rowe tells us that the preparations began in October, two months before the date of the Great Feast or Capac-Raïmi. According to the chronicler Molina, the young men gathered in a ravine near Cuzco where they underwent an initial series of physical endurance tests, such as strokes of the whip and lashes on the arms and legs. They then came back to Cuzco, preceded by a decorated llama, blowing conches known as *huaillayquipacs,* or triumphal trumpets. After the running test, they executed the dance known as *taqui yauri,* from the name of the lances they had just received. Then the inhabitants of Cuzco threw over their shoulders puma skins whose heads, adorned with gold teeth, served as headdresses, and in this costume they attended twice a day the dance known as *taqui coyo* or *colli,* a lively nimble-footed dance, which was executed by young men in long red robes. They were accompanied by four great drums which the Inca Lloque Yupanqui had ordered to be made for these ceremonies. (d'Harcourt)
 Rowe establishes the main preparatory stages and rites of the ceremony proper as follows: In November they went on a pilgrimage to Huanacauri to ask permission of the idol to hold the ceremony. Each of the young novices brought a llama which he sacrificed to the idol. Numerous other offerings were made, followed by sacred dances. The young men then had to help the women to chew the corn to prepare the enormous quantities of *chicha* required for the great day.
 The ceremony proper began with another pilgrimage, accompanied by sacrifices to Huanacauri. After a dance called *wari* (*huari*), the young men rested for six days (probably the six days of fasting referred to by Garcilaso). They were then given new clothes and they ran a race, not to Huanacauri, but on the slope of the other sacred hill (Añahuarque). Rowe tells us that young girls of noble birth awaited the winners on their arrival and offered them goblets of *chicha* to drink. The ceremony then continued until the rite of ear-piercing and the bestowal of the adult male loincloth, as Garcilaso relates. It was at this ceremony that young men gave up their childhood names (given, as we have seen, when their hair was first cut) and took their adult names.
 It should be added that girls also had to observe certain rites at puberty. These included a period of retreat accompanied by taboos on certain foods and purificatory baths,

and resembled many of the rites still practiced by numerous Indian tribes in South America. Unlike the puberty of boys, that of girls did not occasion any public ceremony.

33. As this bird has not been described by any of the chroniclers, apart from the Inca coat of arms depicted by Guaman Poma, Garcilaso's rather vague information is not enough for its identification. According to Gilmore it must be a nightjar, either *Uropsalis lyra* or *Uropsalis segmentata*. It should also be recalled in this connection that the term *capac*, applied to the reigning Incas, meant a falcon, which was the first emblem of the Inca *ayllu*, taken over, according to certain authors, from their enemies, the Chancas.
Gilmore also states, referring to the Markham edition of Cieza de Leon, that Uilcanuta was not a lagoon but a small stream flowing down from the crest of the cordillera into the famous valley of Y'ùcay, where the Incas had their summer residences.

34. Chuquimancu and Cuismancu were the rulers of the valleys between Supe and Cañete. (Krickeberg)

35. See preceding note.

36. The myth of Pachacamac is probably of Chimu or Paleo-Chimu origin. The Incas took it over from the Yuncas. It would seem that originally, in the cosmogonic legends of the Pacific coast, Pachacamac represented the creator-hero Moon, brother of the Sun, and husband of Mamacocha, goddess of the sea. The Paleo-Chimu period appears to have ended around the seventh century, or more than seven hundred years before the beginning of the Inca hegemony. The cult of Pachacamac was perhaps introduced in the Andes cordillera at a very early period by the Collas, who were the first invaders of the Yunca coast. See Rowe.

37. The name of *Rimac* was given to twin valleys, each with a separate language. According to Rowe, the population of these valleys in Inca days was about 150,000.

38. Epiphany.

39. The temple of the idol of Rimac was called Rimac-Tampu. It was this name which, corrupted to Limatambo, was given to the Lima airport.

40. This valley was called Lurin.

41. The idol of Pachacamac. Rosell reproduces this extract from the diary of one of the first conquistadors to visit the celebrated Pachacamac temple: "They [the Indians] took us through a great many doors until we reached the top of the mosque which was surrounded by three or four circular blind walls, like a snail; and so we climbed up in a manner that reminded one more of a stronghold than of the temple of a demon. Right at the top was a small patio in front of the

idol's grotto, made of branches, with a few posts adorned with gold and silver leaf and a roof covered with woven mats as a protection against the sun . . . At the entrance to the patio there was a closed door, with the usual guards . . . This door was variously ornamented with coral, turquoises, and other things . . . Once the door was open there was scarcely room for one person to pass through it. On the other side, all was dark and smelled somewhat unsavory. Accordingly, a candle was brought and we entered a very small grotto, primitive and quite unadorned, with, in the middle, a pole stuck in the ground, the upper part of which was roughly carved in the misshapen form of a man. At its foot were all kinds of small gold and silver objects." Unfortunately Rosell omits to say to whom we owe this description.

42. The Chimus. The Chimu kingdom, with its numerous valleys, was the most powerful state of the Peruvian coast. The Chimu civilization proper was at least as old as that of the Incas and was heir to the Mochica civilization, which dated from about the fifth century A.D. Mochica and Chimu ceramics are among the most celebrated of the American continent. The Chimus were at the height of their prosperity when the Incas attacked them. It is therefore most surprising that Garcilaso should say nothing of them and should not even mention their capital, Chan-Chan, which remains one of the great sites of Peruvian archaeology.

43. It can be seen from these words of Garcilaso's that Parmunca commanded the way into Chimu territory. Parmunca —usually known as Parmonga or Paramonga—was indeed famous for a large fortress which probably marked the frontier of the Chimu kingdom. The following is a description by Cieza de Leon:

"The valley of Parmonga is no less delightful than the others, and I do not think its fertility is exploited by the Indians. If by any chance there are any, they would be at the upper end, where the valley meets the mountain, as at the lower end nothing is to be seen but deserted gardens and woods. There is one thing to be seen in this valley: and that is a fortress, of very fine appearance and well designed for the purpose of those who built it. It is indeed wonderful to see how they brought water by means of channels to irrigate the upper part. The buildings and apartments of this fortress are very well constructed. Their walls are painted with numerous wild animals and birds and they are surrounded by a high, strong wall. The whole place lies in ruins already and has been undermined in various places by treasure seekers. Thus, this fortress can only serve today as a memorial to the past." (Cieza, Part II, Chapter 70)

If we recall that Cieza visited the whole Peruvian coast in 1547, only sixteen years after the arrival of the Spaniards in Peru, it will be realized how rapidly and contagiously destruction was brought about by the first conquistadors. All these valleys, which had been the cradle of one of the finest civilizations of Peru, and which were no doubt extremely prosperous at the end of the Inca rule, were deserted and ruined in less than fifteen years. Even today they have not recovered and the sand borne by the sea winds has completed the work of transforming the whole Yuca coast into one long monotonous desert.

Let us recall once more that the conquest of the Chimus was not the work of Pachacutec but of his son Topa or Tupac Yupanqui, between 1468 and 1471. (Rowe)

44. These old men, employed as guardians of the crops, lived in huts in the fields. They wore fox skins on their heads and frightened away the birds by playing drums, or else with slings, or by waving sticks with bells on them. Male children, from five to twelve years of age, were also employed at this task. See drawings of Guaman Poma.

45. Pachacutec was without doubt the greatest ruler of the Tahuantinsuyu. The following are the chief landmarks of his reign:

1) Before being crowned, he saved Cuzco from the Chancas (1438).
2) Reconnaissance of the southern coast by General Capac Yupanqui. Annexation of the Aimara, Umasuyu, Cotapampa and Chilque territories.
3) Second campaign of Capac Yupanqui, to the north: conquest of Ancara, Huanca, Tarma and other provinces. Flight of Hancohuallu. Execution of Capac Yupanqui.
4) Campaign by Pachacutec in person to the Lake Titicaca basin. Conquest of the powerful Lupacas, which Garcilaso does not mention, although they played a very important part in early Inca history. Prince Tupac then took command of the armies, in 1468.
5) First campaign of Prince Tupac to the north of Quito, and from there into Chimu territory: annexation of all the central valleys.
6) Second campaign of Tupac to the southern coast, from Nazca to Mala. Pachacutec was great not only as a conqueror but also as an administrator and legislator. He codified most of the characteristic customs of the Inca civilization and gave the capital, Cuzco, its final form. He died in 1471, after a reign of thirty-three years.

BOOK SEVEN

Which treats of the Inca Yupanqui,
tenth king of Peru.
With a description of
the third feast of the Sun,
and also of the fourth, during
which the city of Cuzco was
purified of its diseases.
Description of the imperial city
of Cuzco, with its quarters,
its streets, its palaces,
and its schools;
and its prodigious Sacsahuaman
fortress

Every year the Incas celebrated four solemn feasts. We have already described the first one, that is, the feast of Raïmi, and the second, during which the young men were knighted. There remain two others to be described.

The third solemn feast of the Incas was called *Cusquieraïmi,* and it was celebrated after seedtime, when the corn had started sprouting. Many lambs, sheep, and sterile ewes were offered up to the Sun, so that it would keep the frost from destroying the corn, as happens too often in the cold land in and about Cuzco. At such high altitudes as these, it can freeze all year round, and the weather is worse on Midsummer's Day than it is at Christmas, because then the Sun is farthest away. Therefore, when the Indians saw a bright, cloudless sky at nightfall, they feared frost and immediately lighted manure fires to obtain smoke, their idea being that smoke, like clouds, forms a covering that keeps the frost from the earth. I have seen them do this in Cuzco, although I can't say whether or not they still do it, or how efficacious a manner of proceeding it is; I was too much of a child at the time to care about learning everything there was to know about the things I saw the Indians do.

It is comprehensible that the Indians should have had such dread of frost which, when it attacked the corn, threatened their principal foodstuff. This is why they implored the Sun to keep the frost from coming back at the time of year when their seedlings were particularly exposed to the rigors of the weather. Dances and sacrificial offerings succeeded one another, and they drank a lot. The first sheep was burned to ashes, as an offering to the Sun, as were the entrails of other sacrificed animals, the flesh of which was divided among the participants, as it was on the occasion of the feast of Raïmi.

The fourth and last solemn feast of the Incas was called *Citua.* It was impatiently awaited, for on this occasion, the city of Cuzco and its environs were purged of all diseases and any other ills the inhabitants might be suffering from. In other words, it resembled the expiatory ceremonies of the ancient gentiles, by which they purified themselves and washed away their sins. To prepare this feast, the Indians fasted and abstained from intercourse with their wives the first day of the new moon that followed the autumn equinox. The strict fast they observed at this time was similar to the one I described as beginning the novitiate for young Incas, but it only lasted one day. When night fell, the inhabitants of Cuzco kneaded the festival bread called *sancu*. They put it on the fire in earthen pots—for they knew nothing of ovens—and took it off half-cooked. This bread was of two sorts: one mixed with water, and the other with human blood taken from male children five to ten years old, by means of bloodletting between the eyebrows. (I have seen this same blood used elsewhere, for the treatment of certain illnesses.) Each one of these breads was cooked separately, to avoid confusion, since they were used for different purposes. The Indians gathered together in families to make these preparations.

Shortly before dawn, all those who had participated in the fast washed, then rubbed their heads, trunks and limbs with this half-cooked bread, kneaded with human blood, in order to drive out all diseases from their bodies. The master of the house then rubbed the threshold of his main door with a piece of this same bread, which he left stuck on the outside, so it should be known that his house had been purified. The high priest did the same in the Temple of the Sun, and his subordinates visited the convent of the virgins and all the other places they held sacred, in order to perform the same rites: only, more than often, these places were merely those chosen by the demon to outwit mankind, by usurping the rank of God. They made it a point, too, to go to the Huanacauri temple, one league away from the city. This building stood on the very spot where the first Inca, Manco Capac, had come to a halt, before founding the city, as we related at the beginning of this work, and the Indians held it in particular veneration. At the royal palace, the ceremony was led by the king's senior uncle.

As soon as the Sun appeared, the inhabitants of the entire city threw themselves prone on the ground and implored the god-star to banish all their ills, both interior and exterior. They next breakfasted on the other bread, that contained no human blood. Then a richly clad Inca appeared at the gate of the fortress. This was the messenger of the Sun. In his hand he carried a lance, trimmed with a border of multicolored feathers that ran through gold rings from the blade to the end of the shaft. This oriflamme, which the Indians carried in battle, and the fact that this herald appeared at the door of the fortress and not at that of the temple, signified quite clearly that he came as a messenger of war, and not of peace. He ran down the slope of the Sacsahuaman hill, brandishing his lance, until he reached the middle of the main square, where he was awaited by four other Incas of royal blood, carrying lances and, like himself, in war dress. Then, touching the weapons of his four brothers with his own, he ordered them, in the name of the Sun, to go to the four corners of the city and banish disease.

They immediately started running along the four royal roads that lead from there to the four parts of the world. As they approached, all the citizens came out on their doorsteps and shook their clothing, with loud cries and exclamations of joy, as though to rid them of dust. They next passed their hands over their faces, their arms and their bodies, as though they were washing themselves, in order to cast into the street all the diseases in their houses, in the direction of God's herald who would bear them away from the city.

The four messengers ran in this way, with their lances at rest, to within a quarter of a league of the city, where four other Incas, not of royal blood, but privileged, relayed them, carrying their lances for another quarter of a league, after which they handed the weapons and the instructions to the others, and so forth, until the invisible ills had thus been driven back to five or six leagues from the city, where the last warriors plunged their lances into the ground, as though to nail them down and prevent them from returning to the purified city.

A similar ceremony took place the following night to banish all nocturnal ills from the city. Now the lances were replaced by great straw torches, round in shape and slow burning, called *pancuncu,* which the Indians brandished as they ran through the streets and on out into the countryside. There, far from the city, they threw the extinct torches into a stream, along with the water in which they had washed themselves the preceding night, in order that, from stream to stream, the last ills of the city should be carried away till they reached the sea.

Thus the people, the houses and the entire city having been purified by means of fire and sword, there next took place in Cuzco a great festival, that lasted an entire quarter of the moon. To thank the Sun, lambs and sheep were sacrificed, and there was carousing, night and day, with continued singing and dancing, in the people's homes as well as on the public squares.

I have already told how the first Inca, Manco Capac, founded the city of Cuzco,[1] which the Spaniards respected and honored without changing its name, by calling it the Great City of Cuzco, capital of the kingdoms and provinces of Peru. They also called it for a time, New Toledo, a name which was not suitable, since Cuzco is not surrounded by a river as Toledo is, and in no way resembles it. It is rather with Rome that it may be compared: just as Rome was the capital of a great empire, Cuzco was, in fact, also founded by its first king; like Rome, it had a long history of conquests and succeeded in subjugating many very different peoples to its laws; like Rome, it engendered a long line of famous men who covered themselves with glory both in peace and war. But the one advantage that Rome had over Cuzco is that it was fortunate enough to have discovered an alphabet, thanks to which the memory of its sons was perpetuated. What would the glory of our country not have been if, like Rome, it had left, in writing, the story of all the feats of valor and all the noble deeds of its sons, whose good judgment and clear-sightedness in everything was unequaled except by their arts of war! Alas! the precarious oral tradition, transmitted from father to son, has permitted only a meager part of the sayings and acts of our ancestors to survive, and the occupation of our throne by a foreigner, with the change in government that accompanied it, destroyed for all time what might have continued to live on in the popular memory, as always happens when an empire falls and another replaces it.

This is why, actuated by the desire to conserve the heritage of my native land, and to secure the little that remains of it before it should disappear entirely, I, the

Inca Garcilaso, began to write this history of the former kings of Peru, which I shall pursue till the end, even though it be an immense undertaking.

And particularly as regards the city of Cuzco, which was my mother, and mistress of this Empire, I feel that I must keep it from falling into oblivion. I have decided, therefore, to draw a description of it in this chapter, according to the tradition that was passed on to me, as to her natural son, and according to what I have seen with my own eyes. I shall use the old names for the city quarters which were still in their former state, when I left my country, in 1560.

One can understand that King Manco Capac should have decided to found his capital in this beautiful Cuzco valley, when one considers all the natural advantages that are grouped together there: the valley, in this spot, is perfectly flat, and surrounded on all sides by high mountains; it is watered by four small streams and, in the center, flow the waters of a beautiful spring, from which salt was extracted; the land is fertile and the air could not be healthier; the climate is more cold than hot, without its being so cold that one must have a fire to keep warm; it suffices to shut out drafts to forget the cold out-of-doors; if a brazier is lighted, well and good, but if there is none, one doesn't miss it. The same can be said about clothing and beds: winter clothing is bearable, but one can well get along without it, and people who like to sleep with only one cover, sleep well, and those who like three do not suffocate, either. This climate is the same all year round, with no difference between winter and summer, and the same thing is true of the entire country, whether the land be cold, temperate, or hot. Since the cold of Cuzco is particularly dry, meat never spoils there, and if one is careful to hang a joint in a room that is open to the outside air, it will keep for a week, or two, or even a month or three months, until it becomes as dry as smoked meat. Another advantage of this climate is that there are no flies, especially in the houses, as well as no mosquitoes, or other disagreeable creatures; indeed the city is clean and free from all such pests.

The first houses in Cuzco were built on the slopes of the Sacsahuaman hill, which lies between the east and west of the city. On the top of this hill, Manco Capac's successors erected the superb fortress towards which the Spaniards showed greater hatred than esteem because they were not long in destroying it. The city is divided into two parts, Hanan-Cuzco, or Upper Cuzco, and Hurin-Cuzco, or Lower Cuzco, as we said at the beginning of this book. The Antisuyu road, which runs eastward, separates Hanan-Cuzco to the north, from Hurin-Cuzco, to the south. The principal district of the city is called Collcampata, and this is where the first Inca, Manco Capac, built his house, which finally fell to Paullu, Huaina Capac's son. Almost nothing remained of it, however, when I left Cuzco. Continuing eastward, we arrive at the Cantutpata district, which means the district of the Cantut, that is, of a very lovely flower, rather similar to the Spanish carnation. Next comes the Pumacurcu district, which stretches toward the north; *Puma* meaning lion, and *curcu,* beam. There actually were, in this district, a number of heavy beams to which the lions brought in from the country were tied, in order to tame them, before offering them to the king. The Tococachi district, which lies next to this one, is very large. I am unable to say, however, from where the name comes: *toco* meaning window, and *cachi* salt. In any case, the first Franciscan convent was built here. If we turn a bit toward the south —I am describing the city in a circle—we come to the district of Munaicenca, which means, I can't say why, nose-lover, and then to that of Rimacpampa. It will be recalled, in connection with the Pachacamac oracle, that Rimac means he who speaks. Rimacpampa therefore means, the place that speaks, and it was here that all royal ordinances were proclaimed. Also, the Collasuyu royal road runs out from this spot. Finally, in the extreme southern part of the city, lies the district of the Pumapchupan, or lion's tail. (It was given this name because it ends in a point, beside two streams that flow into one.) At more than a thousand feet from the last houses in the city, beyond Pumapchupan, there was a village of some three hundred inhabitants, called Cayaucachi. Now all this was in 1560. Today, in 1562, it seems that Pumapchupan touches Cayaucachi, so rapidly has the city grown. It also, I hear, reaches as far as the suburb of Chaquilchaca, which was about a thousand feet from there, in the same direction, on the Cuntisuyu royal road. Two very clear brooks which were canalized long ago under the earth, flow not far from this road. They are called *collquemachac-huay,* which means, silver snakes. Continuing around the circle, from the south toward the north, we come to the suburb of

Pichu, which also lies beyond the city, like Quillipata, which we reach next. Lastly, far to the north, on the Chinchasuyu royal road, lies the great Carmenca district, followed, on the east, by Huacapuncu. This name means the gate of the sanctuary, because the brook that crosses the main square of Cuzco, enters the city through this district, as does also a long, very wide street that crosses the entire city, beside the brook, and leaves it, at the same spot, to join the Collasuyu royal road, half a league farther on. In order to understand the name of this Huacapuncu district, one must know that it is the gate, not of such and such a temple or sanctuary, but of the whole city which, in its entirety, was considered to be hallowed ground. Passing through Huacapuncu we arrive back in Collcampata, from where we started to tour the different districts of the city, and thus have reached the end.

We have already mentioned the fact that these districts were divided, from the very beginning, according to the four parts of the world, and that the first Inca, Manco Capac, desired that the savages he captured for his service, should be settled there in accordance with their regional origin. Thus those from the eastern regions were settled in the eastern districts, those from the south in the southern districts, and so on.

This principle was always respected, and the land occupied by this great circle of districts, little by little became filled with representatives of the various provinces of the Empire, according to the actual arrangement of these provinces on the map of Peru. And all the curacas, who were obliged to own houses in Cuzco for their court visits, built them to the right or left, or behind his neighbor, according to whether his province lay to the right, to the left, or behind the other's province. These districts, if regarded as a whole, reproduced, therefore, the entire Empire, as though in a mirror.

"The people of each nation," writes Pedro de Cieza de Leon, "settled where the city governors told them to. They retained the customs of their ancestors, and even if there were more than one hundred thousand of them they were easily distinguishable from one another, thanks to the special marks they wore on their heads."

These marks consisted of different ways of dressing their hair that were peculiar to each nation or province.[2]

This was not just an invention on the part of the Incas, whose only wish had been that these customs should be retained, in order that all these lineages and nations extending from Pasto to Chile—which represents over three hundred leagues, according to the same author—should not be confused. It may therefore be said more precisely that this great belt of exterior districts, or suburbs, was inhabited by vassals from every part of the Empire, and only by them, because no Incas lived there. We shall speak later of the center, or of the city itself, however one prefers to call it. We shall describe its streets, its districts, its houses, and the palaces of the kings which the Spaniards distributed among themselves. We shall also tell how this division was made and what each one did with the share that fell to him.

Down the Sacsahuaman hill there flows a little brook which runs north and south to the last district, called Pumapchupan, and separates the city from its suburbs. In the inner city there is a street, today called San Agustín, that follows the same direction, from the old houses that belonged to Manco Capac to beyond the Rimacpampa square. Three or four cross streets, running from east to west, cut through the space that stretches between San Agustín Street and this little brook. The Incas of royal blood lived here, established, they too, according to their lineages or *ayllus*, that is to say, according to whether they descended from this or that king.[3] In San Agustín Street, walking from north to south, were to be seen the Santa Clara convent, the bishop's palace and, on the main square, the cathedral. It was on this same street that the leading conquistadors lived, not only the first hundred and sixty companions of Pizarro, but also some of those who entered the city with Don Diego de Almagro. At the time of the Incas, the main square was occupied by a fine, large covered courtyard, where the festivals took place, in case of rain. This was one of the constructions built under Viracocha Inca, the eighth king. The Spaniards lived there all together, when they first entered the city. I remember seeing it roofed over with straw, which I later saw replaced by tiles. North of the cathedral, behind the square, in a district called Hatuncancha, or the Great District, were the houses belonging to the King Inca Yupanqui. To the south, in the Pucamarca, or Red district, were those that had belonged to the King Tupac Inca Yupanqui. Still farther south, stood the Temple of the

Sun which was preceded by the Intipampa square, or Square of the Sun. The district in which this temple was built, was called Coricancha, that is to say, the district of gold, silver, and precious stones. It touched Pumapchupan which, as we have already written, belongs among the suburbs.

To describe the heart of the city, we must go back to the Huacapuncu district, or the so-called gate of the sanctuary, which was prolonged toward the south by another very large district, the name of which I have forgotten; we might call it the school district, since it was there that King Inca Roca had built the *yacha huaci*, or houses of learning, by which he distinguished himself, as we explained in telling of his reign. Amautas, or philosophers, and harauecs, or poets, lived in these schools with numerous disciples, for the most part, Incas of royal blood. In the two districts that lay farther to the south there were two royal dwellings, the façades of which occupied an entire side of the main square. The one on the east was called Coracora, or the house in the field, there having once been a large green space on this spot, when the square itself was nothing but marshland, which the Incas filled in, as Pedro de Cieza de Leon tells in the ninety-second chapter of his book. I have no knowledge of this house, it having been destroyed before my time, except that when the city was seized, it had fallen to the lot of Gonzalvo Pizarro, the brother of Don Francisco Pizarro, a gentleman I knew in Cuzco. At that time, I was about eight or nine years old and he treated me like his own son. The other royal dwelling, located west of Coracora, was called Casana, which means, the one that freezes. It had been given this name as a sign of admiration, by which they meant that it was composed of such spacious, magnificent buildings that it was enough to "freeze," or cause to swoon, those who looked at it attentively. The great Inca Pachacutec, great-grandson of the Inca Roca, had the palaces erected in the immediate vicinity of the schools, to show the esteem in which he held all learning. In fact, the schools and palaces together formed a solid block of buildings, the doors of which, for the schools, opened to one side, on the street, and to the other, on the brook that ran parallel to them; the kings often passed from one building to the other to listen to the discussions of the philosophers, in which Inca Pachacutec liked particularly to participate, taking the floor himself, for he was a great lawgiver. In my time, the Spaniards opened up a new street to separate the schools from the palaces, and I was able to see a great part of the Casana walls, which were made of richly decorated hewn stone. I remember, too, a covered court there, which was used on feast days, in case of rain; indeed, it was so large that horse tournaments could have been held in it. Juan de Pancorvo, who was one of the first conquistadors, and to whom this palace was allotted when Cuzco was taken, made a gift of the court to the Franciscan Friars, who built a church and their first convent on this site, before settling elsewhere, as we shall see later. Finally, I witnessed the demolition of all the rest of Casana, which was replaced by shops, still seen there today.

The main square of the city, onto which, as we have seen, these palaces gave, was called Haucaipata, which means the festival square. It was a good two hundred feet long by one hundred and fifty feet wide and was bordered on the west by the brook and, on the south, by two other royal palaces. The palace beside the brook, just opposite the Casana, where the Jesuits live today, was Huaina Capac's palace, and it was called, with all its outbuildings, Amarucancha, or the big snake district. I also remember a very handsome round house that stood on the square, in front of this palace, which was taken over by the Spaniards when they entered the city; but of that I shall speak later. The rest of this palace had already been torn down, in my time. The main part of the building, giving on to the square, was allotted to Ferdinand Pizarro, another brother of the Marquis Don Francisco Pizarro, and the rest was divided between Mancio Serra de Leguiçamo, Antonio Altamirano and other conquistadors whose names I have forgotten, not to mention a building that was made into a prison for the Spaniards. East of Amarucancha, on the other side of the Street of the Sun, which led out from the middle of the square, was the Ac-Llahuaci district, which took in the convent of virgins dedicated to the Sun, together with all its outbuildings. The part that gave on to the square was given to Francisco Mejía, and it, too, has since been made into shops. The rest was allotted to various other gentlemen, among whom were Pedro del Barco and the scholar, La Gama.

The open sheds that went all round the square on the three built-up sides—since the fourth side gave on to the brook—were spared by the fire that ravaged the city at the time of the Indian uprising against the Spaniards. The Temple of the Sun and the virgins' convent were also respected. But all the rest was intentionally set on fire by the Indians, in order to burn the Spaniards.

West of the brook, there stretches another square called Cussipata, opposite Haucaipata. At the time of the Incas, the brook at this point was covered with flagstones laid on logs, with the result that these two squares formed practically only one, and indeed, an open space of this sort was quite necessary in order to assemble all the curacas, lords, and vassals who came to Cuzco for the great Sun feasts. Today, the brook is no longer entirely covered over, as it was then, but merely spanned by three stone bridges built by the Spaniards. The houses that occupy the periphery of the Cussipata square did not exist before the conquest, but were built in 1555, when my lord and father, Garcilaso de la Vega, was governor of Cuzco, and given to this poor city that, after having been sovereign mistress and Empress of a vast Empire, had fallen so low that she hadn't so much as a maravedi in revenue.

Today, Cussipata is called Plaza de Nuestra Señora de las Mercedes. It has become a sort of fair grounds or market place, where, in my time, one could see numerous poor Indians exchanging their wares. For the most part, the Spaniards, conquistadors of the first and second groups, settled in the north, beside the brook, while to the south, the convent of Nuestra Señora de las Mercedes covers an entire district, bounded by four streets.

My father, as well as many other conquistadors, lived on another street that went down from the Carmenca district towards the south. His residence faced the square, and on feast days, the leading nobles of the city gathered there, to watch the games, contests and bullfights, from a balcony that ran just above the main door. Continuing southward, the city terminated in a big parade ground on which the cavalry officers exercised. In 1555, or 1556, a fine hospital for the Indians that, today, is famous in all Peru, was built on the end of this land. The credit for this undertaking belongs to a former Franciscan monk, by the name of Friar Antonio de San Miguel. He was a man of great nobility of spirit, from a famous Salamanca family, who was well versed in theology and led such an exemplary life that he later became bishop of Chile.

It so happened that this holy man, while preaching the lenten services in the Cuzco cathedral, declared one day from the pulpit, that it would be well to build a hospital for the Indians, under the auspices of the municipal council, in order, he said, that all Spaniards, conquistadors or others, should repay, in this way, the indefeasible debt they had contracted toward the Peruvian people. He preached on this theme for an entire week, and, the following Sunday, announced, "Gentlemen, today at one o'clock, accompanied by our governor, I plan to take up a house-to-house collection for this purpose. I trust that you will be as liberal and generous on this occasion, as you were strong and brave in the conquest of this Empire."

At six o'clock that evening, my father, the governor, came home and asked me to add up all the contributions that he had written down as he received them. I counted the sum of twenty-eight thousand five hundred pesos, which makes thirty-four thousand two hundred ducats; the smallest gift had been five hundred pesos, or six hundred ducats, and some had gone as high as a thousand pesos. The collection continued, day after day, and, in a few months, it came to more than one hundred thousand ducats.[4] The news having spread over all Peru, contributions and gifts of all kinds, including legacies, kept pouring in for an entire year, so that construction of the hospital could begin. The Indians in the Cuzco jurisdiction came in numbers to help with the work, because they knew that, in the end, they would benefit by it. My lord Garcilaso de la Vega put a gold piece under the first stone of this edifice, one of those we call "double-headed" because it bears the double likeness of the very Catholic King and Queen, Don Fernando and Doña Isabel. This was a matter of great curiosity and something quite new for all those who saw this gold piece, because stamped money had not yet been introduced in Peru, where all affairs were carried on by barter. Everybody was very happy to see something so new dedicated to this cause.

The holy pontiffs have since granted many indulgences to those who died in this hospital. An Indian woman of royal blood whom I knew, having heard this, when she felt her end was near, asked to be taken to this hospital. Her parents having told her that they saw no need to do so, because she could be cared for quite as well at home, she replied that it was no longer a question of her body's health, but of her soul's salvation. They therefore transported her to the hospital, where she refused to be put in the infirmary, requesting that her bed be placed in a corner of the hospital chapel. She then asked to have her grave dug beside her bed, and for her shroud, expressed the wish to wear the Franciscan frock, which they laid over her sheet. She then had brought the wax candles that would be burned at her funeral, she was given the holy sacrament and extreme unction, and, for four days, she remained like that, imploring God, the holy Virgin and all the heavenly host, until, finally, she expired. The entire city wanted to pay homage to this exemplary death, with the result that all the authorities, both civil and religious, followed the funeral procession, in the midst of a great number of nobles, which was a source of pride to the dead woman's family, as well as to all the other Indians. Here we shall end this description of Cuzco, in order to tell now of the life and deeds of the tenth Inca king, through which we shall be apprised of some very admirable things.

After he had donned the scarlet bandeau, and terminated an official state visit of his kingdoms, which took three years, the new king, Inca Yupanqui, informed his counselors of a very bold project he had in mind, which was, to push on toward the Andes, beyond the snow-covered crests of the cordillera that, thus far, had formed the natural eastern frontier of the Empire.[5] These crests being impassable, it was his plan to slip between them by means of one of the rivers that flowed toward the east.

Now these regions had been a frequent topic of conversation at the Inca's court. There were those who said that there were quantities of fine land there, some of which was inhabited and some not. The land of Musu or, rather, of the Mojos, as the Spaniards call it, was known to be one of the richest and most populous in the New World. It was possible to reach it by way of one of the countless rivers that meet in the Andes, east of Cuzco, where, together, they form the vast stream they call Amarumayu. I am not able to say where it flows into the sea. It may be one of the tributaries of the Rio de la Plata, which, in Indian language, is called Parahuay, meaning "follow me," as though the river itself said "follow me and you will see marvelous things." [6]

Mayu means river, and *amaru* [7] is the name they give to the gigantic snakes to be found in these mountains. Thus *Amarumayu* means that this river, which is perhaps the largest in America after that of Orellana,[8] has the same relation to ordinary rivers that these monstrous snakes have to ordinary worms and garden snakes.

The king, Inca Yupanqui, had trees cut down and prepared as many rafts on this river as were needed to hold an army of ten thousand men, with all its supplies. This was a considerable task and it took nearly two years. However, it was finally finished and the entire army embarked, with thirty, forty, or fifty men on each raft. They had hardly started to navigate when they were attacked by clouds of arrows being shot at them from the banks by naked Indians painted red, and on their heads great diadems of macaw and parrot feathers. There was a certain amount of fighting but all these savages ended by surrendering to the Inca, to whom they sent presents of parrots, macaws, monkeys, honey, wax, and a little of everything that is to be found in their hot country. With permission of the Inca, certain of these Indians, called Chunchus, settled in a village near Tono, twenty-six leagues from Cuzco, where their descendants still live today. The Inca army, with its new allies, arrived in the vicinity of the great Husu province, which is said to be some two hundred leagues from Cuzco. This province was as famous for the fertility of its soil as for the fearlessness of its inhabitants.

The Inca dispatched his ambassadors to them, as was his custom, and the people in Musu gave them a good welcome and lent a ready ear to what they had to say. Everything they heard about the Incas, about their government and their beliefs seemed to them to be remarkable and they very willingly accepted to forget their vain idols and adore the Sun. But they refused to become vassals, not having been defeated in battle. A treaty of friendship and confederation was therefore concluded, and the Musus allowed the Incas to settle on their land on this one condition, which the latter were obliged to accept, there being only a thousand or so of them left, after all the wars and diseases that had decimated them on the way. The Musus gave them their highest born girls in marriage and designated ambassadors to accompany them on their homeward journey as far as Cuzco, where the king welcomed his new allies with great kindness. They stayed for some time at court, where they were given further instruction, then finally returned to their own country, after having been showered with presents, extremely satisfied with all they had seen and heard.

People still say in my country that the descendants of the Incas who settled in the Musu province at the time of this campaign, had decided to return to Cuzco under Huaina Capac's reign, but that the news of this king's death, the arrival of the Spaniards and the collapse of the Empire, reached them as they were about to leave, and made them go back on their decision. They therefore remained among the Musus, where they are still greatly revered, and are in charge of all affairs of government, both civil and military.[9]

They say, too, that the river in this part of the world is six leagues wide, and that it takes two days' navigation to cross it in a canoe.

The Indians have many a tale to tell on the subject of this campaign. They speak of heated battles, fabulous exploits, and the surrender of vast provinces, all of which seems scarcely likely, if one thinks of the small number of Inca troops engaged. On the other hand, it is very hard, in this case, to disentangle the legend from the historical facts, as we have done everywhere else, each time putting our fingers on the concrete proofs of what we were telling, because, in contrast to the other provinces of the Inca Empire, these have not yet been conquered by the Spaniards and, consequently, we have no very clear, complete ideas concerning them. It is nevertheless true that, in the last few years, the Spaniards have acquired certain knowledge of these regions, as we shall see.

In 1564, a Spaniard named Diego Aleman, who possessed a little *repartimiento*[10] of Indians near the city of La Paz, decided to undertake exploration of the Musu province, at the instigation of one of its caciques who insisted that gold of a very fine quality could be found there in abundance, and undertook to take him there. So they left together, on foot, with a little band of twelve Spaniards. Their intention was to limit this journey to as complete a reconnaissance of the country as possible, after which they planned to ask for rights of conquest and settlement. They entered the country through Cochapampa, which is near the Mojos' country.

After walking for twenty-eight days through thick forest, the little group arrived in sight of their first village. Despite all the entreaties of the cacique, who advised them to hide in ambush so as to capture a native who could be used as an interpreter, our Spaniard decided to push on, being persuaded that a few words of Castilian, spoken with authority, would suffice to make everyone surrender. And so he walked right into the center of the village with his twelve companions, all of whom were making as much noise as they could, to give the impression that they were more numerous than they actually were. But he had cause to rue this. The Indians discovered the hoax immediately, spread the alarm, and charged at them as one man. In no time, ten Spaniards were killed, Diego Aleman was a prisoner, and the two others had fled. The cacique, not wanting to risk this adventure, had remained hidden in the forest where the two renegades joined him and told him the story. The three of them spent the night on top of a hill from where they could watch the village. The following morning, they saw a column of armed Indians leaving the village, with the sunlight playing on their breastplates, lances, and pikes in a very lovely manner. The cacique explained to the two survivors that all they saw shining like that was of pure gold, because the Indians had no knowledge of any other metal. And taking his poncho, which was made of bands of material sewed one to the other, he added: "The whole of Peru, compared to this country, is no bigger than one of these bands compared to this entire poncho." This was undoubtedly an exaggeration, for this cacique was no cosmographer; the fact is, however, that this land is very extensive.

News of Diego Aleman was brought later by some forest Indians, who had come to Peru for trading purposes. Those who had captured him having found out that he was a gentleman and the leader of his group, had made him their commander-general to lead them in a war against their neighbors, on the other bank of the Amarumayu river. Apparently, they respected and obeyed him very faithfully, and were prouder than anything to have a Spaniard for commander-general.

This event was much talked of in Peru, so much so, in fact, that a certain Gomez de Tordoya soon decided to try his luck at the same adventure. Then, after permission had been granted him, it was rescinded, because of the number of persons who had rapidly decided to join him, the authorities fearing that this might end in some sort of uprising.

Two years later, the governor of Peru granted the same permission to a gentleman from Cuzco named Gaspar de Sotelo. He had a good following, but his best card was no doubt the fact that he had succeeded in interesting the Inca Tupac Amaru, who agreed to undertake the campaign with him, and promised to have all the rafts made that were needed. They planned to pass through the river of Uillcapampa, which is northeast of Cuzco. But projects of this kind always inspire envy, and a certain Alvarez Maldonado succeeded in persuading the governor to change the license previously issued to Gaspar de Sotelo, in his favor. A few more than two hundred and fifty soldiers were soon raised, as well as a hundred or so horses and mares, and Maldonado embarked at their head, on the Rio Amarumayu.

At that moment, Gomez de Tordoya, who had been the first to conceive of this project, and had sacrificed his fortune to it, as well as those of his friends, entered into a manly rage and declared that he too possessed a license in proper form; which was absolutely true, because, although his license had been revoked, no one had thought to make him return the paper itself. He succeeded in raising about sixty men, despite the governor's opposition, and taking their lead across the mountains, he reached the banks of the Amarumayu, downstream from the place where Maldonado had just embarked; here he dug trenches to await his rival, as though he were awaiting a deadly enemy. Although his forces were inferior in number, he believed that he would win, nevertheless, because his men were all bold, trustworthy companions, and each one was armed with two excellent harquebuses.

As soon as Maldonado appeared, the battle began without there having been any question of talking the matter over: for it is well-known that those who have been seized with the rage to conquer will brook no rivals, nor even seconds. They fought for three consecutive days, so cruelly, in fact, that they were nearly all killed; nor were the survivors much better off at this point. However, the Chunchu Indians had watched this battle that had taken place on their territory, and were quite aware that the victor would next turn against them. They therefore joined together and, charging against the men who remained, massacred all of them, including Gomez de Tordoya, with the exception of three whom they took as prisoners. I knew these men well before these events; the first was Maldonado himself, the second a Portuguese monk named Friar Diego Martín, and the third a certain master Simon Lopez, a blacksmith, who was familiar with the functioning of the harquebus. Knowing that Maldonado was the head of one of these two groups, and considering, on the other hand, that he was too old to be of any use, the Indians returned him under escort to the vicinity of Cuzco, where he regained his freedom. As for the monk and the blacksmith, they kept them both more than two years. They brought copper ore to Master Simon, for him to make hatchets and picks, and this work took up all his time. They also showed great respect and consideration for the friar, knowing that he was a minister of the Christian God. And even after they had authorized the two Spaniards to return to Peru, they continued to implore Friar Diego Martín to stay with them to teach them the Christian doctrine. However, he refused. And this was not the only lost opportunity, far from it, of spreading the Holy Gospel without the use of weapons.

When these two men returned to Peru after their long captivity, they told many fresh details concerning the Musus and, especially, concerning what the Incas had done in that distant territory. They declared, for instance, that these Indians still recognized the Inca as their lord, and sent him a handsome present every year. This tradition lasted until the death of Inca Tupac Amaru, which took place several years later. Friar Diego Martín remained filled with remorse; for his conscience reproached him with not having responded to the desire of the Indians by remaining among them to preach the Holy Gospel. He said that he had been unable to accept because he had not had what was needed out there, to say Mass; but very often, he used to be tempted to return there alone, to appease his conscience.

Four years after the events we have just told of, the King Inca Yupanqui decided to organize a new expedition among the Chirihuanas, who live in the Andes, east of the Charca territory. Since nothing whatsoever was known about these people and their country, spies were sent ahead, who declared on their return that they had never seen such poor land, nor a more savage population, which they described as being worse than animals. This entire land, they said, was composed of nothing but steep mountains, separated by lakes and marshes; nothing could be grown there; the inhabitants had neither laws nor religion; they lived like animals, without villages or homes; they fed on human flesh and, not satisfied with attacking their neighbors in order to devour them, they even battened on their own dead, later reconstituting the skeletons which they mourned then buried among the rocks or in hollow trees; they wore no clothing and mated indifferently with either their sisters, daughters, or mothers.

The good Inca Yupanqui (according to Cieza de Leon, this was how he was called), hearing this description, turned to his followers and said: "It is therefore our duty to undertake this campaign, in order that these Chirihuanas may be taught to live like human beings, because our father the Sun did not send us on this earth with any other intention." So the expedition was organized with ten thousand fighting men. It lasted for two years and met with no success whatsoever, this being a bad province that was quite as impossible to enter as it was to colonize. In 1562, the Viceroy Don Francisco de Toledo attempted a second exploration of this same territory. But he had no success, either, and only escaped with his life by fleeing, abandoning arms and baggage, as Father Acosta tells, in the twenty-eighth chapter of his seventh book.[11]

But the failure of this unfortunate campaign did not discourage the good King Yupanqui. His power knew no equal at that time, and his subjects asked only to render service to his greater glory. He decided, therefore, upon a great undertaking, which was to be the conquest of Chile.[12] After having informed his councilors of his decision and made suitable arrangements, he left Cuzco to go and settle in the province of Atacama, on the southern

January

February

March

April

May

June

July

August

September

October

November

December

THE MONTHS AND THE FESTIVALS

January: "The Inca's penance and fasting . . . During that month they offered sacrifices, fasted, made penance, and covered their bodies and heads with ashes, as the Incas still do today, and went in procession to the temples of the Sun, the Moon, their gods, and all the *huacas.*"
February: "They made offerings of great quantities of gold and silver." The Inca is represented kneeling bareheaded, making an offering (perhaps to the stone of Huanacauri). "This is the wet season, it often rains . . . they used in particular to visit the *huacas* of the high mountains and the snows."
March: The Inca is represented kneeling, about to "sacrifice this black sheep. . . . The priests and sorcerers performed many ceremonies, conversed with demons, deprived themselves of salt for I know not how many days, refrained from contact with women, and ate no fruit."
April: Feast of the Inca. They sacrifice "red sheep." This is "a very great feast to which all the lords, the princes, and the poor Incas were invited; they ate, sang, and danced on the main square."
May: The illustration shows Indians carrying supplies of potatoes to the warehouses. It was the feast of the Aimara; there was much singing and drunkenness.
June: The month of Inti-Raïmi. The Inca is represented "drinking with the Sun at the Feast of the Sun."
July: The harvest festival. The illustration shows the High Priest making an agrarian sacrifice before the Inca, who has removed his headdress.
August: The feast of tilling. Four Incas are shown digging while a woman brings them *chicha.*
September: Great Feast of the Moon, wife of the Sun. The town of Cuzco is purified. The illustration shows three purifiers banishing evil from the city with torches in their hands.
October: Procession to ask God for water. "This hungry black sheep helps men to weep and ask God for water."
November: Feast of the dead. The mummies of dead kings are carried in state. They are given food, they are clothed in rich robes, with feathers on their heads; the people sing and dance in their company and carry them through the streets to the main square.
December: Capac Inti-Raïmi. This is "the great Feast of the Sun, which is the king of the heavens, of the planets and stars, and of all up above. Capac means king, Inti means Sun, and Raïmi great feast. Much gold and silver plate is sacrificed to the Sun; five hundred innocent children, boys and girls, are buried alive, standing upright, with these offerings of precious plate and livestock. After the sacrifice, a great feast is held at which they eat and drink to the Sun and dance in the public squares of Cuzco and throughout the kingdom; and those who become too drunk, or who turn their heads towards the women, or who blaspheme and use bad language are all put to death."

border of the Empire, facing the great desert that separates Peru from Chile.

In order to prepare the line of march and the relays for the army, several Incas, who were close relatives of the king, went ahead into the wilderness, accompanied by men from Atacama and Tucma, who knew a little about the region. After having advanced eighty leagues, at the cost of great difficulties, they reached the province of Copayapu,[13] which is well populated, although not very large. It is surrounded by wilderness on all sides, and there is a further distance of eighty leagues to be covered, before one reaches the province of Cuquimpu, where Chile actually begins. Having obtained all possible information, the Inca messengers and their guides retraced their footsteps and returned in great haste to report to the king on what they had seen. Shortly after this reconnaissance, an army of ten thousand men, under the command of a general named Sinchiruca and two camp commanders, started off across the wilderness with abundant supplies loaded on pack animals who, when the time came, would also be used to provide food.

A second army corps of equal size left some time later to support the first one. The inhabitants of Copayapu were much alarmed when they saw the usual Inca messengers appear. At first, they took up arms, but they soon became hesitant, having realized, after the first skirmishes, that they were faced with a very strong opponent.

At that point, they were divided between their desire to preserve their liberty and the fear of losing even more if they should dare to resist the Inca, when the arrival of the second army hastened their decision: with the result that they immediately surrendered, which delighted the Inca, who saw the gates of the great kingdom of Chile swing open before him, without his having struck a single blow. He therefore immediately ordered that a fresh army of ten thousand men should come and join the two first ones, and that together, all three of them should continue their forward march. And thus it was that, after having crossed eighty more leagues of desert, the imperial armies entered the valley of Cuquimpu. Whether there was actual fighting, or whether Cuquimpu surrendered without resisting, I could not say, for the reason that the theater of these exploits is so far from Cuzco that this is all the

Peruvian Indians know about it. What is certain, however, is that Cuquimpu was conquered and the imperial armies, continuing their march southward, subjugated all of the nations they encountered until the valley of Chile, properly speaking, which gives its name to the whole of this kingdom. The campaign is said to have lasted six years and, during all that time, they say that the Inca never stopped sending provisions and reinforcements to his armies, with the result that the day arrived when there were more than fifty thousand combatants in Chile, all of whom were as well supplied and equipped as if they had been in Cuzco.

They extended their conquests as far as the Rio Maulli,[14] fifty leagues south of the Chile valley: which, counting from Atacama, made a strip of new lands more than two hundred and sixty leagues long that they had brought into the Empire. Beyond the Rio Maulli, stretched the territory of the Purumaucas, whom the Spaniards call the Promaucas.[15] These Indians have a very warlike tradition, so that they did not wait for the Inca's messengers before taking up arms to join their neighbors and allies the Antallis, the Pincus, and the Cauquis. And, when the ambassadors arrived, they replied that the victors would be the masters of the vanquished, and that the Incas would soon see how the Purumaucas obeyed them.

Three or four days later, their army of between fifteen and twenty thousand men, pitched camp within sight of the Inca camp, to where they again sent messengers saying that the time for words was passed, and that now it would be for war to decide the victory of those on one side and the death of those on the other. They advised their enemies to put themselves in readiness without waiting any longer, since they would be attacked the next day at dawn.

The Incas and the Purumaucas fought all day long with neither truce nor respite. At nightfall they both retreated to their respective positions, then started fighting again the following morning, as also on the third. Indeed, they were so well matched in daring and tenacity, that after these three days of combat, neither of the two camps had yet gained the advantage. The fourth, fifth, and sixth days, each side strengthened its positions, while waiting for a sortie on the part of the others, but not daring to risk one themselves. On the seventh day, the Purumaucas and their allies returned to their own country, claiming victory, although they had not really won it, while the imperial army retreated to the Rio Maulli, to await further instructions from the Inca. The latter having promptly replied that it was better to hold one's own than to pursue fate in campaigns that were too far distant and too perilous, the war ended there, and, with it, the conquest of Chile. Thus the Empire frontier remained on the Rio Maulli, and the Incas began organization and fortification of their new provinces. All of the Indians in this country yielded with good grace to the laws and customs that were taught them, which they continued to observe faithfully until the Spaniards tried their hand at the conquest of Chile, which was to end so disastrously for them.[16]

At the end of this campaign, King Yupanqui's Empire extended, from north to south, over more than a thousand leagues. The moment seemed to him to have arrived, therefore, when he could abandon all ideas of further conquests and devote himself exclusively to government of his vassals and enhancement of Peru and its capital. Thus he ordered fortresses and Sun temples to be built, as well as convents for virgins, royal warehouses, roads, and irrigation canals. Then, in order to prove that he was the worthy son of his father, he further embellished the Temple of the Sun in Cuzco, which the preceding king had already rendered incomparably beautiful. He also conscientiously visited all his kingdoms, inquiring personally into the needs of his vassals. Lastly, he concentrated his entire attention on the construction of a new Cuzco fortress, for which his father had not only designed the plans, but had also amassed great quantities of rock and hewn stone, as we shall see later.

Thus, he lived several years longer in peace and quiet, surrounded by the esteem of all his subjects. Then, one day, he fell ill, and sensing that death was near, summoned the crown prince and his other sons, and passed away, after having enjoined them to faithfully observe the laws of the Sun, and the customs and traditions of their ancestors. This was his last will and testament. He died at the height of his glory, leaving the Empire larger by five hundred leagues to the south and one hundred and forty to the north, from Chincha to Chimu. He was deeply mourned and his funeral ceremonies lasted a year, as was the custom. He became the tenth god, son of the Sun, having been the tenth king of Peru, and many sacrifices were offered up to him. As his heir and successor, he left his son Tupac Inca Yupanqui, born of Coya Chimpu Occlo, his sister-bride. He is supposed to have had nearly two hundred and fifty other children.

Since it was this king who started to build the Cuzco fortress, we shall now describe it, for it was his exploit of exploits, his trophy of trophies, and not only his, but that of his predecessors and successors as well. Indeed, it is such a marvelous achievement that it would suffice to ensure the glory of all the Inca kings.

Among the many magnificent buildings constructed by the Incas, the Cuzco fortress undoubtedly deserves to be considered as the greatest and most praiseworthy witness to the power and majesty of these kings. Its proportions are inconceivable when one has not actually seen it; and when one has looked at it closely and examined it attentively, they appear to be so extraordinary, that it seems as though some magic had presided over its construction; that it must be the work of demons, instead of human beings. It is made of such stones, and in such great number, that one wonders simultaneously how the Indians were able to quarry them, how they transported them to Cuzco, and how they hewed them and set them one on top of the other with such precision. For they were disposed of neither iron nor steel with which to penetrate the rock and cut and polish the stones; they had neither wagons nor oxen to transport them, and, in fact, there exist neither wagons nor oxen throughout the world that would have sufficed for this task, so enormous are these stones, and so rude the mountain paths over which they were conveyed. They were dragged by sheer numbers of human hands, on the ends of chains, for a distance of ten, and sometimes fifteen, leagues.[17] The *caicusca,* or "weary stone," which the Indians referred to in this way because it would not come as far as the fortress, was taken from a quarry located fifteen leagues from Cuzco, on the other bank of the Rio del Y'ùcay; and those that required the least hauling came from Muina, which was five leagues from Cuzco. They are so well fitted together that you could not slip the point of a knife between two of them:

indeed, such a work defies imagination. And since the Indians possessed no precision instruments, not even a simple ruler, they doubtless had to set these stones on top of one another, then set them down on the ground again a great many times before they succeeded in fitting them together, entirely without cranes or pulleys.

"In Tiahuanaco," writes Father Joseph de Acosta, "I measured a stone that was thirty-eight feet long, eighteen feet wide and six feet thick. The wall of the Cuzco fortress is made of masonry in which I have seen some even bigger ones, and what is most remarkable is that, although these stones are not regular, in fact, they are all of different dimensions, they fit into one another with incredible accuracy, without the use of mortar."

I have already mentioned the fact that this fortress is located north of the city, on a hill called Sacsahuaman. The incline of this hill, which faces the city, is very steep, almost perpendicular in fact, which makes the fortress impregnable from that side. Consequently, all they did was to build a wall of regularly shaped stones, polished on all their facets, and perfectly fitted into one another without mortar. This wall is two hundred spans long. The explanation of the fact that they did not use the mortar we use, made of lime and sand, is that they knew nothing about lime. They did have a mortar, however, made of a very sticky red earth, which they used to replace the stone fragments that they chipped off now and then, when they were cutting it.

On the other side of this wall, the top of the hill forms a vast horizontal plateau which the enemy could easily have reached by a gentle slope. Each one of the enclosures, which are shaped like a half moon, is more than two hundred spans long, and its ends touch the first wall, facing the city. The first, or outer, enclosure is the most remarkable of the three, it being here that the most enormous stones are assembled, and with such imposing workmanship that the very sight of it is enough to frighten the spectator.

I do not believe that these stones, or more precisely, these boulders, originated in quarries, for they do not appear to have been cut at all. Certain of them are concave on one side, convex on another and skewed on a third, while there are some that have no angles, and others with very sharp angles. They were no doubt found, one by one, on the land, and transported just as they were, then fitted according to the shape of each one: the convex side of one filling the hollow of another, and the skewed side of one laid against another of contrary proportions, without there being any need, anywhere, to have recourse to pebbles and stones of lesser dimensions to fill in gaps.

"But what is really remarkable," wrote Father Acosta, "is the fact that these stones, no two of which are alike, fit into each other without mortar, with incredible accuracy."

Only the outer surface of the wall was polished, and only the edges of the stone blocks were finely hewn, along a band about four fingers wide; with the result that, with its rough, irregular surface, its carefully hewn assemblage, and the irregular arrangement of the stones that compose it, this enclosing wall forms a perfect whole, in which there is no detail that shocks the eye.

A Spanish monk, who recently visited Peru, told me on his return, that he would never have believed what people tell about this fortress if he hadn't seen it with his own eyes, because it is even more difficult to imagine than one can say; and that, in reality, it seemed hardly possible that such a project could have been successfully carried out without the help of the Evil One. Those were his very words.

If we think, too, that this incredible work was accomplished without the help of a single machine, is it too much to say that it represents an even greater enigma than the seven wonders of the world? Because one sees quite well how the great wall of Babylon, the Colossus of Rhodes, or the Egyptian pyramids were constructed, with the combined forces of time and countless workers, accumulating, year after year, the necessary material, whether it was a question of bricks and cement, as in Babylon, of bronze, as in Rhodes, or of stone and mortar, as for the pyramids. All of that can be imagined, because, with time, the vastest undertakings can be carried through, if they are merely a matter of repeating gestures and labors of which we know men are capable. But, on the contrary, how may we explain the fact that these Peruvian Indians were able to split, carve, lift, carry, hoist, and lower such enormous blocks of stone, which are more like pieces of a mountain than building stones, and that they accomplished this, as I said before, without the help of a single machine or instrument? An enigma such as this one cannot be easily solved without seeking the help of magic, particularly when one recalls the great familiarity of these people with devils.

Each enclosing wall had a gate cut in the middle, which closed by means of a single big stone that worked like a drawbridge. The first of these gates was called *Tiu-Puncu*, or the sand gate, because it opened on to a sandy plain; the second, *Acahuana-Puncu*, from the name of the architect who designed it, Acahuana; the third, *Viracocha-Puncu*, or the Viracocha gate, through which one reached the inside of the fortress, which was placed entirely under the protection of Viracocha, the god, savior and protector, par excellence, of the Incas. A twenty-five to thirty foot space separated the three enclosing walls from one another. This was filled in with earth to the top of the walls, where a three foot parapet ensured the safety of the guards.

Inside this triple enclosure, three tall towers were erected on a large narrow ground. The largest of them was called *Mayac Marca*, which means the round tower. It was built over a clear, abundant spring, fed by underground canalizations, concerning which nobody knew from where or how they came: the Inca and the members of his supreme council were always the only ones who knew such secrets[18] as these. This round tower contained rooms with gold and silver paneled walls, on which animals, birds, and plants figured in relief, as though in a tapestry. It was here that the king lived when he came for a rest in the fortress, and as much tableware and other service articles of all kinds were kept there as in the other royal dwellings.

The two other towers, which were round, not square, in shape, were called *Paucar Marca* and *Sacllac Marca*, and were used to house soldiers of the garrison, which was composed only of Incas by privilege, ordinary men, even combatants, not being allowed inside this fortress, which was the house of the Sun, both its arsenal and its temple. The commander-general was a blood Inca, who had under his command a galaxy of officers entrusted with precise duties: one was responsible for discipline among the troops, another for supplies, a third for the care and maintenance of all weapons, and another for the clothing and shoe warehouses.

An underground network of passages, which was as vast as the towers themselves, connected them with one another. This was composed of a quantity of streets and alleyways which ran in every direction, and so many doors, all of them identical, that the most experienced men dared not venture into this labyrinth without a guide, consisting of a long thread tied to the first door, which unwound as they advanced. I often went up to the fortress with boys of my own age, when I was a child, and we did not dare to go farther than the sunlight itself, we were so afraid of getting lost, after all that the Indians had told us on the subject.

Since they did not know how to build arches, the roofs of these underground passages were composed of large flat stones resting on rafters jutting out from the walls.

Four master architects contributed to the construction of this fortress, the first and principal one of whom was Huallpu Rimachi Inca, who designed the general plan. He was succeeded by Inca Maricanchi. However, the principal buildings of Tiahuanaco, of which we have already spoken,[19] are attributed to the third one, whose name was Acahuana Inca. The fourth and last architect of the fortress was Calla Cunchuy, and it was in his time that the so-called "weary stone," to which he gave his name, was hauled there. The dimensions of this stone are incredible, and I should like to be able to give them, but unfortunately I do not possess them. This stone remained on the plateau, in front of the fortress, and the Indians say it was so wearied by its long journey that it came to a halt, wept tears of blood, and could go no farther. It has remained unhewn, in the rough state in which it was found. I remember that there were one or two holes in one corner of it, which, according to the Indians, were the eyes with which it had wept blood.

The truth, however, as told by the amautas, is that this boulder was hauled across the mountain by more than twenty thousand Indians, going up and down very steep hills, and that, at a certain spot, it fell from their hands over a precipice, crushing more than three thousand men. Thus it was they and the other slaves who wept blood, and not the stone; it was also the slaves who arrived too weary on the plateau, to be able to hoist their burden up to the fortress. However, all great exploits give rise to legends, and the Peruvian Indians have invented many others, which, like this one, they hand down from generation to generation.

It would have been in the interest of the Spaniards to maintain this fortress, and even to repair it at their own expense, because, quite alone, it gave proof of the grandeur of their victory and would have served as a witness to it for all eternity. And yet, not only did they not keep it up, but they hastened its ruin, demolishing its hewn stones, in order to construct their own Cuzco homes at less cost.

They made their portals and thresholds with the big flat stones that formed the ceilings, and to make their stairways, they did not hesitate to tear down entire walls, provided they were based on a few stones that could be used for steps.

And so, that is how the Spaniards destroyed the Cuzco fortress. Indeed, they did it so quickly that I, personally, saw almost nothing of it, except for the three great enclosing walls, that were too enormous for them to touch, although I have been told that they attacked them recently, in order to discover Huaina Capac's famous gold chain, which they believed had been buried there.

From the time of the good King Inca Yupanqui, under whose reign the first material was assembled, until that of Huaina Capac, the Incas worked for over fifty years to erect this fortress; there are even those who say that they never finished it, and they give as proof this "weary stone" which, according to them, was to have been used for further construction, before civil war and the arrival of the Spaniards put an end to all these projects, and to the Inca Empire itself.[20]

1. Cuzco, as described by Garcilaso, had been entirely rebuilt by order of the Inca Pachacutec, shortly after 1440. According to Sancho, the population of the valley of Cuzco, when the Spaniards arrived, was of the order of one hundred thousand, which is much smaller, it will be noted, than that of the largest coastal valleys.

2. "With regard to the details that can be given of the town of Cuzco . . . it is known that they sacrificed human blood as well as that of numerous sheep and ewes on the sacred hill of Guanacaure (Huanacauri), close to the city. As the town was full of foreigners, often from places very distant

from one another—Indians from Chile, Pasto (Colombia), and members of the Cañari, Chachapuya, Guanca, Colla tribes, and all the other tribes of these provinces, each group was bound to keep to the part of the town allotted to it by the city governors. . . ." (Cieza, Part I, Chapter 93)

3. The following are Krickeberg's remarks on this important subject:

"In spite of its unity and centralization, it must not be thought that the Inca state was an entirely new and original creation, cut off from the general development of pre-Columbian American Society. The Inca Empire was not a 'great socialist state' as certain utopian democrats would have us believe, but the outcome of the continuation and intensification of ancient American social patterns carried to their logical conclusion. For a very long time, no doubt was cast on the statements of the chronicler Garcilaso de la Vega, descended from the Incas, who attributed to the Incas all sorts of institutions which in reality were anterior to the Incas and merely incorporated, unchanged by them, into their system of government, with practical common sense, and an acute awareness of political expediency.

"This is the case of the *ayllus,* in particular. Throughout the high plateaus of the Andes, the tribes were subdivided into clans or *ayllus,* whose members, conscious of their blood relationship, formed agrarian communities, each *ayllu* with its well-defined territory. Internally, these clans were governed on a patriarchal basis, in Inca times at least, although traces of matriarchal institutions have been found at Chinchasuyu and in other regions.

"In Peru, as everywhere else in America, the clan formed a religious, as well as an economic and military unit, each *ayllu* having in its territory its own tutelary deity, regarded as the "creator" or ancestor. There are traces of a totem cult to be seen; Garcilaso, in his description of the Feast of the Sun at Cuzco, speaks of delegates dressed in puma skins or wearing condor wings on their backs, because they considered themselves descended from these animals.

"The clan leaders were called *curacas* . . . In all the tribes of the high plateaus, from the Cañari of Ecuador to the Quechuas of Cuzco, we find the same division of the clan into two groups, *hanan* and *hurin,* which may be compared to the matrimonial "halves" of other American communities.

"The Inca family was originally an *ayllu,* like all the others, in a small tribe of ten or eleven clans. Subsequently, this tribe was to double the number of its clans, for every reigning Inca, with the exception of the *primogenitus,* the crown prince, formed a new *ayllu.* When this tribe settled in the Cuzco valley it did not mix with the indigenous tribes, but became a ruling caste, a situation which continued throughout the history of the Incas, while they extended their empire gradually over the whole country."

However, Rowe disputes the use of the term "clan," accepted hitherto by most modern authors (Bandelier, Baudin, Means, Murdock, etc.). The chroniclers and Spanish historians, he points out, used the term *ayllu* in three entirely different senses: the lineage or descendants of the Inca kings (filiation through the father's line, whereas the concept of a clan implies filiation through the mother's line); social unit (administrative division under the authority of a curaca); and sometimes matrimonial "half." It is very difficult, therefore, to give a definition of this word to cover all its meanings. It would seem to have been, in Quechua, a general word used to describe all related groups, whatever their structure.

4. According to Earl J. Hamilton, the ducat weighed .121 ounces of fine gold. This first collection taken up in Cuzco in one day by Friar Antonio de San Miguel and Garcilaso's father, to build the first hospital for Indians in the New World, thus represented almost 123,200 ounces of fine gold, or about one hundred thousand dollars, at the present rate of gold.

5. It should be remembered that, contrary to what we are told by Garcilaso, the Inca Yupanqui and the Inca Pachacutec were one and the same person, Pachacutec simply being the title given to the king on his coronation for having saved Cuzco from the Chanca invasion. The campaign which Garcilaso is about to describe, in the territory of the Musu (Mojo) and Chirihuana tribes, was led by Tupac (or Topa), son of Pachacutec, after his coronation, between 1471 and 1493. (Rowe) Tupac was the first Inca to penetrate as far as the Gran Chaco. Neither the Mojo nor the Chirihuana tribe, however, was ever annexed to the Tahuantinsuyu. See the chart of the extension of the Inca Empire.

6. Here Garcilaso confuses tributaries of the Amazon and of the Rio de la Plata. This river which he calls Amarumayu is in reality a tributary of the Amazon. The Rio Paraguay—or Parahuay—also flows into the Gran Chaco, but much farther east, flowing not northwards like the Amarumayu, but southwards to join the two other great tributaries of the Rio de la Plata, the Parana, and the Pilcomayo, in Argentina. It is not known how the Incas explored towards the East.

7. The anaconda of Brazil (*Eunectes murinus*), the largest snake in the world.

8. The Amazon, discovered in 1539 by Francisco de Orellana, one of Gonzalvo Pizarro's lieutenants, in the year of Garcilaso's birth.

9. The Mojo tribe is still one of the largest of Bolivia. Their first contact with the whites dates back to the sixteenth century and they have almost entirely lost their cultural characteristics. It is still possible, however, to recognize their Arawak origin and they seem to have escaped all Peruvian influences in spite of their contact with the Inca. (Nordenskiöld)

10. Like the *encomiendas* of sinister memory, the *repartimientos* were concessions of territory and populations, made

on condition that the colonists to whom they were granted feed the Indians and instruct them in the Christian faith. Thanks to the energy and perseverance of Bartolomé de las Casas in urging the Emperor Charles V to action, this legislation was repealed in 1542 by the famous *Leyes Nuevas* which recognized the Indians as "vassals of the crown" of Spain and, consequently, forbade their enslavement. This Dominican father, las Casas, bishop of Chiapa in Mexico, was known as the "father of the Indians." He received a tribute from the French revolutionaries for his struggle against slavery. A defense of him was read at the National Institute on the 22nd of *Floréal,* of the Year VIII. It was forgotten that by securing the freedom of the Indians he helped the black slave trade.

11. At the time of the campaign of Tupac Yupanqui (not of Yupanqui Pachacutec) on the Bolivian plateaus, the territory which later belonged to the Chiriguano (Chirihuana) tribe was occupied by the Arawak tribe of the Chané. It was only some forty years later, in 1525, that the Chiriguanos, a *tupuguarani* tribe, invaded the Gran Chaco and progressed as far as the territory dependent on Cuzco. They were defeated by the Inca armies but never subdued. (Rowe) According to Steward, the Chiriguanos were 48,000 strong at the time of the conquest and their influence is still preponderant in the Gran Chaco to the present day. The reader will gain some idea of their warlike nature from the fact that when they last rebelled, less than thirty years ago, the Bolivian government had to resort to armed force to subdue them. Whatever Garcilaso may say, the Chiriguano Indians, like the Chané tribe, were far from living "like animals." (Note 5, Book IX)

12. This conquest, like the earlier ones, was the work of Topa or Tupac Yupanqui (1471-1493) and not of Yupanqui Pachacutec.

13. Copiapo.

14. Rapel river, just where Santiago, the capital of Chile, now stands, south of the thirtieth parallel.

15. These are the famous Araucan Indians.

16. It will be remembered that Diego de Almagro, in an attempt to conquer territories to the South, outside the limits assigned by the crown to his rival Francisco Pizarro, was halted on the Rio Maulli, as the Inca General Sinchiruca had been, after a savage encounter with the Araucan Indians. In this expedition, which was one of the worst undertakings of the conquest, on the outward journey alone, one hundred and fifty Spaniards and ten thousand of their Indian allies died of exposure while crossing the high desert regions of Atacama.

17. Protuberances, which can sometimes still be seen, were left

on the blocks of stone to give a hold for the levers with which they were raised. Three kinds of stone were used to build the fortress of Sacsahuaman. Two of them, including those which provided the gigantic blocks for the outer wall, were found practically on the spot. Only the third kind of stone (black andesite), for the inside buildings, was brought from relatively distant quarries: the nearest quarries of black andesite were at Huaccoto and Rumicolca, nine and twenty-two miles from Cuzco respectively. (Valcarcel, *Cuzco Archeology*)

With regard to the giant blocks of the outer wall, there is nothing to prove that they were not simply hewn from a mass of stone existing on the spot; this would solve the mystery.

18. In fact, the tower contained a reservoir, which is perhaps the greatest proof left to us by the Inca engineers of their skill. Since this reservoir was at the top of a completely isolated hill, Valcarcel points out, they were obliged to apply the law of communicating vessels and build a conduit with a siphon which probably brought water from the Chakan reservoirs, higher up and approximately two miles away. According to Valcarcel, this reservoir had a capacity of some 12,445 gallons (diameter 30 feet 8 inches, average depth 2 feet 4 inches). Numerous pipes radiated from the reservoir to carry water to the various buildings of the citadel. In the course of his excavations at Sacsahuaman in 1933-34, Valcarcel was able to follow some of these pipes for up to fifty feet. They measure, he reports, between four and five inches in diameter, and are laid in a most interesting manner. Subsidiary distribution tanks are to be observed as well as vertical conduits, elbows, joints, etc. The central reservoir was also linked up with a series of wells for decanting and industrial purposes.

The base of the tower of Muyujmarka (Garcilaso's Mayac Marca) is formed of three concentric circles measuring 30 feet 7 inches, 49 feet 2 inches and 72 feet 10 inches respectively in diameter. (Valcarcel, *Sajsawaman Redescubrimiento*)

19. Here Garcilaso is in the realm of pure fiction, since it is not known who built the fortress of Sacsahuaman and in any case, it has nothing to do with Tiahuanaco.

20. Kelemen gives us the following translation of the name of Sacsahuaman, which he borrows from Squier: "the—high-ground-to-attack-which-provides-corpses-for-the-vultures."

Again according to Kelemen: "The fortress is built of heavy blocks of stone, irregularly hewn, put together without mortar. The first wall is twelve hundred feet long, with an average height of twenty-seven feet. One of the large rocks used in the building is thirty-eight feet long, eighteen feet high and six feet thick. The second terrace is thirty-five feet from the first and is raised to a height of eighteen feet; another eighteen feet separate it from the third, which is fourteen feet high . . . The whole recalls the ruins of the

Moorish fortresses of Spain and Africa. It may be supposed, from certain signs, that this fortress was begun in pre-Inca days and later enlarged and reinforced by the Inca dynasty, of which the Spaniards were to know the last representatives."

Krickeberg's measurements for the three enclosures of the fortress differ from those given by Kelemen: the first, according to him, was 21 feet 4 inches high, the second 16 feet 5 inches, and the third 9 feet 10 inches.

Before it was finally destroyed, this fortress was to change hands three times in the early days of the conquest. Juan Pizarro, a brother of the marquis, died there in 1536 during the Spaniards' last attack on it. In the same engagement the Inca general in command of the fortress, seeing the day lost, committed suicide, rather than surrender, by throwing himself from the top of the main tower.

To conclude, let us once more quote from Valcarcel (*Cuzco Archeology*): "We found the three great fortified towers in the position described by the historian Garcilaso de la Vega in 1560, the year in which he left Cuzco for Spain. These towers, which bear the names of Muyu Marca, Salla Marca, and Paucar Marca, dominate the site of the fortress of Sacsahuaman. Only the base of these magnificent structures is still to be seen. The first tower was cylindrical in shape, on a rectangular base . . . The base of the Salla Marca tower consists of a rectangle measuring 71 feet 6 inches by 33 feet 6 inches . . . The Paucar Marca tower is entirely in ruins and only traces of it are to be seen . . . Our work shows that the whole fortress belongs to the Inca period and there is nothing to show that it might have been pre-Inca . . . The description of Sacsahuaman by Garcilaso is fully confirmed by our findings."

BOOK EIGHT

Which treats of the Inca Tupac,
eleventh king of Peru,
who conquered the Cañaris
and the kingdom of Quito.
With a description of those
rich provinces;
and the exploits of the young Prince
Huaina Capac, until
his three marriages

The Inca Tupac Yupanqui donned the scarlet bandeau and left to visit his kingdoms, as each new sovereign did. This journey took four years, after which, continuing to follow the example of his forefathers, he levied forty thousand fighting men to undertake new conquests. Less than a year later, he took the lead of his army and went to Chachapuya, the land of strong men, according to Father Blas Valera. This province, which lies east of Cajamarca, was as famous for the beauty of its daughters as for the courage of its sons.[1] Their principal weapon was the sling, of which they wore the emblem on their headdress. They worshiped snakes, but also considered the condor as the supreme god. Chachapuya had forty thousand inhabitants and stretched out over particularly steep mountains. In order to reach this famous province, one had to pass through the country of the savage Huacrachucu warriors, who, themselves, lived on steep land that was difficult of access.[2] They, too, worshiped snakes, which they painted on the walls of their temples, and they were recognizable by their headdress, which was made of a black wool cord, dotted with white, and topped by a roe's horn; from whence their name, composed of *huacra,* horn, and *chucu,* headdress.

Being certain of their strength and confident, as well, in the asperity of their mountains, the Huacrachucus went fully armed to the passes the Inca invaders would be obliged to take, to wait for them. There were many battles and many dead. In vain, the Inca tried to convince these bold adversaries with messengers bearing soft words: but although the old people lent a friendly ear, the young ones, carried away by their ardor and their numbers, kept all negotiations from achieving a successful issue. And the war which, for a moment, had been uncertain, flared up again with renewed fury. The Inca had divided his army into three corps, which attacked on three sides at once, and soon he had seized so many passes and strongholds that the enemy was finally obliged to sue for mercy. This the Inca granted with a clemency that was worthy of his ancestors, and the Huacrachucus were treated as brothers by their conquerors. But the war had affected them very cruelly and both their crops and their provisions had been destroyed. The Inca immediately had clothing and foodstuffs distributed among them, and thus, thanks to the victor's generosity, the vanquished forgot their fears and their resentments.

Tupac Yupanqui felt that, after this first success, his army deserved a little rest. However, the country of the Huacrachucus being both arid and very rainy, he commanded his troops to retreat to the frontier and, in order to more diligently carry out the campaign he planned for the following summer, gave orders that this pause should be utilized to send reinforcements of twenty thousand men to his camp.

In the meantime, while royal ministers were instructing the Huacrachucus in the imperial laws and customs, roads and canals were opened up across their country, and all arable land was leveled and brought under cultivation; in other words, everything that might contribute to the prosperity and well-being of these new vassals was done.

The Chachas—which is how the inhabitants of Chachapuya were called—had not remained idle. I have already spoken of their number, their strength, and their determination. Their territory, which measured fifty by twenty leagues, without counting the Muyupampa region, where it was thirty leagues wider still, might well be called a kingdom, rather than a province. Two or three years earlier, having guessed the Inca's intentions from his movements, they had decided to defend themselves, and had begun to fortify their mountains where, today still, may be seen the ruins of their military preparations.

As soon as the Inca had received his reinforcements, he crossed their frontiers and the war began with equal tenacity on both sides. The Incas were determined to continue their advance, at any cost, and the Chachas to die, if need be, rather than give up their independence.

With great difficulty, the imperial army conquered its first city, called Pias, on the top of a slope of the same name, which extends for two and one-half leagues, eighteen leagues from the point where they had crossed the frontier. All the valid men had abandoned this stronghold for others, stronger still, when the Incas arrived. With the result that they found only a few old people and children whose parents had not been able to take them with them when they withdrew. But the great Tupac Yupanqui gave orders that all of these persons should be treated with kindness and consideration.

Thus the forward march continued and the army entered a snowy mountain pass called "the bad gate." It was, indeed, one of the worst, in fact, for those who attempted to go through it, and three hundred picked soldiers, who had gone ahead as scouts, perished from cold in a heavy snowstorm that suddenly buried and froze them all. Here the army was obliged to interrupt its advance momentarily, and when the Chachas heard this, they spread the rumor throughout their kingdom that the Inca had become frightened and withdrawn.

But the blizzard came to an end and the Inca resumed his march. Foot by foot, one might say, he advanced to another big city called Cuntur Marca, which he took with the greatest difficulty, after having conquered several others of lesser importance on the way. In Cuntur Marca itself, the struggle lasted for days, but all the courage and determination of the Chachas was of no avail against the Inca's warriors, who submerged them like a great torrent, forcing them to surrender. The Inca received them with his usual leniency, appeasing their spirits with gifts and kind words, in the hope that, with this gesture, others might be tempted to follow their example.

From now on, conquest was easier and new cities fell at the cost of less difficulty and less bloodshed. The example of Cuntur Marca had borne fruit, and numerous Chachas came to surrender, while others resisted less stubbornly than before. Thus the Inca reached another large city, called Cajamarquilla, which was separated from Cuntur Marca by eight leagues of wild mountains and poor roads. However, after much fighting, Cajamarquilla also fell to the imperial troops.

From Cajamarquilla, the Inca went on to another big city called Papamarca, or the potato city. Then the Raïmi season arrived, just as he was entering still another city, eight leagues from there. He, therefore, celebrated the great Sun feast in this city, and, for this reason, since then the city has been called Raïmipampa, or the place of the Raïmi. Three leagues farther on, the army took a third city, called Suta. By this time, the Chachas, having seen the greater part of their country invested, had ceased to fight with real vigor, and soon the former capital of the kingdom, called Llauantu, surrendered without striking a blow, or almost.

In the entire Chacha kingdom, Muyupampa was the only province that continued to resist. This was the place to which the brave prince Hancohuallu had fled to escape Inca domination, as we recounted in telling the life of the Inca Viracocha. This province, which was located in the Andes, thirty leagues east of Llauantu, was not, properly speaking, part of the Chachapuya kingdom, but they were allied, either by mutual desire through confederation, or through the ties of bondage.

One of the Inca's army corps headed for this province which, realizing that the conquest of Chachapuya was an accomplished fact, surrendered without resisting. Now two other small provinces in this region, the most important of which was called Cascayunca, followed their example. So the army was finally able to take a rest, while the Inca was busy establishing his administration over all the new territories.

The following summer, with forty thousand soldiers, Tupac Yupanqui undertook to conquer the great province of Huancapampa, which was like a mosaic of tongues and small nations, with neither leaders, nor laws, nor cities, nor houses. They fought like animals among themselves over their wives and their daughters; they also went naked, and the males devoured one another.

Even their religion was as brutish as their mores. Each nation, each army unit, each home had its own god: here, it was an animal, there a bird, an herb or a plant, elsewhere a mountain, a spring, or a river, according to each one's fancy. And there were constant battles, between the believers in one god and those who believed in another, to decide which of the two was the greater. It is comprehensible, therefore, that it should have been extremely easy to conquer them, for their resistance consisted merely of running away like wild animals into the mountains and deserts, where the most stubborn among them died of hunger, rather than come down and surrender.

The Inca Tupac Yupanqui promptly had them assembled, and appointed masters to teach them how to live decently, how to settle a village, hide their nakedness and cultivate their land. They also built roads and opened up canals for them, with the result that this province, which thus far had been so wretched, became, in a short while, one of the most prosperous in the Empire. It even had a temple to the Sun and a convent for virgins; also, people stopped eating human flesh and all of them worshiped the Sun.

It is not known how many years after these events the Incas turned their attention to conquering three more provinces that, likewise, contained a multitude of nations, but, in reality, they were much more civil and better organized than the preceding ones. They had no princes, but chose a supreme commander for the three of them, in time of war. These provinces were called Cassa, Ayahuaca, and Callua. The offers made by the Inca as he approached their borders were brutally rejected, and there followed an exceedingly bitter war, in which the Inca lost more than eight thousand men.

Indeed, these provinces had to be taken a foot at a time, by forcing the enemy back, little by little, towards an ultimate corner, in which he fortified himself in the firm intention never to surrender. And these unfortunate people would certainly all have died as a result of this desperate resolution, if a group of their captains, having understood that further struggle was vain, had not come, against the will of the majority, to ask the Inca for peace. Even then, however, peace was not made without a certain number of mutinies taking place.

So many men had perished in this war that the Inca, after having comforted the vanquished, was obliged to displace entire populations, taken from other provinces, in order to repopulate these. He then left for Cuzco, weary and irritated, more by the stubbornness of the people than by any harm they may have done him. He resolved, too, that, henceforth, if he encountered other peoples as dogged as these, he would postpone their conquest until, with time, they appeared to have become less uncompromising.

The Inca Tupac Yupanqui remained for several years in Cuzco, where, for the most part, he continued to work on the fortress that had been started by his father. He then set out again with a view to conquest in the north of the Empire, in the Chinchasuyu district. The province of Huanacu, which was inhabited by several wild, unorganized nations, was subjugated with little difficulty and, in a short time, as a result of the beneficent effects of Inca government, it became so important that it soon commanded many others. A Temple of the Sun and a virgins' convent were built, that employed twenty thousand, some even said thirty thousand, Indians, as Pedro de Cieza de Leon tells, in the eightieth chapter of his book. "The royal dwelling in Huanacu," he adds, "was a splendid palace, entirely built of great polished stones. Here the Inca's majordomos commanded all the other Andes provinces, from which they collected tribute."

But let us not tarry over the details of these conquests, of which I shall give a brief summary. The following year, the Inca levied a very powerful army to undertake subjugation of Cañari, a very large, powerful province that ruled over a great many others. The people in Cañari wore their hair long, gathered together in a knot on top of their heads. By way of bonnets, the nobles wore a sort of cone-shaped sieve, decorated with cascades of different colored ribbons, while the plain people wore a gourd, from whence the name of *matiuma,* or gourd-head, by which they were usually designated.

On the way to Cañari, the Inca seized the province of Palta, which he was obliged to cross. From there comes the delicious fruit of the same name,[3] that today is cultivated and considered a great delicacy in the warm Cuzco valleys. The conquest of this province took place peacefully and easily, thanks to the friendly words spoken by the Inca. The people of Palta had one physical peculiarity; which was a long skull, that was flat both in front and in back. From birth they pressed their children's skulls between two planks, tied together at the ends, which they tightened a little every day. After three years, a child's skull was deformed for life, so they removed the apparatus. This is the origin of the nickname of *Palta uma,* or *palta*-head,[4] used in Peru, and applied to those whose head is too big, or too flat in back, at the nape.

The conquest of Cañari was as easy as that of the people in Palta. After a short period of reflection, all the caciques of this nation replied favorably to the imperial messengers, and they came in great pomp to formally present their surrender to the king, who, after having made them numerous gifts, had their instruction started immediately.

Up until that time the Cañaris had worshiped the Moon, large trees, and certain multicolored stones. But now they abandoned all these false gods to devote themselves to the cult of the Sun; they built a temple in its honor and a convent for virgins; they also erected many palaces for the king. The Inca's administration took great care, as was its custom, to develop agriculture and open up roads and irrigation canals through their territory, for all of which the Cañaris were very grateful. And yet, when the Spaniards arrived, the example of one Cañari sufficed to make them all suddenly take the side of the invaders, and display great hatred for their former masters: all of which goes to prove that the popular saying is a true one, which states that *might makes right!* [5]

The great Tupac Inca Yupanqui stayed a long time among the Cañaris to personally supervise the organization of his administration in their country. Amongst all the things that this great king and, later, his son, Huaina Capac, did for the Cañaris, special mention must be made of the numerous temples and palaces with which they embellished the province of Tumipampa, called, by the Spaniards, Tome Bamba. All these buildings were as rich as those in Cuzco. Their living apartments were paneled with gold and silver, carved with figures of plants and animals, enhanced by emeralds, turquoises, and other precious stones. They also contained numerous accumulated treasures: platters, glazed jars, all sorts of vases made of precious metals, silverware, dazzlingly rich garments, and necklaces of the tiny little gold beads that the Spaniards call *chaquiras*. The latter are real masterpieces, and even the most skillful goldsmiths and jewelers in Seville were astonished by them, when I showed them those I had brought from Peru. They all asked me how the Indians proceeded in the manufacture and, above all, in the welding of these beads, which are thinner than anything one can imagine.

Pedro de Cieza de Leon gives a long account of these Tumipampa palaces and temples, as also of the treasures they contained. He adds the following, with regard to the Sun temple:

"Certain Indians maintain that most of the stones in this temple were brought from Cuzco, on Huaina Capac's orders, or on those of his father, the great Tupac Inca. If this be true, it is quite remarkable, when one thinks of the number and weight of these stones, which had to be dragged with ropes, over such a distance." [6]

The distance between Cuzco and Tumipampa must be nearly four hundred leagues, and the difficulties of the road, which runs through the mountains, are indescribable. And yet, I give my word, I who am also an Indian, that Pedro de Cieza's informers did not lie, but told him the truth. If they had wanted to boast, it would not have been of this work, however incredible this may have been, but of the much more extraordinary favor it betokened. For only those provinces most highly prized by the Inca possessed temples to the Sun, and, no doubt, there was not a single other temple in all the Empire that could compete with the Cuzco temple as this one could, since it was made of the same stone. There was no labor that the Inca's subjects would not have carried out, as though it were child's play, in order to deserve such a reward.

A prince's thirst for conquest, like his ambition, increases with his power. Thus the great Tupac Inca did not remain idle long, and only a few years after his return to Cuzco, he raised a larger army than ever before and set out for conquest on the road that led to the land of the Cañaris, which is fifty leagues from the frontiers of the kingdom of Quito.[7] He crossed the latter without difficulty, subjugating all the little nations he encountered on the way, the principal ones being: Chanchan Moca, Quesma, Pumallacta—or the land of lions, because there were more lions there than elsewhere and they were adored as gods—Ticsampi, Tiucassa, Cayampi, Urcollasu, and Tincuracu. All of these countries were poor, and their populations were so wretched, that the Incas were harder put to it to educate than to subjugate them; indeed, most of them lived in such miserable conditions that the only form of tribute demanded of them was the louse tax.

While the great Tupac Yupanqui was advancing towards these new conquests, other nations, situated west of his path, in the province that the Spaniards call Puerto-Viejo, the principal one of which was that of the Hancahuillcas, came of their own accord to implore him to take them into the Empire and to give them the education that had been of such great benefit to his vassals. He welcomed their ambassadors with the greatest courtesy and sent ministers to teach them how to build roads and canals, how to cultivate the land and how to populate their cities. Nevertheless, these people later assassinated their benefactors, with the basest ingratitude, as Cieza de Leon recounts. I have spoken so frequently of the Inca's kindness, and of all the things they taught their subjects that, just here, in order not to be accused of partiality, I prefer to quote the above-mentioned Spanish author. Here, then, is what Cieza de Leon has to say about these provinces, in chapter forty-seven of his great work:

"The great Topa Inga Yupangue received those who brought him this petition with all the signs of affection, and presented them with pieces of fine wool cloth, woven in Cuzco. And, since he was obliged to return home, where he was impatiently awaited by his subjects who loved him so much that they called him their father, he had to leave without visiting the provinces of these Indians. However, he appointed several governors, who were natives of Cuzco, to go and teach them better customs, to show them how to live properly, and how to develop their agriculture. But not only did the Indians refuse to listen to the good advice of these governors, who had come to their provinces on the order of the Inca, after they themselves had begged for them, but all the thanks they gave for the benefits they might have derived from the presence of these men was to massacre every last one of them, when, in reality, the Inca's envoys had not tyrannized them in any way.

"We are told that the great Topa Yupangue, when he learned this news, preferred not to mention it, being unable to bring himself to punish those who had so basely murdered his captains and vassals."

Now the Inca returned to Cuzco to rest from the toils and cares of war.

After having enjoyed the tranquillity of peace for a few years, Tupac Inca Yupanqui decided to undertake to conquer the kingdom of Quito. This was a large, well-known country sixty leagues long by thirty leagues wide, and endowed with a very rich soil, suitable for all types of agriculture. Its king who, himself, was named Quito, was a powerful lord, as cruel as he was crude and belligerent, and, consequently, dreaded by all his neighbors.

Tupac Inca recruited forty thousand fighting men, went

as far as the frontiers of Tumipampa and sent ahead the usual messengers. But King Quito, who was sure of his own strength, received them arrogantly and let them understand that he refused to listen to them, alleging that he was accustomed to command and not to obey, and that he had no intention of changing, nor would he exchange his gods, which were roe deer and great, tall trees, for the Sun.

The Inca decided to temporize, wishing to avoid war as long as he could. But all his gracious, amiable manners only increased Quito's arrogance, with the result that he had to resign himself to fighting. And so the war started; and it was to last for months, even for years.

Seeing this, Tupac Inca Yupanqui summoned his son and heir, Huaina Capac, together with twelve thousand common soldiers, in the dual intention of reinforcing his army and teaching the arts of war to the young prince who, at that time, was approaching his twentieth year.

Literally translated, the name of this prince means "the rich young man." But, as a matter of fact, and taking into account the manner in which the Incas named and nicknamed their kings, it means "he who, since his youth, has distinguished himself by magnanimous exploits."

Many of his acts of grandeur are cited. And among them, one that struck his contemporaries the most, was the invariably courteous manner with which he received the petitions of women, of whatever age or station. "Mother," he would say, in the case of a woman older than he was, "whatever you say will be done." And to a woman who was more or less his own age, he would say: "Sister, what you desire shall be done"; to one younger than himself, he would reply: "My daughter, what you ask will come to pass." Then, in order to better demonstrate how great was the favor and grace accorded them, he would lay his hand on their left shoulder. As we shall see, he always gave evidence of a similar nobility of sentiment, in the worst of circumstances, even circumstances that concerned his own majesty.

Indeed, this prince behaved so well, and so in conformity with Inca traditions, as soon as he arrived upon the scene of this war, that Tupac Inca Yupanqui decided to put him in supreme command and, himself, return to Cuzco, where many affairs of state awaited him. The conquest of the kingdom of Quito continued, therefore, under the orders of the prince, with the help of able captains. It

Huaina Capac Leaving to Undertake the Conquest of the Canaris

lasted three years, or even five, if we are to believe the inhabitants of Quito. Of course Tupac Inca Yupanqui had conducted these operations over a period of two years, before handing over the command to his son. And, indeed, it was to their common desire to avoid all bloodshed that may be attributed the unusual duration of this campaign. As it was, the imperial armies were obliged to occupy the kingdom progressively, as the enemy withdrew in the face of their advance, and King Quito died of grief when he saw that practically all of his land had been conquered. In fact, in all probability, it was his death that brought the war to a close.

Prince Huaina Capac later gave evidence of great partiality for this kingdom, which he enriched and embellished in a thousand different ways, endowing it, among other edifices, with a Temple of the Sun and a virgins' convent as richly furnished in every way as were the most famous in the Empire. And this partiality increased with the prince's age to such an extent that he carried it to extremes never before indulged in by any of the Inca kings, with the result that the Empire fell into ruin and the royal line became extinct.

Huaina Capac pursued his campaign beyond Quito. He first conquered the Quillacencas,[8] whose name means a metal nose, because these Indians perforated the cartilage that separates the nostrils, to hang, as one would a ring, a small trinket made of copper, gold, or silver. They were dirty, badly dressed, and covered with vermin, and one can say that the only thing they worshiped was meat, which they were so greedy for that they did not hesitate to eat their fill of any dead animals they came across, however rotten and decomposed they may have been. Having brought them to a state of submission without difficulty, the Inca conquered with equal ease the province of Pasto,[9] whose inhabitants were hardly more advanced in their customs, with this difference, however, that instead of being very fond of meat, like their neighbors, they turned from it in disgust, saying, if people tried to force them to eat it, that they were not dogs. All these Indians were quickly subjugated and, as a beginning of their education, they were forced to pay the louse tax, in order to keep them from dying as a result of being devoured by vermin.

After Pasto, the Inca conquered Otauallu, a province that was better organized and more bellicose than the preceding ones, and therefore attempted a certain resistance; then came Caranque, which was a large, more barbarous province than the most barbarous of them all. Here they worshiped the tiger, the lion, and the most frightful snakes, and the only dealings the people had with their neighbors consisted in attacking them in order to capture something to put on their tables, since they battened on human flesh, and on their altars, where they offered still beating hearts to their false gods. These savages resisted the Inca ferociously for a few days, but they were soon obliged to surrender. Huaina Capac took pains to rid them as quickly as possible of their baleful habits, and no doubt this was what was hardest for them, for they were inordinately fond of human flesh.

This, then, was the last conquest made by the Incas, beyond the kingdom of Quito.

Since he had abandoned care of the armies to his son, the great Tupac Inca Yupanqui devoted himself exclusively to government of the Empire, and to pursuing construction of the Cuzco fortress, on which more than twenty thousand Indians were working. Every two or three years, he sent envoys to his governors in Chile, to whom he had delivered quantities of fine vicuña woolen material for the curacas and lords of this kingdom, as also common wool for their vassals. He received, in exchange, gold, feathers, and other fruits of this earth; and things continued like this until Don Diego de Almagro entered the country.

On his return from the Quito campaign, Prince Huaina Capac was received in Cuzco in great triumph. It was then that he married, this being his second marriage, his second sister Raua Occlo, the first wife, named Pillcu Huaco, not having borne him any children. But he was soon to be married a third time, to Mama Runtu, a daughter of Auqui Amaru Tupac Inca, his closest legitimate brother; and, if this time, he wed his niece, it was because he had no other legitimate sisters by his father and mother. The King Tupac Yupanqui and his council recognized these two new wives as legitimate queens, on a par with the first one, and not as concubines, thus ensuring to their issue the right of succession to the throne. Raua Occlo had a son named Huascar Inca, who thus became the future heir; and the third wife of Huaina Capac bore him Manco Inca, who was also, one day, to inherit the Empire, in name, if not in fact, because, in reality, the Spaniards having conquered Peru, one can say that there was no longer an Inca Empire.[10]

Tupac Inca Yupanqui lived several years longer in peace and tranquillity, until the ailment that he was to die of first appeared. Then he called the crown prince, Huaina Capac, and his other sons, who were very numerous, because he had more than two hundred children of both sexes. He said to them what the Incas were accustomed to say by way of farewell, and his last will was that the prince should punish the Huancahuillcas and their neighbors in his name, for the murder of the ministers and captains he had sent them at their own request. "Farewell, my sons," he said in conclusion, "rest in peace, our father the Sun is calling me, and now I must go and take my rest beside him."

Thus died the great Tupac Inca Yupanqui, whose faith, clemency, and gentleness were to leave such an imperishable memory that, thenceforth, he was called Tupac Yaya, which means, resplendent father. In addition to the Crown Prince Huaina Capac, he left five other legitimate sons born of his sister-bride Mama Occlo; they were, in the order of their birth: Auqui Amaru Tupac Inca, Quehuar Tupac, Hualpa Tupac Inca Yupanqui, my maternal ancestor, and, lastly, Titu Inca Rimaohi, and Auqui Maita. His body was so well embalmed that he still appeared to be alive when I saw him, in the year 1559.

Father Blas Valera relates the following reflection, made by this Inca, which I have translated literally from the original Latin:

"Many people say that the Sun is alive and that it created all things. But can one create something without being present at this creation? Now, many things are made in the absence of the Sun. It is therefore not the universal creator. And in view of the fact that it never ceases to turn around in a circle without tiring, we may deduce from this that it is not alive. Because if it were a living thing, it would tire as we do, and if it were free, it would go to visit other parts of the sky that it has never touched. It is like a tied-up animal that walks round and round its stake, or like a javelin that flies where it is sent, and not where it would like to go."[11]

1. The Chachapuya Indians were renowned not only for their fine warriors, but also for their exceptionally fair skins.

2. Garcilaso is the only chronicler to mention this part of the east bank of the Maranon. The name Huacrachucu survives today as that of a town. (Rowe)

3. Palta: local name for the avocado pear; in Spanish *aguacate,* from the Mexican *ahuacatl.* This fruit, now grown in all tropical countries, is of American origin, like the pineapple.

4. There were two kinds of cranial deformity in ancient Peru: one consisting in a flattening of the forehead and the nape of the neck, giving the wide head depicted on many vases of the Pacific coast civilizations. This is the deformity which Garcilaso calls a *palta*-head. The other type of deformity, characteristic of the tribes of the high Bolivian plateau (Aimara), consists, on the contrary, in an elongation of the skull in a sugar-loaf shape, achieved not with boards but by means of tightly twisted turbans. If the word *palta* be taken to mean the fruit and not the tribe, it is rather to this shape of skull that the name would apply.

5. The Cañaris constituted one of the most important nations of the equatorial region. They were related linguistically to the Yuncas of the coast. Before the Incas imposed on them the cult of the Sun, they worshiped natural deities (mountain peaks, lakes, craters, etc.) and plant spirits. Contrary to what Garcilaso says, they never gave up their ancient beliefs. Every year, before the corn harvest, they sacrificed one hundred children at the entrance to a cave said to be inhabited by the corn god (mountain of Curitaqui). This rite was strictly observed until 1775 and traces of it are still to be found today in the folklore of Ecuador. (Krickeberg)

   The alliance of the Cañaris with the Spanish is explained by the fact that they had just been cruelly persecuted by Atahualpa when Pizarro and his companions landed.

6. Over such a distance: "On the grandeur of the rich palaces of Tumebamba, in the province of the Cañaris." (Cieza, Part I, Chapter 44)

7. The Quito campaign was the Tupac Inca's first campaign before he invaded the Chimu kingdom. He was still only crown prince. He was crowned on his return from his conquest of the Chimu kingdom (1471). It was then that, according to Sarmiento, he reached the coast of Ecuador near Manta, and from there set out on a sea expedition lasting nine months: "Tupac Yupanqui," writes Sarmiento, "discovered the islands of Auachumbi and Ninjachumbi and brought

back black men, much gold and a copper chain." Certain authors deduce from this that the Inca had been to Easter Island, which would explain the presence of statues of *orejones* there. But nothing has been found so far either to prove or to disprove this theory.

8. "The Quillacingas are shameless people. Their pastures are as filthy as they themselves and they are held in small esteem by their neighbors." (Cieza, Part I, Chapter 37)
   According to Otto von Buchwald and others, the Quillacingas, like the Cañaris and the Caranques, were of Chibcha origin.

9. The present department of Nariño, in Colombia. It marks the extreme northern limit of Inca expansion, at the height of the Empire, just as the Rio Maulli, in Chile, marks the extreme southern limit. The town of Pasto was close to the second parallel north. The Inca Empire thus extended over more than thirty-two degrees of latitude, or approximately the distance from Paris to the Cameroons.

10. After the deaths of Huascar and Atahualpa, the Incas of Cuzco appointed as their new ruler Manco Inca, the brother of Huascar, while the lords of Quito nominated Tupac Inca, the brother of Atahualpa. Pizarro, who himself had asked for a new king in Quito, resigned himself to recognizing Manco after the assassination of Tupac, probably by the partisans of the legitimate branch. But, some time later, escaping from the vigilance of the Spaniards, Manco fled to the mountains where he gathered together an army of two hundred thousand men with which he came back to lay siege to Cuzco. A fierce battle took place in the fortress of Sacsahuaman. The Spaniards eventually gained the upper hand and Manco disappeared. It was not until 1912 that the mystery of his disappearance was cleared up by the discovery of the great fortress of Macchu Pichu, whose existence was not even suspected by the Spaniards. It was there, probably, that Manco and his sons, the last three Incas, lived on another fifty years or so, unknown to the Spaniards.

11. Tupac Yupanqui was a worthy successor to the great Pachacutec. Practically speaking, he established the final boundaries of the Tahuantinsuyu. The following are the landmarks of his reign (1471-1493):
    1 After his coronation (1471), campaign to the east by Paucartambo.
    2 Conquest of all the Colla territory, after the capture of the fortress of Pucara (the still free Umasuyu and Pucasa tribes had allied themselves with the Collas of the Lake Titicaca basin when the latter rose, taking advantage of the absence of the Inca armies in the forests to the east). As stated in Note 19, Book VI, Cobo describes the triumphal return of Tupac Inca after subduing the Colla rising.
    3 After the above-mentioned campaign, conquest of the high plateaus of Bolivia, then of Chile as far as the Atacama desert and of part of Argentina (province of Tucuman).

BOOK NINE

Life, government, and death of the great King Huaina Capac, twelfth sovereign of Peru. With the surrender of the people of Tumbez, and of the island of Puna; the story of the great gold chain the said king had made, how and why; that of the rebellion and punishment of the Chachapuyas and the Caranques; that of the giants who landed and lived on the seacoast. How Huaina Capac made his son Atahualpa king of Quito; how he was warned of the arrival of the Spaniards; the predictions he made in his testament, and his last will. Huasca Inca becomes king of Peru. His brother Atahualpa makes odious war upon him, and by his cruel actions, prepares the fall of the Empire and of the dynasty of the Incas

The powerful Huaina Capac, who was now lord and master of all Peru, undertook an official state visit of all his kingdoms. His journey began by a triumphal march along a path strewn with flowers, to which the entire people, both lords and vassals, came in throngs to acclaim their new sovereign, mingling their hurrahs with shouts, repeated a hundredfold, of "Huaina Capac, Huaina Capac," there being no more fitting way to pay tribute to this prince than to speak this noble name that, since childhood, he had never ceased to deserve. "All the earlier historians," wrote Father Acosta in the second chapter of his sixth book, "are in agreement in saying that Huaina Capac was worshiped as a god during his lifetime, a thing that had never occurred before in the history of the Incas."

The news of the birth of his first-born son, the future Huascar Inca, reached him during his travels. This event had been so eagerly anticipated by the king that he interrupted his visits to hasten back to his court, where twenty days of uninterrupted festivities followed. Now Huaina Capac began to cudgel his brain to discover some splendid thing, never before seen, that he could invent to lend even greater solemnity to the ceremony to take place when the child would be given his name and have his hair cut for the first time, as was the custom. Thus the idea came to him to order the famous gold chain, that today is known throughout the world, although no foreigner can boast of having seen it. Here is how he happened to think of it: it is well known that each one of the Peruvian nations had its own manner of dancing, which never changed, in the same way that they never changed their headdress. The dance of the Incas was characterized by its solemn, grave nature, and also by the fact that no women took part in it. The men formed in line, facing the reigning Inca, at a certain distance from him, and some two to three hundred in number. Each one held the hand, not of his immediate neighbor, but of the one following him, and thus they formed a sort of chain. They then began to advance little by little toward the king, in slow rhythm, taking, alternately, one step backward and two steps forward, as in those Spanish dances called *double step* and *repeat*.[1] It occurred to the Inca that it would be still more meet, solemn, and majestical, if they were to execute this dance, not by simply forming a chain with their bodies, but by holding in their hands a chain of real, solid gold. This explanation was given me by the old Inca, my mother's uncle, whom I quoted at the beginning of this work. When I asked him the length of the chain, he replied that it went halfway round the edge of the main square in Cuzco, where these dances were held, and which represented three hundred and fifty steps, or seven hundred feet in length. And when I asked him how thick it was, he added that each one of the links was as big as a man's wrist. The general treasurer, Agustín de Zarate, has the following to say about this extraordinary chain in the fourteenth chapter of his first book:

"This chain was so heavy that two hundred Indians had difficulty in holding it. It was in memory of this remarkable masterpiece, created on the occasion of his birth, that the Crown Prince Huaina Capac was given the name of Huasca, which means rope, in the Peruvian language." It is known that the Indians hid this unique invaluable piece, together with other treasures that were never found, after the Spaniards entered Peru. Huascar Inca's real name was Inti Cusi Hualpa, and the appellation of Huascar was given him because of this chain, which the Indians called a rope, not having a more exact term in their language.[2]

But to return to Huaina Capac, it should be added that after having had the idea for this chain, and given the necessary orders to have it carried out, he resumed his visits to his kingdoms for two more years. The feasts in honor of the tonsure and weaning of the young prince were therefore celebrated upon his return to Cuzco, with all the pomp and splendor imaginable.

One year after these festivities, Huaina Capac left for Quito with an army of forty thousand men. It was then that he took as concubine the daughter of the former king of this country, who had been living for some time in the convent for virgins in that city. She was to bear him Atahualpa and other sons, as we shall see later. The

Inca went with his army down to the seacoast, in order to extend northward the conquests of the good King Yupanqui, which had ended with the Chimu country, as we have already told. The inhabitants of the Chacma and Pacasmayu valleys, which were adjacent to the Chimu country, surrendered voluntarily, and their example was followed by the natives of all the valleys that emerge between Pacasmayu and Tumbez,[3] that is to say, Zana, Collque, Cintu, Tucmi, Sayanca, Mutupi, Puchiu and Sullana.[4] The imperial army, which had been replaced several times on account of the insalubrity of this coast, remained here for two years, not to apply force, but to help these new vassals open up irrigation canals and cultivate their land more advantageously.

The Inca next returned to Quito, where he again spent two years developing and enriching this kingdom in every possible way. Then, having assembled fifty thousand fighting men, he went back down the coast, as far as the Sullana valley, from where he sent his ambassadors to Tumbez. The people of Tumbez were more dissolute and inclined to be vicious than all the other inhabitants of the coast. Their chiefs lived lazily surrounded by a court of buffoons, dancers, and mountebanks, and they also indulged in the odious vice of sodomy; they worshiped lions and tigers to which they sacrificed human hearts, and were both strictly obeyed by their subjects and feared by their neighbors. None of these things, however, kept them from surrendering at the Inca's first summons, so great was their fear of his military might. Their surrender was followed by that of the Chunanas, the Collonches, the Yacualls, and a great many other nations living in this region, both on the coast and in the interior.

The Inca entered Tumbez where he ordered construction of a fortress, a Temple of the Sun and a convent for virgins. Once these were finished, he set out for the interior, in order to go to punish, as he had promised his dying father he would do, those who had killed the latter's captains and ministers. He did not actually enter these provinces but settled on their frontiers, from where he sent ambassadors to summon the guilty to come to him, to receive their punishment; and they hastened to obey, so greatly were they terrified both by the heinousness of their crime and by the Inca's arrival.

Huaina Capac had specified that he wanted to see all the curacas, ambassadors, councilors, captains, and other notables in the delegation that had asked his father for the ministers whom, later, they had murdered. And they all came together, as he had bid them to do. They were received by an aide-de-camp, who gave them a long reprimand in the name of the king, pointing out their treason, their perfidiousness, and their cruelty: "You should worship the Inca and his ministers," he said, "because the former sent you the latter to allow you to emerge from your state of ignorance and become men. But you cruelly murdered your benefactors, insulting, by this gesture, the king, who is the son of the Sun. The heinousness of this dual crime demands an equivalently severe punishment. Your nation deserved to perish entirely, without consideration for age or sex. But the great Inca, Huaina Capac, who is by nature, humane and kind, and worthy of the name of Huacchacuyac, or friend to the poor, is willing to forgive all of your humbler subjects. As for you who are present here, however, you who perpetrated and carried out this crime, and therefore deserve to die a hundred deaths, with all your kith and kin, our king grants you, too, unusual grace; for he has ordered that only one out of ten among you should be slaughtered, in order to let it be known that, mercy notwithstanding, there are crimes that bear within themselves their own punishment. You shall therefore draw lots, in groups of ten each, to determine which shall die, in order that none may accuse us of having favored certain among you to the detriment of others."

Such was the Inca's first sentence. Then, addressing himself directly to the Huancahuillca nation, which had instigated this odious crime, he ordered that all the curacas and nobles of this province should have two upper and two lower teeth pulled out, and that henceforth and, for all time, this operation should be performed on their descendants, in memory of and as a witness to their broken vows and the insult they had perpetrated against the great Tupac Inca Yupanqui.

The guilty ones underwent this test with great humility, considering themselves very fortunate to have been so lightly punished: because, to tell the truth, they had all expected to pay with their lives. When it was learned, in the Huancahuillca province that only the nobles and the curacas would have four teeth pulled out, what had been intended for punishment became a favor in the eyes of the people, and, right away, they all voluntarily had their teeth pulled, without anybody or anything, except unforeseeable vanity, having obliged them to do so. Indeed, the custom has endured, and today, still, the people from this province are recognizable by their incomplete dentition. Barbarous, rustic people are like that; and they feel that they have been deprived of a favor if they are spared punishment.

A woman from this province, who worked in my father's house in Cuzco, frequently told a similar story. Like all the people in her country, she had had her nasal cartilage pierced to wear some trinket in it. I remember, too, a bay horse that belonged to one of our neighbors; it was a good creature, but its nostrils had to be pierced when it began to grow short-winded. All the Indians marveled at this innovation and, from that day on, the horse was never called otherwise than Huancahuillca, because its nose was pierced.

Huaina Capac had gone back to Quito, then, from there, to Cuzco, and as far as the country of the Charcas, from where his emissaries went to visit Chile, which continued to produce a great deal of gold, as it had in his father's time. Six years had passed in these travels and pacific works, when the Inca decided to undertake a new campaign. He ordered a strong army of fifty thousand men to be raised in the Chinchasuyu district for assembly in Tumbez, to where he himself would come by way of the coast, visiting, on his way, the shrines of Pachacamac and of the famous talking idol of Rimac. These two oracles, which he had consulted, showered him with flattering words and assured him of success, not only in the undertaking that lay before him, but in all those he might envisage later.

When he reached Tumbez, where his army awaited him, Huaina Capac sent his ambassadors to Puna island, which he had decided to bring into the Empire. This island, which has a circumference of twelve leagues, is very fertile and richly endowed, and also not far from the mainland. At that time, it was governed by a lord named Tumpalla. Neither he nor his predecessors had ever been under the rule of anyone, with the result that he is said to have considered himself to be more the superior than the inferior of his neighbors, the caciques from the coastal country. It must be said, too, that this man Tumpalla was not only arrogant but barbarous and dissolute; he kept both women and young boys, and offered up human sacrifices to the lions and tigers that he adored in addition to the usual gods of these maritime regions, which are the sea and fish, as we explained earlier.

The Inca's demand threw Tumpalla into a state of embarrassment and perplexity. Not knowing what decision to take, he called a special consultative meeting of the principal elders of his island and revealed to them the difficult situation in which he had been placed:

"Foreign tyranny is at our gates," he said. "If we yield to the Inca, we shall be obliged to give up our former freedom, our best land, our most beautiful women and girls, our customs, our laws, and our gods; we shall be forced to build fortresses and barracks for this tyrant with our own hands; in other words, we shall become for all time his vassals and servitors, and I am not sure if it would not be preferable to die right away, once and for all. The fate of us all depends on my decision; it is for this reason, therefore, that I have called you together, in order that you might give the matter your deep consideration, and let me know what reply seems to you to be most appropriate."

The elders discussed the question lengthily. They made an estimate of the forces they could oppose to those of the Inca and realized that, unfortunately, these were quite insufficient. They acknowledged that they could expect no help from the mainland, where their own repeated, savage raids had gained them nothing but enemies. All resistance, on the other hand, would only make things worse, because they would have lost both their lives and their property. Having reached this melancholy conclusion, they decided, as being the lesser evil, to hide their feelings and offer formal surrender, not in the attitude of a people obliged and compelled to do so, but as though nothing could be more agreeable to them. Thus, they thought, we shall be able to gain time and wait until an opportunity for revenge arises.

The curaca Tumpalla, therefore, thanked the Inca's ambassadors in a very submissive, peaceful manner, and he himself sent a delegation, laden with rich gifts, to implore Huaina Capac to be so kind as to come personally to visit the island, where his new vassals would welcome him with joy.

Their wish was gratified. The Inca soon crossed the sound with his army, and landed on Puna without, however, the pomp and ceremony they would have liked. He was invited to live in a superb palace, just recently built, and there were several days of feasting and dancing. Meanwhile, the Inca's ministers had started instruction in the imperial laws, which Tumpalla and his followers swore to obey, under penalty of death.

It was not long, however, before these laws began to seem very harsh to these people who had lived, thus far, in a state of vice and idleness. With the result that a plot was set afoot between Tumpalla and certain curacas from the coast, who found the Inca's domination equally burdensome. The conspirators resolved to await the first opportunity to kill Huaina Capac and his captains; and they would doubtless have tried to carry out this sinister plan immediately, if their soothsayers and sorcerers had not advised patience, in the name of their own false gods.

Huaina Capac could not remain in Puna for long. He was needed in Tumbez for certain important matters, so he soon left, leaving the task of perfecting the organization of the island and its environs to Inca delegates.

An important group of captains and ministers, all Incas, either by birth or privilege, were to return to the mainland shortly after the sovereign, to organize the administration of the neighboring valleys. But the inhabitants of Puna, who were to transport them to the coast, seized this opportunity to take their revenge. Having hidden a certain number of their rafts, they divided these Incas, in view of making two trips. When the first flotilla had reached a spot settled upon in advance, in the middle of the sound, the Puna sailors untied the cords that held together the logs of their rafts, with the result that everybody fell in the water. The Incas knew how to swim, but being hampered by their ceremonial costumes, they were unable to resist their enemies, who were now in their element, like fish, and killed all those who did not drown quickly enough, turning upon them their own arms, which they had seized from them. The rafts, having been quickly repaired, returned to Puna, as though they really had debarked their passengers, and embarked a second group of Inca captains, who soon met the same fate as the first. Indeed, not one escaped. The revolt next infected the island and the seaboard, where it spread to all the nations who had had a hand in the plot, and everywhere, the Inca's captains, governors, and ministers were attacked by surprise and cruelly put to death. Now all of these barbarians celebrated their victory as though they had thrown off for always the yoke of Huaina Capac, and were about to declare war on him and defeat him beyond their frontiers. They hung the heads of their victims at the doors of their temples, and gave their idols the ration of human hearts and blood that they had promised them, should their plans succeed.

The Inca Huaina Capac was cruelly bereft by the death of so many noble companions, who had served to feed the fish. He went into mourning for them, wearing only ash brown, as was the tradition. But soon his spirit was seized with such anger that it made him forget his sorrow, and taking the lead of his army, he returned like a thunderbolt to the shores that had witnessed this heinous crime. He was met by a mere show of resistance, and debarking at Puna, he had the guilty ones brought to him:

"Your crime is too great," he told them, "for me to listen to my heart, which tells me to pardon you. You will all be put to death, and your punishment will be similar to that which you inflicted upon my gentlemen."

Thus, those who had drowned the Incas were thrown into the water; those who had hung their skulls at the doors of their temples, were pierced by picks and lances; others still were hanged or massacred with their own arms, as their victims had been. According to Pedro de Cieza de Leon, who treats lengthily of this affair, there were several thousand dead.

While the Inca was on his way back to Quito, visiting his kingdoms, it frequently happened that caciques from the coastal provinces came to greet him and offer him gifts from their estates. One day he was presented with a tiger and a lion that were both very wild, which so pleased His Majesty that he gave orders for them to be kept for him and given every care. We shall have the occasion to speak again of these two animals, and to show how our Lord Jesus Christ used them as witnesses of the favors he grants to Christians, as a result of which the Indians concluded that the Spaniards were also sons of the Sun, and worshiped them.

The Inca made a long journey, from Tumbez to the Chicha country which was on the Empire frontier,[5] and from there, retracing his footsteps, he returned to Tucma, which the Spaniards call Tucuman, and, from there, to Chile. Everywhere he went he had princely garments distributed among the caciques and the vassal leaders, to the great satisfaction of all concerned. On his way there, and again on his way back, he visited the Cuzco fortress, construction of which was almost finished. These goings and comings, from one end of the Empire to the other, kept him occupied for four years, at the end of which he raised a new army to resume his conquests on the seacoast, north of Tumbez. He was in the Cañari province, with the intention of going to Quito, from where he planned to go down the coast, when messengers arrived to let him know that a serious revolt had broken out in the Chachapuya province: all of his governors and ministers having been killed, along with a great number of soldiers, and others taken into slavery.

The Inca immediately gave orders that all the troops stationed on the coast should turn back to a given point of assembly, near the rebellious province, which it was his intention to punish very severely. He nevertheless sent messengers to the mutineers, ordering them to surrender without delay, if they wanted him to pardon them. But, by way of surrender, his messengers were greeted with threats of death, which made the Inca so indignant that he decided to deal with the offenders, without further ado. He joined his troops on the banks of a river which is usually crossed by means of small rafts that accommodate, at the most, six or seven persons. This manner of procedure appearing to him to be unworthy of both his person and his army, the Inca ordered that all the rafts that could be assembled should be tied end to end across the river, in such a way as to form a bridge. The soldiers themselves set to work with such dexterity that the work was finished in one day. The Inca immediately crossed the river at the head of his army, in battle formation, and took the road for Cajamarquilla, which is one of the most important cities in this province. His intention was to raze the entire country, for Prince Huaina Capac was as severe with traitors and rebels as he was kind and amiable with his loyal subjects.

The mutineers then realized their mistake, and the danger that threatened them, but too late, because the Inca and his powerful army were at their gates. Not knowing what to do, they were seized with panic and fled into the mountains, leaving their cities and all their possessions behind them. The old people, who had not been able to follow them, recalling that the Inca Huaina Capac had never remained indifferent to the plea of a woman, sought out a matron of Cajamarquilla who had been one of the numerous concubines of the great Tupac Inca Yupanqui, and persuaded her to go and implore the Inca to pardon them, because this, they told her, was the only way to appease his anger and to keep the entire province from being put to fire and sword.

The Inca was nearing the city, when the matron went out to meet him, escorted by a large number of women of all ages. She met him two leagues from there and, after throwing herself at his feet, began, courageously, and in a steady voice, to address him as follows:

"O my only lord," she said, "where are you bound for like this? Can't you see that the anger and pride that have blinded you are going to make you destroy a beautiful province which you owe to the labors and genius of your father? Do you not feel that you are doing violence to your filial piety as much as to your own natural generosity? Do you not know that you will regret tomorrow that which your anger and pain incite you to destroy today? Have you suddenly forgotten the noble name of Huacchacuyac, friend of the poor, that, until so recently, was the source of your greatest pride? How is it possible that you should feel no pity for all of these poor in spirit, when you know so well that there is no greater poverty for the human race! And even though they do not deserve your mercy, do you not think that you owe it to the memory of your father without whom these poor people would not be your subjects? Do you not believe that you owe it to yourself, oh son of the Sun? Do not, therefore, allow an angry gesture to sully the pure glory of your past exploits and of all those that you have yet to accomplish. Why punish needlessly all these wretched people, who have already understood their error! Undoubtedly, their crime is a heinous one, but even if it were more so, your pity and your godliness would only be the greater.

Remember all your ancestors, who set generosity and forgiveness of trespasses above all other virtues, and think too that, since you are king, you are the sum of all these kings who are gone. I beg you, forgive, and, should you not be able to do so, grant me, at least, the grace to kill me first, because this is my city and my country, and I do not want to see all my people die."

Having thus spoken, the matron fell silent, while all those who accompanied her gave a deep sigh and repeated together: "Lord, oh, our only lord, Inca, son of the Sun, Huaina Capac, friend of the poor, have mercy upon us, have mercy upon our fathers, upon our husbands, our brothers, and our sons!"

The Inca remained silent and hesitant for a long moment, while this chorus of supplication continued. At last, his natural clemency having appeased the fire of his anger, he bent over toward the matron and, raising her up, replied:

"Woman, it is as though you were the mother of us all, mine as well as that of your own people, you who see from such a distance what is in keeping with my honor and with the memory of my forefathers; allow me to thank you, because, without you, I should surely have regretted tomorrow, as you said, what I was about to do today. You have just acted as though you were my mother, and as though you were the mother of your entire people, because your words have saved their lives and their property. It shall be, then, as you say, and should you have still more to ask of me, speak, and you will be obeyed.

"Now," the prince added, "return to your people, and tell them that you it is whom they must thank. In order that they may be quite convinced that all will be forgotten, four Incas will go with you, as my brothers and your sons, without military escort, but only the ministers needed to restore order."

And the Inca retraced his steps, with all his army; and he gave orders that they should pursue their way to the coast, as though nothing had happened.

The Chachapuyas, from that day on, were the most loyal of vassals. The spot where this meeting took place became a sacred one for them, which they kept watch over, in order that no creature, man or beast, should ever set foot upon it. They surrounded it with three walls: the first of hewn stone, the second of rough stone, and the third of adobe.[6] The ruins of these walls may still be seen today, although, here too, as elsewhere, cupidity has respected nothing, in the belief that there can be no sacred place in the world that does not conceal some treasure.

The first of the seacoast provinces that the Inca sought to subdue, was called Manta, which was where the Spaniards founded the port of Puerto-Viejo. All the inhabitants of this coast, even quite far to the north, observed the same customs and worshiped the same idols: the sea and fish, tigers, lions, big snakes, and all sorts of other wild animals, according to their whims. In the Manta valley, which was the metropolis of this country, they also worshiped a giant emerald, which was said to be as big as an ostrich egg. On important feast days it was taken from the temple and shown to the people, among whom were throngs of Indians, who had come from a great distance to worship it and offer up sacrifices of emeralds that were smaller in size; because the priests and the cacique of Manta had persuaded these poor people that small emeralds were the daughters of the big one and that, therefore, no other offering would be so well received. This selfish reasoning had permitted them to accumulate in Manta an incomparable treasure of emeralds, which was discovered by Pedro de Alvarado and his companions—among whom was my father, Garcilaso de la Vega—at the time of the Peruvian conquest. However, since these conquistadors knew more about war than they did about precious stones, they broke the greater part of this treasure, being unable to believe that it was composed of real jewels, and not of bits of glass, since the stones were not resistant to shock. As for the giant emerald, it had disappeared well before they arrived. Indeed, the persons who hid it, did it so successfully that it has never been found since, no more than have many other treasures that were buried in this same earth.

The people of Manta and the neighboring country practiced sodomy, to the certain knowledge of everyone, with an impudence that had never been seen elsewhere. One of their customs, connected with marriage, was that all of the fiancé's friends and relatives should enjoy the bride's favors before he did. In war, they skinned their prisoners, then filled the skins with ashes to restore their human appearance, and hung them at the doors of their temples, or on the public squares.

The Inca sent his ambassadors to them and, realizing that they could not resist him, they all surrendered, both the inhabitants of Manta and their neighbors.

Huaina Capac crossed their land, after having delegated ministers and governors to them, and arrived in another very large province, by the name of Caranque. Here there were numerous nations and numerous languages, but so little order or government that Caranque, like Manta, surrendered with no resistance.

Beyond Caranque, there lived a more barbarous, bestial people than any of the other nations on the coast. Both men and women carved their faces with splinters of volcanic glass, and they also deformed the skulls of their newborn babies, shaving the tops of their heads. But instead of arranging the hair left on the sides, it was kinked, and left shaggy, in order to increase the monstrosity of their appearance. These savages were excellent fishermen and, in addition to fish, they lived off herbs, roots, and wild fruit. They wore no clothes at all and their gods were the same as the gods of their neighbors. We may mention, among the numerous nations, the Apichiquis, the Pichunsis, the Sauas, the Pecllansimiquis, and the Pampahuacis, all of whom surrendered without resisting. The Inca's army next arrived in the territory of the Saramisus and the Pasaus. The latter, who lived just under the Equator, were perhaps the most barbarous people in the world. They had neither god nor the slightest idea of religion, and they lived in hollow trees, in the heart of the forest; their women were considered as common property and they were unable to recognize their own children; they practiced sodomy openly; they did not know how to till the soil, and went naked; they carved their lips both inside and outside, and painted their faces in quarters of four different colors: yellow, blue, red or black; they never combed their hair, which they allowed to grow long and become filled with straw and dust and vermin, without ever cutting it: in other words, they were worse than animals. I saw them with my own eyes, in 1560, when I left for Spain. Our ship was at anchor for three days off their coast, in order to take on water. They came out on their rafts to sell us enormous fish which they harpooned while we watched, with amazing skill for such backward people. But since they refused our money, they were given meat and biscuits in exchange for their fish. They hid their shameful parts under little aprons of bark or leaves, but this was doubtless more in order not to shock the Spaniards, than out of any natural sense of modesty. One can really say that they were the greatest savages in the forest.

Having seen how unproductive was this dreary, monstrous land, and the barbarousness of its inhabitants, Huaina Capac decided that it would be a waste of his time to stay there.

"Let us retrace our footsteps," he said to his captains, "these people do not deserve to have us for their lord."

So he abandoned to them to their fate.

Before leaving this region, we really must tell a very amazing, admirable story, which the inhabitants say they heard from their most remote ancestors. Apparently, from what they say, in a far-off time, there were giants who arrived by sea and landed on this coast, at the point the Spaniards call Santa Elena, because they discovered it on that saint's day. Many Spanish chroniclers have spoken of these giants, among them Father Acosta and the general treasurer, Agustín de Zarate; but I shall report what Pedro de Cieza de Leon says about them, he who heard their story on the spot, and tells it in great detail. Here, then, is what Cieza wrote, in his fifty-second chapter:

"The natives on this coast relate that in very remote times, a number of large cane rafts appeared one day on the horizon, then came to berth at the point of Santa Elena. These rafts were manned by males who were so tall that a normal person hardly came to their knees, although they were quite well proportioned. All of them were bearded, wore their hair hanging down on their shoulders, and had eyes as big as saucers. Certain of them had clothing made of the skins of animals, while others wore no other costume than the one nature had given them. There were no women with them. They built a sort of village on this point (the sites of their houses may still be seen today), and having found no water, bored wells through solid rock, that were extraordinarily deep. These wells, which contain an excellent water that is always cool, were entirely lined with masonry, executed in such a way that they might resist the wear of time for centuries.

"The food resources of the region were quickly exhausted as a result of the voracity of these men. They also sowed hatred and fear throughout the land, massacring the women in order to rape them, and the men for other reasons. Indeed, the Indians often met together to discuss how they might kill them, but they never dared risk it. So several years passed and the giants seemed to have made up their minds to stay there. Since they had no women to satisfy their desires, they practiced the vice of sodomy among themselves, quite publicly with no apparent sense of shame, and no fear of God. But our Lord God, say the Indians, sent them a punishment that was suited to their crime. Suddenly one day, a heavenly fire appeared above their heads, with a frightful noise, at a moment when they were all paired off together, indulging in their loathsome vice; then there came a shining angel, holding in his hand a sword, who, with one fell swoop of his weapon, killed them all. And in order that God's punishment might be complete, the fire consumed them entirely, leaving nothing but a few bones.

"This, then," Cieza de Leon ends his account, "is what the Indians tell about these giants, and we think they should be believed, because there may still be found in this region bones of a size never yet noted, and certain Spaniards claim to have seen fragments of teeth that were so enormous that they weighed more than half a pound." [8]

A few years after his return from the province of Pasau, the Inca Huaina Capac, happening to be in Cuzco at that moment, was able to participate in the great Sun festival, which they called Raïmi. They tell that on one of the nine days of this festival, the Inca raised his eyes toward the Sun—which was contrary to every tradition—and remained looking at it for a long while, so long, in fact, that his uncle the high priest, who was standing beside him, ended by saying to him: "Inca, what on earth are you doing? Do you not know that it is not meet that you should contemplate our father the Sun in this manner?"[9]

The Inca lowered his eyes, without replying. But a moment later he raised them again and directed his gaze as before.

"Lord," the high priest then said, "not only are you doing what is forbidden, but what an example you are setting to the court and to the entire Empire, assembled here to worship and venerate your father, as our only, our supreme Lord!"

"Allow me to ask you two questions," answered Huaina Capac. "Knowing that I am your lord and king, would one of you dare order me to rise and go a long distance away?"

"He would have to be mad!" cried the high priest.

"Well and good," the Inca continued. "And is there a single curaca of my vassals, however rich and powerful, who would not obey me, if I ordered him to leave here immediately for Chile?"

"No, Inca," said the priest, "there is not a man in all the Empire who would dare to disobey you, even if you asked him to give up his life for you."

"Know, then," said the king, "that the Sun must obey another lord, greater and more powerful than he is. In fact, it is in obedience to an order from this lord that, every day, it accomplishes its long journey during which it may not stop; because if the Sun were its own master, there would be times when it would remain as it is at sunset, or stop to rest on the way, even if this were not necessary."

It is observations of this kind, transmitted by word of mouth, which have made the Spaniards say that if this prince had been taught the Christian doctrine, he would have not hesitated to embrace our Catholic religion, for he was a man of clear, accurate judgment.

The liberty of looking straight at the Sun, which was taken by the Inca, was given a sinister interpretation by the Indians, who were so fearful and apprehensive in their idolatry, that they saw in it an evil omen. No doubt he had permitted himself to make this gesture with, in mind, certain reflections made by his father, Tupac Inca Yupanqui, whose mode of thinking was akin to his own, as we have already seen.

We have told in what a state of barbarity and cruelty the inhabitants of Caranque and the neighboring provinces lived, before Huaina Capac had brought them under the Empire law, thus forcing them to abandon their baleful habits, principally that of relishing human flesh, which they delighted in more than in any other food. But they could not stand this restraint for long, and a few years after their conquest, their chiefs met together secretly

Pizarro and Almagro in Castile

The Spaniards en route to Peru

Challcuchima against the Cañari

Rumiñaui executing the Incas in Quito

He offers maidens to the Christians *The Spaniards visiting Atahualpa*

Atahualpa visiting the Spaniards

Atahualpa is imprisoned

The execution of Atahualpa

The execution of Francisco Pizarro

THE ARRIVAL OF THE SPANIARDS

The first two illustrations represent Pizarro and Almagro in Castile, then at sea. In the second, Guaman Poma shows, to the left of the conquistadors, the pilot, de Solis, at the top of the mast and to their right, Vasco Nuñez de Balboa (?).
The following two illustrations show us General Challcuchima fighting against the "Quito, Cayambi, Cañari, and Chachapuya" Indians; then General Rumiñaui, "the traitor," putting an Inca to death in Quito.
The third shows the same captain offering "maidens" to Francisco Pizarro and Diego Almagro.
The sixth drawing represents the first Spanish diplomatic mission to Atahualpa, at the baths of Cajamarca. Instead of Ferdinand de Soto, the author has represented Sebastian de Belalcazar on the right of Ferdinand Pizarro.
There follows an illustration of the famous "Cajamarca affair." Atahualpa is seated on his throne in the center, with Pizarro kneeling on his left, while Friar Vincent de Valverde raises his cross and his holy book; on the monk's right is the interpreter Felipe, with a ring in his nose.
The three last drawings show, respectively, Atahualpa as a prisoner of the Spaniards, with irons on his feet, seated facing his guard; then the death of Atahualpa, converted to Christianity (he is holding a cross in his hand); his throat is being cut; and lastly the death of Francisco Pizarro who is being pinned to the ground by the young Almagro with his sword.

and decided to collect as many men as might be necessary to murder the governors, ministers, and inmates of all the garrisons that the Inca had stationed on their territory. They were very clever at dissimulation, and, till the end, pretended to obey the Inca's laws and ministers with all the outward signs of the sincerest sort of affection. But this was but a mask, intended to allay suspicion, and to deliver into their hands, when the time came, defenseless victims. The rebellion broke out with extreme violence; all the Inca's ministers and soldiers were killed; their heads, hearts, and blood were offered up to idols; and the Caranques divided up their bodies, which they devoured with all the more pleasure and voracity since they had long been deprived of these feasts, and could now sate their vengeance at the same time that they assuaged their appetites. Huaina Capac was away on a journey, accomplishing what was to be his last visit to his kingdoms, when the news reached him. He immediately assembled an army and marched on Caranque, determined to punish this fresh uprising more pitilessly than ever. At first, there was a real, very cruel war, in the course of which several thousand men were killed on both sides; then, finally, the rebels were obliged to surrender. The Inca immediately had a great many men arrested, among whom were all those who had plotted the conspiracy; that is, more than two thousand men, some of whom were from Caranque, and others from neighboring provinces.

He ordered them all to be slaughtered, to the very last one of them, and their bodies to be thrown into a vast lagoon which bordered on their provinces. Indeed, it was such a massacre that, afterward, it seemed as though the water of this lagoon had been changed into human blood, and from then on, it was never called other than Yahuarcocha, which means the lake of blood. Pedro de Cieza de Leon says that the Inca's soldiers slaughtered no less than twenty thousand persons. I believe that he confuses the number of those who were put to death with that of the total dead of this war, that is, with the losses of both camps added together.

In any case, order was restored, and Huaina Capac returned to Cuzco. As he journeyed along, the prince could not help being sad and disturbed. He was also filled with dark forebodings. Why, he asked himself, had so many rebellions and massacres marked his reign, whereas his predecessors had had no such experiences, with the exception of the Chanca rebellion, under Viracocha Inca.

If one examined it closely, it looked as though one could read in this relentlessness of fate, the portent of an even greater rebellion, in which the entire Empire was destined to disappear, together with the long line of the Incas; and this was not a vain portent, as we shall soon see.

We have read that the daughter of the former king of Quito bore Huaina Capac a son named Atahualpa. As he grew older, this prince became a pleasant gentleman, well built and with an attractive face, as were all the Incas and their sisters, the pallas. He was brave, bold, and courageous and had no fear of combat. His mind was extremely active, his judgment clear, and he was of a shrewd, clever, even wily disposition, with the result that his father loved him very tenderly and liked to have him constantly near him. He would have gladly left him the Empire, if the law of succession had not forbade him to deprive his legitimate, first-born son, Huascar Inca, of the throne. But his love for Atahualpa was such that he resolved to leave him the kingdom of Quito, despite all traditions according to which no one could prejudice the unity of the Empire.

Huaina Capac therefore summoned Huascar Inca, who was living in Cuzco, and having gathered together, with his two princes, all his other sons and numerous head captains and curacas, he addressed the legitimate heir as follows:

"It is well known, Prince, that according to the desires of our ancestor the Inca Manco Capac this kingdom of Quito should fall to you. It has always been thus, and all the land that we have conquered has been annexed to the Empire and subjected to the jurisdiction and power of our imperial city of Cuzco. However, since I love your brother Atahualpa very dearly, and since, too, it pains me to see him poor, it would give me infinite pleasure if you would kindly agree to let me withdraw the kingdom of Quito, which I should like to leave to him, from my conquests to be inherited by yourself. You know, moreover, that this kingdom comes from his maternal ancestors and that, today, it could belong to his mother. In this case, your brother would live there as king, as his virtues merit he should do, and, like the good brother that he is, he would help and serve you much better than if he remained poor. In compensation for this little that I ask of you, many other provinces and vast kingdoms will, with time, be added to all those that you are already certain to receive by inheritance, and your brother will not fail to help you to conquer them, as a loyal soldier and captain; then I shall be able to leave you with a contented heart, when our father the Sun calls me to come and rest beside him."

Prince Huascar Inca replied that it was a pleasure as well as an honor for him to satisfy the desire of his lord and father, and that if the latter wanted to give Atahualpa other provinces as well, he should not hesitate to do so.

Huaina Capac was very pleased with this reply. Huascar returned to Cuzco and Atahualpa took possession of the kingdom of Quito, to which his father added other provinces. He surrounded him with experienced captains, and also made him a present of a part of his army, that he might be served, aided, and advised in all matters. In other words, Huaina Capac acted with this prince like a passionately devoted father, who aims at nothing more than the happiness of his beloved son. He decided to spend the rest of his days in Quito, as much in order not to leave Atahualpa, as to supervise and appease the maritime provinces bordering on this kingdom, and which had remained warlike, barbarous, and constantly on the verge of revolt; finally, in order to entirely appease them, he was obliged to move a large part of their population, and replace them by calm, peace-loving peoples, chosen from distant places. This, as we have already told, was the remedy commonly resorted to by the Inca kings to avoid disorders and rebellion.

It is meet that, in connection with the life of Huaina Capac, we should mention the two great highroads that cross Peru, from north to south, because they are attributed to this king. One of them follows the coast through the plains of the littoral, and the other goes through the mountains of the interior. All Spanish historians have spoken of them, but these two roads constitute, in reality, such a gigantic achievement that no single description suffices to describe them. For this reason, and in the belief that I alone could not speak of them as well as all these others did, I am going to relate literally, what each one has to say on the subject.

"King Huaina Capac," writes Agustín de Zarate, "was the greatest of all the Inca conquerors, and his sense of justice and organization was only equalled by his spirit of enterprise. He knew how to lead people who were so barbarous that they seemed impossible to educate, to a stage of reason and urbanity. His vassals were so devoted and obedient that, at his request, they constructed two extraordinary roads that deserve not to fall into oblivion. None of the seven wonders of the world that the ancients have described to us could possibly have cost such sweat and toil. When he left Cuzco to go and conquer the kingdom of Quito, five hundred leagues away, this king was obliged to surmount great difficulties in order to cross the high mountains that lay between him and his goal, with all his army. And it was the memory of these hardships that determined him, on his return from this campaign, to construct a great, wide highway, all along the cordillera. To do this meant razing peaks and crests, or on the contrary, elevating the road above chasms and valleys, by means of stone walls that sometimes reached fifteen to twenty stades [10] in height. It is said that this road was so flat that one could drive a handcart along it. Unfortunately, the wars between Christians and Indians have destroyed the greater part of these constructions, with the result that, today, the road is impassable.

"Not content with having successfully carried out so exceptional an undertaking, the same Huaina Capac, repeating the journey from Cuzco to Quito—this time by way of the coastal plains—decided to construct an equally important highway there. The work was no easier than it had been in the mountains, because this low land is frequently broken by the wooded valleys of the rivers that flow down from the cordillera, and which widen, often by more than a league, as they approach the sea. But the Indians cleared all these obstacles and succeeded in building a road that was perfectly uniform and continuous, well banked on both sides, and forty feet wide. On leaving the valleys, one had to pass through vast stretches of sand constantly being shifted by the wind, in which the very traces of the road risked being effaced, and the traveler to lose his way; but the Indians remedied this by marking out their road by means of poles planted at regular intervals in the ground. This second road measures five hundred leagues, like the first one. Today, most of these poles have disappeared, because the Spaniards used them to make fires with, but the roads the Indians built across the valleys are still there, and, thanks to their existence, one may measure the considerable importance of the work that construction of this road [11] involved. Thus Huaina Capac went there by one road and came back by the other, and the ground under his feet was entirely covered with branches and sweet-scented flowers." [12]

"This road of the Incas," writes Pedro de Cieza de Leon, with regard to the mountain highway, "is as famous here as the one Hannibal built to cross the Alps; and to tell the truth, it seems to deserve even greater admiration, as much because of the countless stores and warehouses that line it, as of the feat that such an achievement represents, across this precipitous mountain country."

Pedro de Cieza de Leon has nothing more to say about the cordillera road. But here is how he speaks of the lower road, in his sixtieth chapter: "This road was constructed on the orders of Huaina Capac and of his father Tupac Inca Yupanqui, by the caciques from the coast and from the valleys. It is fifteen feet wide and, on one side, rests on an embankment of masonry that is one stade high. The entire road was perfectly smooth and clean. Fruit trees planted on either side, protected it with their shady branches, in which all sorts of birds flew about among the blossoms."

"These two roads or royal highways," says, lastly, Juan Botero Benes, "are two thousand miles long and twenty-five feet wide. Indeed, this matchless construction can easily be set on a par with the Egyptian pyramids and the most celebrated achievements of the Romans."

We should like to add to what these authors have to say that the cordillera highway passed through some very high, open scenery where the Incas built observatories on either side of the road. The Inca's litter was carried up to these outlooks, to which one acceded by means of stone steps, to permit him to rest and, at the same time, to enjoy the imposing spectacle offered by the mountains, some of which were bare, while others were covered with snow. Here, one's eye took in at a single glance fifty to one hundred leagues, with peaks so high that they seemed to touch the sky, and valleys deep enough to open onto the earth's center. None of all this has resisted the ravages of time and war, and today almost nothing remains. Along the coast, too, the only things left, the merest memories of the great highway of yore, are the poles protruding here and there from out the wind-driven sand, to guide the traveler and keep him from losing his way.[13]

Huaina Capac was in residence in his Tumipampa palaces, which were among the most beautiful in Peru, when news reached him that some strange people, of a type that was quite unknown, were cruising in a ship along the coasts of his Empire and had wanted to know what country this was. This naturally aroused the entire attention of the king, who immediately made enquiries as to who these people were and from where they came.

This ship was none other than that of Vasco Nuñez de Balboa, who had just discovered the Southern Sea,[14] and who was later to give the name of Peru to the land of the Incas. These events took place in 1515, and Balboa had crossed the Isthmus of Panama and discovered the Southern Sea two years before, in 1513. A Spanish chronicler wrote that it was Don Francisco Pizarro and his thirteen companions who discovered Peru; but this is to confuse "discover" with "conquer," because Pizarro, his four brothers, and Almagro did not land in Peru to start the conquest of the country until 1531, eight years after the death of Huaina Capac, which took place in 1523, after a reign of forty-two years, as is proven by fragments of Father Blas Valera's papers, and, as everyone knows, the latter was extremely well versed in the history of Peru.

But to return to what Huaina Capac did after he had been apprized of the arrival of the first Spaniards, I shall add that this news was all the more disturbing to him in that it brought to his memory the ancient prediction according to which strangers never before seen would one day land in Peru and despoil the Incas of their Empire and their faith. With the result that, for the rest of his days, he refrained from undertaking further conquests, preferring to govern his kingdom wisely at the same time that he kept an eye on the sea, from where other unknown men might appear. Just here, I think I should also tell that, three years before the arrival of the Spaniards, something happened at court which was interpreted as a very bad omen and sowed fear throughout the Empire. They were celebrating the great annual feast of the Sun, when a royal eagle, pursued by a flock of buzzards, appeared in the sky. The buzzards seemed to be relaying one another around this noble bird, attacking it continuously and giving it such hard and such frequent blows that it ended by falling at the Inca's feet, on the sacred ground where the feast was being celebrated, as though it were imploring his help. It was taken up and fed, and an attempt was made to tend its wounds. But it was so badly off that it died after a few days, without having had the strength to resume its flight. The soothsayers made haste to interpret this event and could see in it only a foreboding of evil. There followed earthquakes of such unusual violence that great rocks were shattered in pieces and mountains collapsed. The sea became furious, overflowed its shores, invading the land, while numerous comets streaked the heavens, sowing terror in their wake. A curious, mysterious fear had seized upon all of Peru, when one unusually bright night the moon appeared with a halo of three large rings: the first one was the color of blood, the second a greenish black, and the third seemed to be made of smoke. Then one of the soothsayers—who were called *llaicas*—came up to Huaina Capac and said to him in a voice that was almost unintelligible, it was so choked with tears:

"Oh, my only lord, know you that your mother the Moon, who is always merciful, warns you that the great Pachacamac, creator and support of the entire universe, threatens your blood and your Empire with great trials that he will soon visit upon us. For this first blood-colored ring, surrounding your mother, means that a very cruel war will break out among your descendants, after you will have departed to rest beside your father the Sun; your royal blood will be shed in such streams that after a few years nothing will remain of it. The black ring threatens our religion, our laws and the Empire, which will not survive these wars and the death of your people; and all you have done, and all your ancestors have done, will vanish in smoke, as is shown by the third ring."

The Inca did not want to reveal the distress into which these words had plunged him: "Leave me," he said to the soothsayer, "all of that is mere folly: you must have been dreaming."

But the magician replied: "Inca, go yourself out into the night, and you will see with your own eyes the signs your mother has made to you; then you can summon all the other *llaicas,* and they will tell you their opinion on the subject."

The Inca went out. He saw the three rings around the moon, and he summoned the *llaicas* who examined the sky and reflected upon it. Finally the most famous among them, who belonged to the Yauyu nation, began to speak, repeating word for word, what the first one had predicted.

"No," replied the Inca, "not until I shall have heard Pachacamac himself, shall I have any faith in your words: for I cannot believe that my father the Sun could hate his own blood to the point of allowing all his sons to perish!"

Thus spoke the Inca, determined that the fear and despair into which he was plunged should not enter into the hearts of his people. But too many convergent signs confirmed the exactness of this prediction, and the arrival of the first Spaniards, in addition to all these recently appeared wonders of nature, showed only too clearly that the time had come for the ancient prophecy of Viracocha to come true; with the result that, from that moment, Huaina Capac lived in fear and anguish. He surrounded himself with a permanently powerful army, chosen among the veterans of his conquests, and he had countless offerings and sacrifices made to the Sun. Throughout the Empire, his seers, sorcerers, magicians, soothsayers, and clairvoyants consulted their familiar demons on his orders, but particularly they consulted the great Pachacamac and the speaking devil of Rimac. The replies of all these celebrated oracles were confused, mingling obscure threats with words that were more favorable. But the majority of the sorcerers replied with ominous forecasts, and the Empire lived in a state of fear, awaiting the direst misfortunes.

Three or four years passed and no disturbing events having occurred, people grew less anxious and, little by little, the Empire recovered its former calm, which it was to retain until Huaina Capac's death.

All of this I learned from talking to the simple people who have retained a very vivid recollection of these events, as also from accounts furnished me by two former captains of Huaina Capac's guard, who died baptized in the Catholic faith when they were over eighty; one of them was named Juan Pechuta and the other Chauca Rimachi. They could not mention this subject without their eyes filling with tears, and I was often obliged to talk of something else, in order to stay their sobbing.

As for the death and testament of Huaina Capac and all that followed, we shall tell it according to the account furnished me by my mother's old Inca relative, named Cusi Hualpa. My mother and her brother, Don Fernando Hualpa Tupac Inca Yupanqui, also told me many details of Atahualpa's cruelty. They were ten years old when this prince's persecutions began, and they bore all the horror of them until the arrival of the Spaniards put an end to them, two and a half years later. We shall explain in due time how they escaped with a very small number of the members of their family. And it will be seen that all these crimes of which Atahualpa was guilty towards his own blood, in the end only served the victory of his enemies.

One day, as Huaina Capac was coming out of a lake in which he had just bathed, near Quito, he was suddenly seized with a sensation of chill, which was followed by one of intense heat. His condition grew worse and worse and, after a few days, he realized that the predictions concerning his death were about to come true.

Further signs had appeared in the sky, amongst which was a huge green comet; lightning had struck in his own house; and the amautas had for several years agreed with the soothsayers in predicting his approaching end which, according to what they said, would constitute the prelude to an avalanche of calamities from which neither the Empire nor the royal line of the Incas would be able to recover. And Huaina Capac knew all that, although these sinister predictions continued to be hidden from the people, out of fear lest the entire nation should pine away of despair.

The king, therefore, summoned his sons, his relatives, and all the governors and captains who could reach the palace in time, and he spoke to them as follows:

"Know ye," he said, "that the moment has come when I must go and rest beside our father the Sun. Already, a long time ago, he made it known to me that he would call me from a lake or from a river. The indisposition with which I was seized upon leaving the water is therefore a sign which I cannot mistake. When I am dead, cut my body open; take my heart and my entrails and bury them in the city of Quito that I have so dearly cherished; then take my body to Cuzco, to lie beside those of my forefathers. I commend to you my beloved son, Atahualpa. May he reign in my stead over the kingdom of Quito and over all the lands that he succeeds in conquering; and you, captains of my army, you shall serve him with the love and loyalty that you owe to your king; obey him in all things, because all that he will ask of you, it is I who shall have revealed it to him, on orders from our father the Sun."

These were the last words that Huaina Capac addressed to his sons and relatives. He then had all his other captains and curacas summoned, all those who were not of royal blood. After making the same recommendations to them, he concluded as follows:

"Our father the Sun disclosed to us a long time ago that we should be twelve Incas, his own sons, to reign on this earth; and that then, new, hitherto unknown people would arrive; that they would obtain victory and subject all of our kingdoms to their Empire, as well as many other lands. I think that the people who came recently by sea to our own shores are the ones referred to. They are strong, powerful men, who will outstrip you in everything. The reign of the twelve Incas ends with me. I can therefore certify to you that these people will return shortly after I shall have left you, and that they will accomplish what our father the Sun predicted they would: they will conquer our Empire, and they will become its only lords. I order you to obey and serve them, as one should serve those who are superior in every way; because their law will be better than ours, and their weapons will be more powerful and invincible than yours. Dwell in peace; my father the Sun is calling me, I shall go now to rest at his side."

The news of this prediction spread throughout all Peru, and the accounts of all chroniclers bear witness to its veracity. According to Pedro de Cieza de Leon (chapter forty-four), the scene took place in the Tumipampa palace, near Quito. It was at the same place, this author adds, that Huaina Capac had received the news of the arrival of the first Spaniards on the coast, in 1515.

Francisco Lopez de Gomara,[15] in the one hundred and fifteenth chapter of his book, relating a conversation between Huascar Inca, Pedro del Barco, and Ferdinand de Soto, at the time of their first visit to Cuzco, tells it in the following terms: "The prince explained that he was the only legitimate lord of the Empire and that Atahualpa was nothing but a tyrant and a usurper, which was why he, Huascar Inca, wanted to speak to the captain of the Christians and ask him to help recover his freedom and his kingdoms: 'Because my father Huaina Capac,' he explained, 'ordered me, on his deathbed, to become friends with the white, bearded men who were going to come, and who would establish themselves as the lords of this land.' "

I remember that one day, while speaking of the arrival of the Spaniards in Peru with the old Inca, who was a relative of my mother's, I asked him the following question:

"Inca," I said, "how does it happen that powerful and numerous as you were and, in addition, being the masters of a country composed of steep mountains which are naturally so difficult of access, you let yourselves be conquered and dispossessed by a handful of Spaniards?"

The Inca had told me a few days before about Huaina Capac's prediction. He told it a second time, then, showing a certain irritation, as though my question implied that the Incas had lacked courage, he said: "You must know that the words spoken by our king were more powerful than all the weapons carried by your father and his companions, and that they it was that subjected us to foreign rule and dispossessed us of our Empire."

Huaina Capac died as he had foreseen, and his last wishes were scrupulously carried out. His heart was buried in Quito and his body, after being embalmed, was taken to Cuzco. All along the road, crowds of people came to pay homage to his remains and to mourn the death of this beloved king. The funeral ceremonies held for him lasted one year, according to custom. He left more than two hundred children of both sexes, and some people even say three hundred. Only a very few, however, survived Atahualpa's cruel treatment.[16]

Four or five years passed calmly after Huaina Capac's death. Atahualpa reigned in peace in Quito, without appearing to have any other concern than the welfare of his subjects, and Huascar did the same in Cuzco.

Nevertheless, when Huascar considered the limits of his Empire and sought by what means he might enlarge it, following the example set by his ancestors, he was seized with doubt, then with fear. With Chile to the south, the ocean to the west, and the cordillera of the Andes to the east, further conquests seemed out of the question; and the road to the north, which was the only one available, was now closed to him by the kingdom of Quito. With the result that, little by little, he began to regret having yielded to his father's desire in giving this kingdom to Atahualpa. Who knew, after all, whether one day this prince, taking advantage of the situation, might not make a campaign of his own and, increasing his power, which was already great, become his rival and threaten to rob him of the Empire?

This fear began to grow in Huascar's mind, to such an extent, in fact, that unable to stand it any longer, he resolved to send one of his intimates with the following message to Atahualpa:

"You are certainly aware of the fact that, according to the laws of the first Inca, Manco Capac, the kingdom of Quito and all of your provinces belong to the crown and to the Empire of Cuzco. By rights, therefore, I was in no way obliged to relinquish the government of this kingdom to you, and if I did so, it was not because I was forced or compelled, but merely not to oppose our father's wishes. Now that he is no longer with us, I am willing, out of respect for his memory, not to go back on this decision, but on two conditions. These are: first, that you will make no attempt to add so much as a particle of land to the extent of your kingdom, since any newly acquired land belongs by rights to our Empire; the other is that, leaving everything else aside, you will swear allegiance to me and acknowledge that you are my vassal."

Atahualpa listened to this message with all the appearances of the most complete humility and submission. He then took three days to reflect upon it and replied, with sly shrewdness, in a very cautious tone that, in his heart of hearts, he had always considered himself to be vassal of his only lord the Capac Inca; that not only would he not increse the kingdom of Quito, however slightly, but that if His Majesty wished to take it back, he would return it immediately, and, like any other of his relatives, would come and live at his court and offer to serve him in peace as in war, according to what it might please his prince and lord to command.

The messenger remained at Atahualpa's court, as he had been ordered to do, to await fresh instructions from the Inca, to whom this declaration was transmitted with the greatest possible celerity by the imperial post. Huascar's reply was not long in coming; being now relieved of his fears, he took pleasures in confirming his brother's titles and prerogatives as king of Quito, and asked him to come to the Cuzco court, at a given date, to pay his homage and take the oath of faithful, loyal allegiance. To which Atahualpa replied that nothing would give him greater pleasure than to carry out His Majesty's wishes; and that in order to give greater solemnity to the taking of the oath he would make to him, he begged Huascar to kindly authorize all the provinces of the kingdom of Quito to come with him in order to celebrate together, in Cuzco, funeral ceremonies for his father Huaina Capac, according to their own traditions and customs; after which they would all take the oath with him.

Huascar agreed to all his brother's requests. He gave him a free hand to organize as he saw fit the funeral ceremonies for Huaina Capac, adding that he would be very happy to see them celebrated in the imperial city according to the customs of the provinces of Quito; and that, in fact, Atahualpa could himself choose the date of this journey.

Thus the two brothers were both equally satisfied; one without imagining that a plot was afoot to rob him of the Empire and even of his life; the other, so taken up with his schemings that, in the end, instead of profiting from them, he became their last victim.

Atahualpa immediately had proclamations made throughout his kingdom to the effect that delegations from each province should be formed and held in readiness to leave soon for Cuzco, where they would celebrate, each one according to its traditions, funeral ceremonies for Huaina Capac, and take the oath of allegiance to the new Inca, Huascar; the delegates should take with them all their insignia, ornaments and gala array, in order that the ceremonies should be invested with all the desired brilliance and solemnity.

At the same time Atahualpa quietly summoned his captains and ordered them to themselves choose the members of these delegations from amongst their most experienced warriors, and to arm them secretly, because, by way of funeral ceremonies, in reality they were off to war. They would travel in groups of five to six hundred men, marching two or three leagues apart. Upon approaching Cuzco, the first groups would little by little shorten their day's march, while the others would lengthen theirs, with the result that they would all be together when they reached their goal.

In this way, more than thirty thousand warriors were raised and equipped in secret. Nearly all of them came from the group of veterans that Atahualpa had received as a gift from his father Huaina Capac at the same time that he was given the throne of Quito. Which means that they were first-class soldiers, perfectly trained.

As for Huascar, even though he had feared, as we said before, Atahualpa's ambitions, he could not doubt his word. An age-old tradition assured the Incas of the loyalty of their vassals, and there was no example in history of a feudal subject having failed to do his duty, especially since he was bound to his lord by blood ties, as Father Acosta emphasizes, in the twelfth chapter of his sixth book. It is understandable, therefore, that Huascar should have had complete confidence in his brother, despite his earlier fears: better still, he generously ordered that these men should be welcomed everywhere as brothers, and that care should be taken to see that they lacked for nothing all along their way.

This, then, was the attitude of both sides: those who were with Huascar were filled with simplicity, and a kindliness that was naturally theirs; while those who were with Atahualpa were marked by the cunning and malice they had learned from him. And Atahualpa counted on this cunning, more than on his strength, to defeat his brother: the latter's confidence would have to deliver him to him unarmed, as otherwise, once the advantage afforded by surprise were lost, he could not hope to win.

So Atahualpa's men took to the road, in the disguise we have described, and they arrived within a hundred leagues of Cuzco without anyone, apparently, having guessed their strategy. However, several Inca governors, all of whom were former captains and, consequently, as well-versed in affairs of war as in those of peace, had been observing them as they passed by and had been astonished both by the large numbers of their groups and by the manner in which these groups were organized. Because five or six thousand men, or at the most ten thousand, would have largely sufficed to give magnificence to the funeral ceremonies they claimed they had come to celebrate; and as for the oath of allegiance, the men of the people to be seen in their ranks were in no way required to take it, only Atahualpa, with his curacas, governors, and captains. Therefore, what were all these people going to do in Cuzco? The Inca governors were familiar with Atahualpa's restless, envious heart; they knew that no really peace-loving, fraternal sentiments could be expected from him. With the result that they grew suspicious and warned Huascar secretly, urging him to be on his guard, because it was not natural for his brother to bring so many men with him.

Huascar suddenly became aware of the danger, as though he had awakened from a dream. He would have to act quickly. He immediately sent messengers to all the governors of Collasuyu, Cuntisuyu, and Antisuyu, ordering them to come to Cuzco as soon as possible, accompanied by all the fighing men they could levy: the enemy army had already occupied the Chinchasuyu, thus depriving the king of the forces in this district, which was the largest and most powerful in the Empire.

Meanwhile, Atahualpa's army was quietly advancing, strong in Huascar's supposed ignorance of its approach. When the front line troops were no more than forty leagues from Cuzco, they began to shorten their day's march in order to allow the bulk of the army to overtake them, with the result that twenty thousand men crossed the Apurimac together, and from that point on, they marched on Cuzco, no longer hiding the nature of their expedition, fully armed with banners flying. Six leagues from the city, the rear guard, composed of ten thousand men, joined them on the Uillacunca hill.

Atahualpa himself was not present; he had preferred to await the result of the first battle, on which he staked all his hopes, on the frontier, at the same time that he hurled a seasoned, well-led army against an adversary that had been weakened by the lack of foresight of its leader.

The inhabitants of Collasuyu, who were scattered over a territory more than two hundred leagues long, had not had time to answer Huascar's call to arms; those from Antisuyu were present, but the small population of this mountainous district had not been able to furnish a very large contingent; indeed, the only force of any size that the Inca could set against his brother was represented by the men from the Cuntisuyu, who came quickly in great numbers with all their curacas: there were more than thirty thousand of them but, after so many peaceful, carefree years, it would have taken long training to make real fighters of them. The Inca, escorted by his personal guard of ten thousand men, had just gone out to meet them when the enemy army, as we said before, began to assemble on the heights of Uillacunca.

Atahualpa's generals had a clear understanding of the situation; their fortunes depended on their speed. So they immediately sought out Huascar, in order to engage him in battle before he should have received more numerous reinforcements. The encounter took place on a broad plateau, some two or three leagues south of Cuzco. No peace offers preceded the fighting, and it immediately became a terrible melee that lasted all day. But Huascar's recruits were unable to resist very long the attacks of an enemy who was superior to them both in numbers and in experience. They became disbanded and the king himself was obliged to flee with what was left of his guard, reduced now to one thousand men, at the most. Atahualpa's army soon overtook and captured him: and thus it was that Huascar, having been made a prisoner by his brother's generals, saw the last of his faithful troops meet death before his very eyes; most of them fell under the blows of the enemy, or took their own lives in order not to witness any longer their sovereign's downfall. Others preferred to surrender, in order to share their Inca's fate and show the sincerity of their loyalty to his cause.

One can imagine the satisfaction of Atahualpa's generals, whose relatively easy victory had permitted such a rich capture as the royal person of the Inca Huascar! They set up a guard composed of four captains and experienced soldiers who never left him, keeping permanent watch over him night and day. The news of his defeat and imprisonment had been immediately proclaimed throughout the Empire, in order to discourage any possible attempts to resist on the part of his followers, and a special courier had carried the announcement of his victory to Atahualpa.

As a matter of fact, the entire history of the war that set these two brothers, Peru's last kings, one against the other, may be summarized in the events of this day. The other battles mentioned by certain Spanish chroniclers were but skirmishes, during which small frontier garrisons clashed with one another; and the story of Atahualpa's imprisonment and miraculous escape is nothing but a romance that this king invented himself to further his cause. Those who have read the chroniclers know that he pretended he had been taken a prisoner by Huascar and that the Sun had come to his assistance, and had allowed him to escape through a crack in the wall, after having transformed him into a snake. This fable, which took advantage of the Indians' natural credulity, had no other aim than to excuse Atahualpa's own tyranny and cruelty, by presenting him as the preferred son of the Sun-god, and therefore the natural heir of the Incas.

Atahualpa's cruelty, for which he was to become so balefully famous, was not long in manifesting itself in the worst possible manner. With his usual deceit, while feigning a desire to return Huascar to the throne, he summoned to Cuzco all the Incas who were scattered about in the different provinces of the Empire as governors and in other official positions, or as camp commanders, captains, or soldiers. The pretext for this gathering was a grand council that he wanted to hold, so he said, with all those of royal blood, in order to promulgate new laws that would determine the future relationship between the two kingdoms, and permit all their subjects to live in lasting peace and fraternity.

This invitation had the effect desired by its author: all the Incas who were not prevented, by age or illness, from traveling, hastened to Cuzco at the date mentioned, except for those—and they were few—who continued to mistrust this prince. And when they were all gathered together, Atahualpa gave orders that every last one of them should be put to death; for, in reality, it was in this way that he intended to make sure that the future would be his.

Before going any further, it would seem necessary to explain the real reasons that impelled Atahualpa to commit these numerous massacres. First, it must be recalled that the laws and statutes of ancient Peru, such as they had been handed down and inviolably respected from generation unto generation, from the first Inca, Manco Capac, to the great Huaina Capac, gave Atahualpa no rights, not only to the Quito throne—since all the fruits of conquest reverted automatically to the imperial crown—but, even less, to the Cuzco throne. In fact, no one could pretend to the title of reigning Inca who was not the son of the last Inca, which Atahualpa was, and of his sister the Coya, or of a palla, that is, a princess of royal blood, which he was not.

Having conquered the crown by force, Atahualpa realized how precarious his situation was. The force of a tradition as old as the Empire itself, necessarily risked, sooner or later, causing the legitimacy of his power to be questioned. And all his strength would be of no avail the day when, all present passions having died down, the entire Empire would demand that the throne be returned to a prince of pure lineage who fulfilled all the conditions required by tradition.

It seemed to him, therefore, in accordance with his own cruel, pitiless nature, that the only way to avoid for all time so serious a risk would be to do away at one time with not only all the legitimate Incas who had a right to the imperial succession, but also with all the illegitimate children of the king who might be tempted to act as he had, now that his bad example had opened the way to their ambitions.

History shows us that all those who had recourse to such remedies had seized the kingdom of another by violence, and that it was essential for them to allow no legitimate pretender to escape if they wanted to retain their throne with any appearance of justification. We might recall, to cite but one example, the sinister custom of the Ottoman royal house, which demanded that each new sovereign should bury his brothers with his father.

But Atahualpa proved to be even more cruel than all the Ottomans, and more thirsty than they for his own blood. Not content with having immolated his two hundred brothers, the sons of Huaina Capac, he felt compelled to sacrifice as well his cousins, his uncles, and all his other relatives, whether legitimate or illegitimate, to the fourth degree of relationship. Some were massacred, some were hanged, while others were thrown in the rivers or lakes with a stone tied round their necks, or hurled from high rocks or steep peaks. Not one escaped from the soldiers whom this tyrant had transformed into executioners. Indeed, his haste to have done with the entire royal line was so great that this huge massacre was accomplished in a few days, while he waited ninety leagues from Cuzco, in the city of Sausa that the Spaniards call Jauja, not daring to make his entry into the imperial city before the whole thing was over. And although poor Huascar was temporarily spared by this rage for destruction, it was only because Atahualpa planned to exhibit him to the people and oblige him to quiet them by force if, in spite of everything, they should happen to revolt. And truly enough, the unfortunate Inca, who was carried from place to place, was obliged to contemplate with his own eyes the massacre of all his relatives; which, for his sensitive nature, was a torture a hundred times worse than death.

Those who had accompanied him to his prison were led on to a broad plain, in the Sacsahuana valley, where they were stood in two lines, facing one another, as though on the two sides of a street. And poor Huascar Inca was made to walk along this entire way, in mourning garb, his hands tied together and a rope round his neck. Seeing their prince humiliated to this extent, and unable to be of any assistance to him, the majority of his loyal curacas began to cry and moan, and threw themselves on the ground in an attitude of worship. This was the last opportunity they had to manifest their loyalty and their devotion to a lost cause, because they were immediately massacred with hatchets and swords.

Once human cruelty has been given complete license, it is unable to put a halt to its havoc, so true it is that its appetite increases in proportion to the amount of human flesh and blood consumed. When there was not a single adult man left of all Huascar's line, or of his principal vassals, Atahualpa turned his vengeance upon the women and children of royal birth. All of those who could be found, in all the provinces of the Empire, with the exception of the virgins dedicated to the Sun, in the Cuzco convent, were gathered together in a large enclosure on the Yahuarpampa, or the so-called blood-soaked plain, which was already famous as a result of the battle that had opposed the Cuzco authorities to the Chancas. They were surrounded by three circles, the first composed of armed warriors, and the two others of sentinels. Having taken these precautions, Atahualpa's cruelty could thus give free rein to all his whims upon these defenseless creatures. They were first subjected to severe fasting. Then, all Huascar's wives, sisters, aunts, nieces, cousins, mothers-in-law were hanged, now to trees, now to gallows built for the occasion, some by their hair, others by both arms, or by one arm, or by the waist, or by still other ways that decency forbids me to relate. They were handed their small children whom they clasped tightly in their arms until the children crashed to earth. The longer the torture lasted, the more delighted were the executioners, who would have considered it a favor to grant a rapid death to their innocent victims. A description of these cruelties of Atahualpa's may be found in chapter five of the third book of the second part of the *History of Peru* by Diego Fernandez, and it will be seen that I have not invented anything. These persecutions and massacres lasted two years and a half, until there was practically no one left who descended from the Incas. The Yahuarpampa battlefield doubly deserves its name, and the Indians themselves say that the blood of the Chancas that soaked it the first time was nothing, either in quantity or in quality, compared to that of the unfortunate Inca women and their tender progeny who were destined to perish on the same spot, on the orders of the usurper, Atahualpa.

A few Incas had the good fortune not to fall into the hands of their pursuers; others succeeded in escaping from the Yahuarpampa encampment, disguised as beggars, thanks to the complicity of their guards who, either because they had finally felt a certain remorse at having continually to shed the blood that they all considered to be divine, or because they had simply grown weary of such bestial, monotonous butchery, helped them to flee. At that time, the survivors were all mere children, boys and girls, ten or eleven years old, at the most. This, in fact, was the case of my mother and of one of her brothers, whom I knew well, and who wrote me recently to Spain. His name is Francisco Hualpa Tupac Yupanqui, and it is from them that I heard the account of these events about which they told me many times when I was young. I also knew two *auquis,* or "infants," one of whom was named Paüllu, mentioned by Spanish historians, and the other Titu. Don Carlos Inca, the son of Paüllu, was a schoolmate of mine. He married the daughter of a Spanish gentleman, who was born over there, and she bore him Don Melchior Carlos Inca who, last year, in 1562, came to the Spanish court to receive the decorations due his grandfather for services rendered to the crown during the conquest and pacification of Peru.

Two ñustas, or "infantas," the legitimate daughters of Huaina Capac, also survived. One of them was named Doña Beatrice Coya, and she married Martín de Bustincia, a gentleman who, at that time, was district collector for Peru in the government of His Majesty Charles V. I went to school with one of her sons. The second "infanta" was named Leonora Coya. She was married twice, to two Spaniards, the second of whom, named Francisco de Villacastín, was among the first conquistadors.

I knew still other Incas and pallas, of lesser rank, but perhaps not more than two hundred in all. My mother was a niece of Huaina Capac, the legitimate daughter of his brother, Hualpa Tupac Inca Yupanqui.

I also knew a son and two daughters of King Atahualpa. One of them, Doña Angelina, bore the Marquis Don Francisco Pizarro a son, who was named Francisco, like his father. He was my rival in racing and jumping, when we were both about nine or ten years old, because his uncle, Gonzalvo Pizarro, took pleasure in watching us compete at these exercises. The marquis also had a daughter, who was quite remarkable, named Doña Francisca Pizarro, whom he married off to his uncle, Don Ferdinand Pizarro. She was a daughter of Doña Inez Huaillas Nusta, herself a daughter of Huaina Capac. After Ferdinand Pizarro's death, she married, for the second time, a Spaniard from Lima, named Martín de Ampuero. I do not remember the name of Atahualpa's other daughter. She, too, was married twice; the first time to a Spaniard, and the second to a half-breed gentleman named Sancho de Rojas. Atahualpa's son was named Don Francisco Atahualpa. He was well built, with a handsome face, like all the Incas and pallas, but he died quite young. I shall relate another time the remarks made to me by the old Inca, my mother's uncle, on the occasion of his death. Another of Huaina Capac's sons, Manco Inca, survived Atahualpa's cruelty. In the absence of any other descendants, the Empire should have reverted to him and, in fact, it did, in title, if not in reality, but only very briefly.

We explained at the beginning of this work how certain villages, which were ennobled by privilege under the first Inca Manco Capac, traditionally furnished the king with the officers and other personnel serving in the royal household. Here, again, Atahualpa's cruel jealousy made itself felt, not uniformly, but with a severity that was meted out according to whether or not the duties of the different persons involved brought them in proximity to the person of the king. Thus the porters, paymasters, cupbearers, cooks and, in general, all those who, because of the nature of their service, came in daily contact with the Inca, were pitilessly slaughtered with their entire families; in addition to which their houses were burned and their villages destroyed. Those who did not approach the king directly, however, such as water-carriers, gardeners, and wood collectors, suffered less. There was, however, not a village within a radius of five or six leagues around Cuzco that entirely escaped these persecutions. Certain of them only lost a quarter of their population, or even a fifth or a tenth, but everywhere there was bloodshed. At the other end of the Empire, the Cañaris were also cruelly decimated for having manifested their loyalty to the legitimate Inca and their hostility to the usurper. "Sixty thousand men perished in the province of the Cañaris alone," Agustín de Zarate writes in his fifteenth chapter, "and the large city of Tumibamba was entirely razed." Francisco Lopez de Gomara and Pedro de Cieza de Leon also insist upon the ravages committed by Atahualpa's soldiers among the Cañaris. "The male population," says the latter, "was so cruelly stricken that today only one man for ten or fifteen women may be seen throughout this province."

But to finish with the accounts of Atahualpa's countless cruel deeds, I shall relate here, as I promised to do in the preceding chapter, the remarks made to me by my mother's uncle, the old Inca, on the occasion of the death of Atahualpa's son, Don Francisco.

It was the day after his death. The dead man being a nephew by a first cousin of my mother's, the few Incas still alive had assembled early in the morning at her house, before the burial was to take place. And one can imagine my astonishment when I saw the old Inca come up to my mother, with an expression not of gravity and earnestness, such as the circumstances seemed to call for, but, on the contrary, beaming and happy as though he were on his way to some feast. But when he offered her his congratulations, instead of his sympathy, saying that he hoped the great Pachacamac would grant her long life in order that she might have the satisfaction of witnessing the death of all her enemies, I was unable to contain my astonishment.

"Inca," I exclaimed, "how can you expect us to rejoice at the death of such a near relative?"

He immediately turned upon me with a look of fury and, seizing the lapel of his mantle, started biting it with rage, which is a sign of intense anger amongst the Indians.

"What!" he shouted, "you consider this traitor and son of a traitor as your relative! Is he who destroyed our Empire, and killed our Inca, your relative? He who dessicated our blood and exterminated our descendants; who committed every crime that is contrary to the traditions of our ancestors! Give that man to me and, dead though he be, I shall eat him raw, without seasoning! He's nothing but a bastard and a son of a bastard! Atahualpa's mother must have sinned with some Quito slave for her to have given birth to such a monster, a man unworthy of the great Huaina Capac whose son he so boldly pretended to be! How can you even suppose that the blood that flows in our veins can have any relation whatsoever to the blood of this man? Do not say such things, for you wrong us all, at the same time that you bring disgrace upon the memory of our ancestors!"

The old Inca continued for a long while in this vein; he recalled once more the interminable list of all the misfortunes Atahualpa had brought upon us, and finally, even forgot his original joy, and all those present fell to weeping and moaning.

The hatred attached to Atahualpa's name had pursued Don Francisco all his life. He could not go out into the street without hearing the word *auca*—which symbolizes all there is to be said about a traitor and a tyrant—being murmured on every side. The result was that he was obliged to resign himself to ending his days between the four walls of his house, the threshold of which he no longer dared to cross. Such unwonted hatred as this was bound to follow him to his grave, and the tears that were shed over his remains were those of hatred rather than love. Indeed, the fate of his two sisters was no more to be envied than was his own.

1. Inca dancing. Contrary to what Garcilaso says, women took part in this dance, either alternating with men in the same line, or forming a separate line parallel to that of the men. (Rowe) Cobo writes that they danced to the sound of a great drum which an Indian of the lower classes carried on his back while it was beaten by a woman. The same author also mentions a dance called Guayayturilla, in which men and women, wearing silver or gold bands on their foreheads, blew into stags' heads which served as flutes (this is the *cachovenado* still used by the tribes of the Orinoco *llanos;* see Note 12, Book VI).

The most interesting Inca dance of which Cobo writes is one in which three people take part: a man, holding a woman by each of his hands, turns continually in and out under their raised arms without the group ever separating. Cobo said it was the most delightful sight he had seen in ancient Peru. This dance was long preserved in the folklore of Peru and perhaps still exists under the Spanish name of *azucena.* Below is the description of a remarkable "historic" *azucena.* It is quoted by d'Harcourt from Vienrich's studies.

"The dance known as the 'dance of the Incas' as performed at Tarma, requires ten to twelve girls, richly dressed (in point of fact only seven people take part in it), wearing the *anacu,* with veils and pearl tiaras on their heads and their hair in long plaits. A *llica* or cloak is held on one shoulder with a bouquet of flowers which is the symbol of the load once carried on the shoulder as a sign of respect and submission when appearing before the Inca: it is called *Inti* (the Sun) and varies in shape from a zither to a quiver or a circle with projecting rays, the center of which is made of *carrizo* (reed) and covered on one side with red, white, and yellow flowers. Its place is taken today by a big bunch of paper flowers. The pallas carry in one hand either a handkerchief or *azucenas,* a kind of tulip or flag iris made from a sheet of tin. The dancers form two groups. In the center of one is the Inca, wearing a short tunic fringed with gold and silver, with a wide band, entirely decorated with coins, covering his chest; on his head he wears a kind of skullcap but his face is uncovered, as the Inca face always is; in one hand he holds a stick or staff. He has one *ñusta* on his right and one on his left. Facing him is Pizarro, masked, dressed in Spanish style, in doublet and hose, with a ribbon on his breast. His uniform is completed by a tricorn and a sword. Two ñustas accompany him in the dance, facing the Inca group. The dancers are joined by an old man called *el brujo* (sorcerer), wearing a leather mask and a white beard. He holds a tambourine (*tinya*). His role is to humiliate and mock the dancer taking the part of Pizarro.

"After dancing in groups, the dancers all join together to sing in unison a song of which the last verse is as follows:

> Traitor Felipillo! Traitor Felipillo!
> Dry the tears of this rock!
> O powerful Inca, let us dance!
> O Señor Juan Pizarro, let us dance!
> All together, let us dance around them.

And Pizarro the conquistador, the marquis, pays homage to the Inca. The childish revenge of an unhappy, humiliated people!

"The special feature we noticed was that throughout the dancing and singing Pizarro is constantly harassed by the sorcerer who keeps moving round him like a gadfly, approaching, striking the tambourine in his ears and then slipping between the ñustas who make a show of hiding him. This pantomime, of which Don Juan is the only victim, is a cause for much laughter, especially when the sorcerer allows Pizarro to take him by the ear and pretend to cut it off with his sword (an act which implies the worst possible insult, since it means enslavement). This incident, somewhat strange in such a serious dance, which evokes such tragic memories, is indeed surprising. There is an explanation, however; the sorcerer in this instance represents the high priest who, in the Inca religion, was at once an oracle and a soothsayer, and accordingly a sorcerer in the eyes of the Christian conquerors. Today, the tambourine struck in Pizarro's ears is supposed to recall the death by treachery of Atahualpa: the high priest prowls around the conquistador like the pangs of his conscience . . . But the Indians have had to mask historical truth until now it has become quite distorted: Atahualpa becomes Huascar; Juan takes the place of Francisco; the sorcerer, that of the high priest . . . Thus they rendered the dance harmless and incomprehensible to their ruthless conquerors."

It should be added that the invocation to Felipillo is addressed to Pizarro's interpreter Felipe, who betrayed Atahualpa at his trial and thus became the accomplice of his executioners. Here, as in the case of the Feast of Inti-Raïmi, it can be said that Peruvian folklore, based at once on ancient Inca tradition and on the memory of historical events which led to the disappearance of the old Empire, partakes of the nature of sacred drama, to be compared to some extent with that of Iran. See Book X and the notes to that section.

2. The golden chain of Huaina Capac. Several other chroniclers have mentioned this famous chain, although none, needless to say, can boast of having seen it. Pedro Pizarro, like Zarate and Garcilaso, asserts that it really existed. Montesinos thinks it is only a legend: "Everything that is said

about the origin of the name of Huascar, especially the story of the golden chain, is pure imagination." However this may be, this legendary chain has remained very popular in Peru, where many seekers of *huacas* still hope to find it some day. It is represented in certain *keros* (M. Valle collection, Lima), but as these are of the colonial period they do not prove that it actually existed. Our present knowledge does not enable us to draw any definite conclusions.

3. On the Gulf of Guayaquil.

4. All these valleys, Mochica-speaking for the most part, had originally been part of the Chimu kingdom, of which Tumbez formed the northern boundary. We have seen that the Chimu frontier to the south was marked by the valley and fortress of Parmunca. See Book VII and Note 42, Book VI. Mochican dialects survived on this coast until the nineteenth century.

5. The Chichas (not to be confused with the drink of the same name) lived in the extreme southwest of the Inca Empire, on the high plateaus of Bolivia, near the northern border of Chile, south of the Charca territory and to the west of the Chiriguano (or Chirihuana) territory. According to Cobo, they paid as tribute to the Inca small, finely carved, red wooden balls for the sacrificial fires in Cuzco. This lightning journey made by Huaina Capac to the south, when he was occupied in the north, and of which Garcilaso offers no explanation, was perhaps due to the fact that the Chiriguano tribe attacked the Inca Empire just at this time. Means, cited by Rowe, states that a Spanish adventurer from the Brazilian coast took part in this attack, with the Chiriguano tribe, and was thus the first European to enter the Tahuantinsuyu.

6. This is the name given to red bricks dried in the sun. Building in *adobe* on a stone foundation is characteristic of the architecture of ancient Peru. It is to be found among the coastal civilizations and those of the mountains alike.

7. Pedro de Alvarado landed on the coast of Ecuador in 1534 and at first was on the point of fighting Pizarro and Almagro . . . But this belongs to another story, that of "honor among thieves," or of the establishment of the Spaniards in Peru.

8. According to certain authors, this legend preserves the memory, in the realm of fable, of a landing on the American coasts by Polynesian invaders, probably from Easter Island. Needless to say this is a hypothesis which cannot be scientifically checked.

9. Although the Inca reigned as an absolute monarch, it would seem that the high priest was so powerful that he could at times pass judgment on the acts of the sovereign and even oppose his decisions.

10. As already stated in Note 13, Book II, the stade is equiva-

lent to seven feet. This masonry supporting the road, must therefore, according to Zarate, have been about 130 feet high. According to Bennett in the *Handbook*, these stone embankments were only about fifteen to twenty feet high, which seems more likely than the height given by Zarate.

11. It was by this coastal road that Pizarro went from Tumbez to Cajamarca to meet Atahualpa and take him prisoner.

12. Agustín de Zarate. (Vol. I, Chapter XIII)

13. The Chinchasuyu highway stretched from Cuzco to the other side of Quito, with a branch to Tumbez via Pachacamac along the north coast; these are the two great highways mentioned by Garcilaso. There were many others just as important.
    The Collasuyu road ran from Cuzco to the Atacama desert (in northern Chile) passing by Lake Titicaca, Lake Poopo, and Mendoza (northern Argentina). A branch to Arequipa ran as far as the Rio Maulli (southernmost boundary of the Empire, in the heart of Chile) via Calama and Copiapo.
    The Cuntisuyu road ran from Cuzco to Nazca and continued along the south coast (towards Arequipa).
    Lastly, the Antisuyu road, which also began at Cuzco, crossed the cordillera and came down again on the northeastern slope, towards the Amazon basin.
    In certain places the coastal road was sixteen feet wide on flat ground, but as narrow as three feet higher up.
    In the mountains, the Indians, to whom the wheel was unknown, cut steps in the rock of the steeper slopes. These special masonry roadworks were many and varied, and the embankments, although their dimensions were not as impressive as claimed by Garcilaso in his enthusiasm, were frequently several yards high. Tunnels were rare, but Cobo mentions one sixteen feet long.
    It is possible, and even probable, that many of these roads dated from pre-Inca days, although no archaeological discovery has yet confirmed this. Even if it is so, it does not detract in any way from the merit of the Incas, who at the very least developed, coordinated and systematized road communications with incomparable skill, in one of the most mountainous and difficult countries of the world. See Rowe and Bennett in the *Handbook*.

14. The Pacific Ocean. The Indian who guided Balboa across the Isthmus of Panama was the first man to speak to the Spaniards of the "rich kingdoms and great Empire of the South." And if the jealousy of his father-in-law Pedro Arias de Avila, had not cost Balboa his life in 1517, perhaps the discoverer of the "South Sea," instead of Pizarro, would also have been the conqueror of Peru.

15. Gomara lived for many years in Mexico, as chaplain to Cortez. His *Historia general* is one of the first comprehensive works on the conquest of America by the Spanish.

16. In point of fact, Huaina Capac was carried off so suddenly, during a violent epidemic, that he had no time to nominate his successor. Atahualpa was Governor of Quito, and Huascar, who lived in Cuzco, was crowned by the high priest as soon as the news reached the capital. In the ensuing war of succession there is no doubt that Atahualpa owed his victory to the presence in Quito of the great army of Huaina Capac who, having just ended his last campaign, had not yet had time to return to Cuzco. Atahualpa took advantage of this circumstance and of the experience of the two greatest generals of the day, Quizquiz and Challcuchima, who supported him. There is no reason to see in these events a kind of nationalist movement on the part of the people of Quito, as might be deduced from Garcilaso's remarks. See Rowe.

The following is a summary, taken from Rowe, of the campaigns of Huaina Capac, who was the last great Emperor of the Tahuantinsuyu:

He extended the province of Chachapuyu (conquest of which had been begun by his father). He took Moyopampa, defeated the Cayambi tribe north of Quito and carried the northern boundary of the Empire to the Rio Ancasmayu. He was doubtless unable to go any farther north (in Colombia) owing to the resistance of the Chibcha Indians. According to Cobo, his intention was to annex the whole of the mountainous region "as far as the North Sea" (Caribbean Sea). He would have needed to know of its existence, and this has not been proved. He conquered the island of Puna and the provinces on the Gulf of Guayaquil (Tumbez).

Huaina Capac died in 1527. Pizarro and the "Glorious Thirteen" had just reconnoitered Tumbez and, five years later, nothing was to remain of the prodigious conquests made by the Incas in the space of three generations, since the reign of Pachacutec (1438).

BOOK TEN

How the Spaniards discover Peru,
land there and take possession of it.
Pizarro makes Atahualpa a prisoner.
Atahualpa has his brother Huascar executed
and promises an unbelievable
ransom in exchange for the freedom that
is not granted him. Sentence
and death of Atahualpa, which put
an end to the tragic history
of the Incas.
The author's conclusions

We left the brute Atahualpa entirely absorbed in perpetrating his crimes. As the list grew longer, the prouder and more pleased this bloodthirsty tyrant became. For it seemed to him that this bloodshed was a guarantee of his supreme power. But, on the contrary, it was to rob him of it, for the benefit of strangers whose very names were unknown to him. The Spaniards knocked on his door at what he thought was his greatest hour, then, after dethroning him, they wrested from him both the Empire and his life. In order to relate these events as they actually took place, we shall have to turn back a few years, in order to follow the stream from its source.

The insatiable thirst for conquest that marked the Spaniards, as soon as they discovered the New World, is only too well known. Nothing discouraged them, nothing repelled them, nothing exhausted them. Neither hunger, nor danger, nor wounds, nor sickness, nor bad days and even worse nights, could keep them from pushing constantly forward, over land and sea, in search of the unheard-of feats that, for all time, have left a halo of glory around their names.

Well, then, there were two gentlemen of very noble lineage living in Panama, both of whom were rich and already famous for their past exploits. The more famous of the two was named Francisco Pizarro, who, although born in Trujillo, had come to the New World when he was still young. He had taken part in numerous affairs, among which were the seizures of Nombre-de-Dios and Panama, under the command of Governor Pedro Arias de Avila, as Gomara points out in chapter one hundred and forty-five of his *History of the Indies*. He was among those who discovered the Southern Sea with that hero of heroes Vasco Nuñez de Balboa. Lastly, he had particularly distinguished himself in the province of Uraba, which he had conquered, settled, and governed in 1512, with the title of lieutenant general, rising above illness and all sorts of privations, as related by Pedro de Cieza de Leon in his sixth chapter. The second of these two gentlemen was named Diego de Almagro. Whether he was born in Malagon, as stated by Agustín de Zarate, or in Almagro, as

Gomara has it, in no way affects the quality of his blood, which could only have been of the bluest if we are to judge by the boldness and generosity of his deeds, because, as the proverb goes, a tree may be judged by its fruit.

There were many rumors going about on the subject of Peru, which people only knew of by hearsay. But what they heard was sufficient to tempt such dauntless spirits as those of Francisco Pizarro and Diego de Almagro. Taking with them Ferdinand de Luque, lord of La Taboga, and a schoolmaster from Panama, they decided to form a company and undertake this conquest. All three of them signed an agreement, and took public oath to the effect that they would neither dissolve nor leave their company, for any reason whatsoever, until they had succeeded in conquering Peru; and that then they would make fraternal division of the profits they might derive from it. They decided that Ferdinand de Luque would remain in Panama to administer the domains of the three associates, while Francisco Pizarro would undertake the part of discovery and conquest, and Diego de Almagro would travel back and forth between the other two, in order to ensure the supplies in men, weapons, beasts of burden, and all sorts of other goods needed by Pizarro.

At that time Ferdinand de Luque was given the nickname of "Mad Ferdinand," and one might even say that he was given it for the three of them. For indeed, what else could people think, at the sight of these three wealthy men, already past middle-age—all three were over fifty—who, after having surmounted countless hardships, threw themselves like blind men into adventures that could only be worse than all those they had ever encountered, since they did not even know where they were going, whether or not this land was rich or poor, nor what means they would need to conquer it. However, the good fortune of those who possess it today was beckoning, and it even forced them to challenge what was then the unknown. But, above all, God, in his infinite mercy, had decided that His gospel should pass through them to these new gentiles who were living in Peru in the gloom of idolatry; a thing that is proven by all the miracles thanks to which this mad undertaking succeeded.

Once their agreement had been signed and their plans made, they built two ships, sparing neither cost nor pains.

The first ship left Panama, under license from the governor, Pedro Arias de Avila,[1] with, on board, Francisco Pizarro and one hundred and fourteen men. After navigating one hundred leagues, they reached a land covered with unbelievably high mountains, where rain fell practically without stopping. The natives of this coast were quite as wild as it was and they came out in such great numbers and shot so many arrows at the Spaniards that several of the latter died, and Pizarro alone received seven wounds, none of which proved to be mortal, however. Almagro's ship, approaching the same coast a short time after, was attacked on the high seas, as though these Indians, having once tasted a Spaniard, wanted more. Again there were several killed, and Diego de Almagro lost one eye. In short, these were the only benefits the expedition derived from the first land it discovered.[2] Almagro joined Pizarro at the latitude of Chinchama, and they decided to continue their way together. However, their second landing was no more successful than the first, man and nature alike proving to be as wild this time as they had been before. Again several men were killed, and Diego de Almagro was obliged to return to Panama, from where he came back with eighty more men, by way of reinforcements. But the coast remained so persistently hostile that, despite their additional strength, they were compelled to sail for a long time yet, without daring to risk a landing. The first peaceful moment came when they reached a place called Catamez, where, finally, there were no more mountains and where they also found abundant supplies. Here they saw Indians decorated with emeralds and turquoises, and with numerous gold nails driven into their faces. Once more they were fired with the hope of profit, and they again saw themselves being favored by fate and soon becoming immensely rich, which made them very happy. But their hope was short-lived. For a large number of armed men suddenly appeared, quite obviously determined to fight, and although the Spaniards numbered two hundred and fifty, by common consent, they reluctantly resigned themselves to withdrawing to an island, which they baptized Rooster Island.[3] They remained there for several days, half fearful, half hopeful, according to whether the situation of the moment appeared to be adverse or favorable. But the determination of the soldiers now began to weaken, and only the leaders remained faithful to their oath to die rather than give up. For this reason, they decided that Almagro would return to Panama again to get fresh reinforcements and that Pizarro would wait for him on this island. Many of the men would have liked to take advantage of this ship to leave, but Almagro refused to take so much as a letter, in order that there should be no risk of besmirching the fair name of Peru.

However, necessity being the mother of invention, despite the watchful eye of the two captains, one of the soldiers succeeded in transmitting a message hidden in a hank of wool, under the pretext that someone in the city was going to knit him a pair of socks. In reality, it was a petition signed by several of them, disclosing the deaths and other hardships endured by the expedition, and imploring that they be given their freedom. It ended on a quatrain which became so famous that all the Spaniards in Cuzco used to quote it in my time. It runs like this:

And so, your honor, the Governor,
Please understand the deal.
They send you forth as a buyer,
Instead you butcher and kill.

When I rediscovered these lines in Spain, in Francisco Lopez de Gomara's chronicle, I felt very happy, because they recalled my youth. In Cuzco, people quoted them rather sententiously, and the old conquistadors said that they had greatly harmed their captains, who had lost everything in this affair.

A year had passed since Almagro had gone back to Panama. He found there a new governor, by the name of Pedro de los Rios, who, having read the soldiers' petition, decided to send a judge to Rooster Island, to restore their freedom to all those who wanted to withdraw from the expedition. As soon as this was known in town, all of Almagro's recruits refused to go with him. It was a great disappointment to this captain, who saw all his hopes about to be shattered. It was also very hard on Pizarro when he realized that, in spite of the oaths they had taken, all of his men were tempted by the judge's decision. Indeed there was soon great confusion among them. Pizarro decided, therefore, to put an end to it with one gesture, which would also show him on which ones

The Poor Indian

he could really count. Drawing his sword, with its point he traced a long line on the ground, which he oriented in the direction of the mysterious land of his heart's desire, Peru.

"Gentlemen," he said, looking directly at his men, "this line represents the toil, hunger, thirst, weariness, sickness, and all the other vicissitudes that our undertaking will involve, until the day when our souls will return to God. Let all those who feel that they are capable of confronting and overcoming these perils cross it and stand beside me, like good, loyal companions. And let those who are frightened by our daring return to Panama, because I do not want to compel anyone against his will: but no matter how few we shall remain, I know that we shall triumph. Divine Providence is on our side, and this force will compensate for the gaps that will be left in our ranks."

He had hardly finished speaking when the Spaniards started to rush towards the boat, so great was their haste to embark before some new event should jeopardize their chances. Thirteen men only dared to cross the fateful line, without allowing themselves to be influenced by the bad example set by the others. On the contrary, with enough daring and faith to pay for all those who no longer had any, they swore again, in unison, that they had confidence in their captain and that they would die with him. Pizarro thanked them as warmly as their generosity deserved, and promised them the better part of the conquests that lay before them. They then took a small boat and landed on another island, which they called Gorgon Island. Many long days passed, during which they suffered cruelly from hunger, living off shellfish and even the snakes and other crawling creatures that abounded on this island, under a sky slashed with lightning, when there was not actually thunder and rain.

Certain it is that God was with Pizarro. Otherwise, it is impossible to explain how human beings could have resisted for months, as they did, the hardships of this waiting. For they experienced a miracle without which the conquest of Peru could never have been achieved. Divine mercy took pity upon the gentiles of the New World; which is why it breathed such ardor and bravery into the hearts of these Spaniards who brought with them the enlightenment of the gospel, just as in other days it had manifested its matchless power through so wretched a thing as Samson's hair.

Almagro's ship reached Gorgon Island after Pizarro and his twelve companions had been waiting for several months.[4] There were enough supplies, but no men, which was enough to discourage them entirely, instead of urging them on. But God was present and they decided to continue their way in order to see with their own eyes what lands, what people, what kind of world existed beyond the equinoctial line, in these regions that, thus far, the Spaniards hardly knew. So they set sail and started to navigate through these perilous waters, serving now as soldiers, now as sailors, according to which were needed. The winds and currents which, in these regions, usually go from south to north, were constantly unfavorable to their progress, and they were obliged to pursue a zigzag course between the coast and the open sea. These currents present such a remarkable spectacle that I should like to describe them for the benefit of those who have never seen them. They appear to be torrential streams rushing landwards with such countless whirlpools, such masses of foam, such noise and raging waves, that the heart of the navigator who risks passing through them is constantly being wrung by the ordeal this presents. Certain currents are broad, while others are narrow, and there are some that are muddy and turbid, like rising rivers, and others that brew a pure, clear water. Days, months, soon more than a year passed in this inhuman struggle. Hunger continued to gnaw at Pizarro and his companions, for the reason that, being few in number, they did not dare risk setting foot on the shore, where hordes of hostile Indians were waiting to massacre them.

Two years after they left Gorgon Island, they finally arrived opposite the great Tumbez valley. One can imagine their wretchedness and the amazement that seized them when they suddenly looked upon this beautiful city, with its fortress, its temples, palaces, and countless houses rising out from a luxuriant, well-tilled valley. During their entire journey, they had seen nothing like it.

They soon became very desirous to know what this country might be. But fear of being massacred kept them from landing and they were undecided as to what they should do. Then it was that God came to their assistance, that He did a marvelous thing, both to help these brave companions and to reveal for the first time to the natives of Peru the dazzling grandeur of the Catholic faith.

Among Pizarro's companions there was a Greek named Pedro de Candia. He was a strong, brave man, a good Christian and of unusual stature. I did not know him, but I well remember his son, who went to grammar school with me. This boy, who was then twelve years old, was twice as tall and twice as corpulent as the other boys of his age; from the son, one can therefore obtain an idea of what the father was like.

So Pedro de Candia approached Pizarro and said:

"Sir, I am going alone to see what there is in this valley. If I die, you will have lost only one man, which is of no importance. But if I succeed, your victory will be all the greater."

He put on a coat of mail that came down to his knees, then he donned the boldest, most gallant looking headdress to be had on board, and buckling his sword, took up a shield of polished steel and, in his right hand, a wooden cross that measured certainly three feet in length, and which seemed to him to be the most dependable of all weapons, since it was the arm of our common redemption. In this outfit, after begging his companions to commend him to God, he took leave of them and went ashore. Step by step, he started off towards the city, with head high and an earnest, lordly mien, as though he were the sovereign master of this land that he was treading for the first time. The Indians, who had been looking at the ship ever since it had arrived, were astonished to see this tall, bearded man coming towards them, because they had never seen anything like him. They did not know what to say, nor did they dare do him any harm, for they asked themselves if he were not of divine rather than human essence. Finally the curaca and the elders of Tumbez decided to unleash on his path the wild lion and tiger that they kept for their King Huaina Capac, as I related in the life of this Inca. But these beasts, which would have immediately torn any other prey to pieces, suddenly lost their natural wildness when confronted with this Christian and, above all, with the cross he was carrying, and came to lie down at his feet, like two faithful dogs.

Pedro de Candia understood the entire significance of this miracle that had just been performed by God our Savior, and grateful faith increased his courage tenfold. Stooping down, he stroked the heads and backs of the two wild beasts, holding the cross above their bodies, to show the Indians that the virtues of this sacred emblem could render harmless the most ferocious animals. And the Indians were quite persuaded by this that he was a son of the Sun and that he had come from heaven; with the result that they started to worship him as such and brought him to the temple, which was entirely paneled with gold, in order that he might see how deeply they revered their god, who was also his father. They led him from room to room and from treasure to treasure, showing him the living quarters of his brothers, the Incas, their sumptuous bedrooms, the stock rooms and kitchens, filled with gold and silver tableware, as also the famous gardens in which every tree, every plant and herb, every animal, every bird and insect, was made out of a precious metal. And although this Christian had amazed the Indians, they, in their turn, amazed him even more.[5]

When Pedro de Candia came back on board ship, he had some difficulty convincing his companions of the truth of what he related to them, for reality in this case seemed quite incredible, in fact it went beyond their wildest dreams. After having been countless times on the verge of death and despair, they had now really discovered a Peru that promised to be richer than anything that had been encountered thus far in the Indies. By common consent, they all decided to return to Panama, since it was unnecessary to pursue any farther this first voyage of reconnaissance which had succeeded beyond all their hopes. According to Agustín de Zarate, three Spaniards, or two, according to Gomara, preferred to remain in Tumbez, in order to see and supervise this incredible wealth with their own eyes, until the return of their companions. No one knows what became of them. Spanish historians claim that the Indians killed them. But the latter retort that they had no reason to take their lives since they worshiped them as gods. No doubt they died of one of the numerous fevers that rage along this coast.

All those who have written about it agree that the discovery of Peru had taken at least three years.

When Pizarro returned to Panama and described to Diego de Almagro and Ferdinand de Luque the incredible riches he had discovered, they decided that he would go to Spain to solicit from His Majesty, the Emperor Charles V, rights of conquest and government of these countries. He was given a thousand pesos for the journey, which were borrowed for the most part, because the expenses of the first one had already gone well beyond the value of the combined estates of the three associates. When Pizarro arrived in Spain, he presented his report to the Indian Council, and promised that he would procure vast treasures and kingdoms for the crown if they would grant him authority over these lands as a recompense for his present and past services. Those who listened to him did not believe that the reality was anything like as bright as he presented it, and yet, a few years later, they were to see him in possession of much more than he had promised. Finally, His Majesty agreed to gratify Pizarro with the title of *adelantado,* that is, governor and commander-general of all the lands that he might bring to the Empire, lands that, before they were called Peru, were first given the name of New Castile, in order to distinguish them from the other Empire, called New Spain,[6] which had just been conquered in the same manner by another group of "stubborn madmen," as they were called by foreigners.

On this occasion, Francisco Pizarro and Diego de Almagro were given the title of "Don" (which will henceforth precede their names in this account), after which Don Francisco Pizarro, having pocketed his letters and his warrants, hastened to embark from Seville, to go and join his companions, accompanied by numerous gentlemen from Estremadura and also by his four brothers.[7] They soon arrived in Panama where Don Diego de Almagro immediately manifested a certain amount of ill humor when he realized that all the responsibilities and honors had fallen to Pizarro, whereas the two of them had shared all the work, all the dangers, and all the costs of the discovery; indeed, he had done more than his share, since he had even lost an eye. The rivalry that followed between the two captains was little by little transformed into undying hatred, which only ended the day when one of the two, constituting himself as judge, obtained the head of the other.[8]

For the moment, their friends intervened, in order that this incipient conflict should not delay the conquest. Don

Francisco's own brother took sides with Don Diego, and Pizarro was obliged to make a solemn promise to the effect that he would renounce the title of *adelantado* in favor of his rival, and would have this confirmed by the king. This oath put a momentary end to the wrath of Almagro, who agreed to give Pizarro one thousand gold ducats, abundant provisions, weapons, horses and all that he had got together, in addition to two ships that belonged to him outright.

Don Francisco set sail with his four brothers and as many Spaniards and horses as his ships would carry. His plan was to follow a direct line without stopping, as far as Tumbez, but the southern wind, which blows continually in these parts, forced him to land one hundred leagues farther north than he had intended. So he sent the ships back to Panama and decided to continue on foot, thinking that in this way he would arrive more quickly.[9]

But an adverse wind was nothing compared to the difficulties that awaited Pizarro and his companions in this harsh, sterile land. They soon experienced hunger and fatigue and, encountering rivers grown wider as they approached the sea, they lost many days building rafts of wood and rush, with which to cross them. They finally reached a beautiful province called Coaqui, where they found food and emeralds. But these uncouth soldiers were no jewelers and, in their ignorance, they broke most of these precious stones, believing that they had no value since they did not resist the hammer. They did likewise in Tumbez, where they destroyed more than four thousand ducats' worth of precious stones,[10] and, later on, Almagro and his men did the same; indeed, I should be unable to estimate the priceless treasures that were destroyed as soon as they were discovered by the Spaniards.

It was at this time that a strange and loathsome malady became prevalent among Pizarro's men, which took the form of excrescences that broke out all over their bodies, but principally on their faces. They thought at first that these were warts, because, at the beginning, they looked like warts. But as time passed, they grew larger and began to ripen like figs, of which they had both the size and shape: they hung and swung from a stem, secreted blood and body fluids, and nothing was more frightful to see or more painful, because they were very sensitive to touch.

The wretched men afflicted with this disease were horrible to look at, as they were covered with these purplish-blue fruits hanging from their foreheads, their eyebrows, their nostrils, their beards, and even from their ears; nor did they know how to treat them. Indeed, some died of them, while others survived. But this ailment must have been prevalent in Peru for a long time, because I remember seeing these same fruits on three or four Spaniards in Cuzco when I was a child. Then it suddenly disappeared, the way it had come, as do bad attacks of grippe.[11]

All these hindrances, however, could not divert Pizarro from his goal. He nursed his friends and his soldiers, and then continued on his way. He soon sent twenty-five thousand gold ducats[12] back to Panama—part of which came from barter, and part from the spoils of war—in order to encourage Almagro, and to prove to everybody that he was a man who did what he promised to do. However, he finally reached Tumbez, where numerous reinforcements that had been attracted from as far away as Nicaragua by the increasing fame of Peru, awaited him. Among these were Sebastian de Belalcazar and Juan Fernandez, both of whom were already famous and destined to become even more so.

Twelve leagues from the shore lies Puna island, which was said to be very rich in gold and silver. Pizarro decided to take possession of it with the help of the newcomers. They crossed the sound on rafts, taking great risks, and were immediately engaged in battle. Among the Spaniards, there were four dead and numerous wounded, one of whom was Ferdinand Pizarro, who received an ugly blow on the knee. They were nevertheless victorious and able to divide rich spoils, composed principally of gold, silver, and valuable clothing. Meanwhile, fresh reinforcements had arrived from Nicaragua, led by Ferdinand de Soto, who was delegated by Almagro. Now Pizarro felt sufficiently strong to attack Tumbez.

In order to enter into the good graces of the city, he had himself preceded by a delegation composed of three Spaniards and six hundred Indians captured on Puna, who had promised to use their good offices in exchange for their freedom. But as soon as the Indians arrived in Tumbez, they forgot their promises and, on the contrary, did everything they could to discredit the Spaniards, accusing them of avarice, fornication, adultery, and all kinds of heinous crimes, with the result that the people of Tumbez were scandalized and turned the three emissaries over to the executioner, without even listening to them.

Meanwhile, Don Francisco Pizarro and his followers, left to themselves, were having great difficulties with their rafts which were continually capsizing in the heavy surf. They finally landed, however, and the battle began. It was bloody but brief, since the people of Tumbez, when they saw their losses, believed that they had been punished by the Sun and gave up the struggle. Their curaca came to pay obeisance to Don Francisco Pizarro, and presented him with rich gifts of gold, silver, and precious stones, in order to appease his wrath. The Spaniards were very pleased with the felicitous outcome of this affair and decided to draw up plans for a Christian city on this spot that would be the first in Peru. They baptized it San Miguel, because it was founded on this saint's day, in the year 1531. Don Francisco Pizarro then sent his three ships to Panama to fetch fresh reinforcements; he loaded them with gold, silver, and emeralds, in such quantities that the metal alone was certainly worth thirty thousand pesos.[13]

When peace returned to Tumbez, the Spaniards set out for Cajamarca where they were to meet Atahualpa, who was said to be fabulously rich, a thing they could well believe after having witnessed and assessed the wealth of Tumbez.

They were obliged to cross a desert of dead sand which extended over more than twenty leagues, and because of their inexperience, they suffered intensely from heat and thirst. Then a series of shady, fertile valleys, following upon these hostile lands, made it possible for them to quickly recuperate the strength they had lost. As they were passing through these regions, an envoy from the unfortunate Huascar Inca sought out the governor, Don Francisco Pizarro. It is not known how this poor king, being himself in prison, had succeeded in doing this. The emissary had perhaps come from one of the curacas who had remained secretly loyal to the legitimate Inca. Be that as it may, with great humility, he asked for help, justice, and amends from the sons of his god Viracocha. The governor replied that he was on his way to put an end to all violence and right all other wrongs that he might encounter.

Two days later, Atahualpa's own brother, named Atauchi, presented himself before the governor, at the head of a solemn diplomatic mission.

"The Inca," he said, "has sent me to welcome the sons of our god Viracocha and to offer them some of the fruits of our earth in order that they might know that we are happy to serve them with all our strength and in every way we can. They have only to ask as they pursue their journey, and they will be served and obeyed as though they were our brothers, the sons of the Sun."

Having delivered this message, the emissary went on talking, but in a different tone, as though he were no longer speaking in the king's name, but in his own.

"Inca Viracocha," he said, "son of the Sun, since it has been my good fortune to present this message to you, allow me, pray, to personally express three wishes which I implore you to grant. The first is that you will consider my Inca and king, Atahualpa, as your brother, and that you will enter into an alliance of permanent peace and friendship with him. The second is that you will forgive whatever offenses we may have committed towards you, through inadvertence or ignorance, and that you will do with us as you will, in order that our great desire to serve both you and yours, may be clearly demonstrated. Lastly, I implore you not to impose, in Cajamarca and the rest of the land, the deadly punishments that you inflicted upon the inhabitants of Tumbez and Puna island. Appease your father's anger and forgive us all, with clemency and mercy, like a real Inca and son of the Sun."

The envoy stopped speaking and, at a sign from him, his captains and curacas came forward with all the presents that Atahualpa had sent to the Spaniards. There were ewes and lambs, tamed animals, wild animals, llamas, guanacos, vicuñas, alpacas, stags, roe deer, deer, rabbits, partridge, ducks, wild fowl, both dead and alive; countless species of small birds; loads of dried meat; corn, in both grain and meal form; quantities of fruit, both fresh and dried; honey, in pots and in the comb; peppers, corn, and resin chicha; green parrots, multicolored parrots, monkeys, and all sorts of other animals, and small creatures peculiar to this region. Indeed, it may be said that everything Peru contains was represented in this offering. There were vases, pitchers, platters, gold and silver bowls, for use in the kitchens and on the table; emeralds and turquoises; rolls of fine woolen goods, and ready-sewn garments, such as the king wore. Among other things, the governor received for himself royal sandals and two gold bracelets, called *chipanas,* one of which was to replace the other, for more than one of these bracelets is never worn at one time. This present emphasized that Pizarro was already renowned, not only as an Inca and son of the Sun, but also as a great captain, because the Incas of legitimate lineage, who are the only ones to wear this insignia, do not receive it until they have distinguished themselves in battle.

The Spaniards renewed their thanks to this emissary, when they realized that he was Atahualpa's own brother. And he went away very pleased and with many a compliment. Don Francisco Pizarro replied, in short, that they had come in the name of the Pope, to reveal to the Peruvians the vanity of their idolatry, and to teach them the real religion of the Christians; as well as in the name of the Emperor and king of Spain, who was the greatest monarch in Christendom, to enter into an alliance with the Inca and all his Empire, and sign treaties of permanent peace and friendship with him; that they would not make war on the Inca and that, in due time, Pizarro would tell him other things that concerned him personally.

In reality, the Spaniards were very divided as to the conclusions to be drawn from this first interview, and as soon as the emissary had left, contradictory opinions began to be expressed. According to some, these gifts were to be suspected, by the very fact of their number and munificence. "The Inca wants to allay our suspicions," they said, "in order to take us unawares and without defense, and thus massacre us more easily. We should be, more than ever, on our guard, because all of that is too good to be true." But others, and they were the most numerous, said, on the contrary, that the Inca deserved to be praised and esteemed for his generosity and the majesty of his ambassadorial mission, and that his brother, the ambassador, had shown great tact and courtesy. "Of course," they added, "the laws of war oblige us to advance with caution, but that is no reason not to acknowledge the grandeur ot a monarch who welcomes us in so gracious a manner."

After a few days' rest, during which they reveled and feasted on Atahualpa's presents, they resumed their march in the direction of Cajamarca, where they hoped to find the Inca. The inhabitants of this city received them in great pomp, as descendants of the Sun and sons of their god Viracocha. The curaca of the province, who was named Cullqui Human, had, himself, organized this reception, on orders from the king. The Spaniards were led to lodgings well furnished with food and drink, and decorated with flowers and sweet smelling branches. Here the Indians began to observe with great curiosity the horses, which they took for heavenly creatures and the equals of their masters. Having remarked that they were continually chewing their bits, they concluded that this was their usual food, and hastened to bring them bars of gold and silver ore, with which they filled their feed-troughs. Then, addressing themselves directly to the horses, they said very kindly: "Do leave your iron aside, and eat this fodder, which is much better!"

And the Spaniards, laughing up their sleeves at their ignorance, encouraged the Indians to bring the horses all the gold and silver they could find, if they wanted to make friends of them.[14]

The very next day, the governor assembled his brothers and his captains in council. Since King Atahualpa was in residence not far from there, in the palaces of a nearby watering place, they decided to send him a diplomatic mission, in order to show their gratitude for all his gifts and the cordial welcome extended to them by his people. Atahualpa's brother having headed the Indian mission, it was decided that Ferdinand Pizarro, brother of the governor, would head the Spanish one, together with Ferdinand de Soto. They also took with them their interpreter, Felipe, who had followed them all the way from Puna island. Felipe's clumsiness in the Inca language was as great as it was in Spanish, but they could not do without him, because they had no other go-between. The curaca of Cajamarca put at their disposal a retinue of two hundred Indian nobles, who were ordered to do everything the Spaniards wished, even to die for them, if need be. One of the leaders among the Indians went ahead, preceding the two gentlemen, to inform Atahualpa of their arrival, and beg His Highness to kindly grant them an audience. The Inca received this messenger very graciously, telling him to reply to the Spaniards that he had been expecting them for some time and would be delighted to welcome them.

He then sent one of his camp commanders to meet them, at the head of an entire company, with instructions to welcome and escort the two sons of the Sun into his presence, with all the respect and veneration due them. This news was somewhat reassuring for Ferdinand Pizarro and de Soto who, at that very moment, had just been informed that the king was surrounded by a guard of more than thirty thousand men, and could therefore not help feeling somewhat suspicious with regard to his intentions.

When Ferdinand de Soto saw the camp commander coming towards him across the plain with all his company, he left his group, and spurring his mount, galloped up to him, as though he meant to show these Indian warriors that, in case their intentions were not of the best, he could exterminate them all, unaided. Just here we are in disagreement with all the Spanish historians who claim that it was not a camp commander, but Atahualpa himself who had come, and that de Soto pulled up his horse and kowtowed to him on the very steps of the throne, so close to the king, people said, that the latter felt the breath of the beast on his face. They added that Atahualpa did not wince, but that, several of the lords with him having been unable to control the fright that this unknown animal inspired in them, he had them executed on the spot, under the very eyes of the Spaniards. All of that seems to me to be purely imaginary; on the one hand, because Ferdinand de Soto would never have thought of making such a thoughtless, discourteous gesture before a sovereign to whom he had just spoken in the name of Charles V and His Holiness the Pope; and on the other, because Atahualpa was far too cunning a politician to give the Spaniards such immediate proof of his bloodthirsty, cruel nature, when his only aim was to win them over to his side. In consideration of which, it is really to be regretted that there should be persons in Spain so eager to appear in a favorable light that, to achieve this, they do not hesitate to say the most fantastic things about others, taking advantage of the fact that they are telling of events and countries that are too far distant for their statements to be easily verified.

The Inca Atahualpa, as we shall see later, was lacking neither in generosity nor in grandeur in confronting the Spaniards. We must grant him this, and, indeed it would be doubly invidious on our part to neglect to mention the remarkable sides of his nature, after having given the description we have of his cruelty and tyranny. The fact is that he possessed a very sharp mind and knew how to be extremely clever as well as tactful in the unusual circumstances in which he was to be placed.

And so, continuing our tale, let us say that the camp commander, after having bowed down with the greatest respect before Ferdinand Pizarro and Ferdinand de Soto, turned towards his soldiers and, pointing to the Spaniards, cried: "These are the sons of our god Viracocha!" Whereupon all the soldiers, stunned with admiration, also bowed down to them, before accompanying them into the king's presence. But the Spaniards too were filled with admiration when, later, they discovered the grandeur and wealth of the royal palace and the company of Inca nobles assembled there: indeed, it is hard to say which of them were the most amazed. The two ambassadors approached the king, who was seated on a solid gold throne, and made him a deep court bow, in the Spanish manner, which seemed greatly to please His Majesty.

Atahualpa rose and embraced them both, very cordially:

"Capac Viracochas," he said, "welcome to my country."

Now gold seats, such as those reserved for the Incas, were brought in, and the three of them sat down. Near relatives of the king were assembled all about them.

Turning towards the latter, Atahualpa said, "You see before you the features of our god Viracocha. This is the aspect, the garb, the very face with which our Inca Viracocha allowed him to be represented in stone, after he had appeared to him."

Then two beautiful young ñustas, accompanied by four young princes, came forward, holding in their hands little gold cups filled with *chicha*. After having bowed low before the Inca, the first one handed him a cup, then, at a sign from him, handed the other to Ferdinand Pizarro. Titu Atauchi, the king's brother, who had headed his mission to the Spaniards, told the interpreter, Felipe, to explain that the Inca was inviting his guests to drink with him, as a traditional sign of love and peace. Ferdinand Pizarro drank first, and

Atahualpa took one or two swallows to join him, before handing the cup to his brother, who finished it. In the same way, he shared the cup handed to him by the second ñusta with Ferdinand de Soto.

The Spanish emissaries believed that the time had come to deliver their message. But the king restrained them from doing so, urging them to rest comfortably, and give him time to look still longer upon the features of his god Viracocha. Meanwhile six pages and six beautifully dressed young girls had entered, with all sorts of fresh and dried fruits, various breads, resin wine, and richly embroidered cotton napkins.

"O, Son of the great Inca Viracocha," said one of them, addressing the Spaniards, "kindly do us the honor of tasting this fruit."

And the two Spaniards were dumbfounded to see such urbanity and courtesy among people who, until then, they had imagined to be rustics and barbarians. Not wishing to seem remiss, they replied eagerly to the invitation of these gracious hostesses, to the great satisfaction of the entire gathering.

Finally, since time was passing, and Ferdinand Pizarro wanted to be back among his companions by nightfall, he urged de Soto to speak, which the latter did, in the following terms, after having greeted all those present, with bared head and a deep bow, in the Spanish manner.

"Most serene Inca," he said, "permit me to tell you that, of all the princes in this world, there are two who are more powerful than all the others. One of them is the Pope, who represents God among men; he administers and governs the guardians of divine law, and teaches the word of God. The other is Charles V, king of Spain and Emperor of the Romans. These two monarchs have been informed of the state of blindness in which the natives of these kingdoms have been living; that is, a state in which, leaving aside the only real God, creator of heaven and earth, they worship his creatures and the demon who deceives them. And this is why they have sent our governor and Commander-General Don Francisco Pizarro, his companions and several priests, God's ministers, to teach Your Highness and all his vassals divine truth and holy law, without which we should not be living on this earth. Thanks to your royal assistance, these men arrived yesterday in Cajamarca, and they have sent us today to Your Highness, in order that we may lay the bases for the harmony, union, fraternity and permanent peace that should reign between us; in order, too, that under your august protection, we might make known here this divine law which Your Highness and all your followers will hear and receive for the great benefit of their spirits and the salvation of their souls."

But, as Father Blas Valera points out, these noble, holy words were translated by the Indian, Felipe, in such a heavy, barbarous manner that not only did the Inca and those close to him not grasp their entire meaning, but they also saw sources of regret and even offense in what was said. And in fact, this poor rendering did destroy all the majesty of Ferdinand de Soto's speech, to such an extent that the Inca exclaimed:

"What is this man driving at with his piecemeal phrases! I understand nothing of what he says, he speaks like a deaf mute."

In the Inca language, this remark was heavy with meaning, and Atahualpa's captains attributed all the confusion of this speech to the poor interpreter, being unable to believe that it might be due to the emissaries themselves, whom they believed to be the sons of God. The Inca replied, therefore, as follows:

"I am delighted, divine lords, that you and your companions should have succeeded in reaching such remote regions as these, and that, thus, you should have confirmed the exactness of the events forecast by our ancestors. However, my soul should mourn, because the fact that you are here, means that the end of our Empire is at hand, your arrival and our downfall being inseparably associated in our ancient predictions. And yet I should like to consider this moment as the happiest we have ever experienced, because our god Viracocha has become manifest through such guests as you, and because the changes that will take place will only be for the greater well-being of our country, as is attested by the tradition of our ancestors and the last will of my father, Huaina Capac, as well as by the unfortunate wars that set enmity between my brother and myself, and could not end otherwise than through divine intervention. For this reason, although I have received daily intelligence of your advance through our land, and of the cruel sanctions you inflicted in Puna, Tumbez, and other places, we have not wanted, my captains and I, either to resist you or to hurl you back into the sea, for we consider that you are the sons of our great god Viracocha and the messengers of Pachacamac. Our father left us instructions to serve and worship you, which, for us, constitutes a law, one that is taught in the Cuzco schools; and no one will dare to take up arms against you. You can therefore do what you desire with us, and if it be your will that we should perish, it will be a source of pride and glory for us to die by the hand of God's messengers. Your deeds and your arrival here give proof indeed that God alone commands you and has sent you to us. But let me, nevertheless, ask you one question, because there is one point in the speech you just made that I did not understand clearly. How does it happen that, although you affirm your desire to discuss peace and permanent friendship with us, in the name of the two princes you claim to represent, you should have so severely handled and massacred the inhabitants of the provinces you passed through, before having spoken to us even, that is, before having discovered whether our intentions were good or bad? You must have acted, therefore, upon the orders of these two princes who, themselves, act in obedience to instructions given by the great Pachacamac. If this then be the case, I repeat, kindly dispose of us as you see fit. I beg you only to have pity on my people, for their suffering and their death would be harder for me to bear than my own."

A chorus of sobbing and moaning greeted the end of this speech, and no one close to the Inca had any illusion but that the promised day had arrived when the Empire would disappear. For Atahualpa himself, the Spaniards were envoys of fate, whom it would be both vain and criminal to resist. For this reason, as we shall soon see, he lost all pride and acted as though he were defeated through resignation to the will of God. But let us not anticipate.

To return to this memorable interview, I shall add that two royal historians took down as best they could the speech made by Ferdinand de Soto and the Inca's reply by means of their cords and knots.

The two Spaniards were quite amazed at the scene

of general affliction that followed Atahualpa's speech. Nor could they understand the cause of it, which was a real misfortune for the Incas, as Father Blas Valera points out, because if the interpreter had been more competent, the Spaniards would have felt compassion and charity towards them. Instead, they were somewhat annoyed by the Inca's speech, just as he had been by theirs, and for the same reasons. They thought, especially, that Atahualpa wanted to be revenged for those they had killed in Puna and in Tumbez, because Felipe mentioned these past events without being able to comment upon them as the king had done. So the inadequacy of this interpreter was twofold: on the one hand, he did not know enough Spanish and Inca words, and on the other, he forgot half of the arguments he was supposed to translate.

Finally, the emissaries asked the king for permission to withdraw. He granted it very graciously, and promised to go himself to Cajamarca very soon, to visit the sons of his god Viracocha and messengers of the great Pachacamac. The two gentlemen from Estremadura left the palace with even greater admiration for this great lord's pomp and kind attentions. When they asked for their horses, two curacas accompanied by a retinue of servants came to beg them to accept a small gift they had brought, even though it were quite unworthy of their divine persons. And this small gift, which was immediately presented to them, was as rich and splendid as the first had been, with lots of gold and silver, both wrought and unwrought. The sight of this dispelled the Spaniards' fears for all time, and they returned to their camp imbued with esteem and regard for the Inca.

When the emissaries arrived back among their own, they described the marvelous things they had seen in the Inca's palace, and the exquisite courtesy that had been shown them. Then they made equal division of the Inca's presents, with which everybody was delighted. But, like all good soldiers, they nevertheless did not neglect to prepare their weapons and their horses for the morrow, in order to be able to fight like Spaniards worthy of the name, despite the crushing superiority of Atahualpa's forces. When day dawned, they divided their cavalry, which only numbered sixty, into three groups of twenty men, commanded respectively by Ferdinand Pizarro, Ferdinand de Soto, and Sebastian de Belalcazar; then each one of these groups went and hid behind a wall, while waiting for the moment to swoop down on the Indians, thus increasing tenfold the effect of terror to which their appearance would give rise. The governor, Don Francisco Pizarro, took command of the infantry, which was composed of hardly more than one hundred men, and went to await King Atahualpa at one end of the main square. Meanwhile, Atahualpa was advancing on a golden litter carried on the shoulders of his men, accompanied by his entire household and his court, and with a degree of magnificence that displayed as much pomp and majesty as it did military power. The litters were preceded by a multitude of servants,[15] who cleared the ground, removing all stones and pebbles and even bits of straw, from the road over which the king was to travel. The military escort was composed of four squadrons, each one comprising eight thousand men. The first preceded the king, two more surrounded him, and the fourth closed the ranks, in the role of rear guard; all of these troops were commanded by General Rumiñaui. There was a distance of one league between the king's camp and the main square of the city, where the Spaniards were waiting for him; however, with all his pomp, it took him more than four hours to cover it. As we shall see later, it was not Atahualpa's intention to fight, but only to listen to the communications from the Pope and the Emperor that had been brought him by the Spaniards. The latter had been described to him as people who were so weak that they could not even climb a hill on their own feet: "That is why they have horses," people said, "some of them ride on their backs while others have to be pulled, hanging on to the horse's tail or to its girth; they are incapable of running as we do, nor can they carry anything heavy."

So all of this information, added to the fact that he considered the Spaniards to be divine beings, made Atahualpa quite unable to suspect the kind of reception that these people had been planning for him.

He entered the square with his three first squadrons, the fourth remaining outside.[16] When he saw the handful of Spanish infantrymen awaiting him, in tightly serried ranks, as though filled with fear, the king said:

"These people are messengers from God. See that no harm is done them, but, on the contrary, treat them respectfully and courteously."

Upon which, a Dominican friar approached the Inca, cross in hand, to speak to him in the name of the Emperor. This was Friar Vincente de Valverde.[17]

Everything in the aspect of this man was calculated to excite the Inca's curiosity, for he had never seen anyone like him. He wore a beard, the tonsure, and the frock of his order; in one hand he held a wooden cross, and in the other, a book which, according to certain chroniclers was *The Summum*, by Sylvester, unless it was the breviary or the Bible.

"What is this Spaniard's estate?" asked the Inca. "Is he the superior, inferior, or equal of the others?"

One of the three dignitaries who had been attached to the Spaniards since their arrival in Cajamarca replied: "Inca, all I know is that he is a captain, a guide who speaks [by which he meant preacher], and a minister and messenger of the supreme God, Pachacamac, which makes him different from the others."

Meanwhile, Friar Vincente had approached the royal litter. He bowed, then began to speak as follows: "O, great and powerful king, in order that Your Highness and all his subjects may learn the genuine Catholic faith, it is advisable that you should hear and believe what I am going to say to you.

"First of all, that God, who is unique although in three persons, created heaven and earth, and that he it is who rewards those who are virtuous, with eternal life, and chastises those who are evil with eternal punishment. In the beginning of time, he created man, with the dust of the earth, and conferred upon him the breath of life, which we call the soul, and which he created in his own image and likeness, with the result that every man is composed of a body and a rational soul.

"This first man, whom God called Adam, is the ancestor of us all: he is the source of our common origin, and we have inherited from him all that goes to make up our nature. He sinned, transgressing the law of his creator, and, like him, all men have sinned, and will continue to do so until the end of the world. No one, whether man or woman, is able or ever will be able to wipe out this original stain, which we all bear, with the exception of Jesus Christ our Lord who, being the son of the real God, descended from heaven and was born of the Virgin Mary, to redeem the human species and deliver it from evil. He finally died for our salvation, on a wooden cross similar to this one that I have in my hand; and it is for this reason that we Christians worship and revere this cross.

"Jesus Christ rose from the dead through his own virtue, and after forty days, he ascended unto heaven, where he is seated at the right hand of God, the Father Almighty. He left his apostles and their successors on earth, in order that they should maintain his rule and show mankind the way of light and how to worship God.

"He willed that Saint Peter, his apostle, should be God's vicar and the prince of all the other apostles and their successors, as of all other Christians; he also willed that the same should be true of all Holy Roman Pontiffs, the successors of Saint Peter, whom we call Popes. And all of them have observed, observe today, and will continue to observe always, with great reverence, the will of Jesus Christ, according to which they must preach and teach men the word of God.

"This is why the Pope, who is the Sovereign Pontiff of Rome, having heard that the peoples and nations of these kingdoms had forsaken the real God, their only creator, to worship idols and images of the devil, granted Charles V, Emperor of the Romans, the right of conquest over these regions in order that this very powerful king, sovereign of Greater Spain and monarch of the entire earth, should subjugate these peoples, their kings and their masters, exterminate all rebels and unregenerates, and in the end, reign over them alone, allowing them to enter into the knowledge of God, and to obey his Church.

"Our great Emperor is very absorbed by the government of his numerous kingdoms and provinces. But he considered that the prospect of salvation of so many souls plunged in error made it impossible for him not to accept the Pope's offer. He decided, therefore, to send his captains and soldiers here, to conquer this land, in the same way that they conquered the large islands and land of Mexico; in order that here, as there, having subjugated these peoples by force, they might lead them to the real religion of Jesus Christ, who, Himself, willed that this should be done.

"For this reason, the great Emperor Charles V chose as his lieutenant and ambassador Don Francisco Pizarro, now present here, as much in order that the same grace should benefit Your Highness's kingdoms, as that he might conclude with you an alliance of perpetual friendship, by virtue of which you and your entire kingdom would become tributary to His Majesty. This means that, since you will pay tribute to the Emperor, you will be one of his subjects, and turn over your kingdom to him, renouncing both government and administration of it, as has been done elsewhere by many a king and powerful lord. This, then, is my first point. Here is the second:

"Once peace has been restored and a friendship pact concluded, either of your own accord or as a result of force, you will be expected to obey the Sovereign Pontiff the Pope in all respects, to accept the faith of Jesus Christ our Lord and to abandon completely and for all time your odious superstitions concerning idols: then you will be given actual proofs of how holy is our law, and how false and demon-ridden was your own.

"And, if you believe me, O King, you will accept all this of your own free will, for the betterment of your people and of your own person. For if you refuse, you must know that we will make merciless war upon you, that all your idols will be cast down, and that fire and sword and bloodshed will compel you, whether you will or not, to reject your false religion, to receive our Catholic faith, pay tribute to our Emperor, and surrender your kingdom to him. But if you persist, you may be certain that God will let your fate and that of your people resemble that of Pharaoh, who perished long ago, in the Red Sea, with all his army. For likewise you will all perish, to the very last one, by the grace of God, and the strength of our arms."

Since what I myself know of this oration corresponds exactly to Father Blas Valera's account, it is the latter that I have given, for, according to him, he memorized it after having read in Trujillo the version set down by Friar Valverde himself. Commenting upon it, Father Blas Valera adds that most historians have mutilated this text, cutting important passages, but that other, reliable men, whose writings may still be consulted, have reported it *in extenso* just as he has told it. He quotes Juan de Oliva and Cristobal de Molina,[18] both priests, well-known preachers, and very conversant with the language of the Indians; Juan de Montalvo, a priest and preacher; Falconia Aragonés, a doctor of both canon and secular law, author of a work entitled *De libertate Indorum servanda;* Friar Marcos de Jofré, a Franciscan monk, and several others. All of these authors are in agreement in saying that Friar Vincente de Valverde's oration was extremely dry and harsh, without a single redeeming word, and that those delivered by Ferdinand de Soto and Ferdinand Pizarro deserve more approval, for the reason that these gentlemen took pains to speak in a more modest, more temperate manner.

But the way it was interpreted by the Indian, Felipe, when he tried to translate this speech for Atahualpa, was even worse. We have already said that this boy, who was of very lowly origin, was a native of Puna island and that his knowledge of both the Inca and the Spanish languages was equally faulty. Nor did the fact that he had been baptized keep him from being quite ignorant of religious matters. The result was that, not at all through malice but rather through incapacity, he could not have made a worse translation of Friar Vincente's oration, repeating parrot-like a series of words not one of which he understood. Thus, in order to say "One God in three persons" he said, "God three and one make four," thinking that he would be better understood. In this way, he rendered unintelligible what he was trying to clarify. In speaking of Adam's generation, he let it be understood that once upon a time all human beings who were born, or yet to be born, were all assembled together, and that they heaped all of their sins upon Adam. With regard to Christ our Lord, he did not mention His divinity, but said merely that He was a great man who died for the human species. As for the virginity, purity, and saintliness of Our Lady, the Virgin Mary, he hardly spoke of them. When he arrived at the second part of the oration, which he understood better than the first, because it had to do with more tangible things, such as war and weapons, he insisted so much on the power of the Emperor Charles V that the Indians believed this king to be superior to God himself, as well as to all the saints in paradise.

King Atahualpa understood from the priest's peroration that the Pope had ordered, and that the Emperor desired him to give up his kingdoms willy-nilly: that he would be compelled to do so by fire, sword, and bloodshed; and that, like Pharaoh, he would be exterminated with all his army. From this he concluded that these guests whom he and his people called Viracochas, considering them as gods, had been transformed into mortal enemies of his people and of his line, since they had nothing but these cruel, pitiless things to say to him. And he felt so sad and so distessed that he could not refrain from uttering out loud the word "*Atac!*" which means, alas! Finally, rising above his sorrow, and restraining as best he could the passions that racked his soul, he, in turn, took the floor and spoke as follows: "Despite the fact that you have refused me all the other things I asked of your emissaries, it would at least have given me great pleasure if you had consented to speak to me through a more learned, more accurate, more experienced interpreter than the one you have; because you must know the incomparable value that words take on for anyone who wants to learn about the customs and the civil and political life of another people; indeed, you might be endowed with the greatest virtues, and it would be difficult for me to appreciate this through what I can see and understand, so long as you do not express yourselves. And how much more pressing still this necessity becomes when the encounter takes place between persons who come from regions that are so remote from one another as ours are. In reality, if such persons attempt to speak and negotiate through the intermediary of interpreters who know neither language, then they might as well choose a four-footed go-between, among their own cattle! I say this, man of God, because I surmise that your words are quite different from those spoken by this Indian; indeed the very reason for our meeting is evidence of this fact. We are here to discuss peace, friendship, and permanent brotherhood, even an alliance between our two bloods, as was stated by your first emissaries when they came to call on me. And these words have a different sound from those your interpreter has just spoken; for he only speaks of war and death, of fire and sword, of banishment and destruction, of extinction of the royal blood of the Incas, of alienation of my kingdom, and, whether I will or no, of my vassalage to someone whom I do not even know. From all of this, I can only conclude two things: either your prince and you yourselves are but tyrants who go about ravaging and destroying everything they encounter in the world, appropriating by force kingdoms to which they have no right, killing, robbing, despoiling those who owe them nothing and have done them no harm; or else you are the ministers of God, whom we call Pachacamac, and He has designated you to punish and destroy us. If this be so, my vassals and I accept death and whatever else you may choose to do with us, not at all through fear inspired by your weapons or your threats, but in order that the last wishes of my father, Huaina Capac, may be fulfilled; for he commanded us, on his deathbed, to serve and honor the bearded men, like yourselves, who would come to this land after he had left it. For many years he had known that these men were cruising in their ships along the coast of our Empire; and he told us that their laws and their customs, their science, and their bravery were greater than our own. This is why we called you Viracochas, meaning by this that you were the messengers of the great god Viracocha: his will and his indignation could not be other than just, and who could resist the power of his arms? But he is also full of pity and mercy, and therefore you, who are his messengers and ministers, you who are not human, but divine, you cannot allow a repetition of the crimes, the robberies, and all the other cruelty that was perpetrated in Tumbez and in the other regions you came through.

"In addition to this, your herald spoke to me of five well-known men, whom I should know about. The first is the god three and one which make four, whom you call the creator of the universe; no doubt he is the same as the one we call Pachacamac and Viracocha. The second is the one whom you say is the father of the human species, upon whom all other men have laid their sins. You call the third one Jesus Christ, who did not burden his fellow men with his sins, as all other men did, but who was killed. The fourth, you call the Pope, and the fifth, Charles. Without taking the others into consideration, you call this latter the all-powerful sovereign of the universe and say that he is above everybody else. But then, if this Charles is the prince and lord of the entire world, how is it that the Pope should have had to grant him permission to make war upon me and usurp my kingdoms? And if this was necessary, this means that the Pope is a greater, more powerful lord than he is, and therefore the prince of the entire universe. I am surprised that I should have to pay tribute to Charles and not to the others; you give no reason for this, and I myself do not see any that would oblige me to do so. Because, if I were obliged, quite frankly, to pay service and tribute to someone, it seems to me that it would rather be to God who, as you say, created us all, and to that first man who was the father of all other men, and to Jesus Christ, who never burdened others with his sins, and, lastly, to the Pope, who can dispose of my person and of my kingdom, to assign them to others. But if you say that I owe nothing to any one of these three, it seems to me that I owe even less to Charles, who was never lord of this land, and has never even seen it. And even if we were to admit that, having received the Pope's blessing, he really had some rights over me, would it not be just and fair that you should tell me this, before proclaiming threats of war, bloodshed, and death? I am neither so foolish nor so unreasonable as not to know how to obey him who exerts authority over me by rights, and justly and reasonably; but how am I to comply with the Pope's desires without knowing what they are?

"Lastly, to come back to that eminent man, Jesus Christ, who refused to burden others with his sins, I should like to know how he died: was it from sickness, or at the hands of his enemies? And was he set among the gods before or after his death? I should like to know whether or not you consider as gods these five men whom you hold up to me, and whom you so venerate. For if this be the case, then you have more gods than we have, for we worship no god other than Pachacamac, who is our supreme God, after whom we worship the Sun, whose bride and sister is the Moon.

"This then is why I should appreciate it exceedingly if a better interpreter would kindly explain these things to me, in order that I might understand them, and conform to your will."

Sayri Tupac receives the viceroy

Don Cristobal Sayri Tupac Inca marries

The allies begin their campaign

Applying the new law

The Spaniards are without shame

An Inca, a half-caste, and mulatto with the corregidor

A Spaniard travels

Private life of Creoles, half-castes, and mulattoes

Private life of their wives

Creole festival

THE SPANIARDS AND THE INCAS IN PERU

In the first illustration, Sayri Tupac Inca is receiving the Viceroy Don Andres, marquis of Cañete: "the king received the viceroy and made him a gift of gold."
The second drawing represents the religious marriage of the same Sayri Tupac, now Don Cristobal, to the Coya Doña Beatrice. The alliance between the Incas and the Spaniards is represented in the following drawing of Martin Arbieto and Don Tomas Tupac Inca setting off together to conquer the Antisuyu. An Indian "mitayo" is then seen being punished for not giving two eggs to the *corregidor.*
Next drawing: "The *corregidors,* the fathers of the doctrine and the lieutenants of the towns and provinces, forgetting that they are there to ensure respect for justice and Christian law, look at the shameful parts of married women and girls."
The *corregidor* invites a half-caste, a mulatto, and a tributary Indian to have supper with him.
The four following drawings illustrate "the misconduct of the Creoles, half-castes, mulattos, and Christian Spaniards of Castile."

In making his reply, the Inca reckoned with the awkwardness of the interpreter, Felipe. He pronounced his sentences slowly, breaking them up into short phrases, so as to give him ample time to understand. And, above all, instead of speaking the language of Cuzco, he chose that of Chinchasuyu, which the Indian understood much better. Despite these precautions, however, the king's thought was nevertheless quite imperfectly and barbarously translated, while the royal historians noted it faithfully on their quipus, in order that it might remain in their archives.

But the Spaniards, who had grown impatient during this long speech, suddenly sprang from their hiding places and attacked the Indians in order to rob them of their handsome gold jewels encrusted with precious stones which they were wearing for this solemn occasion. Other Spaniards climbed up a small tower, on top of which was an idol covered with gold and silver plate enhanced with precious stones. Soon there was immense confusion, the Spaniards struggling to take possession of these treasures, and the Indians to defend them. As soon as the Inca realized what was happening, he gave orders to his men, in a loud voice, not to mistreat or wound the Spaniards, even if they should go so far as to attack him personally. At this point in his account, Father Blas Valera compares Atahualpa with Ahasuerus explaining that, in accordance with the will of our Lord Jesus Christ, the Inca's haughty, savage nature grew humble and gentle before Friar Valverde's cross, in the same way that Ahasuerus had softened in the presence of Queen Esther. And, undoubtedly, divine mercy did intervene at that moment, to make the gentiles in Peru aware of the virtues of Christian doctrine, and of the holy gospels.

Spanish historians say that Friar Valverde himself started the riot by giving a call to arms against the king, who was supposed to have thrown his holy book to the ground; all of which is pure invention, because the king had at no time asked him for his book.[19] What happened was that Friar Vincente, having become alarmed by the shouts that the Indians suddenly started to give, rose from the bench upon which he had been seated talking with Atahualpa, and, at that moment, the book fell to the ground. The priest was about to reply to the Inca's questions, which he considered to be very pertinent, but he was obliged to interrupt himself to go join his people, shouting to them, in vain however, for his voice was drowned by the noise of the crowd, not to do the Indians any harm.

Spanish historians have interpreted this scene quite differently, putting in the mouths of both participants words that neither of them uttered. According to them, the whole thing started with the following question which Atahualpa was said to have put to Friar Vincente: "You say that Christ is God and that He is dead. I worship the Sun and the Moon, both of which are immortal. And what is your authority that God created the universe?"

"This book," the priest is said to have replied.

At this, Atahualpa is supposed to have seized the volume, held it to his ear, shaken it, and finally, seeing that he could not get it to speak, thrown it on the ground.

And this is when Friar Vincente is supposed to have risen and cried: "To arms, Christians! The holy gospel is being trampled under foot! Justice! Vengeance! Up and at these infidels who despise our law and scorn our friendship!"

But all of this is nothing but a fairy tale, as is also the following reply which they attribute to the Inca: "I am free, and I owe tribute to no one, since there is no monarch who is superior to me! I should, assuredly, be delighted to be a friend of your Emperor, who must be very powerful to be able to send troops to such distant lands, but not to obey the Pope, as you ask me to do; because any man who takes the liberty of disposing of my legal property as he does, without even knowing me, in order to give it to his friends, who have no natural right to it, does not seem to me to possess good judgment. And as for my religion, why should I doubt it, when it suits me so well, and the long history of my ancestors is my authority for it!"

As I said before, all these declarations were invented by the Spanish general and his captains to be included in the official report that they were obliged to send to the Emperor: they took great pains to arrange the facts, leaving out everything that did not redound to their honor, and adding what seemed more favorable to them, in order not to pass judgment on themselves. They wanted their feats to be rewarded and for that, they had to gild them, glaze, and enhance them, as best they could.

But, if necessary, many proofs could be furnished as testimony that I have said nothing but the exact truth: to begin with, the quipus kept in the archives of Cajamarca province; and those of the conquistadors who were eyewitnesses of this scene, among them Alonso Valera, Blas Valera's own father.

Shall we say, to summarize, that more than five thousand Indians were killed on that day, among whom were more than fifteen hundred old people, women, and children, who had come out of curiosity to be present at this unprecedented meeting.[20] Some were suffocated in the crowd or trampled to death by the Spanish horses, while others—how many no one can say—died entombed under one of the walls of the square, which collapsed under the pressure of those who were trying to escape. And yet, as I said before, there were on hand more than thirty thousand armed Indian fighters, and the Spaniards only numbered one hundred and sixty! But all these Indians were haunted by the famous prediction of the Inca Viracocha, and they asked themselves if the moment had not arrived when, not only the Empire and its laws, but also their religion and its rites were about to disappear like so much smoke. For this reason, they neither dared to defend themselves, nor to offend the Spaniards whom they considered as gods and the messengers of Viracocha. Spanish historians themselves confirm the fact that Atahualpa forbade his troops to fight.

Thus Francisco Lopez Gomara writes in the one hundred and thirteenth chapter of his book: "None of the Indians fought, although they were all armed; and this is very extraordinary when one recalls their cruelty and how accustomed they were to battle. The reason why they did not fight was that they were forbidden to do so; and they fled purely and simply out of fear, when all at once there was a blare of trumpets, the roar of harquebuses and artillery, and galloping horses, with little bells hung on their girths to increase the fear and confusion."

A little further on, the same author adds: "The reason so many of them died was because they did not defend themselves, and because, too, our men simply cut and thrust with might and main, in order not to break their swords with stabs and backhand strokes, on the advice of Friar Vincente himself."

All the other writers on the subject say the same thing as Gomara, which confirms the fact that Atahualpa forbade his men to fight, through the intercession of Our Lord's mercy, who, on that day, wanted to spare those who were going to preach His holy gospel. Because if this had not been the case, it would have sufficed for the Indians to see their king overthrown and a prisoner, for them all to fight to the death, since they had their arms in their hands; and even with nothing but stones they would have had no difficulty in overcoming one hundred and sixty Spaniards; yet, according to these same historians, there was not a single fatal casualty among the conquistadors, nor even one wounded, with the exception of Don Francisco Pizarro himself, who was slightly wounded in the hand by one of his own men, when he was on the point of seizing Atahualpa.

Friar Vincente de Valverde denied the allegations according to which he himself was supposed to have advised that they keep cutting and laying about themselves, so as not to break their swords. Those are sentences that it is easy to write in Spain, when one is describing an action that took place three thousand leagues away. But how could one believe, or even imagine, that a Catholic father and theologian could have said such a thing, at the most, worthy of a Nero! However, we have spoken enough about this affair, so let us return now to our story.

The Spanish cavalrymen left their hiding places, hurling themselves like thunderbolts at the Indian squadrons, their lances in rest; and they transpierced as many as they could without encountering any resistance. Don Pizarro and his wildly impatient infantrymen had succeeded, meanwhile, in forcing their way to Atahualpa, because at the very idea of so rich a catch they already saw themselves the masters of all the treasures in Peru. The Indians crowded about the royal litter, ready to defend with their own bodies the Inca's sacred person. They were massacred one by one, however, without having made the slightest gesture of defense. Then Don Francisco, who had finally come up close to the king, seized the latter's clothing and, together, they were soon wrestling on the ground.

And thus it was that King Atahualpa became prisoner of the Spaniards, which fact, when the Indians realized it, made them flee in the greatest disorder. Being unable to leave by the only gate of the city, which was in the hands of the cavalry, they hurled themselves with such fury against one of the enclosing walls that they opened up a breach more than one hundred feet wide, through which they were able to escape to the plain. One author wrote that, on this occasion, by yielding to death-hunted men, this stone wall showed more tenderness and pity than the hearts of the Spaniards. Indeed, according to historians, the Spaniards were so angry when they saw the Indians escape, that they dashed across the plain in their pursuit and massacred a large number with their lances, until nightfall forced them to stop. They then pillaged the Inca's camp, where they amassed a considerable amount of booty. Francisco Lopez de Gomara, in the one hundred and fourteenth chapter of his book, gives the following account of this incident:

"In the royal baths, they found five thousand women, of whom they did not fail to take advantage, despite the fact that the women were sad and weary; they also took possession of many fine, large tents and all kinds of provisions: clothing, household linens, valuable tableware, and vases, one of which weighed one hundred kilograms in gold; Atahualpa's tableware alone, which was entirely of gold and silver, was worth one hundred thousand ducats."

When the members of the nobility who had escaped the Cajamarca massacre learned that their king was still alive, they came to offer their services to him in prison. The only one who acted differently was the camp commander Rumiñaui who, as we have already seen, had remained outside the square with the rear guard of his troops. This man had never trusted the promises of the Spaniards and, unbelievably incensed, he fled with his men to the kingdom of Quito with the intention of rapidly levying an army, not only against the Spaniards, but also against Atahualpa whom, secretly, he intended to dethrone for his own benefit, thus following the bad example that this king himself had set. He had hardly arrived in Quito before he seized several of Atahualpa's sons, on the pretext of protecting them; then, as soon as they were in his power, he put them to death, together with Quillascancha, the legitimate brother of the king, the camp commander Challcuchima, and a number of captains and curacas.

Meanwhile, the Inca Atahualpa, finding himself a prisoner, with his feet in irons, had offered to fill with gold the room he was kept in—which was a fine large room—in order to obtain his freedom.

"When he saw that the Spaniards shrugged their shoulders at this proposal, and turned their backs on him, as though they did not consider this possible," wrote Francisco Lopez de Gomara, "he touched the wall of his room, as high as he could raise his arms and, at this height, drew a red line that ran around the entire room.

"The gold and silver of my ransom will make a pile that high," he said, "on condition that you neither break nor smelt any of the objects that I shall have brought, until this limit will have been reached."

A date of payment was set, and once the deal was concluded, gold and silver began to flow into Cajamarca. But such immense quantities were needed that it seemed as though all Peru's resources would not be sufficient, and the time set came and went. Then the Spaniards began to grumble, saying that the Inca was poking fun at them, and that his envoys, instead of collecting gold and silver, were quite simply levying troops to come and free him. Atahualpa was very perceptive, and he soon became aware of the uneasiness that reigned in the camp. He questioned Pizarro, who told him the cause of it.

"What!" the Inca cried, "do you realize the distances that my messengers must cover? Do you know that this gold comes principally from Quito, Cuzco, and Pachacamac, and that there are three hundred leagues from here to Quito, two hundred to Cuzco, and eighty to Pachacamac, which is the nearest of the three?"

He then proposed to the governor to name several Spaniards who, themselves, would go and verify the truth of his statements in these different places, and who could thus accept payment in their own hands.

"You keep me in chains," he concluded, in order to overcome Pizarro's ultimate hesitations, "thus my life will answer for that of your envoys."

They decided, therefore, that Ferdinand de Soto and Pedro del Barco would go to Cuzco, while four other Spaniards would travel to Quito, Huamachucu, Socclapampa, and the Huailla country. In all these places they were to verify the existence of the treasures mentioned by Atahualpa. They would also make guarded inquiry as to whether the Indians were not, here and there, equipping armies to come and free their king. Ferdinand de Soto's departure left Atahualpa very sad, for de Soto was one of the first Spaniards he had known, and he felt he could count on him in any circumstances, as on a loyal, disinterested friend. He nevertheless gave orders that Pizarro's envoys should be well received everywhere, with the result that there was not a single village along the road where they were not welcomed with the pomp that, before, had been reserved for the sons of the Sun. Offerings and sacrifices were made to them, not as to men, but as though they had been gods; for, despite the terrible Cajamarca massacre, news of which had spread throughout the Empire, they still considered the Spaniards as gods, although, from thenceforth, they had assumed the aspect of pitiless, terrible divinities whose perpetual wrath had to be appeased by offerings and sacrifices.

The Spanish envoys traveled in hammocks, which are a sort of hanging bed, made of cotton or string net supported at both ends; it is customary to sleep in them in hot climates, because one feels cooler than on a matting, and one can also travel in them, as these Spaniards did, by fixing the hammock to a pole which two runners, one in front and one in back, carry on their shoulders; if the porters grow tired, without stopping they are relayed by others, so skillfully, in fact, that the traveler is not even aware of the change.

De Soto and Pedro del Barco had left Cajamarca for Cuzco when Ferdinand Pizarro decided to go and visit the famous temple of Pachacamac, about which one heard such wonderful accounts. He left with an escort of cavalry, in case it should be needed. One day, just as their troop reached the top of a hill over which the road passed, the Spaniards stopped, stunned with astonishment, not daring to believe their eyes: for it looked as though the other slope, which they were about to descend, was nothing but a mass of molten gold, reflecting the sun with such brilliance that they were blinded by it. Indeed, they hardly knew what to think. When they had descended a little way, they found the ground covered with pots and cauldrons, cups, vases, pitchers, and countless other objects made of silver and gold: one of Atahualpa's brothers, Quilliscancha, whom we mentioned earlier, was taking all these things—worth two millions—to Cajamarca for the king's ransom; the porters had just laid their loads haphazardly on the ground while they rested, and it was this scattered treasure that, from the top of the hill, had seemed like a dazzling sheet of gold. That excellent man-at-arms, Don Graviel Pizarro, inquisitor of the Holy Inquisition in Cordova, told me this story which he had heard from another gentleman named Juan Pizarro de Orellano, who was a member of Ferdinand's escort on this journey.

We should add that Quilliscancha continued on his way as far as Cajamarca, after which Atahualpa immediately sent him to Quito, to see if Rumiñaui was not organizing some sort of insurrection; the king thought him quite capable of this, and rightly so.

But Rumiñaui had not spent years in Atahualpa's service without learning his methods, with the result that, being apt at dissimulation, he gave the envoy a cordial welcome. Together they bemoaned the king's misfortunes, and they agreed that all the treasures in Quito should be collected as soon as possible in order to permit him to regain his freedom. In short, he behaved like the most loyal of servitors, while awaiting the moment when he could carry out his secret plans—a moment that was not long in coming, as we shall see.[21]

Meanwhile, Ferdinand Pizarro and his companions had arrived at Pachacamac. Their surprise and amazement at the sight of this famous temple, and its unbelievable riches, were unequaled except by that caused by the spectacle of its luxuriant and well-peopled valley. But the astonishment of the Indians was even greater than that of the Spaniards, when they saw these gentlemen with their noble bearing coming towards them, for their faces as well as their dress were, for them, quite new and almost unbelievable. They brought them gifts, made sacrifices to them, and worshiped them in a manner that was inconceivable. Let us say only that they filled their horses' feed troughs with gold and silver, as the natives of Cajamarca had done in similar circumstances.

Meanwhile, Ferdinand Pizarro, having learned that the camp commander, Challcuchima, was encamped forty leagues from there with a considerable army, immediately sent him a messenger, asking him to come and discuss with him important matters on which the peace and security of Peru depended. But since the Indian refused to go to see the Spaniard, Ferdinand Pizarro decided to go to see the Indian, at great risk to his person and his men, for the road was a hard one, very rough and filled with hazards, not the least of which were wide rivers that had to be crossed on the reed bridges I spoke of—and one can imagine what it meant to get the horses over them! This adventure was not at all to the liking of Ferdinand Pizarro's companions, who considered that it was taking a considerable risk to venture forth like that on the word of an infidel, who had a great advantage over them, if one considered the size of his army. But the Spanish captain trusted the signatures and counter-signatures Atahualpa had given him, in case he should encounter one of his captains or camp commanders. And he was right, because in this way he was able to persuade Challcuchima to dismiss his troops and return with him to Cajamarca to see his king. In order to obtain his objective more quickly, the Indian led the Spaniard by cross-country over the snowy mountains, and they would all certainly have died of the cold if several men from the region had not shown them some natural grottoes, of which there are many up there.

The road was so bad that the horses lost their shoes, which was very awkward for the Spaniards because, not knowing that they were going over such a long, hard road, they had brought no others. Here the ingenuity of the Indians came to their assistance; for although they had no iron, they did not lack, on the other hand, for either gold or silver, and thus it happened that, as Gomara says, in his one hundred and fourteenth chapter, "having no iron, they shod their horses with silver, and even with gold, which is more resistant."

They finally arrived in Cajamarca. Before entering the king's chamber, Challcuchima took off his shoes and placed a heavy load on his shoulder, like any wretched Indian, as a sign of submission and humility. Then, in a tone of deep emotion and tenderness, he accused himself before the Inca, saying that it was his, Challcuchima's fault that his august person should have been taken prisoner, because if he had been present, no one could have deprived the king of his liberty. Atahualpa replied that the great Pachacamac had willed that it should be thus, in order that the prophecies of his ancestors and the last words of his father, Huaina Capac, might be fulfilled. He added that, since he had been made a prisoner, he had had his father the Sun consulted, in the Cuzco temple, together with the principal oracles of the kingdom, among them Rimac oracle, which, however, despite its former glibness, had remained silent. The same was true of the Pachacamac oracle, which was even more extraordinary, because it had always proclaimed its unique ability to settle sovereign matters of Empire. From one end of Peru to the other, priests and soothsayers had combined their efforts in using their influence with all their idols, doing their utmost in the way of prayers, gifts, and sacrifices, repeating that the king was in irons and that they were at a loss to know what to do. And all the idols had remained unanimously silent, which filled the king with terror; he thought that the Sun itself must be in distress, for all those who usually spoke in his name to suddenly, and without exception, avoid speaking. "All that," the king concluded, "proves only too clearly, alas! that my end and the end of the Empire are at hand."

The Inca and his camp commander spoke at length about these things, for their hearts were wrung with the same anguish. And that day Atahualpa experienced in his own flesh all the bodily and mental suffering that poor Huascar Inca and his followers had experienced and continued to experience through his fault.

And now the absolute truth: as soon as the sacraments of our Holy Mother the Church, one, Catholic, apostolic, and Roman, came to Peru, all the demons, who thus far had spoken and handled so familiarly with these gentiles, lost their power of speech.

There was first the consecration of the body and blood of our Lord Jesus Christ during the Mass, at which the Christians were present whenever they could be; next there was holy baptism, which was given to all Indians who entered into the service of the Spaniards; then came marriage, which they were made to contract publicly; and lastly, penitence, which was given to all the Spaniards when they confessed their sins while receiving Holy Communion.

These were the first four sacraments to be introduced in Peru, the others following as soon as their need became apparent. And, from then on, no demon dared manifest itself publicly, and the Indians only consulted secretly—and at that, very rarely—the sorcerers who had always cared for them and succored them.

Huascar Inca's partisans, who were the first to become aware of this phenomenon, saw in it, at first, a manifestation of the Sun's anger at the crimes and cruel actions of which Atahualpa had been guilty towards his descendants; but soon this state of affairs became so general that people saw in it a direct consequence of the arrival of the Spaniards, which greatly contributed to developing their prestige. What force these newly arrived men must possess, the simple people concluded, to have succeeded in silencing all the oracles! And they believed more firmly than ever that these were the sons of Viracocha, the god they set over and above all others.

After having walked more than one hundred leagues, Ferdinand de Soto and Pedro del Marco reached the city of Sausa, where Atahualpa's captains held the Inca Huascar a prisoner. The Spaniards wanted very much to see him, and although he was carefully guarded, the Inca succeeded in meeting them. But having no interpreter, they could only communicate by means of signs. It was nevertheless possible to learn the following concerning their interview: having heard that the Spaniards, since their arrival in Peru, claimed to be defenders of law and order, and righters of all wrongs and all villainy, Huascar begged the two captains to stay with him, to protect him from his brother who, after having tyrannized him and deprived him of his crown, now wanted to take his life, which design would undoubtedly be carried into effect as soon as they left, by the captains who had been designated to guard him.

"When your commander-general hears what injustice has been done me," the Inca added, "he will surely return my kingdoms to me, and I shall give him much more gold than my brother could ever have promised him. It will not be up to any line drawn on the wall, but up to the ceiling that I shall fill the room" (which meant three times as much); "because I know where the incalculable riches amassed by my father and all his predecessors are hidden; whereas my brother does not know this, and he is therefore reduced to stripping our temples of their ornaments in order to fulfill his promise."

Pedro del Barco and Ferdinand de Soto replied that, unfortunately, they could not remain with Huascar, having [illegible]ived orders to continue as far as Cuzco, and this [illegible]uld not fail to do; but that they would soon be

How they make their women work

How they marry the Indians

How they apply penitence

How they confess them

They cruelly punish little children

They gamble

They fight

They get drunk with half-castes and mulattoes

There are also some good Christians

A good aged vicar of eighty years

The Franciscans are charitable

A pious hermit begs for the poor

This series of drawings shows first of all the abuses practiced by members of the clergy who beat the Indians to make them work; married them by force; whipped them and took away their children at the age of seven; kicked them into confessing. In the fifth, we see a priest kicking and beating a cacique who has refused him girls and unmarried women. We then see priests gaming, fighting duels, and spending on banquets the "money stolen from the poor Indians." The last four drawings of the series show that there are also good men among the clergy, especially the Franciscans and the holy hermits, who are "poor and beg like the rest of the poor."

back and then they would do everything in their power to help the Inca.

With these words, they departed, leaving poor Huascar more grieved than he had been before they came, because, with them, his last hopes vanished, and he knew that, henceforth, all that awaited him was imminent death —in which he was not mistaken.[22]

So they continued on their way toward Cuzco. When they reached the heights of Carmenca, they had their first glimpse of the imperial city, which, from that point, may be seen in its entirety, and they were immediately filled with deep admiration.

They were welcomed with great pomp, manifested by festivals, dances and triumphal processions under arches of flowers and branches set up in the streets. One of Huaina Capac's palaces, called Amarucancha, had been fixed up in their honor, and it was explained to them that, because of their divine nature, they could not be lodged elsewhere than in the home of their most beloved king. This was a sort of large tower, which I recall having seen in my youth. The walls were about twelve feet in height, but the roof was so high that the whole thing stood above all the towers I have ever seen in Spain, except the one in Seville.[23] On the very topmost point of the roof, instead of a weathervane—for the Indians were not curious about the direction of the wind–there was a tall, sturdy spire, which added greatly to its grace and upward surge. The inside height, from the ground to the top of the roof, was more than sixty feet. It was called Sunturhaci, which means "remarkable house," for it stood out alone from the line of the houses, none of which touched it. It was torn down in my time in order to clear the public square upon which it encroached somewhat. And yet a structure of this kind was not out of place on this square, upon which it occupied so little space. As we said elsewhere, today the Jesuit coliseum is located on this site.

The following day, the Spaniards were carried about the city in litters and shown it in detail. Everywhere they passed the people bowed down before them and worshiped them, with all the demonstrations that are customary to these gentiles. Our two companions were struck by the city's majesty, by the size of its temples and the wealth of its palaces, although all of that had lost much of its luster since the wars between Huascar and Atahualpa: indeed, a great number of the former treasures had disappeared, buried or hidden, no one knows where. The Spaniards were particularly struck by the large flagstones that, as I said before, entirely cover the little stream that runs through the city. And they were also greatly surprised to see so many people, so many merchants and shops—although there was little merchandise left—and the host of servants who surrounded the nobles, hastening to serve them with loving care, as though they had no other desire than to anticipate those of their masters. Ah! what would the Spaniards have said, had they known Cuzco before these fratricidal wars! But their surprise and their admiration were boundless when they noticed that the roofs of the temples and royal houses were topped by Christian crosses. The Indians had had this idea when they had heard the marvelous story of Pedro de Candia in Tumbez. The story had traveled by word of mouth all the way to Cuzco, of how the cross that this Viracocha held in his hand had rendered gentle and harmless the wild animals unleashed on his path. Now, for many years there had existed in the Cuzco sanctuary a bloodstone cross, concerning the origin of which nothing was known. As soon as they heard the story of Pedro de Candia, the priests of the imperial city went in procession to adore this cross, reproaching themselves with not having revered it before as it deserved, since it made possible such great miracles, and imploring it to deliver them from these newcomers who had invaded Peru, as it had freed this man from the wildest of beasts. And thus the idea came to them to place crosses on the temples and principal edifices of the city, in order that they might protect these different sites and the entire Empire from the redoubtable Spaniards.

This is the moment to point out that these idolatrous gentiles, well before anyone had started to preach the Catholic faith to them, came of their own accord, with all their Empire, to the cross, since they placed it on their temples and had recourse to it to combat the terrible fear that had gripped them and not left them, since the death of Huaina Capac, his last predictions, [illegible] frightful war between his sons, and the arrival of the [illegible]iards.

[illegible]and de Soto and Pedro del Barco wrote a detailed report of all they had just seen, and sent it to Francisco Pizarro. They spoke highly of the excellent welcome they had received all along the way, and described the incredible wealth of the imperial city of Cuzco. The conclusions of their report were the same as those of the four other Spaniards who had gone to verify elsewhere the veracity of Atahualpa's statements. Pizarro and his men were delighted to learn that the wealth of Peru really did exist and that it was as fabulous as it had been described. As for the manner in which the Indians worshiped them, in accordance with the wishes of Huaina Capac, they did not want to set too high a value upon it, saying that all that was Indian witchcraft and should not be taken into consideration.

When Spanish historians follow the truth very closely, I prefer to quote their words, rather than give my own version, in order to speak as a Spaniard and not as an Indian.

Here then, textually, is what Agustín de Zarate says, in the sixth chapter of his second book, after telling of the interview between Pedro del Barco, Ferdinand de Soto, and Huascar Inca:

"The two Spaniards then went on their way. But this adventure was the cause of the Inca Huascar's death and of the loss of the great treasure that he had promised them. For the captains who guarded the Inca immediately acquainted Atahualpa with everything that had been said at the interview. The king had enough judgment to understand that if this news were to come to the ears of the governor, he might well be tempted to render justice to Huascar, in view of the latter's generous promises and the immense quantity of gold that he had allowed them to hope for. He had seen clearly the passion of the Christians for this metal, and he therefore feared lest they should deprive him of his kingdom to return it to his brother, and lest, too, they should decide to legitimate the whole affair by putting him to death as an unfair usurper who had taken possession of the throne without having any right to do so. With these reflections, he decided to get rid of Huascar. But one thing embarrassed him and even made him somewhat afraid: he had heard the Christians say several times that, in accordance with one of the laws that they observed most strictly, he who w guilty of murder would be punished with death. He therefore decided to sound out the governor, in order to find out what he thought on this subject, which he did, with great skill, in the following manner: he feigned to be deeply sad, weeping, sobbing and refusing to eat and drink, or even to speak to anyone. The governor urged him to tell him the cause of his suffering. He let himself be begged, in order the better to hide his game, and at last confessed that he had heard that one of his captains, seeing that he was a prisoner, had killed his brother Huascar, because of which he was deeply pained, for he had not only considered Huascar as an older brother, but even as a father, that, although he had taken him prisoner, it was not with any intention of doing him harm, insulting his person or depriving him of his kingdom, but only to oblige him to leave the province of Quito in his, Atahualpa's, possession, in accordance with the last wishes of their father, Huaina Capac, who had, himself, conquered this province beyond the frontiers of his hereditary Empire, and which he had therefore had the legitimate right to dispose of in his favor, as he had done.

"The governor hastened to console this hypocrite, telling him that he should not be so upset, nor torture himself in this manner, because death was the common lot of all men, and that, in this respect, they had little advantage over one another, all of them being obliged to come to it one day, sooner or later; that, moreover, he could assure him that as soon as peace should be restored in Peru, he would find out exactly the names of the persons who had had a hand in this crime, and would punish them as they deserved.

"When Atahualpa saw that the marquis took this affair so lightly, he decided to carry out his plans without further delay. He therefore sent orders to the captains who were guarding Huascar to put their prisoner to death immediately. And this was done so promptly that, later, it was very hard to tell whether Atahualpa's expressions of grief had followed or preceded his brother's death. Most of the soldiers attributed responsibility for this crime to Ferdinand de Soto and Pedro del Barco, not taking sufficiently into consideration the obligation in[illegible]mbent upon these two gentlemen not to diverge from [illegible]rders they had been given. The Indians say that [illegible]uascar realized that he was about to die, he made [illegible]ng declaration: 'I was lord and master of this land for only a very short time, but my traitorous brother, upon whose orders I shall soon die, despite the fact that I am his legitimate lord, will wield the power he usurped for an even shorter time than I did.'

"Such a prediction as this persuaded the Indians that Huascar really was the son of the Sun, when, shortly after that, they learned that Atahualpa, too, was dead."

This, then, was Agustín de Zarate's account. It should be added that Huascar was put to death in a very cruel manner. His executioners cut him in pieces, and it is not known what they did with him afterwards. According to an Indian folk legend, they ate him, out of rage. However, Father Acosta writes that his remains were burned.

And so ended the life of this unfortunate prince, the last monarch of the Peruvian Empire, after he had suffered the maltreatment and persecutions we have described in his person, and in the person of all his followers, even to his servants.

Atahualpa had thought that poor Huascar's death would assure him life and liberty. But he was quite mistaken. Only a few days later, his own time had come, in circumstances that I am not the only one to relate as follows. (They are also described by Francisco López de Gomara and several other Spanish historians.)

The chastisement of heaven is such that it always punishes those who have sided with tyranny and cunning against justice and reason, for God has willed that they should be overthrown and end the victims of their own snares, unless it be of others that are still worse, as we shall see.

In order really to understand these events, which will close the history of ancient Peru, the reader should know that Don Diego de Almagro was at that time navigating on a fine ship in full sail, coming from Panama, to give fresh impetus to the conquest and—if we are to believe his enemies—with the secret intention of arriving in the south before Francisco Pizarro, thus taking advantage of the fact that the royal letters had granted the marquis no territory farther south than two hundred leagues under the equinoctial line. Don Diego's enemies even added that Francisco Pizarro knew of his rival's plans through the latter's secretary, who paid with his head for his imprud talk: Almagro is said to have hanged him by the neck till he died.

However that may be, Don Diego was still navigating when he heard of Atahualpa's arrest, and of the prodigious wealth that the Inca had offered in exchange for his freedom. Knowing this, he decided to keep silent, and simply to go and look up his rival, since, according to their compromise agreement, he had a right to one half of the spoils amassed by Don Francisco.

So he arrived in Cajamarca with his men, who were dazzled by the heaps of gold and silver that had already been collected. But the marquis's followers soon disillusioned them, explaining to them that they need expect no division, since they had had no part in Atahualpa's arrest, or in the deal that had resulted from it. "Not only," they said, "have you no rights to the gold you see here, but you have none either to the gold that will come later, if Atahualpa keeps his promise—which we doubt very much, because all the gold in the world would not suffice for this."

"In that case," Almagro's men said among themselves, "let us kill Atahualpa right away; nobody will be the loser, and everything we get later we shall have earned together, so that they can no longer deny us our share!"

They found all sorts of reasons, slender ones, to be sure, but which nevertheless sufficed for them to decide to put to death so great a lord as Atahualpa, who was really living in anguish because he sensed that his end was near. Every day he observed the displeasure of the Spaniards and the growing uneasiness that reigned amongst them; for they had become obstinate and headstrong, and no longer hid their real sentiments, occasionally going so far as to take one another to task before him, in loud tones. All of that, the Inca thought sadly, will undoubtedly fall upon me. And the silence of the oracles whom he had so frequently consulted, confirmed the fact that he would bear the brunt of their quarrels. His fears increased when even his most trusted followers reported to him that, lately, numerous stars, both large and small, had been seen shooting across the night sky.

Finally, someone told him that an immense greenish-[illegible]lack comet, as long as a pike and as thick as a man's [illegible]y, had just made its appearance. They all remembered [illegible]her comet that had traversed the Peruvian sky dur-[illegible]ast days of Huaina Capac's life. But it was the [illegible]nd Atahualpa's despair was complete. He asked permission of the Spaniards to go out at night, in order to see it with his own eyes; after he had seen it, however, he sank into such stubborn silence that he even stopped talking to those about him, as, until then, he had so loved to do. Don Francisco Pizarro plied him with questions in order to find out the cause of this strange despondency. Out of weariness, and perhaps, too, in order to be left in peace, Atahualpa finally made the following reply:

"*Apu* [which means commander-general], I am now certain that my end is at hand. I know it from this comet, which announced my father's death and now has returned to announce my own. I am sad to think that I shall die so soon, without having had time to benefit from my kingdoms. How should I have any hope? Never have such signs appeared except to presage some great calamity, such as the death of a king or the downfall of an Empire. I suspected my misfortune from the moment I was put in irons, but, today, my fears have given way to ineluctable certainty. So, there: now you know the cause of my despair, and my reasons for being overwhelmed by it."

The governor replied that Atahualpa should not give credence to omens, and that he had no reason not to hope that he would soon be free and back on the throne. But all these cheering words left the Inca as sad as they had found him, for these gentiles had such faith in their omens that this comet was much more convincing for Atahualpa than Don Francisco's fair words.

All that I say about this comet may be found in the sixty-fifth chapter of the book by Pedro de Cieza de Leon, who tells it no differently than I do.

Shall we say, then, in conclusion, as this author does, that Atahualpa had only two weeks to live before the facts had confirmed his dolorous apprehensions. He remained quite hopeless, plunged in such complete grief that nothing could divert him from it.

Don Francisco Pizarro's mental outlook was just the opposite of Atahualpa's. Fortune had smiled upon him so constantly that his ambitions had never been greater, nor his hopes more sanguine. It seemed to him that, in order to assure his future, he could not do better than to send a report to His Catholic Majesty. He therefore informed Don Diego de Almagro and his brothers of his idea, and they all decided unanimously that Ferdinand Pizarro w-head a mission to Spain, in order to make known to His Majesty the feats they had accomplished and to receive the rewards that they felt they had a right to expect. Ferdinand Pizarro took what was needed to cover the costs of his journey from Atahualpa's ransom, since this booty belonged to them all, and since, too, he was going in the name of them all. To cover the king's "fifth" part, he took one hundred thousand pesos in gold and one hundred thousand in silver. These were the first fruits of all the treasures that, from now on, His Majesty would not cease to receive from my native land. The silver was not smelted, but had been chosen from amongst the largest, most remarkable objects that had been brought by the Indians, as Agustín de Zarate specifies in chapter seven of his second book: "There were pitchers, braziers, drums, and sculptures in animal and human forms in such quantities that the value of these treasures was vastly greater than that of their weight in precious metal. Atahualpa was very sad to see Pizarro leave, for he was particularly fond of this gentleman, and talked with him in complete confidence. When Ferdinand Pizarro came to tell him goodbye, the Inca said:

" 'So you are leaving, captain? I am very sorry for that, for as soon as you are gone, the giant and the one-eyed man will kill me.' "

He was alluding to Don Diego de Almagro, who had lost an eye, as we related, and to His Majesty's Treasurer, Alonso Requelme.

Ferdinand de Soto and Pedro del Barco returned from Cuzco shortly after Ferdinand Pizarro had left. They gave their companions a detailed description of all the incredible treasures they had seen in the palaces and temples of the imperial city, and they all rejoiced at the vast fortune that awaited them. Soon, in fact, they only dreamed of the day when they would have taken possession of it. And their impatience could not but weigh upon Atahualpa's fate, because this prince's life seemed to them to constitute the last obstacle that stood between them and their longed-for goal.

Agustín de Zarate and Francisco Lopez de Gomara ... both recounted in an almost identical manner ...pa's last moments; I shall copy, therefore, the ...ven by Gomara in his one hundred and nine... entitled:

"How Atahualpa was put to death
in execution of a legal decision,
after an unfair trial, based on
false witnesses"

"Reasons that no one could have foreseen hastened Atahualpa's death: Felipe, who was the Spaniards' usual interpreter, having fallen in love with one of the king's wives, the lovers resolved to marry as soon as the king's demise gave them their freedom.

"Felipe, therefore, spread a rumor among the Spaniards, which he invented for the occasion, to the effect that Atahualpa was supposed to be raising forces to free himself and to massacre the Christians, and people soon believed this. There were those who said that the prisoner should be put to death without waiting any longer, in order to guarantee both their lives and their seizure of Peru. Others felt that it would be better to send Atahualpa to Spain, because they could not afford to kill so great a king, whatever his offenses. The second proposal was certainly more just. But the authors of the first prevailed, and it was said that this was thanks to Almagro's followers, who considered that they would receive no share of the spoils of conquest as long as Atahualpa lived. Finally Pizarro decided to have him put to death in order to be freed of the responsibilities that Atahualpa's captivity entailed, and also to resume his conquests without further obstacles. Atahualpa was tried for the death of Huascar, and it was also proven that he had wanted to massacre the Spaniards, an accusation based entirely on the malice and dishonesty of Felipe who, taking advantage of the fact that he was the only one who spoke both languages, translated to suit himself what was said by the Indian witnesses called in for the occasion. Atahualpa denied everything to the very end, arguing that he would have been quite incapable of plotting, as they accused him of doing, in his prison cell. He threatened Felipe and begged the judges not to believe what this traitor said. When he heard the sentence condemning him, he reproached Pizarro bitterly for accepting to put him to death after having promised to free him for a ransom. He also implored him to send him to Spain and not to stain his hands with the blood of a man who had brought him a fortune and given him no offense. Before going to be executed, he asked to be baptized, on the advice of those Spaniards who had befriended him, and who explained to him that, otherwise, he would be burned alive. He was baptized, then garroted on a stake driven into the ground, after which he was given a Christian burial, conducted with pomp and ceremony. Pizarro went into mourning for him, and ordered solemn funeral rites in his honor. Today we are unable to feel any resentment towards those who killed him, because life itself punished them in the cruelest of ways.[24]

"Atahualpa died a hard death, and he ordered that his body be taken to Quito, where all the kings, who were his mother's ancestors, had been laid to rest. The fact that he asked to be baptized was fortunate for him because, otherwise, he would have paid for the long list of his crimes. He was a well-built man and lacked neither experience nor courage. He was also frank, always carefully groomed, and extremely clean. He had a number of wives and left several sons. Although he had usurped certain territories from his brother Huascar, he never wore the scarlet bandeau that, before the time that he was made prisoner, had constituted the distinguishing mark of the kings of Peru. He never spat on the ground but always in the hand of a woman of quality, out of dignity.

"His premature death struck the imaginations of the Indians, for they saw in it a proof that Huascar, who had predicted it, was really the son of the Sun."

Thus wrote Francisco Lopez de Gomara. What he has to say about the lies told by the interpreter, Felipe, should be noted, because it confirms all we have written on the subject of this Indian. If we recall, moreover, that Ferdinand de Soto and Pedro del Barco left Huascar to die because they had not understood his reasons for asking them to stay with him, we may conclude that the absence of good interpreters between the Indians and the Spaniards was the main cause of the deaths of these two powerful kings.

The reason Atahualpa asked to be buried in Quito, beside his maternal ancestors, and not in Cuzco among his father's people, was because he knew how he was hated for his crimes throughout the Empire and he feared lest vengeance should be wreaked on his body.[25] As for the fact that he had never worn the scarlet bandeau before his imprisonment, this proves clearly that he could not have considered himself as the legitimate lord of the entire Empire, as long as Huascar, who had more rights than he did to the title, was still living. Once Huascar were dead, he could have had himself proclaimed Inca and Emperor, and then he could have worn this distinguishing mark, even though he had acquired the right to do so through such tyrannical means.

Lastly, shall we say that we should thank the Lord God who allowed an idolatrous Indian, guilty of such great cruelty, to die baptized: divine mercy is infinite and it forsakes not even the guiltiest among us, such as he or I.

He was given the name of Don Juan Atahualpa, and Father Blas Valera says that Friar Vincente de Valverde took the pains to instruct him in the tenets of our Catholic faith, several days before his execution. In all, he had remained three months in irons.

Atahualpa's trial was a solemn one and it lasted a long time. The court was presided over by Don Francisco Pizarro, with Don Diego de Almagro acting as assessor; Sancho de Cuellar filled the role of clerk, another, that of prosecuting attorney, another, that of defense lawyer, to plead Atahualpa's case. Then there were two attorney generals, named by each one of the parties; two investigators, who collected the testimony and presented it to the court, and two barristers, who were simply there to give their opinions. Although I knew several of these men personally, I prefer not to name them.

The examination included twelve questions:

First: Whether the witnesses had known Huaina Capac and his wives, and how many wives he had had.

Second: Whether Huascar was the legitimate son of his father and heir to the kingdom, and whether the bastard Atahualpa was not the son of some Indian in Quito, rather than of the king.

Third: Whether the Inca had had other sons besides those mentioned.

Fourth: Whether Atahualpa had inherited the Empire in accordance with the terms of his father's will, or whether he had taken possession of it through tyranny.

Fifth: Whether Huascar had been defrauded of his kingdom as a result of his father's will, or whether he was, on the contrary, the rightful heir.

Sixth: Whether Huascar Inca was alive or dead, and, in the latter case, whether he had died of sickness or been executed on Atahualpa's orders, and whether this had taken place before or since the arrival of the Spaniards.

Seventh: Whether it was true that Atahualpa worshiped idols and had forced his subjects to offer up human sacrifices, of both children and adults.

Eighth: Whether Atahualpa had made unjust wars, causing the deaths of a large number of persons.

Ninth: Whether Atahualpa had numerous concubines.

Tenth: Whether he had collected, spent and squandered the revenues of the Empire since the Spaniards had taken possession of it.

Eleventh: Whether, to the knowledge of the witnesses, Atahualpa had appropriated crown revenues, since the arrival of the Spaniards, to make gifts and donations to members of his family, his captains, or other persons, and whether he had wasted the stocks of the granaries and public warehouses.

Twelfth: Whether, still to the knowledge of the witnesses, Atahualpa had plotted with his captains, since his imprisonment, to secretly raise armies and collect war supplies, in order to revolt against the Spaniards and murder them.

Ten witnesses were heard. Seven of them had been chosen among the servants of the Spaniards, and three from the outside, in order that they should not all be domestics. As Gomara writes, they said everything that the interpreter, Felipe, wanted to make them say. One of the non-domestic witnesses, named Quespe, who was captain of a company, and the last to be examined, replied each time with one single word, saying *i,* which means yes, or *manam*, which means no. And, in order that the judges might understand him and that the interpreter should not betray him, he raised and lowered his head two or three times when he said yes, and nodded it from left to right, in addition to a gesture with his right hand, when he wanted to say no; and the judges and ministers greatly admired the sagacity of this Indian.

But in spite of all that, they were not afraid to condemn to death so great and powerful a king as Atahualpa, and he was notified of his sentence, as we explained. Many of the Spaniards protested vehemently when they heard the sentence, not only among Pizarro's companions, but also among those of Almagro, because these latter were men with generous hearts, capable of feeling pity. "How can one dare to put to death a monarch who has never done us the slightest wrong, but, on the contrary, has always shown us the most perfect courtesy! If we have something to reproach him with, the only thing we can do is to send him to Spain; for we are not competent to judge a king, the decision belonging to the Emperor. We must consider the question of Spain's national honor. What will the world say when it is learned that we have executed a king who has been taken prisoner, after having given him our word that we would liberate him for a ransom, a substantial part of which we have already collected? People will call us perjurers, tyrants, and bloodthirsty barbarians. We have accomplished great things, and now we are about to sully our glory with this inhuman action. We must fear God, for if we do this He will cease to protect and favor us as He has done until now! Nothing good can come of so barbarous and unjust an action; on the contrary, we must expect the worst disasters and the most relentless of fates. It is not permissible to kill a man without having heard his story and allowed him to present his defense."

And they concluded by saying that they would appeal this sentence before Charles V, but that while awaiting the material possibility to do this, they named Juan de Herrada protector of King Atahualpa. Indeed, they did not only protest by word of mouth, but also in writing, and they notified the judge of their dissent. In reply, they were told that they had conducted themselves as traitors to the royal crown of Castile and to their sovereign, the Emperor, since they were trying to keep the number of his territories and kingdoms from increasing; that the death of this tyrant would ensure all of them their lives and the Empire, whereas if he were allowed to live it would endanger both. They were also told that reports would be sent to His Majesty concerning the mutinies and disorders their attitude had occasioned; and that then it would be seen who were the royal servitors of Spain and who were the traitors; and that the former would be rewarded and the latter punished as they deserved to be.[26]

In fact, things came to such a pass that they would have hurled themselves at one another and all been killed, if God had not stopped it by making others, who were less impassioned than they, intervene between the two groups, and thus succeed in appeasing the Inca's defenders, by telling them to consider the necessities that their own lives and the king's service rendered imperative; that it was not right for quarrels over infidels to divide Christians; and that, lastly, there were only fifty persons sharing their point of view, whereas more than three hundred upheld the point of view of the court; and that, if they should come to blows, they would have nothing to gain from it, but on the contrary, would only destroy themselves as well as such a rich kingdom as this one, which was theirs for all time, if they put its king to death.

These threats—or these good reasons—finally calmed Atahualpa's protectors, and they consented to his execution, which the others carried out.

Once the two kings, Huascar Inca and Atahualpa, who were brothers as well as enemies, were dead, the Spaniards remained supreme masters of both Peruvian kingdoms, there being no one left to oppose or even contradict them, because all the Indians, whether they belonged to Quito or to Cuzco, had remained, after their kings were gone, like sheep without a shepherd.

The war between Atahualpa and Huascar was therefore indirectly the cause of the total downfall of the Inca Empire, from which the Spaniards benefited, as the great Huaina Capac had predicted on his deathbed. But if our Lord God permitted this discord between the two brothers, it was because, in His infinite mercy, He wanted in this way to allow the preachers of His gospel and of His Catholic faith, to more easily bring their enlightenment to the gentiles in Peru.

Having now related the lives of twelve Inca kings who created and governed the ancient Empire of Peru, from its beginnings till its end; having given ample description of their conquests, their generous actions, their government in peace and in war, and of the idolatry that they practiced in their ignorance of our holy religion, I have thus paid the debt that I owed to my country and to my maternal ancestors.

May the divine Majesty, Father, Son, and Holy Ghost, be praised, from century to century, for having granted me the great favor of reaching the end of my task. May it serve the glory and honor of His holy name. And may His infinite mercy, through the blood of our Lord Jesus Christ, and the intercession of His Mother, the Virgin Mary, and of all the heavenly throng, come to my aid and defense, today and in my hour of death, amen, Jesus, one hundred thousand times Jesus.

GOD BE PRAISED.

1. Garcilaso is mistaken by a few months. Pizarro's first expedition left Panama in November, 1524.

2. This was the most inhospitable part of the Colombian coast, north of the Rio San Juan and the present port of Buenaventura, which is the only safe harbor for ships sailing down the Pacific coast from Panama to Guayaquil. The Colombian department of Checo, which extends along the whole length of this coast, is formed of the steep slopes of the western cordillera of the Andes which drop abruptly into the Pacific, and are covered with a tropical jungle as dense as that of the Amazon basin. Garcilaso in no way exaggerates the difficulties encountered by Pizarro and his companions: the rain is such in this region that, according to the popular saying: "It rains thirteen months out of twelve." It is certainly one of the wettest regions of all equatorial America.

3. Gallo (Rooster) Island and the neighboring Gorgon Island, which we shall refer to again later, are situated off the Colombian coast, south of Buenaventura, near Cape Guascama. They have retained the names given them by Pizarro.

4. Pizarro and his companions—who were to be called the "Glorious Thirteen"—had been stranded for seven months on this island. Pizarro's companions were no longer thirteen in number, but twelve, the thirteenth, Bartolomeo Ruiz, the pilot, having escorted to Panama those who had left the expedition. Faithful to his word, however, he rejoined Pizarro on board Almagro's vessel and continued with him.

   The names of the "Glorious Thirteen" are as follows: Alfonso Briseño, Juan de la Torre, Francisco de Cuellar, Alonso de Trujillo, Cristobal de Peralta, Alonso de Molina, Nicolas de Ribera, Garcia de Jerez, Pedro de Candia (the hero of the landing at Tumbez), Domingo de Soria Luce, Pedro Alcon, Martin de Paz, and the pilot Bartolomeo Ruiz —making twelve Spaniards, including three Castilians and four Andalusians, and a Greek (Pedro de Candia).

5. Pedro de Candia ended his days as tragically as did the Pizarros, the Almagros, and most of the early heroes of the conquest. Going over to the camp of the younger Diego de Almagro and being put in command of his artillery in the battle against the government forces of Vaca de Castro, he was transfixed to his cannons with a lance by Almagro in person who suspected him, probably quite rightly, of connivance with the enemy (Battle of Chupas, September 16, 1542).

6. This is of course Mexico, which had just been conquered by Cortez. The vast territory discovered by the Spaniards, from California to Chile, was divided into three main parts,

from north to south: New Spain, New Granada (later Greater Colombia), and New Castile, without counting the captaincies of Central America and "Golden Castile" (Panama).

It was thanks to the intervention of Cortez, the hero of Mexico, that Pizarro was released from prison—where he had been since his arrival, for an old debt that he thought had been forgotten—and obtained the attention and favor of Charles V. These events occurred in 1528 and, as Descola rightly remarks, the court of Spain was still in the state of euphoria brought about by the birth of the future Philip II one year earlier (Valladolid, 1527): this must have made matters easier for the conqueror of Peru.

7. They were in fact his three brothers, Ferdinand, Gonzalvo, and Juan, and his half-brother Martin de Alcantara.

8. Pizarro did, indeed, obtain Almagro's head, but the latter's supporters were not long in taking their revenge by assassinating the old marquis in his palace when he was at the height of his glory. He fell, arms in hand, striking out at several of his aggressors, who were much younger than he, thus, to the end, remaining worthy of his reputation for valor. The same was true of Almagro, old as he was, who disdainfully mocked his jailers a few minutes before his execution.

9. They had landed in the Bay of Ancon, in northern Ecuador, halfway between the towns of Esmeraldas (Ecuador) and Tumaco (Colombia).

10. See Note 4, Book VII.

11. Verruga, or Clarion's Disease, has never been reported except in Peru. Even there it is only to be found in certain valleys of the western slope of the first cordillera, at an altitude of between three and ten thousand feet. It is caused by Barton's bacillus (*Bartonnella bacilliformis*) which was isolated only recently. These warts can also appear internally and may cause hemorrhage. (d'Harcourt)

12. Around 3400 ounces of fine gold. See Note 4, Book VII.

13. Thirty thousand ducats, that is, about 3700 ounces of pure gold. See Note 4, Book VII.

14. The Spanish made their entry into Cajamarca on November 15, 1532 "at the hour of vespers." (Siegfried Huber)

15. Three hundred people, according to the chroniclers.

16. Indeed only Atahualpa's personal escort, five thousand strong, went with him into the citadel of Cajamarca.

17. This Dominican was chaplain to the expedition.

18. Undoubtedly Cristobal de Molina of Cuzco, chaplain of the

Cuzco hospital. He left several works, including the *Relación de las fabulas y ritos de los Incas.* This author is not to be confused with his homonym, Cristobal de Molina of Santiago.

The chronicler referred to by Garcilaso as Juan de Oliva is doubtless the Jesuit, Anello Oliva, of Italian origin. He left the *Historia del reino y provincia del Perú.* According to Dorsey, he lived in Peru from 1597 to 1642.

19. Certainly, this is an example of a specific instance of the liberties Garcilaso takes with history, as much to exculpate the Church, in the person of Father Valverde, as to tone down the violent character of Atahualpa, whom he does not spare elsewhere, but whom he now seeks to defend as the last representative of the Inca dynasty. Everything indeed goes to prove that the story of the breviary being thrown to the ground is true. There was a concerted plan among the Spaniards, Father Valverde included, to provoke hostilities on any pretext that the priest could find. Valverde is said to have withdrawn hastily, as soon as the breviary had fallen to the ground, as if in the presence of an unpardonable sacrilege, crying out to the Spaniards, *"Salid a el! Os absolvo!"* ("Attack him! I give you absolution!") Whereupon the Spaniards charged to the famous cry: *"Santiago y a ellos!"* ("St. Jacob [help] and [now up and] at them!")

20. These figures are not entirely to be relied on. According to Jerez, who took part, the Indians numbered eight hundred dead. Other chroniclers estimate their losses at one thousand, two thousand, and three thousand.

21. The chronicler Oviedo relates that Rumiñaui killed Quillascancha and made a drum of his skin "in such a way that his back formed one side of the instrument and his belly the other."

22. Challcuchima, under whose guard Huascar was placed, had every reason to get rid of his prisoner: "He treated him so barbarously—among other forms of torture, he had held him fast by means of a rope tied to his collarbone—that he would have signed his own death warrant by releasing him." (Huber) Challcuchima was later to be burned at the stake, by order of Pizarro.

23. The Torre del Oro is one of the most celebrated monuments of Seville.

24. We have already described the tragic end of Pizarro and Almagro. It should be added that Father Valverde was assassinated by the Indians.

25. "When the Spaniards had left Cajamarca, the Indians entered by night the church in which the Inca's body had been placed; they took it away, embalmed it as was the custom, and buried it. It was never found."

26. It should be pointed out that at the very time when this

decisive page in the history of the New World was being so brutally turned, a Dominican, Father Francisco de Vitoria, a professor at the University of Salamanca, was writing: "Religious differences do not justify war . . . Christian princes, even when they are upheld by the Pope, can neither prevent barbarians from sinning nor punish them for it . . . The existence of Europe is not a just cause for war."

TRADITIONAL LIST OF INCA SOVEREIGNS

Based on Rowe. The dates, from 1438 to 1532, are derived from the manuscript of Cavello de Balboa, in the New York Public Library. According to information supplied to Baudin by Means, the New York manuscript is a copy, made in the early eighteenth century, of an original which has since been lost, and may be in a monastery in Spain. Cavello de Balboa, who arrived in America in 1566, lived first in Bogota, then in Quito, where he wrote his *Miscelanea austral* between 1578 and 1586.

Manco Capac *?*
Sinchi Roca *?*
Lloque Yupanqui *Thirteenth century*
Maïta Capac *Thirteenth century*
Capac Yupanqui *Thirteenth century*
Inca Roca *Fourteenth century*
Yahuar Huacac *Fourteenth century*
Viracocha Inca *Fourteenth-Fifteenth century*
Pachacutec (or Pachacuti) *1438–1471*
Tupac (or Topa) Yupanqui *1471–1493*
Huaina Capac *1493–1527*
Huascar *1527–1532*
Atahualpa *1527–1532*

We recall that, according to Garcilaso, Tupac was not the son of Pachacutec but of Yupanqui, who was himself the son of Pachacutec. This confusion is probably due to the fact that Pachacutec was also called Yupanqui before his coronation. See the portraits of these kings by Guaman Poma.

APPROXIMATE CHRONOLOGICAL TABLE OF ANCIENT PERUVIAN CIVILIZATIONS

(BASED ON LEHMANN)

	Andean Regions	North Coast	Central Coast	South Coast
3000 BC				
			Chilca?	
		Huaca Prieta		
			Aspero	
1500 BC				
800 BC	Chavin	Cupisnique	Ancient Ancon	Cavernas
200 BC				
		Salinar		Necropolis
	Chanapata			
	Chiripa			
	Recuay B			
	Recuay A	Gallinazo		Nazca A
	Ancient	Mochica A	Ancient	
	Tiahuanaco	Mochica B	Lima	Nazca B
	Pucara			
1000				
	Classical Tiahuanaco	Coastal Tiahuanaco		Pacheco
1200				
	Epigonal Cajamarca	Epigonal Chimu	Late Ancon Chancay	Middle Ica
1450				
	Inca	Chimu? Coastal Inca	Chancay Inca	Late Ica Inca
1532				

GLOSSARY

Accla: chosen woman.
Accla-Huaci: house of the chosen women (convent).
Aillu or ayllu: lineage, clan. See Note 3, Book VII.
Amaru: large snake (anaconda). See Note 9, Book IV.
Amauta: philosopher. See Book II.
Apu: Lord, or captain. Honorific title preceding a name. Example: Apu Inti, the Lord Sun.
Asa: beverage prepared for the Inca and his relatives on the occasion of the Sun ceremonies.

Caicusca: "weary stone."
Cantut: the Inca flower. See Note 30, Book VI.
Capac: chief (from the Aimara kapak: falcon).
Caparec Tempu: the inn of the morning.
Chacra: field.
Chacu: halt. Ceremonial hunt attended by the Incas once a year.
Chasca: head of hair. Designates the planet Venus.
Chasqui: state couriers.
Chicha: corn beer. See Note 24, Book VI.
Chuspa: purse which the Inca wore swung over his shoulder to keep his coca leaves in.
Citua Raïmi: one of the four great Sun festivals.
Cocha: sea, lake, any body of water.
Corequenque: very rare bird that furnished the feathers for the royal headdress. See Note 33, Book VI.
Coricancha: the "golden quarter" of Cuzco.
Corpahuaci: public hostels situated along the royal highroads, in which travelers could obtain a meal and be cared for in case of illness.
Coya: the queen, sister-bride of the Inca.
Cuntur: condor.
Curaca: official. Non-Inca public servant. See Notes 4, 5, 6, Book II.
Cusquieraïmi: festival celebrated after the sowing. See Note 2, Book V.
Cussipata: the square in Cuzco reserved for curacas during the festivals.
Cuzco: capital of the Empire. The world's navel.

Hanan-Cuzco: Upper-Cuzco.

Harauec: Indian poet. Literally, inventor.

Haucaipata: the main square of Cuzco reserved for the king and his relatives at the time of the festivals.

Huaca or Guaca: term applied to all sacred objects or places (a totem stone, a grave, the crest of a mountain, could also be called huaca). Today this word has become the synonym of a treasure, because of the frequent presence of wrought gold and jewelry in or near the ancient huacas.

Huacamayoc: soothsayer.

Huachacuyac: "friend of the poor." Title given to the Inca kings.

Huacra: horn.

Huara: loincloth made of a piece of cloth or linen; triangular in shape and fastened to the belt both in back and in front.

Huaracu: to dub a knight. See Note 32, Book VI.

Huata: year, annual movement of the Sun. As a verb, it means: to fasten.

Hurin-Cuzco: Lower-Cuzco.

Illapa: thunder and lightning. See Note 15, Book III.

Inca Capac: the reigning Inca.

Inti: the Sun.

Inti-chacra: the sacred field of the Sun.

Inti-Raïmi: the feast of the Sun.

Kero: goblet in form of an animal's head.

Llaicas: soothsayers.

Llautu: scarlet insignia of supreme power.

Mamacocha: Our mother the sea, divinity.

Mamacuna: concubine of the Inca, or virgin dedicated to the Sun. See Note 2, Book IV.

Mamapacha: the earth-mother, divinity.

Mamaquilla: Our mother the Moon, divinity.

Mama Runtu: "mother-egg."

Mascapaicha: a pompon of gold threads that hung down over the Inca's eyebrow; with the scarlet *llautu* this was the principal sign of supreme power.

Mayu: river.

Mitimac: displaced populations (colonies). The word *mitayo,* meaning Indian servant, derives from it.

Nusta: infanta.

Occlo: woman of royal blood, who lived in the palace and observed the vows of chastity.

Orejones: "Long-ears"; name used by the Spaniards to designate the nobles (Incas either by blood or by privilege).

Pacha: the earth.

Pachacamac: the master of the world, supreme divinity. See Note 36, Book VI.

Palla: princess of royal blood.

Pampa: square or flat countryside.

Pampairuna: prostitute.

Pucara: fortress.

Puma: American lion.

Puna: the high plateaus of the Andes (at an altitude of 1900 feet or more).

Quilla: the Moon.

Quinoa: small Peruvian cereal.

Quipu: literally: knot. This has been extended to mean an accounting apparatus made of knotted strings of different colors and thicknesses. See Note 25, Book II.

Quipucamayoc or quipucamayu: imperial accountants in charge of the quipus.

Raïmi: festival.

Rimac: he who speaks (oracle, herald, etc.).

Rimac pampa: square in Cuzco on which proclamations were made (forum).

Runa: people.

Sairi: tobacco.

Sancu: special bread sacrificed during the Sun festivals.

Sinchi roca: "the brave."

Sunturhuaci: "the remarkable house."

Tampu or tambo: state warehouse (storehouse), road relay.

Tahuantinsuyu: the Inca Empire (the four parts of the world).

Tiupuncu: the sand gate.

Tupu: agrarian measure.

Tupuy ricoc: "the men who see everything."

Uchu or aji: pimento.

Uilac-umu: the high priest.

Uncu: the Inca's shirt.

Uruya: cable suspended above running water, to which a basket is hung that makes it possible to cross from one bank to the other.

Usuta: traditional shoes made of a leather or string sole, fastened about the ankle with a fine cord.

U'yaca: little sticks which, when rubbed together, produce sparks with which a fire may be lighted.

Viracocha: supreme divinity, with Pachacamac. Name given to the Spaniards when they arrived in Peru. See Note 13, Book IV.

Yacha huaci: schools.

Yacolla: the Inca's square-shaped cape.

Yahuar: blood.

Yahuarcocha: lake of blood.

Yahuarpampa: blood-soaked plain.

Yunca: inhabitant of the coastal valleys.

BIBLIOGRAPHY

Chroniclers and Historians of the Spanish Conquest

ACOSTA, JOSE DE — *Historia natural y moral de las Indias.* Seville: 1590. Mexico: Fonda de Cultura Económica, 1940.

ARRIAGA, PABLO JOSE DE — *Extirpación de la idolatría del Perú.* Lima: Geronymo de Contreras, 1621. Buenos Aires: 1910.

BETANZOS, JUAN DE — *Suma y narración de los Incas.* ("Biblioteca hispano-ultramarina," vol. V.) Madrid: M. G. Hernandez, 1880. (Manuscript dated 1551.)

CABELLO DE BALBOA, MIGUEL — *Histoire du Pérou.* Paris: A. Bertrand, 1840. (This is the third part of the *Miscelanea antartica* written from 1576 to 1586. The entire work was published by the Universidad Nacional Mayor de San Marcos, Instituto de Etnologia, Lima: 1951.)

CIEZA DE LEON, PEDRO DE — *La crónica del Perú*—Part One. Seville: J. Lacio, 1553. Buenos Aires: Espasa-Calpe Argentina, S.A1, 1945. *La crónica del Perú*—Part Two. (Biblioteca hispano-ultramarina, vol. V.) Madrid: N. G. Hernandez, 1880. Buenos Aires: Ed. Argentinas Solar, 1943.

COBO, BERNABE — *Historia del Nuevo Mundo.* Seville: E. Rasco, 4 vols., 1890-5. Madrid: Ed. Atlas, 2 vols., 1956. (Written between 1596-1653.)

GOMARA, FRANCISCO LOPEZ DE — *Historia general de las Indias.* Saragossa: 1552-3. Madrid: 1932.

GUMILLA, JOSE *El Orinoco ilustrado.* Madrid: M. Fernandez, 1741. Bogota: Ediciones ABC, 1955.

GUTIERREZ DE SANTA CLARA, PEDRO *Historia de las guerras civiles del Perú.* ("Colección de Libros y Documentos Referentes á la Historia de América," vols. II-IV, X, XX-XXI.) Madrid: V. Suarez, 1904-29.

LAS CASAS, BARTOLOME DE *Brevísima relación de la destrucción de las Indias.* Seville: Casa de Sebastian Trugillo, 1552. Mexico: Sec. de Educación Publica, 1945.

MOLINA, CRISTOBAL DE (CUZCO) "Relación de las fábulas y ritos de los Incas," *Revista Chilena de Historia y Geografía* (Lima), vol. V.(1913.) (In 1916 a newly edited version appeared in Lima in the Colección de Libros y Documentos Referentes á la Historia del Perú, vol. I. The work itself was written between 1572-1591.)

MOLINA, CRISTOBAL DE (SANTIAGO) *Relación de la conquista y población del Perú.* ("Colección de Libros y Documentos Referentes á la Historia del Perú," vol. I.) Lima: 1916. (Written ca. 1552.)

MONTESINOS, FERNANDO "Memorias antiguas, historiales y políticas del Perú," *Revista de Buenos Aires,* (Buenos Aires), vols. XX-XXII (1870). Madrid: Marcos Jimenez de la Espada, 1882. Lima: Libreria e Imprenta Sil, 1930. (Written in 1644 or 1652. Montesinos, who was known to be opposed to Garcilaso, is the most disputed of Spanish historians.)

MORUA, MARTIN DE *Historia del origen y genealogía real de los reyes Incas del Perú, de sus hechos, costumbres, trajes y manera de gobierno.* ("Colección de Libros Referentes á la Historia del Perú," 2nd series, vols. IV-V.) Lima: 1922-1925. Madrid: Condejo Superior de Investigaciones Cientificas, 1946. (Written in 1577 or 1590.)

OLIVA, ANELLO *Vidas de varones ilustrés de la Compañia de Jesus de la provincia del Perú.* Lima: Ed. Juan Pazos Varela y Luis Varela y Orbegoso, 1895. (Ms. dated 1631.)

OVIEDO Y VALDES, *Crónica de las Indias. La Historia general*

GONZALO FERNANDEZ DE — *de las Indias.* Seville: Cromberger, 1535. Salamanca: Casa de Juan de Junta, 1547. (An independent work with a similar title was published in Toledo in 1526.) *Natural History of the West Indies.* Chapel Hill: University of North Carolina Press, 1959.

PIZARRO, PEDRO — *Relación del descubrimiento y conquista de los reinos del Perú (1571).* ("Colección de Documentos Ineditos para la Historia de España," vol. V.) Madrid: 1844. *Relation of the Discovery and Conquest of the Kingdoms of Peru.* New York: The Cortes Society, 1921.

POLO DE ONDEGARDO, JUAN — *Relación de los fundamentos acerca del notable daño que resultó de no guardar á los Indios sus fueros.* ("Colección de Libros y Documentos Referentes á la Historia del Perú," series 1, vol. III.) Lima: 1916. (Ms. dated 1571.)

Relación del linaje de los Incas, y como extendieron ellos sus conquistas. ("Colección de Libros y Documentos Referentes á la Historia del Perú," series 1, vol. IV.) Lima: 1917. *Narratives of the Rites and Laws of the Incas.* London: 1873.

De la orden que los Indios tenían en dividir los tributos y distribuirlos entre sí. ("Colección de Documentos Ineditos del Archivo de Indias," vol. XVII.) Madrid: ?

POMA DE AYALA, FELIPE GUAMAN — *Nueva crónica y buen gobierno.* Paris: Institut d'Ethnologie, 1936. Buenos Aires: Ed. Nova, 1943. La Paz: Ed. del Instituto Tihuanacu, 1944. (This work was probably completed in 1613 after 20-30 years of hard work and is the only illustrated Peruvian codex.)

SANCHO DE LA HOZ, PEDRO — *Relación para S.M. de lo sucedido en la conquista y pacificación de estas provincias de la Nueva Castilla y de la calidad de la tierra, después que el capitán Hernando Pizarro se partió y llevo a su Magestad la relación de victoria de Caxamalca y de la prisión del cacique Atabalipa.* ("Colección de Libros y Documentos Referentes á la Historia del Perú.") Lima: 1917. *An Account of the Conquest of Peru.* New York: The Cortes Society, 1917. (Written in 1534. The English translation is from an 1847 Spanish translation by Joaquin Garcia Icozlalceta from a 1556 Italian translation by C. B. Ramusio of Venice.)

SARMIENTO DE GAMBOA, PEDRO *History of the Incas by Pedro Sarmiento de Gamboa, and the execution of the Inca Tupac Amaru by Captain Baltasar de Ocampo.* Cambridge: Hakluyt Society, 2nd series, no. XXII, 1907. (This work was first published in 1906 by Weidmann in Berlin under the title *Geschichte des Inkareiches.*)

VILLAGOMEZ, PEDRO DE *Exhortaciones e instrucción acerca de las Idolatrias de los Indios del Arzobispado de Lima.* ("Colección de Libros y Documentos Referentes á la Historia del Perú," vol. XII.) Lima: 1919.

XEREZ, FRANCISCO DE *Verdadera relación de la conquista del Perú y provincia del Cuzco, llamada la Nueva-Castilla, conquistada por Francisco Pizarro.* ("Biblioteca de autores Españoles," vol. XXVI.) Madrid: 1853 and 1947. In English translation: Chicago: 1936. (Written in the middle of the sixteenth century, there is some evidence of the work having been published in Salamanca ca. 1547.)

ZARATE, AGUSTIN DE *Historia del descubrimiento y conquisto de la provincia del Perú, y las guerras y cosas señaladas en ella, acaecidas hasta el vencimiento de Gonzalo Pizarro y de sus secuaces, que en ella se rebelaron contra Su Magestad.* Antwerp: 1555. Seville: A. Escrivano, 1557. ("Biblioteca de autores Españoles," vol. XXVI.) Madrid: 1853. *A History of the Discovery and Conquest of Peru.* London: Penguin Press, 1933.

More Recent Works

ANDELIER, ADOLPHE FRANCIS *The Islands of Titicaca and Koati.* New York: 1910.

BARBAGELATA, HUGO D. *Histoire de l'Amérique espagnole.* Paris: Librairie Armand Colin, 1936.

BAUDIN, LOUIS *The Socialist Empire: the Incas of Peru.* New York: Van Nostrand, 1961.

BENNETT, WENDELL CLARK *Archeology of the Central Andes.* ("Handbook of South American Indians," Bulletin 143, vol. II.) Washington: Bureau of American Ethnology, 1946.
Engineering. ("Handbook of South American Indians," Bulletin 143, vol. V.) Washington: Bureau of American Ethnology, 1949.
Ancient Arts of the Andes. New York: 1954.

CASSOU, JEAN *Les Conquistadors.* Paris: Gallimard, 1941.

DESCOLA, JEAN *The Conquistadors.* New York: Viking, 1957.

DORSEY, GEORGE AMOS *A Bibliography of the Anthropology of Peru.* ("Anthropology Series," vol. II, no. 2.) Chicago: Field Museum of Natural History, 1898.

GILMORE, RAYMOND M. *Fauna and Ethnozoology of South America.* ("Handbook of South American Indians," vol. VI.) Washington: Bureau of American Ethnology: 1950.

GARCIA ROSELL, CESAR *Los monumentos arqueológicos del Perú.* Lima: La Cotera, 1942.

HARCOURT, RAOUL D', AND MARIE D' *La musique des Incas et ses survivances.* Paris: P. Geuthner, 1925.
La medicine dans l'ancien Pérou. Paris: Librairie Maloine, 1939.

HUBER, SIEGFRIED *The Realm of the Incas.* London: R. Hale, 1959.

IZIKOWITZ, KARL GUSTAV *Musical and Other Sound Instruments of the South American Indians: a comparative ethnographical study.* Göteborg: 1935.

KELEMEN, PAL *Medieval American Art.* 2 vols. New York: Macmillan, 1943.

KRICKEBERG, WALTER *Ethnología de América.* Mexico: Fonda de Cultura Económica, 1946.

LEHMANN, HENRI *Les ceramiques précolombiennes.* Paris: 1959.

MARKHAM, CLEMENTS ROBERT "On the geographical positions of the tribes which formed the empire of the Incas," *Journal of the Royal Geographical Society* (London), vol. 41 (1871).
A History of Peru. Chicago: C. H. Sergel, 1892.

MEANS, PHILIP AINSWORTH "A study of ancient Andean social institutions," *Transactions* (Connecticut Academy of Arts and Sciences), vol. 27 (1925).
Ancient Civilizations of the Andes. New York: Scribner's, 1931.

METRAUX, ALFRED *Warfare, Cannibalism and Human Trophies.* ("Handbook of South American Indians," vol. V.) Washington: Bureau of American Ethnology, 1949.

MURDOCK, GEORGE PETER *Our Primitive Contemporaries.* New York: Macmillan, 1934.

NORDENSKIOLD, ERLAND "The ethnography of South-America seen from Mojos in Bolivia," *Comparative Ethnographical Studies* (Göteborg), vol. 3 (1924). "Calculations with the years and months in the Peruvian quipus," *Comparative Ethnographical Studies* (Göteborg), vol. 6 (1925). "The secret of the Peruvian quipus," *Comparative Ethnographical Studies* (Göteborg), vol. 6 (1925).
"Modifications in Indian cultures through inventions and loans," *Comparative Ethnographical Studies* (Göteborg), vol. 8 (1930).

OLSON, RONALD LE ROY *Clan and Moiety in Native America* ("University of California Publications in American Archaeology and Ethnology," vol. 33, no. 4.) Berkeley: 1933.

PARDO, LUIS A. *Ruinas del santuario de Huiracocha.* (Cited by García Rosell, n.d.)

ROWE, JOHN HOWLAND *Inca Culture at the Time of the Spanish Conquest.* ("Handbook of South American Indians," Bulletin 143, vol. II.) Washington: Bureau of American Ethnology, 1946.

SQUIER, EPHRAIM GEORGE *Peru; incidents of travel and exploration in the land of the Incas.* New York: Harper & Bros., 1877.

STEWARD, JULIEN HAYNES — *The Native Population of South America.* ("Handbook of South American Indians." Bulletin 143, vol. V.) Washington: Bureau of American Ethnology, 1949.

VALCARCEL, LUIS EDUARDO AND MALDONADO, ANGEL — "Sajsawaman redescubrimiento," *Revista del Museo Nacional* (Lima), vol. III, nos. 1-2 (1934).
Cuzco Archaeology. ("Handbook of South American Indians," Bulletin 143, vol. II.) Washington: Bureau of American Ethnology, 1946.

VALDIZAN, HERMILLIO, AND MALDONADO, ANGEL — *La medicina popular peruana.* Lima: Torres Aquirre, 1922.

VIENRICH, ADOLFO — *Azucenas quechuas por unos Parias.* Tarma: 1905.

WASSEN, HENRY — "The Ancient Peruvian Abacus," *Comparative Ethnographical Studies* (Göteborg), vol. IX (1931).

YACOVLEFF, EUGENIO, AND HERRERA, FORTUNATO L. — "El mundo vegetal de los antiguos Peruanos," *Revista del Museo nacional* (Lima), vol. IV (1935).

Dictionaries and Encyclopedias

LITTRE, EMILE — *Dictionnaire de la langue française.* Paris: Pauvert, 1956-8.

REAL ACADEMIA ESPANOLA — *Diccionario de la lengua española.* Madrid: 1956.
Histoire des litteratures. Vol. II. Paris: Gallimard, 1956.
Histoire universelle. Vol. II. Paris: Gallimard, 1957.
Literatura Incá. Paris: Desclée, De Brouwer, 1938.

INDEX OF INCA LIFE

as found in the Commentaries of Garcilaso the Inca

D

E

F

G

H

DISCUS BOOKS

DISTINGUISHED NON-FICTION

Title / Author	No.	Price
THE CONCISE ENCYCLOPEDIC GUIDE TO SHAKESPEARE Michael Rheta Martin and Richard A. Harrier	16832	2.65
CONSCIOUSNESS AND REALITY Charles Museous and Arthur M. Young, Eds.	18903	2.45
CONVERSATIONS WITH JORGE LUIS BORGES Richard Burgin	11908	1.65
CORTES AND MONTEZUMA Maurice Collis	40402	2.50
DISINHERITED Dave Van Every	09555	1.25
DIVISION STREET: AMERICA Studs Terkel	22780	2.25
EINSTEIN: THE LIFE AND TIMES Ronald W. Clark	44123	3.95
ESCAPE FROM FREEDOM Erich Fromm	47472	2.95
THE FEMALE IMAGINATION Patricia Meyer Spacks	28142	2.45
THE FEMINIZATION OF AMERICAN CULTURE Ann Douglas	38513	2.95
FRONTIERS OF CONSCIOUSNESS John White, ed.	24810	2.50
GAY AMERICAN HISTORY Jonathan Katz, Ed.	40550	3.95
GERMANS George Bailey	44917	2.95
GERTRUDE STEIN: A COMPOSITE PORTRAIT Linda Simon, Ed.	20115	1.65
THE GREAT POLITICAL THEORIES, VOL. I Michael Curtis	23119	1.95
THE GREAT POLITICAL THEORIES, VOL. II Michael Curtis	23127	1.95
THE GREEK WAY Edith Hamilton	37481	2.25
GROTOWSKI Raymond Temkine	12278	1.65
THE HEBREW GODDESS Raphael Patai	39289	2.95
HENRY JAMES: Five Volume Biography Leon Edel	39636	14.75
HOMOSEXUAL: LIBERATION AND OPPRESSION Dennis Altman	14214	1.65
THE HUMAN USE OF HUMAN BEINGS Norbert Wiener	21584	1.95
THE INCAS Garcilaso de la Vega	45542	3.50
INTERPRETATION OF DREAMS Freud	38828	2.95
JESUS IN BAD COMPANY Adolf Holl	19281	1.65
THE LIFE AND DEATH OF LENIN Robert Payne	12161	1.65
THE LIFE AND WORK OF WILHELM REICH M. Cattier	14928	1.65
LIFE IN A CRYSTAL PALACE Alan Harrington	15784	1.65
THE LIFE OF JOHN MAYNARD KEYNES R. F. Harrod	12625	2.45
LOUISA MAY: A MODERN BIOGRAPHY Martha Saxton	40881	2.95
MALE AND FEMALE UNDER 18 Nancy Larrick and Eve Merriam, Eds.	29645	1.50
POE, POE, POE . . . Daniel Hoffman	41459	2.95
MAN IN THE TRAP Elsworth F. Baker, Ph.D.	18809	1.95
MAWSON'S WILL Lennard Bickel	39131	2.50

(2) DDB 10-79